The Extreme Right

The
Extreme
Right

Freedom and Security at Risk

edited by
**Aurel Braun and
Stephen Scheinberg**

 **WestviewPress**
A Division of HarperCollins*Publishers*

Copyright © 1997 by Westview Press, A Division of HarperCollins Publishers, Inc.

Published in 1997 in the United States of America by Westview Press, 5500 Central Avenue, Boulder, Colorado 80301-2877, and in the United Kingdom by Westview Press, 12 Hid's Copse Road, Cumnor Hill, Oxford OX2 9JJ

Library of Congress Cataloging-in-Publication Data
Braun, Aurel.
    The extreme right : freedom and security at risk / Aurel Braun,
Stephen Scheinberg.
      p.   cm.
    Includes bibliographical references and index.
    ISBN 0-8133-3150-1 (hardcover).—ISBN 0-8133-3151-X (pbk.)
    1. Fascism.   2. Radicalism.   3. Right-wing extremists.
4. Democracy.   I. Scheinberg, Stephen J.   II. Title.
JC481.B694   1997
320.5′33—dc20
                                                                            96-35186
                                                                                 CIP

The paper used in this publication meets the requirements of the American National Standard for Permanence of Paper for Printed Library Materials Z39.48-1984.

10   9   8   7   6   5   4   3   2   1

To our wives,
Julianna Braun and Sandra Scheinberg,
and our children,
Daniel, David, Ellen, and Martin

Contents

Acknowledgments

We are grateful to our main funding source, the Cooperative Security Competition of Canada's Department of Foreign Affairs. Roger Hill and Grazyna Beaudoin were the dedicated professionals of that agency who helped us at all stages.

This project was initiated under the auspices of the Institute for International Affairs of B'nai Brith Canada. Paul Marcus, its director at the time, played an absolutely crucial role. A remarkable individual with a keen interest both in human rights and in scholarship, Paul Marcus was instrumental in pulling together the contributors and the Advisory Committee, applying for funding, and helping to organize public seminars across Canada. He was, in addition, consultant, friend, traveling companion, and the essential aegis of our work.

B'nai Brith Canada, directed by its executive vice president, Frank Dimant, and its national president, Brian Morris, was essential to the success of the project. The organization's long-term commitment to human rights inspired our work. A second B'nai Brith agency, the League for Human Rights, and its director, Karen Mock, gave us valuable assistance in our endeavors. We also thank Len Butcher of the B'nai Brith *Tribune,* who copyedited an early version of the work.

The Advisory Committee members did much more than lend their names to this effort, and for their participation we thank Frank Dimant, Ian Kagedan, Paul Marcus, David Matas, Thelma McCormack, and Mark Webber. Of course, we assume responsibility for errors and omissions.

Michi Ebata and David Cooper ably served as project coordinators. David Cooper's input during the second phase of the preparation of the manuscript was invaluable. Talia Klein, research associate, provided crucial help toward the completion of this book.

We wish to thank also all those diverse experts and members of the public who attended seminars in Montreal, Toronto, Ottawa, and Winnipeg and gave us the benefit of their responses to our initial formulations. This process was an interesting and perhaps unique experience in the gestation of a scholarly work. The Department of Canadian Heritage helped us to provide translation services at our Montreal and Ottawa seminars.

We would also like to express our gratitude to Susan McEachern, former senior editor at Westview Press, for her encouragement, suggestions, and patience and to Rebecca Ritke, Melanie Stafford, and other members of Westview Press as well as Diane Hess, the copy editor, who have so ably helped us to bring this work to completion.

Finally, we want to thank our families, who not only provided us with encouragement but graciously coped with a great deal of disruption.

Aurel Braun
Stephen Scheinberg

1

Introduction

Aurel Braun

During a visit to Moscow in May 1994 I asked an old academic acquaintance about his perceptions of the political conditions in Russia. He lamented the disarray among the democrats and was perturbed by the economic hardships and the all too visible poverty. But overall he remained optimistic. The transition was painful, but he assured me, "We are perfecting democracy." In a society that had spent more than seven decades "perfecting communism," this Russian democrat, a proponent of fundamental transformation, was employing, almost amusingly, Marxist language to describe the process of democratization in Russia. There was a kind of pride in his remarks that somehow Russia was catching up to the West. "We are joining," he added, "what President Boris Yeltsin has called the ranks of the civilized nations." His remarks, though, raised two issues: one about the understanding of the core characteristics of democracy and the other about the state of democracy in Western nations.

It is reassuring to see the tremendous interest in democratic theory in Russia. Many Russian intellectuals, for instance, have been reading the *Federalist Papers*. Yet it is surprising how many misconceptions about the nature of democracy remain. First, the belief that a political system can be perfected is deeply rooted in some ideologies but not in democracy. Democracy, as Thomas Jefferson and others have contended, is a continuing struggle. It is a system that involves checks and balances to compensate for human frailty and ambition. Unlike totalitarian ideologies, it does not represent a "once and for all solution." It requires patience, commitment, and participation. It relies not only on institutions and processes but also on a vigilant and vibrant civil society. Therefore, an assumption that democracy can be perfected endangers the continuing commitment to the struggle to keep democracy viable and diminishes the will to deal with those who would undermine it.

Second, the notion that democracy somehow has been perfected in Western states is a misunderstanding of the character of political systems in pluralistic democracies. In the established democracies, institutions and processes have continued to evolve in order to ensure the protection of basic human rights and have indeed involved a continuing struggle against forces that in a variety of ways have challenged democratic ideals or have sought to diminish human dignity. The horrific carnage caused by right-wing extremists when they exploded a bomb in Oklahoma City in the United States in 1995 or the spectacle of millions of French citizens giving the right-wing demagogue Jean-Marie Le Pen, the leader of the Front National, a record 15 percent of the vote in April 1995 are but two of the manifestations of the continuing dangers of extremism in long-established democracies. In both emerging and established democracies, then, there is the need to deal with threats to freedom and security.

There is a need for balance and prudence, though, in analyzing such threats and risks. It is not the contention of this book that democracies are in mortal danger. Also, the authors are not involved in an attempt to measure the performance of governments either in emerging or established democracies on the basis of some strictly construed version of political correctness. Rather, they seek to identify threats to freedom and security, assess the responses to such threats, and suggest some means of dealing with the potential dangers.

Traditionally, the gravest threats to democracy from the right emanated from fascism. In most democracies, there are at least small groups that reject democratic institutions and idealize the old fascist regimes. But among the larger radical right groups, the resemblance to fascism is superficial. This applies to Jörg Haider's Freedom Party in Austria and Gianfranco Fini's National Alliance in Italy, which are more radical rightist parties than fascist ones. Fascist ideology was based on an integrated set of concepts that combined antiliberalism and xenophobic forms of nationalism and echoed the intellectual ferment in Europe in the post–World War I era. Scholars such as Stanley G. Payne have argued persuasively that the Western world has been inoculated against that kind of fascism.[1] That classical fascism is not a probable threat in established democracies and probably not even in emerging ones, however, is not sufficiently comforting. There are numerous other threats.

As Oxford's philosopher John Gray has written, in the liberal democracies the principal danger has come from the revival of the radical right.[2] There are, of course, threats from violent skinheads and small neo-Nazi organizations, but it is the radical rightist parties whose members are populists and doctrinaires of the antigovernment right—who, as John Gray has argued, combine economic Darwinism with a deeply reactionary view of family life— that pose the greatest danger by widening social divisions, deepening political alienation, and fostering cultural warfare.[3]

Still, the existence of these parties is not a cause for panic. None of these radical right parties or individuals propagating these views have a good chance of gaining power in the established democracies. Jean-Marie Le Pen has virtually no chance even of sharing power nationally. In the Austrian elections in December 1995, Haider's party failed to make gains for the first time in a decade.[4] The issue, then, is not one of imminent danger but rather of the need for awareness of the potential for danger. Democracies should deal early with threats to freedom and security across the entire political spectrum, whether these emanate from skinheads, neo-Nazi groupings, or an antidemocratic radical right.

In the emerging democracies, though, the danger is graver. The absence of a deeply rooted legal system that can offer citizens protection, the fragile emerging democratic institutions, and the uncertain political processes all create an environment where opportunities for extremism exist. Furthermore, in the postcommunist states, the lines between extreme left and right become blurred as prevailing political extremism combines features of both. The slower the transition in these postcommunist states, the more strength the antidemocratic seem to enjoy. But even in the more difficult situations, democratic forces can and should fight those of extremism. It would be most unfortunate if in any of these states, including Russia, the democratic forces were to become paralyzed with fear and abandon the fight. But to counter extremism effectively in the established and the emerging democracies, we must understand the nature of the threat clearly. This book is first, therefore, an effort to provide some conceptual clarification of the problem.

Conceptual clarification is essential to the process of finding a balanced approach to countering extremism. There is a problem in defining right-wing extremism, in part because much of the salient analysis has come not just from the left but from that part of the left that believed threats to freedom and security emanated exclusively from the political right. In established democracies this blinkered view of threats should not pose an insurmountable problem because with the collapse of communism in the former Soviet Union and East-Central Europe not only the external threat but also the internal possibilities for the extreme left have diminished or disappeared entirely. However, in assessing the threat to freedom and security in the postcommunist states, we must remember that not only is the division between right-wing and left-wing extremism difficult to define but an analytic separation may be misleading and counterproductive.

From the beginning of the imposition of communist regimes in Eastern Europe, there was a blurring of lines. In the German Democratic Republic (GDR) it was not uncommon for loyal members of the Nazi Party to "convert," becoming equally loyal members of the Communist Party or even working for the dreaded GDR secret service. During communist rule, in certain cases such as Romania under Nicolae Ceaușescu, ultranationalism was used as a legitimating factor, thereby giving rise to a virulent type of national communism that in its xenophobia incorporated elements of both the extreme left and right. In the wake of the collapse of the Soviet Union one could also witness the blending of the extreme left and right in the reestablished Communist Party. The threat to Russian democracy comes from a "red-brown" combination of ultranationalism and the desire for central control. Often these tendencies are manifested in the same individual. This may indeed explain the facility with which some of these extremists can move from the Communist Party to an ultranationalist one and back.

In the postcommunist states the differences in attitudes and the rate of success in transition also points to another problem. In the Eastern and Central European states communism has been largely discredited. Surveys of attitudes show that the vast majority of individuals do not want the communist economic and political systems back. The highest number of those who did was recorded in Bulgaria at 29 percent and the lowest number in Poland at 8 percent.[5] These low numbers are quite remarkable given the enormous amount of stress that the transition engendered. This transition, as one of the keenest analysts of change in Eastern Europe, Laszlo Csaba, noted, involved not merely some improvement of a prevailing system but rather implied the destruction of the traditional economic and political order under socialism and its replacement with multiparty democracy as well as a new set of coordination mechanisms and openness to economic, technological, and cultural exchange with the outside world.[6] Thus in much of Eastern and Central Europe, democracy is taking root.

In Russia, however, the reaction to the attempts at fundamental political and economic transformation has been considerably less encouraging. Surveys show that a majority consistently gives a positive rating to the regime in power *before* the start of perestroika.[7] Russia, therefore, does not appear to have reached the takeoff point for democratization that most of the East European states have. Russia has not reached the same measure of transformation. Therefore, the possibilities for extremism are enhanced. This is not to suggest that there is a danger of a return to the old hard-line communist regime. Rather, there are possibilities of various combinations of "red" and "brown" forces coalescing to push for an authoritarian agenda. Thus the concept of extremism as applied to the emerging democracies needs to take into account the dangers posed by the inability to reach a takeoff point for democratization (as in Russia) and the possible loss of transformation momentum in all postcommunist societies.

A second goal of this work is to examine the actual manifestations of extremism. The authors do not restrict their analyses to blatant acts of hatred and antidemocratic activity but also look at the subtle challenges to democracy that may in fact pose the most insidious long-range threats. Moreover, since the book is predicated on the notion of democracy as a continuing struggle, it is assumed that there is a perpetual danger in both emerging and established democracies that needs to be addressed calmly but decisively. Within this context the book touches in its various chapters on the issues of political will, that is, the willingness of both governments and populations to be vigilant and recognize the early warning signs of extremist threats to democracy and, further, to engage in a sustained effort to counter such threats. The authors also examine the mechanisms for dealing with extremism. Their examinations involve an assessment of tendencies, institutions, legislation, and attitudes. These analyses highlight what is common in the threats to freedom and security and the differences not only between the established and emerging democracies but also among the states in each category.

For this single-volume work, the selection of states for close examination was both a difficult and an important task. The overall coverage is from Vancouver to Vladivostock because this not only allows the contributors to examine most influential established democracies but also presents them with an opportunity to analyze the democratic process and the dangers posed to it by extremism during a historically remarkable period of transition in what had been the communist world. For a single-volume work the selection of states had to be prioritized and parsimonious. The rise of the right in Austria and Italy at first made these states tempting subjects. But in Austria, Jörg Haider's Freedom Party, despite its clever anti-immigrant and nationalist oratory, has reached a plateau in its support. In Italy, Gianfranco Fini's National Alliance is unlikely to access power even as a junior partner in a coalition.[8] More significant, however, is the fact that in comparing the importance and influence of these states with the others selected, the contributors found them to be less urgent choices.

The United States, as a superpower and a long established democracy that has sought to build a multiethnic society, was an obvious choice. Right-wing extremism, moreover, has a long history in America. But concern here was not only with the most blatant manifestations of extremism (whether it came from skinheads or the Ku Klux Klan or even the lunatic fringe that was responsible for the Oklahoma City bombing). It was also essential to examine threats from the radical right. This radical right differs from the conservatism of Ronald Reagan or Margaret Thatcher because it rejects important elements of the democratic consensus in the United States. The candidacy of individuals such as David Duke and also of the much cleverer and more credible radical rightist Pat Buchanan raises issues about ultimate threats to freedom and security.

Canada, a country that Stephen Scheinberg calls the "peaceable kingdom" in Chapter 3, at first seems to be a state characterized by harmonious pluralism and multiculturalism. Yet here too there are right-wing extremists who wish to undermine democracy. Neo-Nazis have engaged in violence, and some have become involved in a large-scale propaganda effort that seeks to deny the Holocaust through an efficient distribution network that spews hate literature beyond Canada's boundaries. In this "peaceable kingdom," a separatist movement nearly succeeded in wrenching the country apart on the basis of ethnic dissatisfaction. When the proponents of separatism in Quebec lost the 1995 referendum the (separatist) provincial leader bitterly blamed it on the ethnic minorities and a business conspiracy.

Britain and France were also logical choices. Both headed huge empires, and they still wield considerable influence in the Commonwealth and in "La Francophonie," respectively. They are members of the United Nations Security Council and are nuclear powers. Long-established democracies but with somewhat different legal systems, they also have large minorities, many of which came from the former empires. Both states need to acknowledge multiethnicity, emphasize the notions of citizenship, and yet deal with the problems of seemingly intractable unemployment and social dislocation that so easily play into the hands of the extreme right.

Germany is not only the economic engine of Europe and the largest and wealthiest state in the European Union but is also a state recently reunified. It must integrate 16 million people who lived in nondemocratic political cultures under the Nazis and the communists. It is also a country that has taken in huge numbers of foreigners, first as guest workers, second as immigrants from former communist states beyond the Elbe, and third as asylum seekers. Germany, therefore, can teach and at the same time needs to learn many lessons in reinforcing democracy and in achieving a successful political and economic transition in what was East Germany. Last, what happens in Germany has a significant effect on the Eastern and Central European states because here Germany has the greatest economic impact and it is in the process of reestablishing, at least to a considerable degree, its former cultural influence.

Among the postcommunist states, Russia was the first and natural choice. It not only occupies an enormous area, stretching over eleven time zones, and has a population twice that of Germany but it retains thousands of potent nuclear weapons. It is also a multiethnic federation struggling to achieve democracy. There are over 25 million non-Russians living in the Russian Federation and there are a similar number of Russians living beyond the borders of the federation in what has been called the "near abroad." Moreover, what happens in Russia has a profound effect on the states in the near abroad and potentially also on those in Eastern Europe.

After more than seven decades of communism, with a devastatingly mismanaged economy and with enormous unresolved ethnic issues, Russia seemed ill equipped to embark on the road to democracy. But even though monumental obstacles remain, remarkable progress has been made. This is why Russia is a kind of "land in between." Given Russia's importance, the way in which the government and the people of Russia deal with the problems of extremism—which, as noted, tends to be a vile cocktail of right-wing and left-wing demagoguery and subversion—will have an effect not only on the fate of the citizens of the Russian Federation and of the near abroad but on much of Eastern Europe and ultimately on international peace and security.

The small state of Hungary was selected because it was at the cutting edge of reform when communist regimes were in power in the region and then in 1990 moved quickly toward fundamental transformation. Before embarking on fundamental political and economic transition, Hungary thus had the longest experience with reform of any communist state and thus a head start in dealing with issues such as questions of legality and the treatment of minorities. Currently, Hungary is eagerly seeking membership in the European Union and in NATO. There is one other factor that is also relevant: Minorities constitute 10 percent of the population of Hungary, and this state has more of its co-nationals living in neighboring states than does any other country in the region (up to 5 million, or about 50 percent of the population of the state).

Therefore, there ought to be several restraints on extremism in Hungary. First, from a domestic perspective, the building of democracy in a period of transition requires a great deal of vigilance and sustained commitment to counter antidemocratic forces. Second, Hungary's desire for membership in the Western organizations, such as the European Union and NATO, means that it must meet the criterion for pluralistic democracy that these organizations stipulate for membership. And third, the fact that so many millions of ethnic Hungarians live in surrounding states means that Hungary needs to set an example in the treatment of its own minorities in order to be able to occupy the moral high ground in asking for fair treatment of its co-nationals in the region.

Poland was selected not only because it is the largest postcommunist East European state but also because of the special conditions in that country. It is ethnically more homogeneous than the other countries in Eastern Europe, but it also has a strong sense of historical victimization. The Solidarity union has brought together workers and intellectuals in what at first seemed to be an endeavor to protect workers but that ultimately constituted the beginnings of the rebuilding of civil society. The church in Poland also played a unique role in preserving national identity over centuries of Polish struggles to reconstitute the state and under communist rule. Moreover, the church frequently provided a haven for political discussion and dissent. With the fall of the communist regime, Poland was the first to embark on a policy of "shock therapy" with all of the potential social dislocations that such a policy can create. In the postcommunist era the behavior of some of the players has changed. Some authoritarian tendencies have reemerged. The role of the church has been increasingly questioned. Thus Poland should reveal much both about the nature of extremism in the region and about the possibilities of countering it in order to protect freedom and security.

*   *   *

The contributors examine both the literature on right-wing extremism and, in their case studies, the political and economic structures and processes that either foster or enable extremism to flourish. Moreover, they assess the responses of governments, nongovernmental organizations, and populations to manifestations of extremism and include interviews with important policymakers, thinkers, and even some of the most important leaders of extremist forces, such as Vladimir Zhirinovsky.

Michi Ebata in Chapter 2 begins to probe the conceptual problems by examining the definitional parameters, assessing the literature, and also speaking to some of the causes of right-wing extremism and its effects. She also points out that although right-wing extremism entails a rejection of democracy, it can also be a product of democracy.

In Chapters 3 and 4, Stephen Scheinberg examines right-wing extremism in Canada and the United States, respectively, and highlights the remarkable longevity of the phenomenon in North America. Canada has a long history of right-wing extremism before World War II. Though there has been a moderation of extremism in the postwar era, problems with integrating immigrants and with separatism have meant that right-wing extremist groups, small as they may be, have nevertheless found an audience. Furthermore, despite anti-hate legislation, hatemongers and Holocaust deniers such as Ernst Zundel have managed to build a web of hate through racist and anti-Semitic literature that can reach beyond the boundaries of Canada. In the United States too there are manifestations of blatant right-wing extremism from skinheads, members of the Ku Klux Klan, and octher hate groups. In general the law has been crucial in keeping the Klan and other fringe elements in check. But, as noted, there are threats from radical right leaders who seek public office and manage to retain various degrees of public respetability. David Duke, an ex-Klan leader, ran for various offices in Louisiana. Pat Buchanan, a radical rightist who made numerous statements that can be interpreted as anti-Semitic and who has consistently pushed an anti-immigration viewpoint, has managed to appeal to significant numbers on the right of the Republican Party. Thus extreme forms of populism as well as some of the elements of religious fundamentalism singly and in combination do present a threat to freedom and security that democrats need to address.

In chapter 5, David Matas compares the extreme right in the United Kingdom and France. The extreme right has enjoyed greater success in France than in the United Kingdom. Jean-Marie Le Pen's Front National has enjoyed considerable electoral success, though it is highly unlikely to form part of any coalition government. Nevertheless, it has been able to virtually monopolize the political extreme right. In the United Kingdom the extreme right has been characterized by factionalism. Both governments have tended to downplay the threat, though the French response appears to be more rigorous. The author points out that each of the three forms of the French response, namely resistance, recuperation, and repression, carries some danger. Important questions remain about the effectiveness of the response to the danger from the extreme right both in the United Kingdom and in France.

Ian Kagedan, in Chapter 6, examines developments in Germany between 1945 and 1989 and also the danger from right-wing extremism since reunification. He assesses the response of the government and of the public in light of the special problems Germany has to deal with. These derive from the history of Nazism and from the difficulties of the unification and the need to deal with large-scale immigration and the numerous seekers of asylum.

Aurel Braun's Chapter 7 is the bridge between the study of the established democracies and the emerging ones. The postcommunist states present a special problem because there is no historic precedent for such transformation. Though it is important to recognize the common elements of established and emerging democracies, it is equally essential to be cognizant of the differences. In the postcommunist states, at least during the transition period, extremism cannot be clearly delineated as either right- or left-wing. The combination of the two is what poses a danger, and Braun proposes that the best way to analyze the issue is by looking at such elements as momentum, majorities as victims (victimology), status of minorities, laws and legality, and the efficacy of these states in coping with refugees.

In Chapter 8 Braun examines Russia as a "land in between" where the battle between the forces of democracy and those of reaction continue. Though the former have won some decisive victories, many other battles have been inconclusive. In the areas of momentum, majority victimization, status of minorities, laws and legality, and coping with refugees, important questions remain. Russia simply has not reached the "takeoff point" for democratization. This is not to suggest that the status quo ante can be reestablished. Rather Braun suggests that in Russia the forces of extremism continue to pose a grave danger of detouring, if not altogether stopping, the process of democratization that began with the collapse of communism.

In Chapters 9 and 10, Braun provides a more optimistic assessment in his analyses of conditions in Poland and Hungary, respectively. In both states democracy has taken off and the communist parties have been transformed into credible social democratic ones. Yet in each case, in all five areas of analysis applied to the postcommunist states there are some question marks. In Poland, as in Hungary, there remains a strong sense of majority victimization that poses problems for building political consensus, protecting minorities, and dealing with refugees. In Poland manifestations of authoritarianism both from some of the political leadership and from elements in the church have had a negative impact, and there are concerns about the ability and the willingness of at least some of the policymaking elites in Poland to recognize and act on the early warning signs of danger from political extremism. In Hungary, two successful democratic elections give cause for optimism, but at the same time there has been increased polarization. There are also questions about issues of momentum, laws and legality, and attitudes to refugees.

In Chapter 11, Ebata examines the internationalization of the extreme right. The extreme right and the "red-brown groupings" draw inspiration from a similar ideological heritage. It is not entirely surprising that one of the luminaries invited to Zhirinovsky's birthday party was Le Pen from France. Extremism, though, poses a danger not only to individual states but to the international community as a whole, and Ebata argues that it flourishes because it takes advantage both of domestic debilities and the weaknesses and tensions in the international system. The international community, therefore, should have an interest in combating extremism. The participation and political will of governments; of nongovernmental, intergovernmental, and regional organizations; and of the population at large are all required.

The balance sheet shows the dangers to freedom and security from extremism but also the possibilities of combating it. Violence against Roma, which has included beatings, arson, and even killings, in the East European states and the bombing of a federal building in Oklahoma City are not isolated incidents but symptoms of the threat posed by antidemocratic forces. It is essential to recognize the early warning signs and continue to struggle against extremism. The dangers must be identified and clearly understood. And there has to be the political will on the part of governments, of nongovernmental organizations, and of the citizenship at large to engage in a sustained effort to fight for democratic freedoms, to protect peace and security. And the struggle will need to go on indefinitely, for sadly it does not appear that democracy is perfectible.

Notes

1. Stanley G. Payne, *A History of Fascism, 1914–1945* (Madison: University of Wisconsin Press, 1995).

2. John Gray, "Defining Evil," *New York Times Book Review*, February 25, 1996, 15.

3. Ibid.

4. *Globe and Mail*, February 9, 1996.

5. *New Democracies Barometer IV* (Vienna: Paul Lazarfeld Society, 1995).

6. Laszlo Csaba, *The Capitalist Revolution in Eastern Europe: A Contribution to the Economic Theory of Systemic Change* (Aldershot, UK, and Brookfield, Mass.: Edward Elgar, 1995).

7. Centre for the Study of Public Policy, University of Strathclyde, "New Russia Barometer," sample surveys 1 (N: 2106), 2 (N: 1975), 3 (N: 3535), 4 (N: 1943); and Richard Rose, "Russia as an Hour–Glass Society: A Constitution Without Citizens," *East European Constitutional Review* 4(3), Summer 1995: 34–42.

8. *Economist*, October 21, 1995, 55–56.

2

Right-Wing Extremism:
In Search of a Definition

Michi Ebata

Definitional Parameters

The recent upsurge in racist violence in Europe and North America and the electoral successes of radical right parties in the former have heightened awareness of what was once the fringe phenomenon of right-wing extremism. Not endemic to any particular country, right-wing extremism is clearly evident throughout the European and American continents. Many observers, however, are dismissive of what they consider an unfortunate but still peripheral problem. In stark contrast, other commentators seize upon the Oklahoma tragedy or draw parallels to the Nazi accession to power, invoking the specter of the Third Reich. The irreconcilability of these two perspectives underscores the need for a deeper examination of the problem and an adequate response to it. Clearly, arriving at a coherent and consistent understanding of right-wing extremism begins with the search for a definition of the problem itself.

References to right-wing extremism have been heard more and more frequently since the mid-1980s. The term has been applied to individuals, parties, movements, and organizations across the world from North America to Europe, Eastern Europe, Russia, and the Middle East. It has also been used in reference to a wide range of phenomena from skinhead youths to football hooligans, neo-Nazis, white supremacists, militia groups, extremist fringe political parties, and more successful radical political parties. Thus right-wing extremism consists of many different forms. It can refer to an ideology, a form of observable behavior, various kinds of political activities, or personal attitudes and dispositions. Right-wing extremism is not confined to politics. It is part psychological, part sociological, sometimes political, and, unfortu-

12

nately, often criminal. The consequences of accounting for such a wide variety of phenomena under one concept are twofold. First, there is the danger of diluting the meaning of the concept by including too many phenomena. Second, there is the risk of reducing and rigidifying the concept by deductively seeking an essentialist quality binding these phenomena.

Notwithstanding these problems, several attempts have been made to offer a serviceable definition of right-wing extremism.[1] Michael Billig captures its duality when he says, "The term 'extreme right' is a particularly troubling one to use in political analysis. At first, (it seems) to be an obvious label but it is one that can so easily cause a misleading impression. The term is obvious to the extent that there are a number of political parties, movements and individuals which it seems entirely appropriate to label as 'extreme right' to distinguish them from the traditional right or extreme left-wing."[2]

As with any "ism," right-wing extremism is a broad concept that is not static or precise; nor should it be, since this would imply a coherence and simplicity that is not reflected in reality. But although determining the essence of right-wing extremism seems impracticable, we can arrive at a nominal definition that serves as a guide in applying the concept to particular groups and situations. As with any label, there is the danger of using the concept as a political weapon to discredit opponents. The value judgments imbued in a concept associated with reprehensible crimes from the not too distant past compel careful examination of the conditions under which the concept of right-wing extremism can be legitimately applied. Specifying the conditions for the concept's proper usage is a question of how narrow or how broad a phenomenon it is. Four approaches will be taken to address this question. In the first section I attempt to identify right-wing extremism by examining its most salient features. In the second section I explore the ways in which the extreme right is different from other similar phenomena. In the third, right-wing extremism is defined in terms of its causes, and in the last, I assess the impact of right-wing extremism and its ultimate significance.

Identifying the Problem

Common usage suggests that right-wing extremism refers to the violent skinhead, white supremacist, and neo-Nazi gangs or the radical right parties that have gained such prominence in recent years. After an examination of such groups generally classified under this category, certain common and constant themes of right-wing extremism are discernible. Right-wing extremists are identified foremost by their fundamental expression of hatred, bigotry, or prejudice rooted in an "ideology of inequality."[3] This hatred is an expression of a worldview that divides society into those who belong and those who do not. It is specifically manifested as racism, xenophobia, homophobia, misogyny, and religious intolerance. In most cases it is also directed specifically against the state. As such, hate is an integral value that infuses the ideology, motivates the actions, and serves as a source of solidarity for right-wing extremists. But hatred is far more than just an expressed sentiment; it is a source of action dedicated to expelling the offending outsider from society in order to remake society into its "purer historical" form. On the basis of their resentment and hostility toward those with perceived or actual differences, right-wing extremists mobilize against those who do not belong to their particular in-group. This mobilization can be taken to its logical extreme of physically destroying the out-group, an outcome that is accomplished through the incitement of hatred in the form of hate speech, hate propaganda, and hate crimes. Such propaganda often relies on pseudoscientific theories and has religious and cultural overtones. In fact, the out-group is central to right-wing extremists in their hierarchical conception of the world; it provides a means of maintaining their sense of superiority, thus giving meaning and purpose to their lives.

This focus on the out-group has made immigrants the most popular and visible target. According to right-wing extremists, immigrants are responsible for all that ails society from unemployment to crime to the general malaise of the country. Both France's Front National and Germany's Republikaner Party employ the slogan "eliminate unemployment, stop immigration." Consequently, most of the vicious attacks by right-wing extremists in various European countries have targeted members of large immigrant communities: Arabs in France, Turks in Germany, Asians in Britain. This deep hostility directed toward outsiders has made immigration the most prominent issue on the platforms of the extreme right. Its success at seizing and manipulating popular fears of the "foreigner" has prompted established political figures to appropriate the issue themselves, reinforcing its apparent relevance and urgency. The issue of immigration also reinforces the importance of the status of citizenship, which conveys belonging and acceptability. This focus on immigration and its converse, citizenship, reveals the extreme right's nationalist impulse, the second common identifying theme.

Based on the premise that the nation is the primary unit of social and political organization, extremist nationalism has been invigorated since the demise of communism. Unlike civic nationalism, which stresses equality and solidarity, the exaggerated, chauvinistic, and aggressive nationalism of the extreme right upholds the sanctity of the nation and national identity against any other value. Each person is defined by membership in primordial ethnic and cultural groups that are hierarchically arranged according to the "natural order." In the extreme right's view, violating this natural order through racial intermingling leads to decadence and decay in society, culminating in the destruction of civilization. Consequently, the extreme right portrays itself as the defender of the nation, protecting society's integrity and purity from the onslaught of foreigners and unwanted change. National identity, therefore, is primary and prior, subordinating all other identifications; it divides good from evil and friend from enemy. It is a source of pride that right-wing extremists feel has been denied them by the state and liberals. Right-wing extremists stridently speak of "keeping France French," a "Germany for Germans," "real and true Hungarians," "pure Russians," "loyal Americans."

This ethnocentrism is often translated into an expansionary and territorially aggressive foreign policy. Italian neofascists have demanded the return of Dalmatia in the former Yugoslavia to Italy; Zhirinovsky has called for a greater Russia from Alaska to Germany; German extremists have insisted on a return to pre-Yalta borders with Poland. Nationalist right-wing extremists were also at the forefront of opposition to European integration when the Single European Act was propelling the European Union inexorably forward. Similarly, prior to the 1989 collapse of socialism and the popular urge for reunification, right-wing extremists demanded a unified Germany based on 1938 borders. When these issues were initially unpopular, those on the extreme right succeeded in combining nationalist rhetoric with a populist emotive appeal to the common people that addressed their frustrations, anxieties, and disenchantment. In France, this national populism is personally reflected in Jean-Marie Le Pen, who is depicted as "the hero of the city dweller, the person who feels oppressed by bad housing, immigration, the threat of unemployment and a general sense that something has gone wrong with his country."[4]

In Hungary, Istvan Csurka, the anti-Semitic poet-playwright and leader of the *nepi* (folk) wing of the Hungarian Democratic Forum, is the author of numerous poems and songs that protest modernization's erosion of the "true Hungarian consciousness."[5] "That's why we need a new authentic people so that we can defend ourselves all the more passionately to save ourselves."[6]

The radical religious right in the United States has similarly combined patriotic entreaties with populist oratory, winning significant support and endorsement. In upholding the heroism and virtue of the nation, the extreme right has defined and propelled itself onto the front pages of U.S. newspapers.

Although immigrants today are the main targets for right-wing extremist attack, they still have not replaced one constant object of attack: the Jews. Anti-Semitism, the third theme, is widespread throughout the extreme right. It sometimes manifests in casual insults to Jews; more often, the attacks are obscene, graphic, and violent, even sophisticated and conspiratorial. In spite of the very small number of Jews in many European countries, the popular condemnation of anti-Semitism, the political disadvantages of such prejudice, and the availability of other victims, strong anti-Semitic currents constantly materialize on the extreme right. On one extreme, Jewish communities have suffered numerous violent attacks because of their Jewish identity. In 1985, Seattle attorney Charles Goldmark was murdered along with his wife and family because the perpetrator, a follower of the extreme right, believed him to be Jewish.[7] Right-wing extremists have also claimed responsibility for torching Jewish synagogues in Berlin in March 1994 and Moscow in December 1993, in addition to more frequent acts of cemetery desecration and vandalism. Nevertheless, in comparison to immigrant and foreigner communities, Jewish communities have been spared the greater portion of direct attack, "primarily because the immigrant is a more visible, convenient and effective target, and the immigration issue produces a more substantial opportunity for mobilisation."[8]

In contrast, according to much of the extreme right's propaganda, Jews are the ultimate source of evil. Anti-Semitism, thus, performs a special function for the extreme right. Jews are convenient and residual targets, easily vilified on the basis of past propaganda, preempting the need for new and original bigoted doctrines. As a tool and device, anti-Semitism is critical for indoctrinating new recruits, furthering internal solidarity, and conferring continuity and endorsement from the past. Anti-Semitism also provides an ideological justification and purpose joining right-wing extremist movements from different countries that otherwise target nationally specific immigrant groups. For right-wing extremists, Jews represent the unidentified enemy behind the state, behind politicians, behind any position of power. Moreover, the emergence of Holocaust denial as an "academic" enterprise has obfuscated the boundaries of anti-Semitic hate speech, bringing ostensible credibility and legitimacy to the extreme right. It is not that every right-wing extremist must be anti-Semitic; neither is the reverse true, that all anti-Semites are right-wing extremists. The point is that anti-Semitism is central to right-wing extremist discourse, having developed beyond personal prejudice to a way of thinking that structures outlook. Hence, the presence of anti-Semitism can be a useful indicator of hostility toward other minority groups and "also serves as a barometer of the threat to a nation's political democracy."[9]

Anti-Semitism to some extent also reflects the final identifying factor of right-wing extremism, its propensity to disregard accepted norms of public behavior. The extreme right is neither restrained nor bounded by constitutional rules and procedures but is unabashedly committed to violence, explicitly and implicitly. Right-wing extremists have gained their notoriety through frequent attacks, murders, terror, and the destruction of property in every country under study. Unlike other kinds of political terrorism, "what is striking about many of the extreme right terrorist attacks is that they are not followed up by the issuing of demands or attempts to justify their action to the public at large."[10]

The purpose of violence appears to be to display the virility and power of right-wing extremists, along with the vulnerability of others; to instill fear and panic; and to earn respect. Extremists accomplish this objective partly through their intimidating and belligerent style and antagonistic attitude. The Nazi symbols frequently used by right-wing extremists, such as the swastika and the Seig Heil salute, are identified with the atrocities committed in the past. Neo-Nazi gangs have also instigated incidences of football hooliganism, such as intimidating crowds by attacking rivals and spreading their racist creed at the football game. Some of the more purposeful groups have engaged in organized violent and paramilitary activity. One need only mention the 1995 Oklahoma City bombing and its alleged connection to the Michigan militia, one of many militia groups in the United States. Such groups are not a recent phenomenon. The *Turner Diaries,* an opus for the race war, inspired the creation of the Order, a fraternity of racists who terrorized the Northwestern United States. Another example is the bombings in California in 1993.[11] The Austrian neo-Nazi leader Gottfried Küssel and his associates were filmed by German journalist Michael Schmidt practicing military exercises and claiming assistance from members of the German army.[12] It has also been widely reported that bomb-making manuals on CD-ROM have been circulating throughout Europe.[13]

A commitment to violence need not be confined to the execution of violent acts but can also be implicitly reflected in strategic considerations. Within the seemingly political ranks of the extreme right, violence is an intrinsic element encouraged and manipulated by leaders and often condoned by alliances with those who commit violence.[14] Radical right parties seeking electoral success do not obviously embrace and participate in physical violence and thus jeopardize their success, but their rhetoric justifies such action. The strident emphasis on the nation, the preservation of the race, the commanding word of God, or the call to war presupposes the notion of sacrifice, the need to take any and all measures necessary to achieve their ends. Inflammatory statements such as "Expect confrontations that will be not only unpleasant but at times physically bloody. . . . This decade will not be for the faint of heart, but the resolute"[15] clearly indicate that the means are subordinate to the goals—and unrestricted means inevitably lead to the use of force. Moreover, their platforms and specific policies rest on assumptions of extraordinary state powers, thus sanctioning the future use of state violence directed against segments of society. In contrast to mainstream norms and standards, violence is not unthinkable but is a "legitimate" option and necessary strategy for the extreme right.

The most outstanding characteristics of the extreme right are, then, the centrality of hatred toward outsiders, nationalism, anti-Semitism, and violence. Selecting these themes provides a point of departure for contrasting and comparing the variety of manifestations of the extreme right. Recognizing and elaborating upon these factors is useful; however, the purpose of the exercise is to identify the extreme right, and that is usually not very problematic. Journalists, politicians, academics, and other observers generally refer to the same groups when they describe the extreme right. Further, it cannot be proven that the identified themes constitute the basic properties whose presence is necessary and sufficient for the right-wing extremist label to be affixed. Because these themes are more suggestive than conclusive, they are not criteria at all. Hate, nationalism, anti-Semitism, and violence are not unique to right-wing extremism but are shared by neoconservatives, left-wing radicals, and others. Moreover, not all right-wing extremists are the same; some, particularly at the political end, have moderated their positions to achieve other objectives. To escape the dilemma of using these themes, it is necessary to probe deeper beneath the surface of the extreme right to find and trace the borders that outline the phenomenon of right-wing extremism.

Differentiating the Right

After specifying the salient features of right-wing extremism, I want to now determine some parameters of the phenomenon. The object of this approach is to establish a line that distinguishes what is right-wing extremism from what is not. The very terms employed, "right-wing" and "extreme," suggest that there are criteria that demarcate the right from the left and the extreme from the normal. If right-wing extremism is situated within the locus of ideas associated with "the right," we may draw upon the most commonly and popularly understood classification of political life. The distinction between left and right has its origins in the Assembly of revolutionary France, where the right represented support for the status quo and the left, change. Positions on either side revolved around three sets of issues, political decisionmaking, economic relations, and cultural authority and tradition. Originally, the left was seen as a champion of equal representation and universal suffrage, the free market, and autonomy from religious and cultural authority; the right defended the monarchy, a feudal economy, and the role of the Catholic Church. More generally still, the left is associated with the working classes and the right with the privileged classes. Over time, the issues, the actors, and the policies have evolved such that the simplicity of this spatial schema belies the contentiousness of what left and right have come to mean. Concepts once differentiating left from right such as democracy, order, justice, freedom, the market economy, equality, individualism, the state, and so on no longer correspond to clear identifications of the left and the right. Compounding this confusion is the contextual development of left and right whereby the left-right paradigm of the West has a different conception in non-Western countries such as those in postcommunist Eastern Europe. Some scholars also point to a more profound value shift transforming the left and right, caused by the conflict between the old, materialist politics and the new, postmaterialist politics.[16]

If we put the left and its philosophical traditions aside, this conceptual ambiguity is further complicated by the paucity of political thought in support of the right. There are few notable philosophical inquiries on the right, perhaps because, as a recent example finds, "the concept of the right is extremely elusive."[17] According to Roger Eatwell and Noël O'Sullivan in *The Nature of the Right,* the right should be conceived of as not one monolithic right but a collection of "rights." In place of an ideological core, the right represents an assortment of different responses to developments on the left. These various styles of thought can be coalesced into categories of the reactionary, moderate, radical, extreme, and new rights. This approach can accommodate differences arising over specific issues that otherwise would invalidate a more static and unyielding schema. Within this schema, the authors contend that the extreme right developed in reaction to the rise of socialist and communist movements in the nineteenth and early twentieth centuries. What distinguishes this extreme variant from the other styles of the right is the persistence and preservation of anti-Semitism. Specifically, the ideology of anti-Semitism, contained in an elaborate conspiracy theory, is intrinsic to the extreme right. Michael Billig argues that the anti-Semitic conspiracy tradition "represents a common theme linking extreme right-wing groups from different countries and linking them to pre-war fascism."[18]

According to this conspiracy theory, an insidious cabal has been plotting to take over the world by positioning its members in places of power in the media, government, finance, business, and so on. In such positions of influence, members are able to control worldwide events to advance the cabal's evil purposes. Only a very few, according to the adherents of this conspiracy theory, have knowledge of this evil plot, having grasped the truth by rejecting the ignorance of conventional thinking. Since the first conspiracy theories first emerged centuries ago, different conspirators have been accused of directing the plot. Gradually, the conspiracy has become inextricably linked to Zionism and Jews, inspired and strengthened by the forgery *The Protocols of the Learned Elders of Zion.* However, the conspiracy tradition has developed beyond a rather incredible theory into a "revisionist" enterprise that purports to refute the veracity of the Holocaust. Holocaust denial, as the name suggests, claims the Holocaust was a myth or hoax fabricated by the leaders of the "conspiracy" in order to elicit sympathy for the creation of Israel. In this version, the conspiracy tradition serves a number of critical functions for the extreme right. Not only is it an important indoctrinating device, it has become a self-generating industry and a convenient tool, justifying and explaining the failures of the extreme right and conferring upon its successes an even weightier import. The conspiracy theory "implies a complete and novel way of looking at politics; the new member has to learn that the political ideas he has acquired from conventional sources are not what they seem."[19]

If Billig distinguishes the extreme right by the anti-Semitic conspiracy theory, the definition he is offering is extremely narrow and open to criticism. By positing the conspiracy theory as a unique component essential to the extreme right, he is reducing the phenomenon and emphasizing the role of the leadership as opposed to its lay members. The cognitive and political implications of conspiracy thinking, furthermore, marginalize the extreme right, relegating it to the fringes, whereas some proponents have successfully penetrated the political mainstream. It must also be questioned whether the conspiracy theory is by itself a necessary feature of right-wing extremism considering the political objectives of many activists and given the geographical diversity of extremist groups. This raises the further question of the centrality of anti-Semitism to right-wing extremism as opposed to the issue of immigration and foreigners. However, it should be assumed that this category of the "extreme" right is necessarily restricted because it is distinguished in relation to other particularized styles found among rightist groups. Billig himself concludes that the spectrum of ideas on the right is inherently problematic because of the notion of extremism that "seems to imply that such movements are rather like the non-extreme right, but just a bit more so."[20] However, within the broader scheme set forth by Eatwell and O'Sullivan, the categories of "rights" are themselves hazy and particularly problematic when various right-wing groups are categorized. The Republikaner Party of Germany, the Poujadists of France, and the John Birch Society of the United States are included in the radical right variety rather than the extreme right. Jean-Marie Le Pen and the Front National (FN) are described as extreme right; but Le Pen was once himself a Poujadist, and he advocates ideas and policies that could easily fall under the rubric of the moderate, reactionary, or new right. The classification of American nativist groups is also contentious, displaying some of the attributes of the reactionary right, but not necessarily enough of them to qualify under this category. Many leading white supremacists in the United States were also onetime Birchers. Where would militia groups now be placed? If the essence of the "right" is unclear, the problem, then, is how to specify and qualify the categories of moderate, radical, extreme, and reactionary.

The idea of extremism originated with the rise of absolutist or activist politics toward the end of the nineteenth century and the beginning of the twentieth century. With the inception of absolutism or activism, the strict linear conception of the left-right spectrum was gradually replaced by a circular model that remains confused to this day. As a result of this transformation, an alternative conceptual approach to organizing political and social life developed according to ideal types. The extreme variants of these ideal types are totalitarian communist systems, equated with the extreme left, and fascist regimes, synonymous with the extreme right. Subsequently, fascism is considered to be the prototypical example of right-wing extremism, with the result that today's right-wing extremists are frequently labeled fascist or neo-fascist. This means that a definition of fascism would suffice for a definition of right-wing extremism.

Fascism and neofascism "are classic concepts derived from the name of one political movement and one political party."[21]

According to Noël O'Sullivan, among others, fascism is defined as an ideology based on natural history, the pursuit of an expansionary and aggressive geopolitical policy, and corporate statism. The state serves one homogeneous ethnic grouping and aims to reincorporate and reunite any members of that grouping located outside its borders. Fascism is furthermore identified with a cultist worship of and obedience to a charismatic leader, total devotion to the state, an admiration of strength accompanied by a fascination with militarism, and an overwhelming reliance on propaganda. As such it seems to denote little more than a violent and authoritarian style of a young and virile male-dominated movement. Parallels can easily be drawn linking today's right-wing extremists to their fascist ancestors. The contemporary extreme right is predominantly male, largely youth-oriented, and clearly violent. Propaganda is more evident than ideas, and militaristic fantasies are ubiquitous. Undeniably, fascism is an inspiration for the extreme right.

However, inspiration and parallels do not necessarily lead to the conclusion that contemporary right-wing extremism is the same phenomenon as fascism. The value of equating the two is limited by the implied conclusion that there has been a historical continuity of ideas, people, and goals between the past and today's right-wing extremists. Parallels also presuppose cultural and political similarities and antecedents that suffer in a pan-European, cross-Atlantic definition. Moreover, many scholars hold the view that fascism was a historically specific movement resulting from a particular configuration of forces not likely to be repeated and therefore irrelevant in this contemporary context.[22] Clearly, fascism is too narrow a definition for right-wing extremism, especially given that fascism and Nazism themselves are differentiated. Such a definition would also exclude one of the most successful right-wing extremist organizations in the world, the American-bred Ku Klux Klan. More important, the automatic association of fascism with the interwar regimes in Europe and their subsequent alliances with Nazi Germany have infused the concept with a tremendous amount of repugnance and condemnation, thereby severely discrediting its utility. "It is also a matter of moral and political responsibility: those who exaggerate the nature and scale of a contemporary problem by reference to the rich history of past evils run the risk of eliminating all meaningful distinction."[23] It is more useful to treat fascism as a historical source and inspiration for today's collection of right-wing extremists. In this function, fascism can serve as a useful indicator of political purposes and perhaps also of political fortunes and dynamics of extreme-right organizations.[24]

Whether we array the right along a spectrum of different rights or operate from ideal types, establishing clear and certain boundaries to distinguish the extreme right is not possible. Isolating right-wing extremism is not viable without oversimplifying and reducing it to a very particularistic and specific phenomenon. Therefore, this approach has the opposite failing of the first by presenting too narrow a definition and thus excluding a number of phenomena. However, discerning the contours of right-wing extremism need not follow just a spatial and static delineation but should include a dynamic and temporal conception. Rather than reducing the phenomenon to its parts, we should reconstruct right-wing extremism in order to understand it as a whole phenomenon and then contextualize it to determine its overall importance.

Understanding the Causes

A discussion of right-wing extremism would be incomplete without an exploration of its causal factors, but all too often this proceeds in a cursory and often deterministic fashion. Not surprisingly, the complexity of right-wing extremism is reflected in the explanations that account for it. In the following section, I attempt to sketch the four models usually offered in explanation of right-wing extremism: social-psychological theories; socioeconomic theories; political theories; and international, or global, theories.

Social-psychological explanations are predicated on the assumption that certain personality attributes predispose individuals and, summarily, social groups to certain ideas and modes of behavior. Focusing on the personality structure involves an exploration of the attitudes that explain an individual's affinity to right-wing extremism. This sociopsychological approach is most closely associated with the 1950 study by Theodor Adorno and colleagues, *The Authoritarian Personality*. In the introduction, Adorno argued that "since fascism was not economically in the interests of the masses it sought to attract, 'it must therefore make its major appeal, not to rational self-interest, but to emotional needs.'"[25]

Originally a project on anti-Semitism, the study became primarily concerned with the personality forces of the potential fascist. On the basis of their results, Adorno and colleagues were able to develop a profile of the fascistic individual and provided a fascism scale, or f-scale, by which this potential could be measured. The authors concluded that

> anti-Semitism is a symptom of a deeper psychological malaise which can, and does, manifest itself in prejudice towards other outgroups; and, secondly, that a crucial component in the psychology of prejudice is cognitive rigidity. . . . Furthermore, the typical prejudiced individual was said to have possessed an authoritarian syndrome, whose features included a rigid adherence to conventional values, a resistance to introspective self-examination, an admiration of

power, an exaggerated and prurient concern with sexual goings on, a tendency to think in rigid categories, and a belief in the inferiority of outgroups. . . . In consequence the authoritarian needed to experience the world in rigid categories—people or social groups were to be classed as wholly good or wholly bad, and each had their allotted place in a strictly hierarchical perception of the world. The authoritarian's own repressed, bad feelings would then be projected on to inferior outgroups, such that it was always the Jews, or the blacks, or any other convenient scapegoat who were sex-obsessed, violent, anti-social and so on.[26]

Adorno, as a member of the Frankfurt School, located the source of authoritarian prejudice in the impact of family upbringing on the development of the personality, but also more generally in capitalism's structuring of relationships according to authority and obedience. However, given that Adorno was associated with the Marxist tradition, *The Authoritarian Personality* has been criticized for generalizing conclusions that were based on an ideological bias against "the right." In *The Open and Closed Mind,* Milton Rokeach ignored political orientation by studying the authoritarian mind in general. Through an examination of the structure of belief systems and disbelief systems, Rokeach presented the idea that there were two ideal-type cognitive styles, the open mind and the closed mind. Extremist and moderate orientations reflect how information from the outside world is assimilated. Rokeach postulated that the more closed the system, "the more sensitive should [the subject] be to communications, reinforcements, warnings, prohibitions and promises issuing forth from his own group or authorities and the more should he be dependent on such positive authorities for information he accumulates about a particular disbelief system."[27]

The closed-minded person is unable to evaluate and act on information received from the outside on its own intrinsic merits, relying instead on a source to which he or she accords authority. The extremist is unduly receptive to information, representing his or her own beliefs regardless of contradictions while utterly rejecting as false any contrary information. Thus the extremist style of thinking is characterized by an image of unity that is potentially conducive to conspiracy thinking.

Other studies have specifically focused on the emotional factors that contribute to the propensity to believe in conspiracy theories. It has been suggested that conspiracy thinking results from emotional repression, mental stress, "the need for defensive ascription enabling people to protect their own sense of self-esteem and to justify their own apparent failings,"[28] and the need for psychological compensations, that is, a feeling of superiority over others. These factors are usually encapsulated in the "scapegoat theory," whereby those in an economically and politically depressed position elevate themselves by targeting more vulnerable groups that reflect their own predicament. For example, the documentary on the Rostock attack produced by *Der Spiegel* showed bitter and resentful East German bystanders complaining about the condescending treatment received from West Germans.[29] In venting their frustration on the more vulnerable foreigners, they were able to derive a sense of personal pride from national pride.

These sociopsychological theories address the questions of why ordinary people subscribe to right-wing extremism, why some join the extreme right, and why others willingly abandon normal existence for life on the fringes. However, by focusing solely on the individual actor and on the importance of the personality and attitudes in determining the actor's behavior, these explanations can be reductionist and deterministic. There is an element of unjustified causal certainty linking prejudice to fascism and also a sense of psychological fallibility implying deviant mental faculties. On their own, sociopsychological theories also fail to address the dynamics and developments of the phenomenon of right-wing extremism as a social and political movement. Within *The Authoritarian Personality* itself, there is a tension between the primacy of personality needs and the importance of economic forces. Adorno wrote, "It seems well understood today that whether or not anti-democratic propaganda is to become a dominant force in this country depends primarily upon the situation of the most powerful economic interests, upon whether they, by conscious design or not, make use of this device for maintaining their dominant status."[30] Thus even in the beginning, the psychological argument was bridged with socioeconomic arguments.

Socioeconomic theories begin with the premise that right-wing extremism is a movement of "modernization losers" who have lost their status and economic security as a result of the uneven processes of industrialization. Increasing economic and social competition has created a pool of resentful castoffs who seek gratification and social acceptance. Erwin K. Scheuch and Hans-Dieter Klingemann, after studying the NPD (Nationaldemokratische Partei Deutschlands) success in West Germany, declared right-wing extremism to be a "normal pathological condition of industrial societies."[31] They argued that the potential for right-wing extremism exists in all industrial societies because of the contradictory processes of modernization that result in tremendous economic and cultural upheaval. In reaction to these pressures, those who cannot keep pace "tend to build up a variety of inner-defence mechanisms such as, for example, a rigid, cognitive personality structure which in turn in certain circumstances predisposes them to vote for parties promising the restoration of a better past and the elimination of structurally-induced social tensions."[32] Thus it is in response to economic forces that the psyche becomes susceptible and vulnerable to the message of the extreme right.

In a complete departure from the psychological approach, the sociologist Seymour Martin Lipset in collaboration with Earl Raab gave greater consideration to economic factors in *The Politics of Unreason*. This book, representing a mainstream status quo orientation, offered a historical-sociological account of right-wing extremist movements in American history. Lipset and Raab contended that "right-wing extremist movements in America have all risen against the background of economic and social changes which have resulted in the displacement of some population groups from former positions of dominance."[33]

Demographic shifts and successive waves of immigrants create new pools of people striving to achieve the American dream. In this quest, they encounter and hence threaten to displace the status and security of those who most recently attained such success and have the most to lose by this new influx. Thus Lipset and Raab defined right-wing extremism as the "politics of backlash" resulting from despair and as rising "in reaction against the displacement of power and status accompanying change."[34] Rather than emphasizing psychological deviance and abnormality, Lipset and Raab argued that "extremist movements are not primarily the product of extremists. The critical ranks in extremist movements are not composed of evil-structured types called extremists, but rather of ordinary people caught in certain kinds of stress."[35] Lipset and Raab disagreed with the explanation that bigotry and conspiracy thinking were primary sources of right-wing extremism rather than surface expressions of a deeper structural problem. Many scholars have agreed with this general postulate, providing supporting evidence in their own studies. In a study on the Republikaners in Germany, it was found that "right-wing extremism is more strongly represented in rural areas and small towns, among the less educated, within low-income groups, among members of the so-called middle class and among older groups."[36] Christopher Husbands, an expert on the extreme right in Europe, also concluded that support for the British National Party was older and drawn from the petite bourgeoisie. This same argument is applied with respect to the skinhead phenomenon and youth participation in the extreme right. It is commonly argued that skinheads come from broken homes and that their opportunities and prospects are restricted and bleak. Therefore skinheads are characterized as frustrated, demoralized youths who turn to violence, venting their frustration as a form of rebellion. According to Mark Hamm, who espouses this view, "The skinhead subculture provides its members with an environment where status ascriptions can finally be achieved."[37] Nevertheless, it has been shown that skinheads often come from stable middle-class families and that neo-Nazis often hold steady employment and are regarded to be "reliable, hard workers, who, when facing trial, never had trouble getting their foreman or factory director to testify that they were stellar workers."[38] To retain some of the economic thesis's validity, some authors have focused less on the actual loss of economic status than on the perception of decline and the accompanying feelings of threat. In an opinion study of political supporters of German political parties, "compared with the general population, twice as many REP [Republikaner Partei] supporters feel disadvantaged"[39] and "nearly twice as many perceive their present economic situation as being bad."[40]

According to socioeconomic theories, right-wing extremism is a product of stressful and demanding times; it is a product of extraneous social factors. But this characterization as a reaction and backlash obscures the possibility of right-wing extremism as a phenomenon independent of social forces. Lipset and Raab and Scheuch and Klingemann have suggested that right-wing extremism is an unavoidable and predictable reaction to processes that periodically disturb society. The extent of the problem should then vary upon the amount of stress; the more structural and transformative the changes are, the more destabilizing the potential for right-wing extremism. But right-wing extremism should also be a temporary phenomenon that should not be sustained once stable conditions prevail. In promoting the idea of a backlash, Lipset cannot account for the constancy of right-wing extremism and its continuity through prosperous times such as the 1950s and mid-to-late 1980s and for the fact that membership in the Klan began to disintegrate at the *advent* of the Great Depression, not to mention the fact that Western Europe has elected more extreme-right candidates than Eastern Europe. According to this evidence, right-wing extremism has become a perennial and constant backlash. If the conditions that result in this backlash are always present, then Lipset is not offering a theory of causation at all. Instead, he is offering a thesis on the probability of right-wing extremism that has little in the way of predictive value. Klaus von Beyme found that although the thesis that "the less well-educated lower middle classes are always in danger of being attracted towards right-wing extremist parties was upheld in many studies, . . . these social strata did not show the same voting behaviour every time."[41] Again, this socioeconomic explanation is too deterministic. As with the sociopsychological approach, it presupposes the presence of a social strain, a predictable reaction, a ready ideological remedy, and an available right-wing extremist organization. In other words, these vulnerable middle classes fall under the sway of right-wing extremists who already exist and whose presence must perforce be explained. How were parties of the extreme right in a position to offer an alternative to available political actors, where did they come from, what forms do they take, and what kinds of success do they enjoy?

The transformation of the extreme right from negligible fringe group to mainstream political alternative occurred as a result of an opening of political space, which encouraged the entry of new parties and actors. A process of political radicalization was initiated with the rise of the new left and corresponding development of the new right. The resulting and ongoing polarization between left and right increased the opening for even more radical parties to maneuver into the political fray. This newfound exposure coincided with the public's growing disenchantment with the available political parties, perceived to be unresponsive to popular concerns and priorities and too like each other to present any noticeable alternative to the status quo. Across Europe and North America,

> intraparty volatility has progressively accelerated in the 1980s and "there is little evidence that this flux is likely to abate." At the partisan level, a series of indicators show the accelerated process of "decomposition of established party ties." The decline of party identification, of the number of party members and of the degree of partisan involvement all indicate that the previous enduring ties between the electorate and established parties are progressively fading away, thus enabling the emergence of new parties and or new agencies for the aggregation of demands.[42]

While traditional parties neglected popular concerns, the radical right parties presented themselves as political alternatives by articulating ideas on subjects that were considered prohibited, such as German history, German unification before 1989, nationalism, immigration, and religion. By addressing this void, the extreme right mobilized support at the expense of traditional parties. Similarly, specific policies and events also contributed to the tensions fueling the development of the extreme right, particularly the policies of immigration and of integrating the foreigner. This general sense of disillusionment extends to the political system as a whole and is manifested in a growing lack of confidence in the functioning of its institutions. There is a growing sense of a "moral [crisis] of democracy, . . . compris[ing] a flight from politics, . . . a weariness with its debates, disbeliefs about its claims, scepticism about its results, [and] cynicism about its practitioners."[43] This perception dominates those on the extreme right. In Germany, "compared with the general population, only half as many REP supporters, or less, trust the main political institutions of parliament, government and the established parties."[44] Thus the vote of endorsement for the extreme right is sometimes interpreted as reflecting political discontent rather than ideological sympathy. Similarly in France, "the vote [for the FN] appears as a whole to be the manifestation of protest against the policies of the government. More particularly, 31 percent admit the vote [in Dreux, where the FN won close to 30 percent in a 1989 by-election] was specifically meant to be a warning to the government, and 23 percent suggest it was meant to show opposition to the government."[45] According to a national sample of voting, Nonna Mayer and Pascal Perrineau discovered that 67 percent of those close to the FN and 52 percent very close to the FN think people vote for an FN candidate "to protest against today's political system."[46]

A final causal explanation might focus on some of the international processes that have been creating conditions favorable to the development and success of the extreme right. Rapid social change has increased insecurity and instability for many people, contributing to feelings of alienation and resentment. One such change is the end of the cold war. The trauma and crisis resulting from the complete collapse of a social and political system undoubtedly enhanced the potential vulnerability and susceptibility of Eastern European societies to right-wing extremism. The deprivations in the East also affected Western Europe by triggering an influx of refugees to the European Union member states; this influx fueled xenophobia by contributing to a sense of siege, again enhancing the appeal of the extreme right. However, these events, as dramatic as they are, have not taken place in a vacuum but have occurred amidst the larger processes of globalization and fragmentation. The authority of the state has diminished as greater interdependence and interaction amongst peoples have expanded beyond the control and scope of the state. Ironically, this erosion of state sovereignty has taken place in conjunction with the rise of the welfare state, which is entrusted with a tremendous degree of intrusive responsibilities. This intrusiveness has objectified a monolithic and omnipresent state, thus adding to the sense of alienation some people feel. The globalization of culture has also diminished the capacity for people to differentiate amongst themselves, threatening people's identity and no doubt resulting in a backlash, a reactionary defense of the strong nation and strong state. It has also reshaped the labor market, increasing social and geographic mobility and making it more and more difficult to secure one's existence economically and socially. The increasing individualization amidst a greater lack of stability and durability in social relationships has heightened feelings of isolation and powerlessness. These upheavals and transformations have been feeding a sense of insecurity and trauma that culminate in a spiritual malaise. A crisis of disillusionment and despair regarding the modern condition is permeating many societies. It is sometimes argued that

> modern society is characterised by a persistent and escalating degree of individ-
> ualisation which results from the weakening of the social ties that connect indi-
> vidual human beings to collectivities (e.g. the family, place of work, religious
> communities, etc.). The resulting isolation gives rise to anxiety and the absence
> of clear objectives. . . . In order to resolve this anxiety, so the argument contin-
> ues, atomised individuals seek and find security in right-wing political pro-
> grammes and organisations. The latter are characterised as offering a new iden-
> tification with a national community which is defined negatively by reference to
> "alien elements" who "belong" somewhere else.[47]

Rapid social change has undermined the categories by which people think and look at the world. This uncertainty has predisposed some to look to the extreme right.

Clearly, no explanatory model is sufficient unto itself; each focuses on different aspects of the extreme right without explaining the whole. Rather, in each country, a specific configuration of forces and conditions coalesced to produce particular manifestations of right-wing extremism. Since it is not possible to accurately predict the conditions leading to the emergence of right-wing extremism, we can only generally conclude that some disillusioned and discouraged people will turn to the extreme-right alternatives for the simple solutions they provide.

Assessing the Impact

Understanding the nature of right-wing extremism through its causes still offers only a partial perspective on the extent of right-wing extremism. In this final section I explore the significance of right-wing extremism by focusing on its various impacts. From the viewpoint of the victim and the potential victim, the extreme right poses a very obvious and violent threat to society. The security and safety of ordinary citizens and communities have been jeopardized by the violent actions committed by the rank and file of extreme-right groups. To the people who are terrorized and intimidated, the criminological danger is the most visible threat facing the public and politicians. This threat is compounded by the climate of hostility incited and manipulated by the extreme right. Depicting these out-groups as the burden and bane of society, the extreme right has struck a sympathetic chord with sections of the population, creating an inhospitable and forbidding environment for some. The violent release of extreme hatred through the particular energies of the extreme right has to some extent shattered accepted standards of restraint and released inhibitions regarding personal prejudices and opinions. However, "the greater visibility and increased awareness of racist violence should not be confused with an assessment of the extent of its occurrence."[48] The "undoubted energy of neo-fascist activities continues to result in constant organisational splits and a multitude of competing organisations and movements. Their effect is therefore constantly dissipated."[49] This criminal element is still relatively small and is a threat only to civil peace. The more abhorrent crimes have also provoked condemnation and galvanized shocked citizens and opponents to strike back at the advocates of hatred. A good example of this is the spontaneous demonstrations in Germany voicing outrage and a renewed commitment to democracy and tolerance.

On the basis of the increased activity of the political wing of the extreme right, it is far too easy to extrapolate the possibility of an organized takeover of the state by neo-Nazi and neofascist political parties. However, the prospects for a neofascist takeover seem remote, at least in Western Europe, notwithstanding the election of numerous fascist and extremist candidates. With some exceptions, the central and national corridors of power continue to be impervious to the extreme right. Right-wing extremist candidates have been very successful in winning seats in municipal, state, and European parliamentary elections. As for the exceptions, in Austria the formerly named Freiheithliche Partei Östereichs (FPÖ) is one of the three main political players on the Austrian political landscape, as is Le Pen in France, whereas neither is necessarily a force in the European Parliament. At all levels, extremist political parties have successfully made incursions into the political mainstream. The more entrenched they are in the political system, the greater the danger extremism poses, particularly if the support is stable over a long period of time and, worse, increasing. In France,

> since at least the mid-1980s there has been a persisting fear that the FN would at some time make a successful breakthrough to win control of a city like Nice or Marseille. For the first time, in the municipal elections of 18 June 1995, in the afterglow of Le Pen's first-round Presidential success in April, the FN was able to do that; in three towns in the south, Toulon, Marignane and Orange the FN won up to 37 per cent of the second-round vote, enabling the party to nominate the mayor. In Nice, Jacques Peyrat, formally independent but ideologically close to the FN and a former member and confidant of Le Pen, won the mayoralty with 44 per cent of the vote.[50]

Success, moreover, reproduces itself. "Certainly, nobody who has seen the obvious professionalism and extensive resources in the national offices of parties like the FPÖ, the VB (Vlaams Blok) and the FN can doubt their potential for major influence or the dedication of those involved. . . . Instead, they are young, hard-working, professionally oriented political ideologues with a clear understanding of both their goals and also of strategy for their attainment. It is that distinctive feature which makes them a danger."[51]

In addition to accessing a public podium from which to voice their views, extremists have won a measure of influence with opposition politicians and have had an impact upon governance at all levels of power. The most blatant example of the pressure the extreme right has exerted is the manipulation of the immigration issue. Taking advantage of the fears and apprehensions permeating society concerning the presence of foreigners and different races, the extreme right helped to dictate the terms in which the issue was debated with the collaboration of most other politicians. In place of a serious discussion on racism, nationalism, culture, or the economic and societal malaise, many immigration laws were hastily and restrictively rewritten. Simply on the policy level, the extreme right sustained a climate hostile to foreigners, minorities, and refugees. Specific groups targeted by the extreme right suffer the immediate threat, but clearly the implications extend beyond the particular energies of the extreme right to the impact of the movement in general. In operating from the mainstream, right-wing extremist groups threaten the effective functioning of the liberal democratic system of governance. In this case, the authority of established intermediate structures such as political parties, interest groups, and the media is seriously undermined by the extreme right. "Their very presence in the midst of functioning democracies raises a cruel dilemma of how far to tolerate the intolerant without seriously compromising the institutions of free speech and full freedom of political action and association . . . and of where to draw the line between the values of ethnic identity and exclusiveness, on the one hand, and liberty and human rights, which are the essence of liberalism, on the other."[52] Paradoxically, right-wing extremism may serve democracy by encouraging serious reflection on the underpinning tenets of democracy. Eatwell agrees that "the analysis of small parties on the political fringe, beyond the bounds of conventional political respectability, can illustrate more important issues about the nature of political beliefs, and in particular, about the nature of irrational racial prejudices."[53] This challenge, of course, only compounds the fears cast by right-wing extremism, because it casts doubt on the capacity of liberal democracy to sustain itself. For societies already in the throes of political and economic upheaval, such doubts and concerns can be overwhelming.

But is the threat posed by right-wing extremism limited to the institutions of the liberal democratic system? Is it possible for the extreme right to be, as some authors argue, "a movement which seeks a comprehensive ideological change, *without*, however, questioning the legitimacy of the constitution and established institutions of the state?"[54] Does not the challenge to these structures convey a more fundamental attack upon the values and principles upholding liberal democracy? Richard Stoss has defined right-wing extremism as the "totality of anti-democratic attitudes and behaviour patterns directed against parliamentarian/pluralist systems of government."[55] The nationalist principle and the worship of natural history expressed by the extreme right subordinates and hence contravenes democratic rights and freedoms. Right-wing extremists do not recognize the supremacy of the rule of law and the constraints that it imposes, advocating instead a suprapowerful state that would be under the control of an elite group. The principles of pluralism, equality, and tolerance are clearly not respected by those on the extreme right who frequently act outside of the bounds of constitutional restraint. In place of political compromise and accommodation, the extreme right advocates violence, authoritarianism, and the elimination of all forms of opposition.

Right-wing extremism is, then, a rejection of democracy and the liberal democratic state. However, in challenging democracy, right-wing extremism seems to strike people as something outside of democracy, threatening to destroy it. This idea can be misleading. Right-wing extremism is very much a product of democracy and can flourish and attain its objectives only in democratic states. It may be argued that the countries of Eastern Europe, particularly Russia, are not yet democratic systems and that, therefore, this argument is untenable.

In many ways, right-wing extremism is directed not only at the foreigner but also at the pillars of liberal democracy and the liberal democratic state:

equality, individual identity, pluralism, tolerance, and capitalism. Right-wing extremism acts upon democracy, transforming and challenging accepted notions of political life, and then is itself further transformed. Right-wing extremism represents an alternative worldview, a worldview in which progress means the end of democracy. In place of progress and rationality, right-wing extremism defends a social order supposedly predetermined by nature. In fact, right-wing extremists are redefining this "natural" order according to their own prejudices. They do not want to simply change the world; they want to recreate it.

Understanding and accepting the role right-wing extremism plays in liberal democracy is problematic for reasons similar to those that make explanations of fascism inadequate. Noël O'Sullivan has argued that the reaction to the appearance of the fascist regimes and subsequent events was one of general surprise and a degree of bewildering shock. He states that liberals and conservatives alike were unprepared for fascism because of the problem of understanding fascism as "a modern ideology which is wilfully destructive."[56] The first step toward grasping fascism and, similarly, right-wing extremism must be an acceptance of the fact that there are people who deliberately and determinedly wish to harm other people.

The danger of right-wing extremism lies not in the articulation of ideas we might consider abhorrent, which is natural in an open and free environment, but in the inhibition of the free contest of ideas to the detriment of political discourse. Liberal democracy is founded on the free expression and debate of all ideas, but the extremist style "hampers our understanding of important issues, muddies the waters of discourse with invective, defamation, self-righteousness, fanaticism and hatred and impairs our ability to make intelligent well-informed choices."[57]

In its transition from the fringe to the mainstream, the extreme right eliminated some of the obvious vitriol from its rhetoric, using politically acceptable language instead. The obfuscation of its purposes has tainted discussion and reduced the complexities of reality to a false simplicity. The extreme right pollutes and subverts the notion of truth, repudiating reason. As such it must be seen as a challenge to the Enlightenment project of rationality, tolerance, and progress in favor of a destructive, supremacist, racial project. Whereas modern democratic politics is about the open contest of ideas, right-wing extremism is about closing minds and politics to ideas.

Conclusion

Upon exploring the extreme right's multifaceted traits, boundaries, causes, and impacts, we see clear evidence that this is a phenomenon that cannot be lightly ignored in the hope that it will simply disappear. Although to some extent the extreme right refers to a narrow and specific movement, its implications are broader and deeper, touching upon fundamental values, human rights, and the very fabric of democracy. Right-wing extremism serves as a point of entry to the wider-ranging problems of hatred, xenophobia, and nationalism that frustrate the healthy functioning of democracy. Identifying right-wing extremism is not so much a matter of specifying these manifestations as it is of identifying elements that challenge some of the basic tenets of democracy and the democratic state. There may be numerous strands of right-wing extremism that combine in different ways and in different places, but in the end what right-wing extremism seeks is the elimination of the modern democratic state.

Perhaps the extreme right cannot be sufficiently understood as a singular phenomenon; such a perception obscures the different extreme-right traditions. One option might be to follow the example set forth by Roger Eatwell and Noël O'Sullivan: conceiving of an array of extreme rights and developing a taxonomy of extreme-right categories. Notwithstanding the restrictions of such an approach, it would allow for the inclusion and differentiation of various extreme-right manifestations, their multiple causes and potential impacts. It would certainly enable a more comprehensive discussion of the distinction between the political element of right-wing extremism and the explicitly violent movement and, especially, the relationships between the two.

In the end, it is more than evident which groups and individuals belong to the extreme right. They are the groups and individuals who feed and live off hatred, inequality, and violence. It is the responsibility of the journalist, scholar, and politician to understand the conditions for legitimately designating who belongs in the extreme right and refrain from manipulating the label for political purposes. Right-wing extremism is not a trivial phenomenon, but neither is it a perilous threat.

Notes

1. For a systematic discussion of the definition of right-wing extremism, see "The Cutting Edge: The Extreme Right in Post-War Western Europe and the USA," introduction to Paul Hainsworth (ed.), *The Extreme Right in Europe and the USA* (London: Pinter, 1992).

2. Michael Billig, "The Extreme Right: Continuities in Anti-Semitic Conspiracy Theory in Post-War Europe," in Roger Eatwell and Noël O'Sullivan (eds.), *The Nature of the Right* (London: Pinter, 1989), 146–166.

3. Kurt Moller, "Right Wing Extremist Orientation Among Young People in Reunited Germany," lecture at York University, March 11, 1994.

4. Geoffrey Harris, *The Dark Side of Europe: The Extreme Right Today* (Edinburgh: Edinburgh University Press, 1990), 89.

5. Paul Hockenos, *Free to Hate* (London: Routledge, 1993), 114.

6. Ibid., 130.

7. Leonard Weinberg, "The American Radical Right: Exit, Voice and Violence," in Peter Merkl and Leonard Weinberg, *Encounters with the Contemporary Radical Right* (Boulder: Westview Press, 1993), 186.

8. Harris, *The Dark Side of Europe,* 69.

9. Randolph Braham, as quoted in Anti-Defamation League, *Hitler's Apologists: The Anti-Semitic Propaganda of Holocaust Revisionism* (New York: ADL, 1993), 57.

10. Harris, *The Dark Side of Europe,* 101.

11. "California Teen-Ager Is Arrested in Bombings Aimed at Minorities," *New York Times,* November 8, 1993, A10.

12. Michael Schmidt, "The Truth Shall Make Us Free," TV documentary appearing on "Human Edge," TV Ontario, November 24, 1992.

13. *Searchlight,* January 1994: 4. See also Anti-Defamation League, "Extremist Groups Strengthen International Ties with Hi-Tech Communications: Poses New Threat of Anti-Semitism," press release, June 24, 1994.

14. "Hard-Core Nazis Will Throw Their Weight Behind the Electoral Fascist Republikaner Partei (REP) in This Year's German Parliamentary Elections," *Searchlight,* April 1994: 18.

15. Anti-Defamation League, *The Religious Right: The Assault on Tolerance & Pluralism in America* (New York: ADL, 1994), 4.

16. Michael Minkenberg, "The New Right in Germany: The Transformation of Conservatism and the Extreme Right," *European Journal of Political Research* 22, 1992: 59.

17. Roger Eatwell and Noël O'Sullivan, *The Nature of the Right* (London: Pinter, 1989), viii.

18. Billig, "The Extreme Right," 156.

19. Michael Billig, *Fascists: A Social-Psychological View of the National Front* (London: Harcourt Brace Jovanovich, 1978), 297.

20. Billig, "The Extreme Right," 146.

21. Jaroslav Krejčí, "Neo-Fascism—East and West," in Luciano Cheles, Ronnie Ferguson, and Michalina Vaughan, eds., *The Right in Western and Eastern Europe* (London: Longman, 1995), 1.

22. See, for example, Robert Miles, "A Rise of Racism and Fascism in Contemporary Europe?: Some Sceptical Reflections on Its Nature and Extent," in *New Community* 20(4), 1994: 548.

23. Ibid.

24. Piero Ignazi, "The Silent Counter-Revolution: Hypotheses on the Emergence of Extreme Right-Wing Parties in Europe," *European Journal of Political Research* 22, 1992: 3, 16.

25. Michael Billig, *Ideology and Social Psychology: Extremism, Moderation and Contradiction* (New York: St. Martin's Press, 1982), 103.

26. Ibid., 102–106.

27. Milton Rokeach, *The Open and Closed Mind* (New York: Basic Books, 1960), 61.

28. Billig, "The Extreme Right," 161.

29. "The Truth Lies Behind Rostock," *Der Speigel,* TV documentary appearing on "Human Edge," TV Ontario, May 25, 1995.

30. Theodor Adorno et al., *The Authoritarian Personality* (New York: Harper & Row, 1950), 7.

31. Erwin Scheuch and Hans-Dieter Klingemann, "Theorie des Rechtsradikalismus in westlichen Industriegesellschaften," *Hamburger Jahrbuch für Wirtschafts- und Gesellschaftspolitik* 12, 1967: 11–29.

32. Jürgen Falter and Siegfried Schumann, "Affinity Towards Right-Wing Extremism in Western Europe," in *West European Politics* 11(2), April 1988: 97.

33. Seymour Martin Lipset and Earl Raab, *The Politics of Unreason: Right-Wing Extremism in America, 1790–1970* (New York: Harper & Row, 1970), 485.

34. Ibid., 3.

35. Ibid., 484.

36. Falter and Schumann, "Affinity Towards Right-Wing Extremism in Western Europe," 103.

37. Mark Hamm, *American Skinheads: The Criminology and Control of Hate Crimes* (Westport, CT: Praeger, 1993), 80.

38. Hockenos, *Free to Hate*, 75.

39. Bettina Westle and Oskar Niedermayer, "Contemporary Right-Wing Extremism in West Germany: 'The Republicans' and Their Electorate," *European Journal of Political Research* 22, 1992: 96.

40. Ibid.

41. Klaus von Beyme, "Right-Wing Extremism in Post-War Europe," *West European Politics* 11(2), April 1988: 14.

42. Ignazi, "The Silent Counter-Revolution," 3.

43. Charles Maier, "Democracy and Its Discontents," *Foreign Affairs,* July-August 1994: 59.

44. Westle and Niedermayer, "Contemporary Right-Wing Extremism in West Germany," 97.

45. Pierre Brechon and Subrata Kumar Mitra, "The National Front in France: The Emergence of an Extreme Right Protest Movement," *Comparative Politics* 25, October 1992: 77.

46. Nonna Mayer and Pascal Perrineau, "Why Do They Vote for Le Pen?" *European Journal of Political Research* 22, 1992: 132.

47. Miles, "A Rise of Racism and Fascism in Contemporary Europe?" 558.

48. Ibid., 552.

49. Ibid., 557.

50. Christopher Husbands, "Racism, Xenophobia and the Extreme Right: A Five-Country Assessment," revised lecture given to the Faculty of Social Sciences at the University of Amsterdam, May 9, 1995, 15.

51. Ibid., and 19.

52. Brechon and Mitra, "The National Front in France," 63.

53. Eatwell and O'Sullivan, 149.

54. Brechon and Mitra, "The National Front in France," 64 (emphasis added).

55. Richard Stoss, *Politics Against Democracy: Right-Wing Extremism in Western Germany* (New York: Berg, 1991).

56. Noël O'Sullivan, *Fascism* (London: JM Dent, 1983), 2.

57. Laird Wilcox, "What Is Extremism? Style and Tactics Matter More Than Goals," in John George and Laird Wilcox, *Nazis, Communists, Klansmen, and Others on the Fringe: Political Extremism in America* (Buffalo, N.Y.: Prometheus Books, 1993), 55.

3

Canada: Right-Wing Extremism in the Peaceable Kingdom

Stephen Scheinberg

A jogger made his way through Montreal's Angrignon Park on a late November day in 1992. He probably had no apprehension of danger when he was suddenly assaulted by three skinheads who, believing their victim was gay, viciously beat him to death. The oldest of the three juvenile perpetrators was found to have connections to neo-Nazi organizations. That this was not an isolated incident was underlined a month later when another small band of skinheads brutally attacked a school teacher, whom they also believed to be gay. This second attack took place at a highway rest stop in Joliette, Quebec. These murders had their grim companion in Canada's West. On January 28, 1991, a Cree trapper, Leo LaChance, took his pelts into Prince Albert, Saskatchewan. There he had the misfortune of entering a pawn shop owned by a leading white supremacist, who shot and killed him. These events should have warned Canadians that all was not well in the land.

The year 1993 arrived in Montreal, especially in the Jewish community, in a striking way. Seven area synagogues were daubed with swastikas and, in one case, the feared Nazi warning "Juden Raus" (Jews Out!). These acts took place in a community that is home to perhaps the highest percentage of Holocaust survivors in North America. Right-wing extremists have been active not only in Quebec but across Canada. Hate lines operated in British Columbia, Manitoba, Ontario, and Quebec, spewing out their messages of white superiority. British Holocaust denier David Irving, offering anti-Semitism as serious scholarship, appeared in Toronto and Victoria before being shown to the exit. Unknown perpetrators vandalized a Hindu temple in London (Ontario), threw a Molotov cocktail into a Haitian church in Montreal, and painted a star of David on the door of a Lebanese-owned restaurant in Charlottetown.[1]

These incidents demonstrate that peaceful Canada is not immune to the viruses of racism and violence, but one must also have perspective and some context for evaluating their impact on this society. Canada is not pre-Hitler Germany; and its extreme right does not come close to rivaling the racist movements of today's Western Europe or even the United States. There is, for example, no Canadian political expression of racism or anti-Semitism such as one finds in most other nations (no Republikaners or National Front), despite the sporadic attempts by a few extremists to infiltrate its major parties. There is no Canadian parallel to a David Duke, a Klansman competing for high office. Yet from time to time antiracist organizations and journalists have depicted a Canada ready to fall under the fascist jackboot. A misleading map showing extremist organizations across the nation does not indicate that a dot in Saskatchewan may represent only five individuals. Similarly, a chart showing the interlocks between extremist groups may look impressive but encompasses only a few hundred members of the radical right. The point is not to minimize the danger of extremism in Canada. Murder, assault, and desecrations are not matters to be taken lightly, but it is important, nevertheless, to maintain perspective on their source.

Membership in hate groups is notoriously difficult to document, but it is probably safe to say that it is proportionally lower in Canada than in the United States. The Anti-Defamation League (ADL) makes some informed estimates on the size of particular organizations in the United States; Klan-watch, a division of the Southern Poverty Law Center, prefers to track groups. Ephemeral organizations and transient membership characterize the extreme right and make it notoriously difficult to chart membership.

It would be helpful, for the purpose of perspective, if one could compare the incidence of hate crimes in Canada with those in other nations. Some of Canada's police forces have begun keeping such data but there is as yet no mandate for a national collection system. Perhaps the only comparative, quantitative measures other than attitudinal surveys are the annual reports on anti-Semitic incidents issued by the ADL in the United States and the League for Human Rights of B'nai Brith (LHR) in Canada. These reports, employing similar methodologies, yield one usable measure. In its report for 1992 the ADL listed 1,730 incidents across the United States; in the same year the LHR total was 196. For 1993 the American group reported 1,867 incidents and the Canadian, 256.[2]

These raw data may be indicative, although they must be tempered by the following observations. First, not all anti-Semitic incidents are hate crimes, but many are. For example, the statistics on such crimes kept by the Intelligence Squad of the Montreal Urban Community Police for 1993 were close to those of the LHR. Second, the perpetrators of anti-Semitic incidents are not necessarily adherents of the extreme right; freelance bigots also do such ugly work but without direction. Third, the numbers at first glance may indicate that the Canadian proportion of incidents keeps within range of the roughly ten-to-one population ratio. However, Canada's Jewish population, the target group of these incidents, is far smaller proportionately, slightly more than 1 percent of all Canadians; the figure for their American coreligionists is 2.5 to 3 percent. Given that most anti-Semitic incidents occur in areas of substantial Jewish concentrations (although the phenomenon of attitudinal anti-Semitism without the presence of a Jewish community is well known), the figures indicate that Canadian Jews are getting far more than their share of such undesired attention, perhaps two to three times as much.

The picture is ambiguous with hard and comparable data in short supply. Hence, one must rely at present on historical studies, one major sociological survey of the extreme right in Canada and contemporary journalistic accounts, to make an informed assessment.

The Extreme Right Before World War II

Nativism certainly played a strong role in Canadian society right up to World War II, and elements of it linger to this day. In British Columbia anti-Oriental sentiment flourished, as it did in the American Pacific states. Prairie nativists were particularly anti–French Canadian. Ontario's Orange Order, a powerful political force in the late nineteenth century, supported the prairie nativists against the métis and believed in a Protestant, British Canada. In Quebec, Jewish immigrants were seen as a particular threat by French Canadian Catholics. Maritime nativists were catholic in their scapegoating. Yet although bigotry was strong across the land, it functioned within the parameters of political democracy and worked through the system to impress its will within the parliamentary process.

In the 1920s the U.S.-based Ku Klux Klan came to Canada. The revived American Klan of that era was an economic enterprise, a fraternal order, and a major political power in several states. Some studies of the Klan of that era have maintained that its most prominent targets were blacks, Catholics, and Jews. Despite the Klan's secret rituals, exotic titles (Kleagles, Klaverns, etc.), robes, hoods, cross burnings, and occasional acts of terror, it was not unambiguously an extremist organization. The Klan was as much a welcome part of many American communities in the 1920s as the Rotary or Kiwanis. Its leaders were known and respected, and Klan membership could even be vital to a political career within the system. An Alabama lawyer, Hugo Black, joined the Klan in 1923 mainly as a business and political proposition and then went on to become a liberal U.S. senator and later one of the great champions of civil rights on the Supreme Court bench.[3]

Recent American studies of the Klan contend that the organization was not so much "extremist" or "terrorist" but rather "populist." "The Klan," writes Professor Leonard Moore, "appears to have acted as a kind of interest group for the average white Protestant who believed that his values should be dominant in American society."[4] The new school of Klan historians may be too impressed by the representative nature of the local groups they have studied, but they are surely correct in stressing how different modern groups are from the Klans of the earlier Reconstruction or later civil rights eras.

Those wonderful old photographs of cross burnings in Kingston, Ontario, or Saskatchewan that appear in Canadian texts should not evoke an image of the terrifying night riders of the post–Civil War American South. Professor Martin Robin says of the Klansmen in Ontario that they were for the most part "mundane fraternalists." There were Klaverns in Toronto, Ottawa, Hamilton, Welland, Niagara, and other cities. Some staged cross burnings; there were even a couple of church desecrations attributed to the Klan, but no wave of terror there or anywhere else in Canada.[5]

The KKK had its greatest success in Saskatchewan, where by 1929 there were a reported 129 Klan locals and 25,000 members (other estimates run from 15,000 to 40,000) sustained, in Robin's words, by "prayers, patriotism, fraternity, and hate."[6] Saskatchewan Klansmen had some political clout through ties to local Tories, but these were perhaps exaggerated by the provincial Liberals. In any event, it seems evident that Saskatchewan's Klansmen, like their American counterparts, were political and community insiders working within the system. They capitalized on anti-Catholic and anti-French phobias that were part of the local landscape, but Robin understands as irony that the Klan was a "Yankee import" and hence as "an alien institution in British North America the Klan could hardly feed on anti-alien sentiments."[7] Yet it is clear that, for a time, many Canadians did not regard this white, Protestant organization as an alien intruder but as a brother standing shoulder to shoulder against new and unacceptable values identified with immigration and modernization.

It was only in the 1930s that the first truly right-wing extremist organizations appeared in Canada. In Quebec the journalist Adrien Arcand teamed with the printer Joseph Menard to publish three anti-Semitic and profascist weeklies—*Le Goglu, Le Miroir,* and *Le Chameau.* Financial backing came from French small businessmen and professionals as well as subsidies from Montreal mayor Camillien Houde and the federal Conservative Party of R. B. Bennett.[8] Arcand and his Order of Goglus were natural recruits to the Nazi cause, and one of Hitler's agents in America, Kurt Ludecke, was the contact person.

In 1933 the Tories withdrew their support from Arcand's three weeklies, but he and his partner, Menard, found financing for the new *Le Patriote.* It was forthrightly antidemocratic, antiliberal, antisocialist, and anticommunist and notably anti-Semitic. At least two prominent Quebeckers, Senator P-E Blondin and J. E. Laforce (president of the St. Jean-Baptiste Society) intervened with Prime Minister Bennett on Arcand's and *Le Patriote*'s behalf. But the journalist, evidently buoyed by Hitler's rise to power, was moving further to the extreme and founding his own Nazi style Blueshirt movement and National Social Christian Party (NSCP). Yet even at this point the Bennett Conservatives recruited Arcand as Quebec publicity director for the Conservative campaign in 1935.[9]

There were also pro-Nazi grouplets west of Quebec. Arcand's Ontario lieutenants were John Ross Taylor and then Joseph Farr. They gathered no appreciable number of followers. In British Columbia there was the Canadian Union of Fascists, which chose to wear black shirts; it had no more than thirty members. Another British Columbia fascist formation, the Praetorian League, had somewhat less than 100 members. Arcand's NSCP had less than 2,000 members at its height. There were also Italian and German Canadian adherents of fascist groups, but certainly for many of the former and for some of the latter, affiliation was more an expression of national pride than an endorsement of totalitarianism.[10]

Robin offers an interesting contrast that illuminates the size of the fascist menace in 1930s Canada. Arcand and Farr attempted to reorganize their political forces around the new National Unity Party in 1938. They were able to attract 1,500 to a Massey Hall meeting in Toronto that July, but the Canadian League for Peace and Democracy, a communist front organization, brought out 10,000 to Maple Leaf Gardens to hear the antifascist message of Professor William E. Dodd, former American ambassador to Germany.[11] In terms of numbers, the Canadian fascists were never a force to be reckoned with.

It is also notable that although the various shirt movements undoubtedly appeared threatening, there are few recorded incidents of fascist violence in Canada. The Christie Pits riot in Toronto on August 17, 1933, was an outgrowth of anti-Semitism, the so-called Swastika Club, and the increasing militancy of young Jews. The riot began during a baseball game when someone waved a swastika flag and cries of "Heil Hitler" were heard. There is no evidence that any organized fascist group was responsible, although the Christie Pits gang might have made good recruits for the movement.[12] Perhaps some oral history within the Jewish community might yield a few more incidents of fascist-like violence in the 1930s, but it would seem that the Canada of that era was not very welcoming to right-wing extremists.

Many Canadians did turn to right-wing solutions, but to those that functioned within the established order. Social Credit in Alberta was one such manifestation that harbored within it an important anti-Semitic element, but Premier William Aberhart and his successor, Ernest Manning, were neither anti-Semitic nor antidemocratic.[13] There was an important strand of right-wing clerical nationalism in Quebec within which anti-Semitism played an important role, but there is little evidence of links to Arcand. In all probability such nationalists did not approve of his pan-Canadian fascism. *Le Devoir,* representing this viewpoint, did not even mention Arcand or report on his party through all of the 1930s.[14]

Thus even in those "ten lost years" of Canada's Great Depression with up to half the workforce unemployed at one point, a prairie dust bowl, thousands of transients, and so-called Bennetburgs, or shantytowns, no substantial number of Canadians turned to the desperate solutions of the extreme right. The more substantial sectors of the citizenry required no "führer" to restore order, poor farmers preferred the solutions offered by Social Credit or the socialist Cooperative Commonwealth Federation (CCF), and blue-collar workers looked to a revived trade union movement or options on the left. In any case, the scattered seeds of the extreme right failed to take root in Canada's inhospitable soil in what should have been the most welcoming of times.

Stanley Barrett on Canada's Right Wing

The single most substantial study of Canada's right-wing extremists was carried out by Professor Stanley Barrett about a decade ago and published as *Is God a Racist? The Right Wing in Canada* in 1987. Barrett looked at nearly 100 organizations and 600 individuals and classed them as either "radical right" or a "fringe right" that does not openly condone violence and often refuses such labels as "racist" or "anti-Semitic."[15] In the latter group Barrett includes such individuals as Paul Fromm and Ron Gostick, who although not violent skinheads, surely fit within the careful application of this volume's preferred, and widely used, category of right-wing extremists. Barrett's designations may arise from an overly zealous scrupulosity or a fear of libel actions, but segmenting the already minuscule ranks of Canadian extremism does not appear to be too useful.

Professor Barrett's geography of the right is very important. He found the majority of his organizations in only one or two provinces with 68 percent of them in Ontario. Of his 586 individuals, 448, or about 75 percent, lived in Ontario. British Columbia and Alberta followed far behind. He found Quebec "relatively free of organized right-wing activity," which he attributed to two factors, the primacy of the nationalist issue and the fact that the language of North American racism is English.[16]

Men dominated the ranks of the right with 390 members; only 58, or 13 percent, were females. His most surprising findings were in the areas of education and occupation. Sixty-two percent of his "radical right" group had attended university, technical school, or college; the figure rose to 84 percent in his fringe right group. Similarly, 60 percent of the radical right and 85 percent of the fringe group were in professional or white-collar jobs.[17] The extreme right was not evidently recruited from some lumpenproletariat or economically marginal sector of the population. They were Canada's middle-class neighbors or their children.

Barrett never estimates the numbers involved in the right wing of the mid-1980s except to state that his sample "is a gross underestimate" and that a more inclusive definition would have captured "thousands of individuals, and not a mere 586." Later he concludes that Canada's "organized right wing is substantial, but not out of proportion with that in other countries."[18] However, he never makes any comparison to other nations.

The bulk of Barrett's study was ethnographic, descriptive of the various leaders and groups that made up the extreme right of the early- and mid-1980s. Many of them are, unfortunately, recognizable a decade later; some of the organizations and players have changed, and some of these changes are striking: (1) at the time Barrett's book was published, skinheads were primarily a British phenomenon and had barely penetrated our consciousness, (2) the extreme right now seems to have made some incursions in the province of Quebec, and (3) Barrett's contention that Canada's right was proportional to that of other countries (the United States and Western Europe?) seems an even more dubious proposition today.

Hate Crimes in Canada

Although antiracist groups have been demanding a uniform, national reporting system for hate crimes, previous governments were not responsive. There appears to be a commitment from the Liberal government of Jean Chretian to introduce such a system in the near future. In the meantime there is no reliable statistical basis for judging the extent of hate crimes in Canada.

There is available, however, a survey compiled from "mediascan files" by Multiculturalism and Citizenship for the year 1992 and the first four months of 1993. Thus what we have is a compilation of those events that made it into the newspapers in a sixteen-month period. These included two murders, twenty-two assaults, and two death threats, all categorized as "physical violence against a person." There were thirty-one instances of hate propaganda noted, but it is doubtful that most of them would have been criminally actionable. Four hate telephone lines were in operation, and there were four weapons-possession cases. Thirty-two instances of vandalism were reported, including seven cemetery or place of worship desecrations, seven cases of arson or bombing, three of theft and vandalism, and fifteen of racist graffiti. Eight cases of hateful remarks were also recorded, but again, it is unlikely that they would be actionable as hate crimes.[19]

Barrett's optimistic 1987 view of Quebec might have to be altered by the data in this report. Both murders took place in Quebec, and both victims were thought to be gay. Thirteen of the twenty-two assaults and all four cases of weapons possession were in Quebec. Cases of vandalism against property were more evenly spread, largely among Ontario, Quebec, and Manitoba.

Twelve of the twenty-one identified perpetrators of violence against persons were either neo-Nazis or skinheads. The four weapons charges were brought against eleven skinheads, three Klansmen, and a neo-Nazi. None of the desecrators of cemeteries and synagogues were identified, but experience would indicate that many of the perpetrators were right-wing extremists.

These figures are not entirely satisfying, and one should regard them at best as indicative rather than as definitive. For one thing, the figures on the geographic distribution of hate crimes are suspect. The League for Human Rights reports on anti-Semitic incidents have always shown a far different distribution. In 1991 the League reported 171 incidents in Ontario and 31 in Quebec; in 1992, 137 and 28, respectively; and in 1993, 170 and 56. Not all incidents are hate crimes, but the League's vandalism statistics (vandalism is a criminal act) approximate the same ratios.[20]

Perhaps some Quebec newspapers that specialize in crime reporting tend to skew the data, or perhaps the covered sixteen-month period in Quebec was an anomaly. There are also undoubtedly more extremist groups and individuals operating in Quebec today than during Barrett's period of study, but Ontario is still the hate group center of Canada.

A newspaper database is deficient in one other area. Gay bashing has undoubtedly become too familiar in Canada and is probably vastly underreported. Many gay bashes go unreported by victims who fear the socioeconomic repercussions of coming forward or suspect the police of being unsympathetic to them. Not one of the twenty-two assault targets noted in the study was reported as gay! This was not the fault of the compilers but an evident weakness in the data they were using.

A spokesman for the Ottawa Hull Lesbian and Gay Task Force on Violence stated that in its first year of operation it received twenty-four reports of crimes against gays, lesbians, and bisexuals. Eleven of them involved some form of physical assault, but significantly, only six of the assault victims reported to the police. In Vancouver a local gay group estimated 600 verbal and physical attacks on gays every year. The gay community there felt that these were not reported due to the cavalier attitude of the police toward gay bashing. Whatever the reasons, it is clear that antigay crimes are a serious issue across Canada and that they have barely dented the public consciousness.[21]

The Hate Groups

The Ku Klux Klan

The Ku Klux Klan is the oldest of the radical right organizations both in Canada and in the United States. South of the border it is in disarray. Criminal prosecutions and civil litigations have left the Klan's various manifestations in a weakened position both in terms of resources and membership.

Then too, it has been weakened by the desertion of those such as David Duke who seek to take their bigotry to the mainstream bigotry and others, in the more radical camp, who regard the KKK as old and ineffectual. Its weakness below the 49th parallel significantly reduces the ability it once had to organize in Canada or at least to attract young Canadians. Of course, to a very limited extent the Klan can still capitalize on name recognition and the media lure of its hoods and robes, when it can get them.[22]

The Klan of the early 1980s was strongest in Ontario under Alexander McQuirter and in British Columbia under Al Hooper. There were numerous estimates of its size at that time ranging from a few hundred to several thousand. However, such figures should be compared to the assertion of then Ontario Attorney General Roy McMurtry that there were 30 Klansmen in Toronto and of Neil Louttit, a reporter who infiltrated the Klan, that there were about 200 in the province. Deduct the number of journalists, Royal Canadian Mounted Police (RCMP) agents, and the merely curious from these totals and the resulting figure is small. Barrett managed to locate 149 members in Ontario, 62 in British Columbia, and a handful elsewhere. One should keep in mind that the American Klansman David Duke had given the Klan a great deal of media exposure, and although he formally left the KKK in 1980, he had undoubtedly aided its cross-border notoriety.[23]

The Canadian Klan of the 1990s has shown few signs of life in its former "strongholds." Wolfgang Droege and other Toronto extremists were once Klansmen but apparently believe the organization has outlived its usefulness. In recent years, however, the Klan has shown signs of life in Manitoba and Quebec. Bill Harcus, a young Manitoba racist, seems to have shopped around the Canadian and American extremist marketplace searching for the most likely business to enter. According to Warren Kinsella, "Harcus reasoned, correctly, that a new Klan formed by him would whip up a massive controversy in his home province."[24] Harcus was like a prospective franchisee considering the relative merits of McDonalds, Wendys, and Harveys and making his 1989 decision based on the notoriety of his product.

Harcus built a small nucleus of about thirty followers, who put out a magazine titled *Maximum National Socialism*, established a hate line, and distributed hate propaganda. There may have been some connection between his group and increasing attacks on visible minority group members. In December 1991 Harcus and two of his followers were arrested and charged with a variety of offenses, ranging from weapons possession to advocacy and promotion of genocide. At the same time the LHR, Manitoba Intercultural Council, Manitoba Coalition Against Racism and Apartheid, and Wade Williams filed human rights complaints against the Klan hate line.[25]

The criminal charges were thrown out when Klan lawyer Doug Christie was able to demonstrate that one of the two police who had infiltrated the Klan testified not from notes she had taken immediately following her meetings with Harcus but from police transcripts of electronic surveillance. The Human Rights Tribunal, however, found for the complainants and in a wide ruling barred both Harcus and the KKK from operating such lines anywhere in Canada.[26] The wind may have been temporarily taken out of the sails (sheets?) of the Manitoba Klan, but one may expect to hear more of the Klan and young Mr. Harcus there or elsewhere.

Quebec has, strangely enough, been the second scene of Klan activity, strangely because Catholics had been a major scapegoat for the KKK in its post–World War I incarnation. But in 1990 Michel Larocque established Longitude 74 of the Invisible Empire (Montreal is located on the 74th longitude), and a second Klan group under Eric Vachon was organized in the Sherbrooke area. The American Invisible Empire group was then under the leadership of a Catholic, James W. Farrands of Connecticut.

These Quebec Klansmen probably number only slightly more than their Manitoba counterparts, but they have been very active distributing *The Klansman* and other literature, holding Konklaves, and demonstrating. One measure of their strength was a July 31, 1992, Aryan Fest, which attracted a total of eighty, including skinhead allies and Ontario friends. There have been many unsolved hate crimes in the Montreal area and at least one cemetery desecration in the Sherbrooke region that may have been Klan sponsored.

The Quebec KKK has achieved its greatest notoriety when it was able to capitalize on local and spontaneous episodes of racism. The most notable was in August 1990 during the "Mohawk Crisis," when the KKK propagandized already angry residents of Chateauguay who deeply resented the barricade on the Mercier Bridge, their link to Montreal. Later, when an attempt was made to evacuate 100 native women, children, and the elderly from Kahnawake, some fifteen Klansmen and others stoned their vehicles. The attack resulted in serious injuries to six of the Mohawks. This event was seen by millions of television viewers, most of them undoubtedly revolted by what they saw, but some twisted few may have been attracted to the Klan.[27]

There have been sightings of the Klan in Ontario, but the few Klansmen there are probably only those who prefer not to accept the leadership of Wolfgang Droege and his henchmen in the Heritage Front.

The Heritage Front

The Heritage Front, writes Bill Dunphy, "is the most powerful racist gang to hit Canada since the real Nazis, back in the Dirty Thirties."[28] If anything, Dunphy understates the case. Arcand, Farr, and others may have had more followers but did not have the records of crime and violence that Droege and his associates bring to the racist cause.

Droege himself has been convicted and served time for weapons charges, cocaine possession, assault, and conspiracy to violate the U.S. neutrality act. The last offense grew out of his participation in a bizarre coup attempt, staged by white racists, to take over the Caribbean island of Dominica. He served two years of imprisonment for his role in that enterprise and four and a half for the other violations.

This Bavarian-born racist has been around many of the major North American hate groups—the Klan, Western Guard, Nationalist Party—and has even consorted with members of the Order, the most important American terrorist organization of the 1980s. He now claims to be peaceful and law abiding, just a lover of white people and not a hater of others. This is the path taken by his old friend David Duke, although Droege has not yet gone the whole distance.

In 1989 on a trip to Libya, as guests of Colonel Khadafy, several Canadian racists conceived the Heritage Front (HF) as an alternative to Don Andrews's Nationalist Party. On September 25, Droege, Gerald Lincoln, James Dawson, and Grant Bristow held the formative meeting in Toronto. At a November meeting of Rita Ann Kelly Hartmann's Ottawa-based Northern Foundation, the Heritage Front was first revealed to extremist circles, but CSIS (the Canadian Security and Intelligence Service) was already well informed.[29] The HF's first public assemblage was a "martyr's day" (December 8, 1990) commemoration of the death of Robert Matthews, the leader of the Order who was killed resisting the FBI.

Despite its peaceful protestations, the HF has ties to many of the most violent and some of the most vile racists in North America. Its Toronto visitors have included Tom and John Metzger of WAR (White Aryan Resistance), Dennis Mahon of the Klan, and Sean Maguire of the Aryan Nations. Droege and company may have their preferences among American racial extremists, but perhaps to enhance their own status they seem to value their links to all of them. Through George Burdi, a.k.a. Reverend Eric Hawthorne, the HF is linked to the Church of the Creator.

In its few short years the HF has operated hate lines in its own name or through individual members. It has staged street marches and concerts featuring Burdi as the lead singer of RAHOWA (Racial Holy War). None of these events drew more than 200 persons, but small numbers can create large problems:

- October 26, 1993—"Two members of the Heritage Front . . . were arrested by Durham police last week and charged in separate armed robberies and a variety of weapons offenses." (*Toronto Sun*)
- June 19, 1993—George Burdi "was charged yesterday with beating a woman in Ottawa during a street brawl." (*Toronto Sun*)
- June 10, 1993—"The security chief of the racist Church of the Creator was arrested yesterday after a 22-year-old man was kidnapped tortured and threatened with death. . . . Police seized evidence and a 13-gauge shotgun, a .22 calibre pistol and a .45 calibre semi-automatic handgun." (*Toronto Sun*)

- May 31, 1993—"The bloodshed began with neo-Nazis hurling bottles into the anti-racist crowd on Bronson St. It ended with savage beatings on Wellington St." (*Ottawa Sun*)
- February 12, 1993—"Hate groups in Toronto have recently grown bolder, as signified by a march on Jan. 25 by about 50 Heritage Front members—young men and women with punk hairstyles and heavy boots, brandishing swastikas and Ku Klux Klan symbols. . . . They chanted 'Equal rights for whites!' When they were confronted by anti-racism protesters, a melee ensued." (*New York Times*)

These reports are only a sample of their work. A recent HF defector, Elisse Hategan, said that the leaders encouraged young members to get firearms acquisition certificates, join the armed forces, and take self-defense training.[30] HF members also attempted to infiltrate the Reform Party of Canada, evidently drawn to a party that advocated immigration restriction and attacked multiculturalism. The party, to its credit, quickly expelled known HF members.

At the moment the future of the Heritage Front is uncertain. First there was the defection of Elisse Hategan, who was being groomed by Droege for a leadership role. Then it was revealed that Grant Bristow, one of the major organizers of the HF, was a source for the government security agency CSIS. The Security Intelligence Review Committee's thorough report on CSIS's involvement in the Heritage Front has, at least in most quarters, ended speculation that Bristow planned the HF's infiltration of the Reform Party or that CSIS actually indirectly funded Droege's activities.[31] In 1995 the Heritage Front seemed to almost disappear from public view, and its prospects seem poor. However, hard-core racists of the Droege variety will undoubtedly find new forums through which to pursue their chosen work.

Skinheads

Neo-Nazi skinheads are undoubtedly the shock troops of right-wing extremism. These violence-prone youth are a relatively new phenomenon on the Canadian hate scene. It is no surprise that the word "skinhead" does not even appear in the index of Barrett's 1987 study, but by 1990 the LHR would issue a full-scale report on them, including a two-year "rapsheet" of skinhead-related incidents. It was already apparent by then that what had begun in England as a stylistic but class-related youth revolt had taken on ominous new baggage in the form of racist and neo-Nazi ideology.

The skinheads sought out the older leaders of right-wing extremism to give meaning to their rebellion, and the old guard reciprocated eagerly, seeking fresh recruits for its cause. Paul Fromm would appear with thirty skinheads as bodyguards. A David Irving Holocaust denial lecture in Ottawa's Chateau Laurier was protected by skinheads. Terry Long, the Alberta leader of the Aryan Nations, welcomed skinheads to one of his gatherings. More recently they have been evident in the retinues of Wolfgang Droege and Michel Larocque. Although the extremists benefit through access to sturdy new recruits, the police may also gain because they can more easily identify those associated with otherwise small, elusive youth groups.

Desecrations of synagogues and cemeteries, assaults on antiracists, gays, and members of visible minorities, and murders have marked the trail of Canada's neo-Nazi skinheads. The most notorious examples were (1) the Nazi-style graffiti on seven Montreal area synagogues, a Jewish community center, and Jewish homes in January and February 1993, which was attributed to skinheads; (2) the vicious assault in 1990 on former radio broadcaster Keith Rutherford at his Edmonton home, necessitating hospitalization and causing permanent damage to one eye; (3) an attack on a man "thought to be gay" in the vicinity of the Manitoba legislature; (4) the murders of two Quebec men, also thought to be gay, in November and December 1992; and (5) a 1993 assault on a Sri Lankan immigrant in Toronto that left the victim brain damaged and partially paralyzed. This list is not meant to be exhaustive but to provide a sample of skinhead criminal acts.

Skinhead numbers are notoriously difficult to document, but ADL has offered a ballpark figure of 3,500 for the United States. There is no reason to believe, based on various reports from around the country, that Canada has more than its proportion of neo-Nazi "skins"; a recent estimate of 350 hardcore neo-Nazi skinheads is probably somewhat high.[32] Some of them are organized into loosely knit organizations such as the Aryan Resistance Movement (ARM), centered in British Columbia, or the Northern Hammerskins, operating out of Minneapolis–St. Paul. The former has claimed something on the order of thirteen chapter affiliations in as many Canadian cities, but that seems an exaggeration. As for the Hammerskins, a recent ADL report reveals a low level of activity at their home base with signs of them appearing in the Minnesota hinterland. In Canada a couple of post office boxes in Winnipeg and Montreal, a slight appearance in Toronto, and members in Winnipeg and British Columbia (where they compete with ARM) may be all there is. Antiracists often transform contacts into extremist networks, but their effectiveness is questionable.

Over the past few years the skinheads, along with other extremists, have held conclaves at Provost (Alberta), Minden and Metcalf (Ontario), and La Plaine (Quebec). The numbers attending varied from around 35 to 200; usually attendees also came from outside the province and represented many assorted extremist groups. Of course, some of those who did not attend these gatherings may have reckoned that police with their cameras would also be nearby, but skinhead attendance was encouraged and often catered to by featuring racist rock bands. These Aryan fests have vividly demonstrated that there are linkages between the skins and older extremists, but with these contacts there are also undoubted jealousies, competitiveness, and resentment of paternalism. The danger from Canada's racist skinheads is not, at present, in their connections but in their isolation. Effective police work, through agents, wiretaps, and surveillance, is facilitated when the criminal elements are well known to them and connected.

It is now some ten years since the skinheads made their appearance in North America, and the economy has witnessed dramatic ups and downs that cannot be correlated to skinhead activity. That should convince us that facile economic explanations of the skinhead phenomenon are not useful any more than the equally facile notion that they are products of dysfunctional families. In Professor Mark Hamm's sample of thirty-six American skinheads, only five reported friction in their family backgrounds and only one admitted to violence in the family. Hamm also usefully validates what other observers have remarked on, that the skinhead is no longer tied to the traditional blue jeans, T-shirts, Doc Marten boots, leather jacket, and, in the case of males, shaved heads.[33]

It is too early to tell whether this youth, terrorist subculture will persist in Canadian or North American society. The terrorism associated with the leftist Weathermen of the late 1960s was not long lived. It remains to be seen whether the youth terrorism of the right has any deeper roots or staying power, but if its core values of homophobia, racism, and anti-Semitism are encouraged by coded messages from Canada's "legitimate" right in the form of attacks on multiculturalism, calls for non-European immigration restriction, or opposition to gay rights, then the skinheads could be with us for a long time.

Ideologues of Extremism

Despite Canada's Hate Propaganda Law, extremist publications are still plentiful. The Supreme Court did, by a close margin, uphold the law in the cases of Keegstra and Andrews, but the ruling was narrowly constructed to protect free speech concerns. Provincial attorneys general, even with this positive decision, have seemed reluctant to apply the law. These officials have their own free speech concerns and also perhaps fear making martyrs of the hatemongers. Finally, although anti-Semitic or racist publications may be commonly viewed as hate propaganda, that same recognition does not seem to extend toward homophobic works.

James Keegstra, a former mayor and school teacher of Eckville, Alberta, has retreated to his work as a garage mechanic. He was probably too preoccupied during his prolonged defense to make more than the occasional appearance before extremist gatherings. A Moncton, New Brunswick, teacher, Malcolm Ross, has been writing and publishing his own anti-Semitic works since 1978, attacking Zionism, international Jewish conspiracies, and Jewish abortionists. Despite prodding from B'nai Brith and Canadian Jewish Congress, in the mid-1980s the New Brunswick attorney general refused to prosecute. Of course, Ross's publications preceded the Supreme Court's Keegstra decision, but the attorney general's inaction left Ross free to publish yet another book in 1988. He was subsequently relieved of classroom duties by the Moncton School Board.

The foremost anti-Semitic propagandist in Canada is undoubtedly Ernst Zundel. His Samisdat Publishing Company in Toronto is unfortunately one of the world's major sources of Holocaust denial material, including German-language publications that feed the fires of hatred in Central Europe. Zundel emigrated to Canada in 1958 and came under the tutelage of the aging Quebec fascist Adrien Arcand. He moved from Montreal to Toronto in the mid-1960s but did not commence his publishing career until 1976. Through Samisdat Zundel distributes not only his own rather negligible works but all of the "classic" Holocaust denial literature of Arthur Butz, Richard Harwood, Robert Faurisson, and others. He reportedly takes in more than six figures per annum from this enterprise.

As was the case in New Brunswick, the Ontario attorney general's office was also reluctant to use Section 319(2) of the Criminal Code prohibiting the willful promotion of hatred. In 1983, Sabina Citron, a Holocaust survivor, took matters into her own hands and filed against Zundel under the "false news" provision of the Criminal Code. The attorney general could have still blocked the case, but it was now a public matter, and rejection of Citron would have been perceived as a blow against the Jewish community. Attorney General Roy McMurtry therefore chose to have his office take the case itself. There were two Zundel trials. The verdict against him in the first trial was referred to the Ontario Court of Appeal, which although upholding the constitutionality of the law, ordered a new trial based on procedural errors. A second trial ultimately led to the Supreme Court, which struck down the false-news section as unconstitutional. The trials as well as the decisions allowed Zundel to publicize his cause and pose as a martyr to free speech. More recently a buoyant Zundel increased his potential audience through weekly radio broadcasts and satellite television shows aimed at a German audience.

In Quebec a small band of nationalist intellectuals, Cercle Jeune Nation, has issued an extreme-right journal, *Jeune Nation*, which vigorously attacks immigration and multiculturalism from a stance not unlike that of Jean-Marie Le Pen. *La Presse* columnist Francine Pelletier has referred to the group as "nazis in ties," a characterization that, though vivid, is perhaps somewhat extreme. The journal has applauded the resurgence of the European right, attacked minority appointments, defended the antiquated notion that the Quebecois are all of pure Norman stock, and sees present immigration policies as the subversion of Quebec's march to sovereignty. The group's best-known figure is Universite de Montreal history professor Pierre Trepanier, who referred to Le Pen as "a courageous man leading an important battle." Cercle Jeune Nation is not an influential group in nationalist circles and is perhaps an anachronism within the movement of today. It is nevertheless important in that it confers an aura of intellectual legitimacy on racist currents in contemporary Quebec.

The Christian Right

There is also another set of organizations that should be considered within any survey of extremism in Canada. In the United States there is a burgeoning phenomenon known as the Christian right. Insofar as Christians, Jews, Muslims, and other religious groups participate in politics and seek to influence the legislative process, their activities are entirely legitimate. There are, however, at least two major areas in which such activities shade over into extremism. The first is obviously the troubled American politics of abortion, which has spilled over into harassment, arson, and murder. The second is homophobia when it becomes the ideological and propagandistic equivalent of racism and anti-Semitism. Thus the now familiar line of the American Christian right that gay rights are "special rights" becomes a direct challenge to a more generous Canadian pluralism.

Religious fundamentalists are the core constituency of the Christian right, and it is not the purpose of this study to smear the values of millions of Americans and Canadians with the "extremist" label. However, the movement does have an extremist element.

The soft side, the nonextremist element, of the American Christian right's advance into Canada is James Dobson's Focus on the Family. That organization is now well established in Vancouver and Ottawa. Dobson's "pro-family" broadcasts may be heard not only on Christian radio stations along the border but on local stations across Canada. The low-key Dr. Dobson appeals to many who value the family as an institution, favor discipline, and oppose pornography, but he also furthers an antigay agenda. Other such American organizations also have established beachheads in Canada, including the Rutherford Institute in Prince George, British Columbia, and Pat Robertson's American Center for Law and Justice in Ottawa.

One of the most radical of the antiabortion groups in the United States is Human Life International (HLI), founded and chaired by Father Paul Marx. It operates now in twenty-five American states and promises to expand into twenty-five more and every Canadian province. The organization is strongly linked to elements of the extremist right in Europe and to lawbreakers such as Operation Rescue's Randall Terry. One of HLI's leaders recently wrote that "lethal force will be the only reasonable action for some and those of us who stood by and did nothing will have the least right to cast stones."[34] This is the language of fanaticism rather than of the reason and civility that have generally characterized Canadian debate. HLI also sponsors appearances of noted American homophobes Stanley Monteith and Paul Cameron. This organization's anti-Semitism, anti-Masonry, homophobia, nativism, and contempt for the legal protection of those seeking reproductive counseling pose a threat to Canada's democratic and civil traditions.

American nativist and extremist organizations have often spawned their Canadian branch plants, and it would be surprising if some of the extremist elements that function within the Christian right did not find their way there. It is hoped, however, that Canadians will recognize that American brands of hatred do not fall under the free trade provisions of NAFTA. In the recent "same sex benefits" debate in Ontario the most visible opposition to the legislation came from the Catholic Church, and thus, for the most part, the contest was not marred by the virulent homophobia of the recent Oregon and Colorado antigay referenda. There has been no reported outbreak of gay bashing in Ontario similar to that accompanying the American initiatives. The good sense and reason of the Canadian Catholic Church with its dedication to democracy and civility offer a strong bulwark against the intrusion of zealotry.

Conclusion

Canada is not immune to the virus of extremism and the damage it can cause. Extremist acts of murder, assault, arson, desecration, and hate propaganda are all too well known to those who follow the news in Canada. One such act is too many.

Yet the peaceable kingdom has not become pre-Hitler Weimar, the France of M. Le Pen, or even the United States of Pat Buchanan. Despite some historical efforts to exhume the KKK in Canada's West or Arcand's fascism in 1930s Quebec, twentieth-century Canada has not been home to much in the way of right-wing extremism. That is also true today. Canada is not home to a mass party of the extreme right, its hate groups are small, and no major Canadian figure openly espouses a politics of bigotry.

"Across Canada, in every region, in almost every town and city, the web of hate continues to spread," writes Warren Kinsella.[35] There is no doubt that one can find individuals as well as small groups of extremists across Canada; they know one another and communicate. But my own view is that there is no strong, united extremist network functioning here. Still, though the evidence on whether right-wing extremism is a growing problem is thin, there is no doubt that the menace is real, as attested to by a trail of hate crimes across the land. A conservative perspective on the numerical strength and the prospects for extremism in Canada must not lead to paralysis.

Notes

1. Multiculturalism and Citizenship Canada, "Reported Incidents of Overt Racism in Canada," January 1, 1992, to April 30, 1993.

2. League for Human Rights of B'nai Brith Canada, *Audit of Anti-Semitic Incidents, 1992, 1993* (Toronto: LHRBBC, 1992, 1993). Anti-Defamation League, *Audit of Anti-Semitic Incidents, 1992* (New York: ADL, 1993).

3. David M. Chalmers, *Hooded Americanism: The History of the Ku Klux Klan* (Durham, N.C.: Duke University Press, 1987), 314–315. Black was also a member of the American Legion, Knights of Pythias, Masons, Civitans, Odd Fellows, Moose, and Pretorians.

4. Leonard J. Moore, "Historical Interpretations of the 1920s Klan: The Traditional View and Recent Revisions," in Shawn Lay, ed., *The Invisible Empire in the West: Toward a New Historical Appraisal of the Ku Klux Klan in the 1920s* (Urbana: University of Illinois Press, 1992), 34.

5. Martin Robin, *Shades of Right: Nativist and Fascist Politics in Canada, 1920–1940* (Toronto: University of Toronto Press, 1992), 14.

6. Ibid., 44.

7. Ibid., 85.

8. Lita-Rose Betcherman, *The Swastika and the Maple Leaf: Fascist Movements in Canada in the Thirties* (Toronto: Fitzhenry & Whiteside, 1975), 4–11.

9. Ibid., 36–43.

10. Robin, *Shades of Right,* 162.

11. Ibid., 267.

12. Cyril H. Levitt and William Shaffir, *The Riot at Christie Pits* (Toronto: Lester & Orpen Dennys, 1987), 2.

13. Howard Palmer, "Politics, Religion and Antisemitism in Alberta, 1880–1950," in Alan Davies, ed., *Antisemitism in Canada* (Waterloo: Wilfrid Laurier Press, 1992).

14. Pierre Anctil, "Interlude of Hostility: Judeo-Christian Relations in Quebec in the Interwar Period, 1919–39," in Davies, *Antisemitism in Canada,* 157.

15. Stanley R. Barrett, *Is God a Racist? The Right Wing in Canada* (Toronto: University of Toronto Press, 1987), 9.

16. Ibid., 27–32.

17. Ibid., 35–38.

18. Ibid., 355.

19. Department of Multiculturalism and Citizenship, "Reported Incidents of Overt Racism in Canada," January 1, 1992, to April 30, 1993.

20. League for Human Rights of B'nai Brith Canada, *Audit, 1991, 1992, 1993.*

21. *Ottawa Citizen,* May 15, 1993; *Vancouver Sun,* September 3, 1992.

22. One Toronto Klansman complained of how difficult it was to get robes made in Canada.

23. Barrett, *Is God a Racist?* 133.

24. Warren Kinsella, *Web of Hate: Inside Canada's Far Right Network* (Toronto: HarperCollins, 1994), 36.

25. *Vancouver Sun,* December 21, 1991; Helmut-Harry Loewen and Mahmood Randeree, "White Hoods: The Klan in Manitoba," *Canadian Dimension,* March-April 1993.

26. *Globe & Mail* (Toronto), September 9, 1992; *Winnipeg Free Press,* December 28, 1992.

27. Kinsella, *Web of Hate,* ch. 10; Canadian Centre on Racism and Prejudice, *The Presence of the Ku Klux Klan in Quebec,* August 1991, 10 pp.

28. Bill Dunphy, "Canada's White Rights Groups Readying for Racial War," *Toronto Sun,* n.d.

29. Security Intelligence Review Committee, *The Heritage Front Affair: Report to the Solicitor General* (Ottawa: SIRC, 1994), ii, 10–15.

30. *Canadian Jewish News,* December 23, 1993, 5.

31. League for Human Rights of B'nai Brith Canada, *The Heritage Front Report: 1994* (Toronto: LHRBBC, 1994); SIRC, *The Heritage Front Affair.*

32. ADL, *The Skinhead International: A Worldwide Survey of Neo-Nazi Skinheads* (New York: ADL, 1995), 19.

33. Mark S. Hamm, *American Skinheads: The Criminology and Control of Hate Crime* (Westport, Conn.: Praeger, 1993), 114, 127–129. Hamm, I believe, puts too much emphasis on the role of the Metzgers as catalysts for the movement.

34. Karen Branan and Frederick Clarkson, "Extremism in Sheep's Clothing: A Special Report on Human Life International," *Front Lines Research* 1(1), June 1994, 3.

35. Kinsella, *Web of Hate,* 349.

4

Right-Wing Extremism in the United States

Stephen Scheinberg

Terror and mass murder have reawakened Americans to the dangers of right-wing extremism. On April 19, 1995, the Alfred P. Murrah Federal Building in Oklahoma City was destroyed by a huge bomb that took the lives of 168 people. The alleged perpetrators, Timothy McVeigh and Terry Nichols, were connected to the militia movement, then little known to the American public, but in preceding months several warnings that the militia organizations were armed and dangerous had been issued by antiracist groups.[1] Their warnings were not heeded, at least in part because many Americans believed that the menace from the right had disappeared.

In his comprehensive 1988 study of extreme-right movements in American history, David Bennett, the author of *The Party of Fear*, was optimistic in his conclusions. Antialienism, or nativism, which had been at the root of such movements since the days of the early republic was, in his view, a spent force. "Nativist and anticommunist conspiracy theorists still remained active in the mid 1980s working on the frayed edges of a lunatic fringe."[2] Movements that had once enjoyed the support of tens or hundreds of thousands of Americans had, he believed, shriveled into insignificance.

According to Bennett, demographic, social, and economic changes had undermined the extremist appeal to antialien sentiments. Their binding tradition had been a "common vision of alien intruders in the promised land"; the American Israel had to be protected at various stages in the past from Catholics, Jews, Communists, and others. The decline of the Soviet Union and increasing racial and religious tolerance in the United States promised a nativism-free United States. To cap it off, "the very religious and ethnic profile of New Right political leadership reminds us that nativism is dead."[3] Undoubtedly, the prominence of Jews and Catholics on the new right of the mid-1980s inspired his confidence. Anti-Semitism, that most telling indicator of extremism, is also in decline, argues Leonard Dinnerstein, the author of *Antisemitism in America*. He contends that "by comparing the strength of antisemitism in the United States today with what it had been in previous decades or centuries, the obvious conclusion is that it has declined in potency and will continue to do so for the foreseeable future."[4]

As a prognosticator, Bennett seems to have been right about some of the lunatic fringe elements. The numbers and influence of traditional racist groups such as the Klan, the John Birch Society, and the Liberty Network have decreased; but the racist skinheads gained support in the early 1990s, and the militant Aryan Nations organization has revived with new leadership. Some of the groups and individuals of the classic extreme right have, however, only taken on new forms. For example, the Klan leader David Duke has transformed himself into a Republican politician, and many, now more than ever, cloak their extremism in religious garb.

Perhaps Professor Bennett's nativist vampire seemed to have a silver stake firmly planted in its well-interred body in 1988, but such scripts always take a not very surprising turn. Thus, today various American commentators and academics see the revival of some familiar forms of antialienism as well as new variations on the theme.

Cornell University political scientist Benjamin Ginsberg is one such pessimist who sees the signs of a new mainstream anti-Semitism in the land. Most American Jews shared the progressive faith with many of their compatriots, and after World War II they believed that they were growing ever more secure. The final victory over the forces of bigotry could not be far off. In the early 1990s it was even more apparent that America's Jews enjoyed enormous success, constituting half of all the billionaires and a substantial portion of the faculty in elite universities. Ten members of the U.S. Senate and thirty-two members of the House are Jews; three major networks have Jewish CEOs, and Jews are prominent in the Clinton White House circle (Robert Reich, Mickey Kantor, Ira Magaziner, and others). However, Ginsberg did not believe these numbers gave cause to rejoice.

His model of the Jewish relation to the state rests on three scenarios giving rise to anti-Semitism. First, a state such as Stalin's Russia, in an attempt to consolidate a regime with significant Jewish participation, might use anti-Semitism to characterize a supposed enemy. Second, an existing state (tsarist Russia) could use anti-Semitism against antiregime forces that included Jews. Finally—the scenario relevant to the current American case—when Jews are prominent in the state, anti-Semitism offers an attractive weapon to challenge the state.

Ginsberg has obviously been jarred by Republican Pat Buchanan's willingness to take anti-Semitism back into the political battleground; Buchanan has made biting references to the U.S. Congress as "Israeli occupied territory" (not very different from catch phrase Zionist Occupied Government, or ZOG, beloved by the skinheads) and charged that while men with obvious Jewish surnames such as Rosenthal, Kissinger, Perle, and Krauthammer beat the Gulf War drums, it was boys with names like "McAllister, Murphy, Gonzales and Leroy Brown" who would risk their lives. Buchanan is perhaps the most blatant of the Republican paleoconservatives (a term used to describe the party's far right, what used to be its McCarthyite wing), but he has "demonstrated," says Ginsberg, that "one wing of the Republican party is already quite comfortable with Duke's ideas, if not with Duke."[5] Ginsberg's point is that anti-Semitism has been newly relegitimated and stands available if the Clinton administration fails and the United States slides into economic distress.

The second major challenge to Bennett's premature optimism is the rise of the Christian right in the United States. Undoubtedly, great care must be taken before affixing extremist labels, and it is not intended to indiscriminately include all evangelicals, fundamentalists, or socially conservative Christians within the scope of this study. There is a "culture war" taking place in the United States, and the heated battles over abortion, homosexuality, and creationism are just some of the fronts on which it is waged. An observer must take care not to be drawn into the battle and adopt the views or the terminology of the combatants.

Yet some of the Christian right well deserve the extremist appellation. Of course, true believers are by definition not pluralists and thus challenge a fundamental tenet of modern democracy. There is an extreme wing of the Christian right active in the United States, and it will be examined later, in some detail. A major focus of this Christian extremism is on homosexuality. Believers have every right to maintain that homosexuality is inconsistent with their theology, but when antihomosexual campaigns move outside of the church and in the public arena characterize gays as sick, disease ridden, perverted by choice, and unfit as comrades for clean-living American soldier boys, then they express a clearly extremist view. Gay Americans have become the major new scapegoat in their country, perhaps to an extent unknown in other democratic nations, and it can be argued that just as surely as Julius Streicher's *Der Sturmer* was a direct contributor to Nazi anti-Semitism with all that it led to, so the homophobic outpouring from religious extremists leads to gay bashing and murder.

Religion affords what amounts to a privileged sanctuary for bigotry. Homophobia in America is generally expressed in terms of religious values. Just as the churches once labeled Jews as Christ killers or blacks as bearers of the curse of Ham, they now provide a cover for prejudice directed against homosexuals. The medical profession has long since stopped describing homosexuality as an illness and for that matter so have most of the churches. Unfortunately, a bible, a collar, or the title of Reverend, Father, or Rabbi are no guarantee against extremism.

Two other contemporary issues also must be considered, as they seem to run counter to Bennett's optimistic conclusion. The first issue is the rise of terrorism and hate crimes that, to be fair to Professor Bennett, are not necessarily manifestations of the mass movements he is concerned with. However, the second issue—nativism—is one of his major themes. In the words of one of the leading American students of immigration, Nathan Glazer, "The immigration debate is becoming more and more agitated." He warns, "Every time anti-immigration sentiment rises, there is something new as well as much in the way of prejudice, ethnocentrism and racism that is old."[6]

The Klan, Skinheads, and American Law

By 1994 the Ku Klux Klan had fallen on hard times. Once the strongest hate group in the land, it is now a splintered, faction-ridden, though potentially dangerous, manifestation of its dubious past glories. The modern Klan, in its anti–civil rights heyday, boasted a membership of 55,000 in 1967 and had of course, many more supporters. Today, the divided Klan has probably no more than 4,000 members nationwide.[7] There are a number of factors that contributed to the decline of the Klan:

1. The contextual: Included here are the triumph of its enemy the civil rights movement, declining racism even in the Klan's southern base, strong condemnation by the political right (from individuals and groups once the Klan's covert supporters or recruitment base), and the modernization of the South (sun-belt industrialization).
2. The strategic: As some of the old Klan stalwarts discovered the counterproductiveness of violence, they, perhaps like David Duke, stored their Klan robes in the attic and donned three-piece suits.
3. The legal burden: The Justice Department, state agencies, and private civil rights institutions such as the Southern Poverty Law Center (SPLC and its Klanwatch) and the Anti-Defamation League (ADL) all brought constant pressure against the Klan and its members.

The legal offensive against the Klan merits particular attention. The high point of federal Justice Department activity against the Klan came in the conservative Reagan administration. When Reagan campaigned for the presidency in 1980 he made a stop at Philadelphia, Mississippi, where he made an appeal for conservative southern votes by emphasizing his support for states rights, a position identified with the support of segregation. His choice of Philadelphia seemed ill chosen to supporters of civil rights because that town had been the scene of the now historic murder of three civil rights workers in 1964. Democrats naturally castigated Reagan's insensitivity, but

Klan leader Bill Wilkinson used the incident to give the Klan's dubious support to the Republican candidate.[8]

Ronald Reagan did not need the Klan and eventually repudiated its endorsement. Perhaps Wilkinson should have looked at some of Reagan's backers before giving his support, for although Reagan was certainly appealing to many conservative Southerners, he also won to his side prominent Jewish neoconservatives. Part of the agenda of the latter group was certainly the active prosecution of the Klan and like organizations. Yet the administration was perceived by the National Anti-Klan Network in 1983 as being reluctant to prosecute the Klan. A year later, however, the Network reported that the Justice Department had begun to move against the Klan. From 1979 to 1989 the Justice Department prosecuted at least 114 individuals for crimes of racially motivated violence.[9]

Whether successful or not, the weight of federal prosecutions in terms of the exposure of individual Klansmen and the financial loads inflicted heavy burdens on the Klan. Members of the Klan, the Order, Aryan Nations, and other groups were convicted of or indicted for synagogue bombings, murders (the best known being that of Denver talk-show host Alan Berg), armed robberies, paramilitary training, threats to public officials, and other offenses. Thus the full weight of the Justice Department, which had too often been invisible in the civil rights years, now helped to keep the Klan and its associates on the run.

The major nongovernmental institution in the war against the Klan is the Southern Poverty Law Center of Montgomery, Alabama. Morris Dees and his partner, Joseph Levin, were young Montgomery lawyers when they founded the SPLC in 1971, and through it carried on then conventional civil rights litigation. In 1980 it added the affiliated Klanwatch project, which maintains, as does ADL, a major hate group database. Dees and his associates have also pioneered in bringing civil suits against the Klan. One of their most notable triumphs was in a suit brought against the United Klans of America for damages resulting from the murder of a black teenager by three Klansmen. Dees used the concept of agency, derived from corporate law, to hold the United Klans responsible for the deeds of its officials. An all-white jury held the organization responsible for the act of its members and awarded damages of $7 million. The Klan's headquarters building was seized in partial payment, and the efficacy of civil actions against hate crime perpetrators was now a matter of record.[10]

More recently Dees, this time in cooperation with the ADL, brought suit against the notorious Tom Metzger, a former "grand dragon" of the California Klan, who left the white sheets behind to found his own WAR (White Aryan Resistance) in the early 1980s. A skinhead murder of an Ethiopian immigrant, Mulugeta Seraw, in Portland, Oregon, was linked to Metzger by an informant who came to the ADL. SPLC recognized this as the opportunity for another civil action. In 1991 a Portland jury awarded the Seraw family $12.5 million, a judgment upheld on appeal. Metzger lost his home, which was seized, and the courts are to supervise future payments, though Metzger and his son John continue to operate. Nevertheless, the verdict should effectively limit their expansion, as a healthy share of any WAR profits will be directed to the victim's family.[11]

SPLC civil actions put financial pressure on the Klansmen and bring well-trained investigators into play who draw on the Klanwatch database. In addition, Dees and associates have often stepped in when law enforcement agencies have not acted. Thus organizations such as ADL, SPLC, and the Atlanta-based Center for Democratic Renewal bring pressure on both the hate crime perpetrators and sometimes complacent or lethargic government authorities.

Legal action has been an essential element in keeping the Klan and other violence-prone fringe elements in check. The Order, responsible for the assassination of Alan Berg and a Ukiah, California, Brink's robbery in 1984, seems to have been put out of business after a trial that resulted in sentences ranging from 40 to 100 years in prison for nine men and one woman. Posse Comitatus and various Nazi movements have also seriously declined. Richard Butler's Aryan Nations encampment at Hayden Lake, Idaho, persists and in the mid-1990s was revived by former Klansman Louis Beam. In 1995 it was reportedly operating in twenty-two states. One should also note that all of these groups exchange their personnel, who may be attracted to another leader, a more violent style, or even another location. Such interchangeability between the Klan, Aryan Nations, the Order, and neo-Nazis often leads to the Church of the Creator (COTC) or the Christian Identity movement.

The COTC, organized by the late Ben Klassen some twenty years ago, attacks Christianity itself as a Jewish invention. Klassen and his followers called for a "racial holy war" (RAHOWA) against Jews and those he termed the "mud races" (visible minorities). In the late 1980s and beyond, the "church" had some success in recruiting within the world of white supremacy, especially among young skinheads. Spokesmen claimed a circulation of 20,000 to 40,000 for their monthly *Racial Loyalty* and members throughout the United States and in thirty-seven other countries. Prison-based members number about 180, many of them doing time for hate crimes including terrorism and murder.

The recent suicide death of Klassen, instability in COTC leadership, and intense pressure from Klanwatch (which filed suit against COTC following the murder of a black sailor) make the future of the organization uncertain. Before he died, Klassen sold his North Carolina property at far below its value to one of America's most notorious racists, William Pierce. Pierce authored the *Turner Diaries,* which served as an inspiration for the Order and perhaps for the Oklahoma City bombing. Thus in some form Klassen's legacy will survive him, but unlike the Identity movement, the COTC has no public links to the Christian right.

Identity churches first came to public notice in the late 1970s and early 1980s, although their roots go back to the nineteenth century Anglo-Israel movement. That movement contended that the British themselves were the true Israelites and thus God's chosen people, the fruits of imperialism being one mark of his favor. In its American variation anti-Semitism became a strong element, for if the British were the true Jews, then those who called themselves Jews must be Khazars (a central Asian people) and certainly the devil's offspring. Only whites are held to be the children of Adam, and they must struggle for their heritage against all the inferior races.[12] Identity gives the radical right "a philosophical center of gravity." Richard Girnt Butler, an Identity leader, is also the organizer of the Aryan Nations in Hayden Lake, Idaho, and enjoys the support and affection of America's most notorious racists, including the jailed members of the Order.[13] Pete Peters, another well-known Identity minister, functions out of LaPorte, Colorado, and spreads his message via cassettes, videos, and his *Truth of the Times,* which is carried twice weekly on the Keystone Network in 120 cities. Peters gained some notoriety when it was learned that members of the Order had attended his services in 1984. Pastor Thomas Robb of the Knights of the KKK presides over Identity's Church of Jesus Christ in Harrison, Arkansas. ADL estimates that 200 to 300 small Identity-oriented churches operate in the United States; the number of their followers, according to Leonard Zeskind of the Center for Democratic Renewal, is probably around 25,000 with 150,000 others who have attended meetings, purchased materials, or been involved in some way.[14]

Both Identity and Church of the Creator give a spurious religious cover to the essentially political activities of the neo-Nazi fringe. They may also capture some unwary souls attracted to their weird but essentially racist theologies.

The skinhead movement is one of the exceptions among the violence-oriented movements because it experienced marked growth in the late 1980s and early 1990s. Skinheads originated in Great Britain in the early 1970s. They were shaven-headed young men sporting tattoos and wearing combat-type boots. Their appearance, as well as their chosen hard rock "Oi" music, could be seen as a kind of youth culture revolt against the long-haired middle class of the day. Chauvinism and xenophobia were imbedded in the style.

American skinhead gangs using Nazi insignias appeared in the mid-1980s. Not all skinheads were Nazis, but too many were. Their violent attacks on blacks and Jews in particular caught the attention of ADL, which issued its first report on them in 1987. At that time it was hoped that the skinheads would not be around for long because youth culture seems to change so swiftly. Unfortunately, this movement, which may have had less than a thousand members in 1987, was estimated to be approximately 3,500 strong in 1993. Klanwatch estimates thirty-five skinhead killings since 1988 and hundreds of assaults. "Not even the Ku Klux Klans," states the ADL, "come close to the skinheads in the number and severity of crimes committed in recent years."[15] In the mid-1990s ADL maintained that skinhead numbers were holding constant, but Klanwatch reported a steep decline in the number of racist skinhead groups from 144 in 1991 to 87 in 1993 and only 34 in 1994.[16] Klanwatch director Danny Welch attributes the decline to the impact of the Metzger conviction and especially to effective police work. It is, however, much too early to celebrate the skinhead demise, and even if the allure of its particular racist culture fades, many of its graduates will move on to other organizational forms.

The Militias

In the wake of the Oklahoma City bombing, the American media and justice officials began to take serious note of the militia movement. The two accused bombers, Timothy McVeigh and Terry Nichols, seemed to have been associated with the Michigan militia, and many questioned whether these gun-loving weekend warriors who drilled and trained in camouflage outfits were a major threat to American security.

Paramilitary groups on the extreme right have a long history, but the groups calling themselves militias came to notice only in 1994. In its first report on the militias the ADL found them functioning in thirteen states, but by 1995 reports had come in of operations in forty states with an estimated 15,000 members. Klanwatch figures reinforced this image; they estimated some 328 militia and support groups functioning in forty-four states.[17]

Not all of the groups and individuals associated with the movement are racist or anti-Semitic. Some of the militias even have black members, and many of the militia recruits, at least before the Oklahoma City bombing, would have been surprised to learn that they were consorting with notorious extremists. However, the militias do attract Klansmen or Aryan Nations sympathizers who may attempt to indoctrinate or recruit the militia men and women. It would be an error, then, to cast all militia groups and members as extremist, but they do harbor such potential.

Most of the members seem to have been attracted by a range of conspiracy theses united by mistrust of the federal government. At the top of their list of suspicions is the belief that the Brady gun-control bill was the first step to disarm Americans, thus leaving them vulnerable to some foreign conspiracy (the United Nations or something they term the new world order) that would destroy their liberties. The federal government killings of the Branch Davidians in Waco, Texas, and of the wife and son of Randy Weaver at Ruby Ridge, Idaho, are the two incidents usually cited by militia leaders as evidence of the conspiracy.

The militia members are largely white and rural. One Michigan militia training session attracted small businessmen, executives, auto workers, and nurses. Ten of the 100 or so attending were women.[18] These apparently ordinary Americans are, however, in many states in violation of the law.

Seventeen states have antimilitia laws, seventeen have anti-paramilitary-training laws, and seven states have both. The former make all unauthorized militias illegal, and the latter make paramilitary training with an intent to cause civil disruption a crime. Although the laws are available and tested, they are not enforced. Danny Welch contends that "no modern country in the world allows private armies. . . . If we let fanatics run around the countryside plotting armed resistance . . . we are flirting with anarchy."[19] Welch is correct, but the fault is not in the laxity of particular law enforcement personnel but one deeply imbedded in the culture.

James William Gibson's *Warrior Dreams* persuasively presents a strong American culture that is based on "the warrior role as the ideal identity for *all* men."[20] He contends that the culture is a reaction both to the Vietnam War's adverse impact on older American traditions of masculine identity and to the "threats" posed by the feminist movement, civil rights, and the new immigration. The Rambo films, *Soldier of Fortune* magazine, Tom Clancy novels, and the like provide a steady stream of a new mythology that validates "the ordeal of combat" as "the principal culturally certified path toward manhood."[21] One need not subscribe to Gibson's pervasive attribution of the warrior myths, but at the least, one should recognize that an important American subculture provides a ready-made recruitment base for the militias and other armed groups.

The Liberty Lobby

Aside from the well-known purveyors of violence discussed previously, there are several organizations dedicated to the propaganda of extremism and to political action. The best known and perhaps most effective are Willis Carto's Liberty Lobby (and its publication, the *Spotlight*) and, until recently, the associated Institute for Historical Review.

Carto's early career took him through several far-right and anti-Semitic organizations; for a brief time he was an organizer for the John Birch Society. In 1961 Carto launched the Liberty Lobby to reach out to members of Congress, testify before congressional committees when appropriate, and tabulate voting records from a rightist viewpoint. A few years later, in 1966, Carto acquired the old *American Mercury* magazine and turned it into an anti-Semitic quarterly that has now ceased publication. The *Spotlight*, founded in 1975, is the Lobby's major weekly publication. Its reported circulation of 300,000 in 1981 has fallen to 100,000 or less today. Carto also established the Institute for Historical Review, in 1979, which publishes *IHR Newsletter* and the scholarly appearing *Journal of Historical Review.*[22]

Through the years the Lobby and its associated publications and organizations have promoted an agenda, under the guise of patriotism and anticommunism, that uses anti-Zionism and Holocaust denial as vehicles for the promotion of anti-Semitism. "International Bankers," the Trilateral Commission, and, of course, the ADL figure prominently in the Lobby's defense of the American way of life. The Populist Party, which ran candidates in the 1988 and 1992 presidential campaigns, was heavily backed by Carto and the Lobby. The party also attacked the income tax, the Federal Reserve Board, and immigration. David Duke was the none-too-successful presidential candidate of the Populists in 1988.

It would be overly simplistic to write off the Liberty Lobby as merely a lunatic fringe expression. The Lobby has money, an estimated $4 million budget per year; it has a staff of around fifty and a substantial circulation of its assorted publications. In the late 1980s numerous radio stations were acquired; in 1989 the Lobby boasted 147 stations with 1.5 million listeners. It also reaches abroad through World Wide Christian Radio of Nashville, which carries its *Radio Free America* program. Liberty Lobby has an audience, members (25,000 of them), and undoubtedly financial supporters.[23]

The First Amendment free speech protection seems to hamper any government or private legal effort against Liberty Lobby. There has been one exception: Holocaust survivor Mel Mermelstein sued to collect an Institute for Historical Review reward of $50,000 for anyone who could prove that Jews were really gassed at Auschwitz. IHR settled for the reward plus an additional $40,000 for Mermelstein's pain and suffering. The settlement may have helped to further discredit Carto, but it was not large enough to put him out of business.

In 1993 there was a fracturing within the Liberty Lobby camp; a group split from the IHR and denounced the Holocaust denial journal, for of all things, being in league with the ADL. Carto's group subsequently founded the *Barnes Review*, which carries on in the same vein.

Programmatically the Lobby has been active on two fronts. Tricia Katson, its legislative representative, returned to the organization after working for David Duke in Louisiana and tried to insinuate the Lobby's agenda into the anti-NAFTA campaign, with little discernible impact. The Lobby and its *Spotlight* have also developed links to the militia movement, especially the extremist Montana group. ADL researchers revealed that McVeigh, using the alias T. Tuttle, placed an ad in *Spotlight* for the sale of a "military style launcher."[24]

The Klansman and the Columnist

Right-wing extremists in the modern United States have not typically found much success through their own fringe political parties. Third or minor parties have enjoyed little attention from voters. Access to the ballot in many of the fifty states necessitates near-heroic efforts, the nonparliamentary structure provides little recognition for even victorious minor party candidates, and the American political culture tends to regard a third-party vote as a wasted ballot. Thus the right-wing extremist seeking a political base generally looks to the established major parties.

Earlier in the twentieth century the Democratic Party gave shelter to Klansmen, and a party convention in 1924 was almost ripped apart on the Klan issue. Even after World War II and into the 1960s racist and segregationist members of Congress, advocates or defenders of lynching, were an important element of the party. The modern Republican Party has been home to extremist elements such as the pre–World War II America First movement, most notably Senator Joseph McCarthy and some of his more fanatic supporters in the 1950s. These examples are not comprehensive but offered merely to illustrate an American tradition of right-wing extremism within the two-party framework.

There are within the Republican Party of the 1990s varieties of conservatism, including "neoconservatism" and the "traditional right," that eschew all forms of racism and anti-Semitism and have a profound commitment to the democratic norms of American society. Yet the party is also the home of racist, homophobic, antidemocratic, and perhaps anti-Semitic figures, such as David Duke and Pat Buchanan and their followers. Most Republicans were outraged by Duke's appropriation of their standard in three Louisiana races, and some were uncomfortable with Buchanan's intemperate outbursts as well as his opposition to George Bush in 1992. Duke is a former American Nazi, a onetime Klan leader, and a distributor of racist and anti-Semitic materials. As a student at Louisiana State University in the early 1970s Duke not only paraded as a Nazi brownshirt on one occasion but organized a youth affiliate of George Lincoln Rockwell's American Nazi Party. He graduated to the Knights of the Ku Klux Klan as Imperial Wizard and then later took the title of national director, the change in nomenclature indicating Duke's desire to modernize and mainstream the Klan and white supremacy, his persistent trajectory.[25]

Duke learned to make effective use of the media, especially television. He claimed that a 1974 appearance on the NBC *Tomorrow* show with Tom Snyder brought in 5,000 new members to the KKK. Although Duke exaggerated his impact, this first national television appearance and others that followed not only made Duke the best-known advocate of white supremacy in the country but also gained him a following. He either caught ill-prepared television hosts by surprise when he eschewed the ranting style of a previous generation of southern demagogues for a soft-sell couched in the rhetoric of white people's rights or he capitalized on television's inability to devote sufficient time or resources to presenting his background.[26]

His first entry into politics was in a race for the Louisiana State senate in 1975. Running in a conservative Baton Rouge district, he received 33.2 percent of the vote. Four years later in another state senate race he received 26 percent of the ballots cast. One must keep in mind that in both contests Duke was still well known as a Klan leader. Perhaps Duke recognized the limits of the Klan identification when he then ostensibly left the Klan, appointing his friend Don Black as his successor, and founded the National Association for the Advancement of White People (NAAWP).

Duke's *NAAWP News* was used as a vehicle to attack Blacks, Jews, immigration, and welfare, but in a new and shrewd manner.[27] Despite his hatreds, Duke made a breakthrough on the racism front when he switched from the most overt attacks on minorities to an assertion of white rights, appealing in a more subtle manner to the fears of his constituency.[28]

Since 1988 Duke has been a persistent candidate for office. He began with the Democrats, the classic home of white supremacy in the American South, but that party had changed too much for the likes of Duke, including too many black voters. He announced as the extreme right-wing Populist Party candidate for president in 1988 but received only 47,047 votes nationwide. Duke does not like to be marginalized, and less than a year later he reappeared, this time as a Republican Party candidate for the Louisiana State legislature.

He ran in the white-flight suburban District 81 of Metairie, outside of New Orleans, and survived in a field of seven to narrowly win a runoff against a prominent Louisiana Republican, John Treen. This victory came in the face of national media attention and denunciations from prominent Republicans, including George Bush and Ronald Reagan. One Duke biographer sees him as the "teflon racist,"[29] but a student of Louisiana politics more persuasively argues that his "extremist history ironically renders him a more powerful voice for 'white people' than anyone without his baggage could possibly become."[30] The Duke constituency in Metairie is perhaps somewhat more racist than suburbanites elsewhere, but the voters responded to his appeals on issues of crime, welfare, and affirmative action (not white supremacy), opting for the man they most trusted to represent their concerns.

Encouraged by this show of support, Duke entered two races for higher offices in 1990 and 1991. In his 1990 try for the U.S. Senate he attempted to unseat incumbent Democrat J. Bennett Johnston and received 43.5 percent of the total vote but 57 percent of the white vote. The next year he ran for governor and in a three-way race edged out the incumbent to face former governor Edwin W. Edwards in a runoff. Edwards was victorious in this rather ambiguous contest, which became known as "the Crook versus the Klansman," but Duke's 43.5 percent included 60 percent of the white vote.

Is Duke a local phenomenon? Is Louisiana a kind of unique backwater of American politics? One of the South's leading contemporary novelists, Walker Percy, had this message for his fellow Americans: "If I had anything to say to people outside the state I'd tell them, 'Don't make the mistake of thinking David Duke is a unique phenomenon confined to Louisiana rednecks and yahoos. He's not, and don't think that he or somebody like him won't appeal to the middle class of Chicago or Queens."[31]

Two political scientists, Susan Howell and Sylvia Warren, have compared national with New Orleans data to answer the question of whether Duke could have run successfully elsewhere. They conclude that his issue appeal could reach elsewhere in the United States, but there was no way to know if his past might alienate votes outside of Louisiana or the South.[32] In 1992 Duke tested the presidential waters in the Republican primaries but never raised sufficient funds to seriously challenge President George Bush or the better-financed Pat Buchanan.

Since 1992 Duke himself has not been as visible, but there are certainly other American political figures who have proved willing to pick up the Duke issues and appeal to much the same constituency. For better or worse, those who follow in his footsteps do not have Klan robes or Nazi uniforms in their attics, but their objectives may be much the same.

Today's leading political light of the extreme right is undoubtedly Patrick J. Buchanan, former Nixon and Reagan staff member, syndicated columnist, and well-known television figure. He never shared Duke's enthusiasm for the Klan or the like but makes no secret of his admiration for the late Senator Joseph McCarthy, the spearhead of America's anticommunist inquisition of the 1950s. To Buchanan, Joe was a populist who knew that "the governing American Establishment, our political elite, was no longer fit to determine the destiny of the United States." McCarthy, like Nixon, was a victim of his crusade against these "illegitimate usurper(s)."[33] Buchanan, like McCarthy, is an outspoken and contentious gutter fighter, but should he be classed as an extremist? One prominent student of American extremism interviewed for this study questioned the classification because Buchanan is a Republican (thus presumably not on the fringe) and does not carry Duke's Klan baggage. Yet as Harvard law professor Alan Dershowitz has said, "It is precisely because Buchanan was never a member of the Ku Klux Klan or a Nazi sign-carrier that he is so dangerous. His views on many issues are almost indistinguishable from Duke's."[34]

In 1990 American conservatives of various stripes went through a painful debate on the subject of whether Buchanan was an anti-Semite. His enthusiasm for championing those accused of Nazi war crimes had been long observed without raising such accusations, and he had never displayed any personal animus toward Jews. It was in the context of the Gulf War that the debate was touched off. Buchanan had charged that "there are only two groups that are beating the drums for war in the Middle East—the Israeli defense ministry and its 'amen corner' in the United States." He described Congress as "Israeli-occupied territory," blamed four prominent American Jews for leading the nation into war (A. M. Rosenthal, Richard Perle, Henry Kissinger, and Charles Krauthammer), and "said that when the U.S. went to war, the U.S. kids 'humping up that bloody road to Baghdad' would have names like McAllister, Murphy, Gonzales and Leroy Brown," all notably not Jewish names.[35]

His comments stimulated an unparalleled barrage from Rosenthal, the Canadian conservative David Frum, and numerous others, but certainly the most serious pronouncement came from the conservative doyen William F. Buckley in *National Review*. His consideration of a comrade who had "occupied the same ideological foxhole" was undoubtedly painful. In measured language he declared Buchanan "to be insensitive to those fine lines that tend publicly to define racially or ethnically offensive analysis or rhetoric." In sum, Buckley concluded, "I find it impossible to defend Pat Buchanan against the charge that what he did and said during the period under examination amounted to anti-Semitism."[36] Other critics were certainly less restrained than Buckley, but why did it take them so long to challenge Buchanan?

The answer probably lies in the political and ideological configurations of the modern Republican Party. Nixon, Ford, Reagan, and Bush had offered a new home for the so-called neoconservatives. They were militant cold warriors, some former Trotskyists, many of them Jews and extremely protective of Israel. *Commentary* and the *Public Interest* were two of their major outlets. In the Republican Party they coexisted with moderate conservatives, John Birchers, old McCarthyites, and those who had manned the bulwarks of segregation. It was probably a sometimes uncomfortable alliance but not an anomaly in American politics. Perhaps on the one side, it was the perceived anti-Israel outlook of Secretary of State James Baker that led some neoconservatives to look for the exit, but Buchanan, who escalated his rhetoric in search of a core constituency on the far or extremist right of the party, may also have been an influence. In any case, the Buchanan record was now becoming painfully clear.

There were those, including even some Jews, who defended Buchanan against the charges of anti-Semitism, and one cannot loosely label him an extremist based solely on the flurry of rhetoric during the Gulf War, his advocacy for accused war criminals, or defense of the Carmelite convent at Auschwitz. Patrick Buchanan meets almost all the standard tests for right-wing extremism, and it is important to establish this point in order to show that at least his most fervent supporters also should be counted in that camp.

Following are selections from the Buchanan record:

- Nationalism: "He [Bush] is a globalist and we are nationalists. He believes in some Pax Universalis; we believe in the old Republic. He would put America's wealth and power at the service of some vague 'new world order'; we will put America first."[37]
- Democracy: "Of IBM, the Marine Corps, the Redskins and the D.C. Government, only leaders of the last are chosen by democratic procedure; only the last is run on democratic, not autocratic principles. Yet who would choose the last as the superior institution?"[38]
- Nativism: "High rates of non-European immigration, even if the immigrants come with the best of intentions in the world, will swamp us. Not all, I hasten to add, do come with the best intentions. . . . Does this First World nation wish to become a Third World Country? Because that is our destiny if we do not build a sea wall against the waves of immigration rolling over our shores."[39]
- Also on Nativism: "What Americans are being asked to decide . . . is whether the United States of the 21st century will remain a white nation."[40]
- On the L.A. riot of 1992: "Foreigners are coming into this country illegally and helping to burn down one of the greatest cities in America."[41]
- On white supremacy: "Multiculturalism is an across-the-board assault on our Anglo-Saxon heritage . . . Our culture is superior to others . . . Robert Frost will be remembered when Maya Angelou is forgotten."[42]
- Race: "I think God made all people good, but if we had to take a million immigrants in, say Zulus, next year, or Englishmen, and put them in Virginia, what group would be easier to assimilate?"[43]
- Homosexuality: "A visceral recoil from homosexuality is the natural reaction of a healthy society wishing to preserve itself. A prejudice against males who engage in sodomy with one another presents a normal and natural bias in favor of sound morality."[44] "Amidst the moral crud of the Weimar Republic, the Nazi bullies must have had a certain appeal."[45]
- AIDS: "nature's retribution on gays."[46]
- Conspiracy: "Not only did the KGB acquiesce in the collapse of the old order, the KGB orchestrated it; 1989, says one East European, was 'one of the largest puppet shows in the history of mankind.'"[47]

This selection of Buchananisms is not out of the ordinary. A comparison of his rhetoric with the more guarded statements of the French extremist Jean Marie Le Pen might prove instructive to those who deny his extremism. The man tends to express himself vigorously and perhaps more candidly than others who might share his general assumptions, and he is now probably the unrivaled leader of the extremist right in the Republican Party. His primary races against George Bush in 1992 and Bob Dole in 1996 may have been electorally unsuccessful, but they established him as the national champion of an important sector in American life. He has received the most enthusiastic receptions at the meetings of the Christian Coalition.

Christian Extremism?

The religious right has been recognized as an important element in American politics over the past fifteen years, but although sporadic alarms have been sounded on the linkage of Armageddon preachments and nuclear policy or the ability of a so-called moral majority to translate its particular morality into national policy, mainstream condemnation of its activities has not resulted. In fact, there is clear resistance to any attempt to fasten the extremist label on any but the most outrageous sectarians. Indeed, one recent student of American extremism regards such attempts as "academic McCarthyism."[48]

Sociologists James Davison Hunter and Sara Diamond, two of the leading students of the Christian right, also reject the label. In his *Culture Wars*, Hunter depicts "orthodox" and "progressivist" camps as "labelling the opposition an extremist faction that is marginal to the mainstream of American life. . . . Each side struggles to *monopolize the symbols of legitimacy*."[49] For Hunter, the religious orthodox spokespersons represent a major tradition of American culture, a tradition that is now engaged in uncivil battle with an equally valid progressive culture. Diamond seems to reject the label not only because liberals use it as a tool to mobilize votes and funds but also because it is, in her view, ideologically motivated by their desire to use the extremist label as a means of maintaining a liberal status quo. She also questions how one can define millions of Americans who are members of a Christian right that "genuinely represents a solid minority of Americans. In some parts of the country that minority is a majority. Last summer, six Oregon counties passed preemptive measures banning civil-rights protections for gay citizens. The measures were sponsored by the activist Oregon Citizens' Alliance, but they won because thousands of voters share the Christian right's homophobia. To call them all 'extremists' will not change the vote tallies."[50]

Both Diamond and Hunter are rightly troubled by categorizing millions of Americans as radicals or extremists, but surely the history of many other nations includes episodes in which millions of adherents of "legitimate" traditional cultures have been mobilized for extremist ends. In the United States, the most religious nation in the Western world, one would presume that the churches would be subject to assaults from all shades of political opinion and that they would reciprocally affect political and social doctrine.

Embattled liberal groups such as People for the American Way and Planned Parenthood have not indeed refrained from such rhetorical confrontation with the religious right. In 1994, the politically moderate Anti-Defamation League entered the fray with a major attack, *The Religious Right: The Assault on Tolerance and Pluralism in America*. This volume, researched and written by the ADL's David Cantor, is a substantial contribution to our knowledge of the movement.

One may, then, adopt the scholarly relativism of Hunter, the excessive caution of Diamond, the partisanship of the liberals, or alternatively try to sort out those movements or elements within the religious right that unambiguously deserve inclusion in this study. Dominion theology (sometimes referred to as reconstructionism) represents the most extreme end of the religious right.

The movement's founder, Rousas John Rushdoony calls for a kind of theocratic state based on the Mosaic law. Thus the death sentence might apply to crimes such as adultery, blasphemy, and homosexuality with enslavement as a lesser penalty. Rushdoony, a onetime John Birch Society activist, has in his books "maligned Jews, Judaism and Blacks and [has] engaged in Holocaust 'revisionism.'"[51] Gary North, a reconstructionist minister and Rushdoony's son-in-law, is based in Tyler, Texas; two other leaders of the movement, Gary DeMar and Joseph Morecraft, are based in Atlanta.

ADL is particularly disturbed by the reconstructionist's ties and influence in the mainstream Christian right. It is, however, difficult to set out these links without falling into a kind of guilt-by-association strategy. Thus the fact that Rushdoony and North have made several appearances on Pat Robertson's *700 Club* cannot be taken as an endorsement of all of their views. However, since Robertson does not practice Giraldo-style journalism, their appearances indicate some acceptance and bestowal of credibility. Rushdoony is close to the Rutherford Institute, a mainstream Christian right educational enterprise, and to John Whitehead, its founder. North and Rushdoony have both been members of the far-right Council for National Policy along with Christian right stalwarts such as Robertson, Jerry Falwell, James Dobson, and Phyllis Schlafly, among others. This only tells us that those named are willing to consort and ally with the reconstructionist theocrats.

Influence is a notoriously difficult thing to measure. The movement claims only 40,000 core followers. In 1981 *Newsweek* called Rushdoony's Chalcedon the religious right's leading think tank. However, it is doubtful that it occupies that position today. What can be said is that some reconstructionist doctrine has influenced the mainstream religious right. ADL fairly concludes that "the religious right is not primarily reconstructionist and most of those who do adopt some reconstructionist teachings reject its more extreme views."[52]

This brings us to the mainstream of the religious right—Pat Robertson and his Christian Coalition, James Dobson's Focus on the Family, Paul Weyrich's Free Congress Foundation, Donald Wildmon's American Family Association, and many other like organizations. Planned Parenthood condemns not only their opposition to abortion and birth control information but their alleged encouragement of harassment, violence, and murder of abortion clinic patients and workers. People for the American Way denounces their threat to pluralism and hence to the liberal's understanding of the essence of democracy. ADL is disturbed by their attempt to "Christianize" (or even "Judeo-Christianize" America) and to challenge the separation of church and state. All of these are important issues but not central to this study.

Racism, anti-Semitism, and anti-Catholic bigotry are three of the most important bricks in the traditional edifice of American extremism, but it has become ever more difficult to make the extremist case against the religious right on those grounds. The clearest case of change for the Protestant religious right is on Catholicism. As late as the Kennedy election of 1960, there were still Protestant, fundamentalist clergymen who denounced a Catholic running for president. But the old order has surely changed. Robertson's Christian Coalition followers enthusiastically welcome Catholic heroes, including Pat Buchanan, Phyllis Schlafly, and Colonel Oliver North. The antiabortion movement has brought Catholic and fundamentalist together in common cause, and the growth of a conservative Catholic charismatic movement has also bridged some of the differences.

In the 1960s, today's leading figures of the religious right often denounced Dr. King and the civil rights movement, but now they have even appropriated his name for their own ends, including a desire for black support against gay rights. An important pragmatic stream is represented by Christian Coalition director Ralph Reed, who actively seeks black and Hispanic support rather than concede these groups to the liberals. Black and Hispanic conservatives may indeed respond to such appeals. There are several notable black figures now active on the religious right, and although they may represent a kind of tokenism, their presence surely has antiracist educative value within the constituency. For many years the black Ben Kinchlow served as Robertson's cohost, sending an important message to fundamentalist America.

This is not to say that there are not still important areas of race relations in which the religious right does not meet the standard of tolerance. Even in recent years the religious right has continued to oppose civil rights measures, but that may also be attributed to an antistatist bias common to most conservatives.

As for anti-Semitism, one may trust that the ADL has dredged up as much as its unmatched resources can offer for its recent study of the religious right. Its study cites a few, probably careless but revealing, remarks of Falwell and Robertson. Certainly Don Wildmon has been more overt in his attacks on the Jewish media. Sara Diamond sees no problem in her identity as a Jew studying the religious right. She finds that "most of the Christian right is not overtly anti-semitic. . . . In fact, . . . their love for the state of Israel is so overwhelming that if the subject of my being a Jew were to come up, they would be really supportive."[53]

Until recently the religious right has been an ardent backer of Israel, along with those political figures it supports such as Colonel Oliver North and up to his pronounced turn with the Gulf War, Pat Buchanan. Perhaps it is revealing that Buchanan continues to be a favorite of the religious right, a group that did not join other conservatives in denouncing his anti-Semitic remarks.

In any case, there is a latent anti-Semitism in the religious right. Their demons, especially since the collapse of the Communist system, have been the "secular humanists," a kind of conspiracy that they see as dedicated to undermining the allegedly religious foundations of the American republic. A scapegoat conspiracy is better left not too well defined in terms of organizations, names, and numbers, but certainly the American Civil Liberties Union (Jewish Lawyers?), "the media" (Jewish dominated?), the feminists and abortionists (prominent Jewish participation?) are at its core. Some on the religious right have estimated that the "conspiracy" numbers only 3 percent of all Americans, a convenient figure that just happens to be the approximate representation of Jews in the American population. Pat Robertson evidently sees only *some* Jews as the enemy, "a strident minority within a minority of only 5,000,000" dedicated to "the systematic vilification, weakening, and ultimate suppression of the majority point of view from society." He has warned of "*a Christian backlash of major proportions*" against them.[54]

A traditional American Jewish stake in pluralism and the religious right's theocratic leanings are difficult to reconcile. The latter has been able to make common cause with some few among Orthodox Jews; the latter will be more useful as window dressing than as a bridge toward conciliation.

Pat Robertson is undoubtedly the major figure of the religious right today. His *700 Club*, Christian Broadcasting Network, and the Christian Coalition as his political arm make him a formidable figure in American life. By 1985 he had built a television network of some 200 stations with a $230 million budget, and he was broadcasting into sixty foreign countries.[55] His father, Senator Willis Robertson of Virginia, evidently gave him a taste for politics, and in the mid-1980s he launched a campaign for the 1988 Republican presidential nomination. That effort was unsuccessful, but through it he built the base of the Christian Coalition, which is now proving itself a formidable force in Republican politics.

Pat Robertson is like Pat Buchanan, in the mainstream of Republican politics, and he is also arguably an extremist in several respects: as a devotee of conspiracy theories, as an ardent supporter of global antidemocratic forces, and as a homophobe.

His conspiracy theorizing leads him to the myth of the Masonic Illuminati who brought about the French Revolution, to conspicuously Jewish bankers who supposedly financed the Russian Revolution, and even to speculation that John Wilkes Booth was in the employ of these same European bankers. His anti-Masonic claptrap is clearly derived from the late-nineteenth- and early-twentieth-century classics of anti-Semitism. These are not, however, the harmless musings of a crank but of a leader whose words reach millions of Americans, who imparts to them the wisdom of his wife, Dede: "I don't trust anyone running the foreign affairs of America who speaks with a foreign accent."[56] The connection between foreign-based conspiracies and Messrs. Brzezinski and Kissinger are obvious.

Robertson has been the most active agent of the religious right in foreign affairs and still is. He was an ardent supporter of the pro-apartheid regime in South Africa, but Central America was the area in which Robertson showed the greatest interest. His Christian Broadcasting Network was one of the large private donors to the Nicaraguan contras, working closely with John Singlaub's World Anti-Communist League. El Salvador's death squads had a friend in Robertson, who dined with their late leader, Roberto D'Aubbuisson and characterized him as a "very nice fellow." The *700 Club* claimed that El Salvador's regime was a victim of liberal media distortion. Robertson was particularly close to General Efrain Rios Montt in Guatemala and flew there to support his "born again" friend who carried on a genocidal campaign against the mostly native population.[57] Recently, Robertson's organizers have been prominent in the Ukraine and allegedly work with the remains of the extremist Banderist forces there. Mere anticommunism does not make one an extremist, but Robertson's consistent attachments to the most authoritarian forces on the world scene go well beyond realpolitik.

Homophobia is in the United States of the 1990s the "miner's canary" (the early warning) of bigotry and extremism. Overt racism and anti-Semitism are now taboo in the larger American culture, but public expressions of homophobia, especially from ministers of the gospel, is rarely if ever denounced. Certainly one might regret but yet tolerate the doctrinal exposition of biblical sources on homosexuality. But when Robertson and his fellows leave the confines of their churches to fight an alleged homosexual conspiracy, they become hatemongers just as surely as were the racists of an earlier day.

Robertson has promoted the circulation of *The Gay Agenda,* an antigay video that features Dr. Stanley Monteith, a Christian Coalition member. Monteith "rattles off a long list of extremely precise statistics indicating the exact percentage of gay men who participate in a variety of sexual activities— e.g., fisting, rimming, and the ingestion of feces." Monteith's source was antigay activist Paul Cameron, who resigned or was expelled from the American Psychological Association.[58] Cameron has suggested that AIDS carriers might be branded or banished and links gays to mass murder and child molestation. Robertson assembled the religious right forces for a "Battling Gay Rights" conclave in September 1992, which targeted eleven jurisdictions for antigay referenda that would—like the well-known Oregon and Colorado efforts—prohibit the locality from acting against gay or lesbian claims of discrimination.

One Christian Right group that is prominent in the antigay and antiabortion front is Human Life International (HLI), headed by two priests, Father Paul Marx and Matthew Habiger. Monteith and Cameron are part of the HLI entourage as well. Father Marx and other HLI writers persist in identifying their Jewish—not their Unitarian, Episcopalian, or other—opponents. "Notice," writes Father Marx, "how many Jews helped lead the infamous 1971 abortion planning meeting in Los Angeles."[59] HLI also warns of the "Moslem threat to the world," and Father Marx tells the story of Turkish doctors in Germany who in order "to support large Moslem families, work overtime aborting German women."[60] As is the case with Pat Robertson, Father Marx takes up the anti-Masonic line, and HLI distributes at least two tracts on the subject. HLI is, according to Canadian scholar Michael Cuneo, one of the "smaller, more volatile groups," in the pro-life camp, but his appraisal did not include their extremist bent.[61]

Robertson, HLI, and their ilk set the ideological climate for antigay hate crimes just as Nazi Party propagandists once did for the SS thugs. "Anti-gay violence—usually assaults, frequently very brutal ones is epidemic," says Danny Welch.[62] Gay-bashing attacks rose markedly in those locales in which the antigay referenda were introduced. Martin Hiraga of the National Gay and Lesbian Task Force believes that "the political rhetoric gave permission to people who don't understand, and don't care to understand, to do horrible things." His organization claimed that in the three months before Oregon's measure 9 went down to defeat, antigay violence climbed an extraordinary 600 percent.[63]

Seattle writer Eric Scigliano has given a name to this phenomenon of perpetrators stirred to their violent deeds by ideologues; he terms it the "Smerdyakov defense," after the patricide in Dostoyevsky's *The Brothers Karamazov*. Smerdyakov placed the responsibility on his half brother, the religious Ivan, whose words inspired the deed.[64] The foes of hate propaganda have long understood the crimes of both Smerdyakov and Ivan.

Pat Robertson is the preeminent figure in the religious right today and representative of much of its leadership. He is not as rhetorically extreme as Don Wildmon of the American Family Association and not quite as smooth as Dr. James Dobson of Focus on the Family. Thus in more than one sense one can place him at the center of the religious right. It would be an error to

infer that Robertson's extremism necessarily extends to the larger constituency of the religious right—the televangelists' audience, the contributors to the Christian Coalition, or even the active foot soldiers in its political
efforts. It would also be a mistake to exempt these groups only because we
are concerned about labeling as extremists millions of Americans. Millions of
Frenchmen support Le Pen, and large numbers of Austrians support Jörg
Haider. Unfortunately, extremism need not be confined to pathetic neo-
Nazis and the like.

McCarthyism of the 1950s, it has been argued, was not in fact a popular
movement of the extreme right. Governor George Wallace in the late 1960s
seemed on his way to building such a movement. In the mid-1990s United
States, the religious right seems poised to effect major changes in American
politics and build an extremist, populist movement within the Republican
Party. The Christian Coalition claims to be adding thousands of new adherents each month with membership approaching 1 million. In early 1996 the
coalition had seemingly achieved ascendancy in five state organizations of
the Republican Party and nominated candidates opposed by the party establishment. It has money, media, and votes, which can translate into power,
and it has artful demagogues like Colonel North and Buchanan to capitalize
on this base.

Jewish Extremists

Extremism does not recognize sectarian limitations. In fact, a kind of religious orthodoxy—Protestant, Catholic, Islamic, or Jewish—may link religious zealotry to the goal of secular dominion. In the Jewish case, the organizations spawned by the late Rabbi Meir Kahane give credence to this
linkage.

On February 25, 1994, Baruch Goldstein, a follower of Kahane (he had
been an elected Kach member of Kiryat Arba's town council and had managed Kahane's Knesset campaign), shocked the world when he killed
twenty-nine Muslim worshippers at the Tomb of the Patriarchs Mosque in
Hebron. It was an act calculated to disrupt the fragile movement toward
peace in the Middle East and finds its mirror image in Islamic terrorism directed against not only Israel but Jews around the world.

Meir Kahane established the Jewish Defense League (JDL) in 1968 to defend the American Jewish community from its enemies, who, some have
suggested, were in Kahane's eyes primarily black. In the following year the
Kahaneites established a summer camp to train young Jews in using firearms
and in hand-to-hand combat. Through the 1970s and 1980s the organization and its followers were involved in numerous terrorist and disruptive actions against Arab representatives, the Soviets, and mainstream Jewish organizations, which they viewed as ideological enemies. Kahane emigrated to

Israel in 1971, and although the JDL fractured, the Rabbi maintained contact with his American followers through speaking tours and fund-raising.

Kahane found a fertile field to cultivate in an Israel besieged by its Arab enemies; the temptation is strong there to reply in kind against acts of terrorism. The rabbi or his followers were arrested on numerous occasions for arson, arms smuggling, shootings, and disturbances. In 1985 his Kach (Thus) Party was officially banned by the Israeli Knesset for "inciting racism" and "endangering security." In November 1990 the Rabbi was assassinated in midtown Manhattan. Neither the banning nor the assassination have stopped the Kahane movement's extrapolitical activities.

Kahane Chai (Kahane Lives), one of the offshoots of the JDL, held a summer 1993 training camp, Camp Meir, in New York's Catskill Mountains. Israeli reserve officers and sergeants allegedly trained the youth in arms use and guerrilla tactics. Some of the trainees were subsequently slated to go to Israel for work on the West Bank. Two early 1994 bomb incidents directed against Jewish organizations supporting the peace process were met by the Kahaneites traditional denial of responsibility along with a refusal to "condemn anybody targeting Jewish groups which in our opinion, caused the deaths of so many Jews at the hands of Arab terrorists that they embrace." Kahane Chai, the Jewish Defense Organization, Jewish Direct Action, and the JDL (the California branch that retained the name) claim thousands of members, but their claims seem vastly inflated.[65]

Fund-raising for the extremist movement in Israel is a principle activity of Kahane Chai and its front groups in the United States, which include Operation Adopt a Settlement, American Friends of Yeshiva Harave Meir, and the American Friends of the United Yishuv Movement. The three groups share the same Brooklyn phone number with Kahane Chai. Kach International also conducts similar fund-raising efforts, and a recent ad flagrantly asked for contributions "to ensure that Dr. Goldstein's work on behalf of Israel and the Jewish people continues."[66]

The work of the JDL and its various offshoots demonstrates that even relatively small extremist organizations can have an important impact on international peace and security. In this case a reciprocal relationship between extremist zealots in the United States and Israel reinforces efforts in each country. Israel has responded with debatable bannings of Kahaneite groups, and in the United States authorities are looking beyond law enforcement efforts to possible violations of Internal Revenue regulations giving tax exempt status to nonpolitical, charitable contributions. These Kahaneite offspring were in winter 1995 included by the Clinton administration on a list of suspected supporters of Middle East terrorism. It was none too soon.

Yitzhak Rabin's murderer, Yigal Amir, was associated with the Israeli extremist organization known as Eyal, centered at Bar Ilan University in Tel Aviv. It appears to be one of several Kahane-Kach offshoots that until the assassination was known only for threatening behavior rather than terrorist operations. Following the assassination Israel took extra security precautions that included the exclusion of known Kahaneites seeking to emigrate from the United States to Israel. This measure may help within Israel, but there is no shortage of targets within the United States for those intent on the violent disruption of the Middle East peace process.

Black Extremism: The Nation of Islam

Extremism has now broken down not only the sectarian barriers but also the racial ones. It may seem a strange world in which groups among the oppressed have adopted the mode of the oppressors, but it was the populist anti-Semitism among sectors of the German working class that led the Social Democrat August Bebel to refer to anti-Semitism as the socialism of fools. Louis Farrakhan and the Nation of Islam (NOI), which he leads, also exploit the frustration of the downtrodden and have not only reversed racial stereotypes but appropriated a strident brand of anti-Semitism common to the Klan and its ilk.

Farrakhan's organization is now undoubtedly the most potent anti-Semitic force in the United States and is extending into Canada. On Monday, October 16, 1995, an enormous crowd of black men variously estimated at anywhere from 400,000 to over 1.5 million gathered in Washington, D.C., at the call of one of America's most effective demagogues. Even at its height in the 1920s, the Klan could muster only 45,000 in Washington, D.C., and Dr. Martin Luther King's great rally in 1963 drew only 250,000.

It is quite clear that a great proportion of those who attended the 1995 event had little interest in Farrakhan or his anti-Semitism but seized an opportunity to demonstrate against drugs, for an upright and moral black manhood, and against a congressional economic program that targets America's most vulnerable. Yet the only clear result of the march is that it enhanced Farrakhan's position as perhaps the preeminent leader of black Americans.

The NOI emerged in the 1930s and first achieved prominence under the leadership of Elijah Muhammad in the 1960s. Muhammad's doctrine of racial separatism and antiwhite hatred was given its greatest voice by the late Malcolm X. Malcolm's formidable charisma carried the NOI to its height in the mid-1960s when it had schools and temples in forty-six cities and perhaps as many as 500,000 adherents. Malcolm split with Elijah and was later murdered by assassins connected to the NOI. When Elijah died in 1975, his son Wallace Deen Muhammad rejected his father's separatist doctrines and led a following into orthodox Islam. In 1978 Farrakhan, then a minister of the New York mosque, rejected the turn to moderation and reorganized the Nation of Islam as a separatist and racist organization.

The NOI's racism is now more subdued than its anti-Semitism, which plays a central role in its efforts. Farrakhan and the NOI depend on anti-

Semitism to accomplish different ends. First, it guarantees publicity to a not very large organization with a membership that may be as low as 10,000 and not higher than 100,000.[67] A black radical denouncing the "honkeys" will not get the same attention as one labeling Jews as "bloodsuckers." Jewish defense organizations such as the Anti-Defamation League will respond vigorously to such provocations. Second, because many established black leaders have previously found a great deal of both political and financial support in the Jewish community, anti-Semitism is a useful means of undermining them in the American black community and challenging their positions. Finally, standing up to "the man," in this case the "powerful" Jew, helps to establish Farrakhan and his supporters as the meanest, toughest defenders of their community.[68]

Racist and anti-Semitic language from a white demagogue may find a small minority with receptive ears, but unfortunately Farrakhan is exploiting an already broadly based outlook. Survey after survey has established that anti-Semitism is firmly rooted among American blacks, and unlike the case with most other groups, education enhances rather than mitigates this prejudice.[69] Thus, Farrakhan and his deputy Khalid Abdul Muhammad are the most favored performers before black college student audiences, whom they regale with homophobic and anti-Semitic witticisms.[70]

In a three-year period (1993–1995) Farrakhan has maneuvered the Nation of Islam and himself into a leadership position in the black community. He had been excluded from the observance of the thirtieth anniversary of Dr. King's march, but since then the opposition to him has crumbled, first with the Congressional Black Caucus entering into a covenant with him and then with the massive support of his march by almost all the major players in the black community.[71]

It remains to be seen what Farrakhan will do with his striking victory. If he has further and, especially, political ambitions, he might feel the need to now assume a more statesmanlike stance and drop the uglier side of his rhetoric, although not so quickly as to alienate his following.[72] The political route, given his rhetoric of self-help, could even lead him into some unusual alliances with white extremists. Or he may choose to consolidate his leadership position, retaining the rhetoric of hatred as an effective bond to his people. In either case, Farrakhan and the NOI will persist to either further poison American political life or, through their rhetoric, to encourage the black-on-white hate crimes that are a growing and disturbing phenomenon.

Conclusion

Traditional right-wing extremism in the United States, the skinhead movement excepted, appears to be on the decline at least in numbers. Law enforcement efforts, civil suits, and a general decline in popular racism and anti-Semitism have all contributed to the decline of the Klan and like groups. The skinheads, however, seem to have thrived on the economic dislocations and youth underemployment of the late 1980s and 1990s. In general, traditional extremism does not promise to be an attractive option for many Americans in the near future. However, small numbers of individuals are capable of terrible acts of violence. Thus, law enforcement agencies cannot afford to relax their scrutiny of such individuals and their organizations.

At the same time, American extremism has mainstreamed. In the words of one wag, "The John Birch Society didn't die, it was 'born again.'" Important elements of the religious right are infected with extremism, and there are substantial ties between them and powerful, radical demagogues on the American political scene. Thus a politicized extremism with a popular base and operating within one of the two major parties is appearing in the United States for the first time in many years.

Its advent is coincident with the end of the Cold War and the demise of international communism with its base in the Kremlin. The conspiracy theorists of the right had for decades seen the evil hand of Moscow in all they despised. In recent years the menace of a rather amorphous "secular humanism" has proved a pale substitute for the communist conspiracy. The Manichean worldview of the extremists demands an enemy, an anti-Christ, to serve as the source of evil. As long as the great enemy resided abroad, albeit with its agents perceived even in the White House, the extremists were merely the most militant of cold warriors. However, the emerging but as yet ill-defined new enemy resides at home, and that change could ultimately disturb the domestic tranquility of Americans.

Notes

1. See, for example, Anti-Defamation League [hereafter ADL], *Armed and Dangerous: Militias Take Aim at the Federal Government* (New York: ADL, October 1994); Klanwatch, *Intelligence Report*, June 1995, 5. Klanwatch's Morris Dees had alerted Attorney General Janet Reno and her counterparts in six states on the militia ties to hate groups in the same month that ADL issued its report.

2. David Bennett, *The Party of Fear* (Chapel Hill: University. of North Carolina Press, 1988), 346.

3. Ibid., 401.

4. Leonard Dinnerstein, *Antisemitism in America* (New York: Oxford University Press, 1994), 250.

5. Benjamin Ginsberg, *The Fatal Embrace: Jews and the State* (Chicago: University of Chicago Press, 1993), 242–243.

6. Nathan Glazer, "Debate on Aliens Flares Beyond the Melting Pot," *New York Times,* April 23, 1995, 3.

7. ADL, *The KKK Today: A 1991 Status Report* (New York: ADL, 1991).

8. Wyn Craig Wade, *The Fiery Cross: The Ku Klux Klan in America* (New York: Simon and Schuster, 1987), 387–388.

9. Southern Poverty Law Center, *The Ku Klux Klan: A History of Racism and Violence* (Montgomery, Ala.: The Center, 1991), 52.

10. Bill Stanton, *Klanwatch: Bringing the Ku Klux Klan to Justice* (New York: Grove Weidenfeld, 1991), 191–246.

11. Morris Dees, *Hate on Trial: The Case Against America's Most Dangerous Neo-Nazi* (New York: Villard Books, 1993).

12. Michael Barkun, "Racist Apocalypse: Millennialism on the Far Right," *American Studies* 31, 1990: 122–126.

13. Ibid., 132.

14. *New York Times*, November 16, 1993.

15. ADL, *Young Nazi Killers: The Rising Skinhead Danger* (New York: ADL, 1993).

16. ADL, *The Skinhead International: A Worldwide Survey of Skinheads* (NewYork: ADL, 1995); Klanwatch, *Intelligence Report 77*, March 1995.

17. ADL, *Armed and Dangerous;* ADL, *Beyond the Bombing: The Militia Menace Grows* (New York: ADL, 1995); Klanwatch, *Intelligence Report 79*, August 1995.

18. *New York Times*, November 14, 1994, A1.

19. Klanwatch, *Intelligence Report 78*, June 1995.

20. James William Gibson, *Warrior Dreams: Violence and Manhood in Post-Vietnam America* (NewYork: Hill and Wang, 1994), 9.

21. Ibid., 305.

22. Frank Mintz, *The Liberty Lobby and the American Right* (Westport, Conn.: Greenwood Press, 1985); ADL, *Extremism on the Right* (New York: ADL, 1988).

23. ADL, *Liberty Lobby* (New York: ADL, 1990).

24. ADL, *Liberty Lobby: Hate Central. A Case Study in the Promotion of Anti-Semitism and Extremism* (New York: ADL, 1995).

25. Michael Zatarain, *David Duke: The Evolution of a Klansman* (New Orleans: Pelican, 1990); Tyler Bridges, *The Rise of David Duke* (Jackson: University of Mississippi Press, 1994).

26. Gary Esolen, "More Than a Pretty Face," in Douglas Rose, ed., *The Emergence of David Duke and the Politics of Race* (Chapel Hill: University of North Carolina Press, 1992).

27. Bridges, *The Rise of David Duke*, p. 18, makes the point that Duke, like the rest of the extreme right, "has always viewed Jews as a far greater threat to the white race than blacks."

28. ADL, *Dukewatch 1992: The Failed Campaign of an Extremist* (New York: ADL, 1992).

29. Zatarain, *David Duke*, 41.

30. Lawrence Powell, "Slouching Toward Baton Rouge," in Rose, *The Emergence of David Duke*, 18.

31. Ibid., 12.

32. Susan Howell and Sylvia Warren, "Public Opinion and David Duke," in Rose, *The Emergence of David Duke*.

33. See Buchanan's chapter "As We Remember Joe," in Patrick Buchanan, *Right from the Beginning* (Boston: Little, Brown, 1988).

34. *Los Angeles Times*, November 22, 1991.

35. ADL, *Anger on the Right: Pat Buchanan's Venomous Crusade* (New York: ADL, 1991), 2.

36. William F. Buckley, "In Search of Anti-Semitism," *National Review*, December 30, 1991.

37. *Boston Globe*, January 5, 1992.

38. Patrick Buchanan, "Worship Democracy? A Dissent from the Right," *Washington Inquirer*, January 25, 1991.

39. Patrick Buchanan, "Today Canada, Tomorrow USA," *Washington Inquirer*, July 6, 1990.

40. Patrick Buchanan, "Immigration Reform or Racial Purity?" *Washington Inquirer*, June 15, 1984.

41. *Los Angeles Times*, May 14, 1992.

42. *Right-Wing Watch*, October 1993.

43. *Washington Post*, December 9, 1991.

44. Patrick Buchanan, "Marching to the Wrong Tune," *Washington Inquirer*, March 29, 1991.

45. As quoted by Alan Dershowitz, *Los Angeles Times*, November 22, 1991.

46. *Newsweek*, January 27, 1992.

47. Patrick Buchanan, "'Democratization' of Eastern Europe Is KGB Scam," *Washington Inquirer*, April 19, 1991.

48. Leonard Weinberg, "The American Radical Right: Exit, Voice, and Violence," in Peter Merkl and Leonard Weinberg, eds., *Encounters with the Contemporary Radical Right* (Boulder: Westview Press, 1993), 185.

49. James D. Hunter, *Culture Wars: The Struggle to Defend America* (New York: Basic Books, 1991), 147.

50. Sara Diamond, "Watch on the Right," *Humanist*, March-April 1994.

51. ADL, *Religious Right*, 120.

52. Ibid.

53. Michael Slaughter, "An Interview with Sara Diamond," *Z Magazine*, January 1993, 29.

54. ADL, *The Religious Right: The Assault on Tolerance and Pluralism in America* (New York: ADL, 1994), 21.

55. Sara Diamond, *Spiritual Warfare: The Politics of the Christian Right* (Boston: South End Press, 1989), 13.

56. Pat Robertson, *The New World Order* (Dallas: World Publisher, 1991), p. 255.

57. Diamond, *Spiritual Warfare*, ch. 6.

58. *The Dignity Report*, August 1, 1993.

59. Paul Marx, *Confessions of a Prolife Missionary* (Gaithersburg, Md.: Human Life International, 1988), 269.

60. Pat Buchanan, *Washington Times*, August 21, 1989.

61. Michael W. Cuneo, *Catholics Against the Church: Anti-Abortion Protest in Toronto 1969–1985* (Toronto: University of Toronto Press, 1989), 71.

62. *Klanwatch Intelligence Report*, June 1992.

63. *Klanwatch Intelligence Report*, February 1993.

64. James Coates, *Armed and Dangerous: The Rise of the Survivalist Right* (New York: Hill and Wang, 1995), 166–167.

65. ADL, *Extremism in the Name of Religion: The Violent Legacy of Meir Kahane* (New York: ADL, 1994).

66. Robert I. Friedman, "The Brooklyn Avengers," *New York Review of Books,* June 23, 1994.

67. Don Terry, "Minister Farrakhan: Conservative Militant," *New York Times,* March 3, 1994, B9. This reporter declares that "no one seems to know for sure how big the Nation of Islam is."

68. The black journalist William Raspberry has said: "I don't know what accounts for this gratuitous antisemitism, nor do I fully understand why so many Blacks—even those who studiously avoid expressing it themselves—see it as somehow gutsy to say these hateful things." *Washington Post,* October 30, 1989.

69. Dinnerstein, *Anti-Semitism in America,* 209–210.

70. I attended Muhammad's speech to a crowd at Montreal's Concordia University on May 3, 1993.

71. Clarence Page, "Bringing Farrakhan into the Fold," *Chicago Tribune,* September 19, 1993. Page understands this display of black unity as "a sign of despair, a sign that mainstream black leaders are so desperate and confused over how to win back the respect of ghetto blacks that they will tarnish their long-held commitment to coalitions and desegregation by embracing the nation's leading black separatist."

72. Don Terry, "Seeking Statesmanship, Farrakhan Softens Tone," *New York Times,* October 25, 1995, 14. Terry reported that Farrakhan in a postmarch speech said he would endeavor to become more statesmanlike in his rhetoric "because the march had elevated his stature and his responsibility."

5

The Extreme Right in the United Kingdom and France

David Matas

Historically, the extreme right both in England and in France has always been marginal in terms of popular support. In England, the extreme right has also been insignificant politically. In France, however, the extreme right managed to frame a political issue that monopolized public debate for years—the Dreyfus affair. It also managed to seize political power and govern at least that part of the country within the Vichy regime.

Alfred Dreyfus, a Jewish officer of the French general staff, was convicted by court martial of communicating military secrets to a German military attaché and sentenced to life imprisonment. The true author of the communication was Major Walsin-Esterhazy, who had forged the communication in the handwriting of Dreyfus on orders of his superior, Colonel Sandherr. Esterhazy fled to England and revealed his forgery there. The Court of Cassation in July 1906 annulled Dreyfus's sentence and acquitted him.[1]

The Dreyfus case was more, however, than a miscarriage of justice. It became a rallying point for the extreme right in France. Anti-Dreyfusards used the polemics around the case to promote their agenda of anti-Semitism and antirepublicanism. The army general staff, among whom was Marshall Pétain, future head of the Vichy regime, was solidly anti-Dreyfus.

Despite all the polemics and the considerable anti-Semitic mob violence it generated, the anti-Dreyfusard movement never amounted to much politically. At its peak, the anti-Semitic anti-Dreyfusard movement elected nineteen members to parliament.[2] The right-wing extremist group with the largest membership between World Wars I and II, Le Parti Populaire Français, founded by Jacques Doriot in 1936, had at most 250,000 members.[3] Tolerance in France was sufficiently widespread before World War II to allow the election of a Jewish prime minister, Léon Blum, who served from June 1936 to June 1937 and from March to April 1938.

Germany defeated France in June 1940 and occupied its northern region. In the southern part, on July 2, 1940, a collaborationist regime was installed with a capital in Vichy and Marshal Henri-Philippe Pétain at its head.[4] The prime minister under Pétain was Pierre Laval.

Before the war, there were an estimated 350,000 Jews in France. With the German occupation of northern France, many Jews fled to Vichy France. The Germans demanded that the Vichy regime hand over for deportation the Jews in its jurisdiction. The Vichy government distinguished between French and foreign-born Jews, rounding up the foreign-born Jews for the Germans but refusing to hand over the French born. In November 1942, the Germans occupied all of France and proceeded to round up the French Jews whom the Vichy regime had refused to hand over.

Although the Vichy regime dragged its heels on deportation of French-born Jews, it was otherwise enthusiastically and autonomously anti-Semitic. The Vichy regime had its own anti-Jewish campaign, not in response to German demands but as a result of long-term priorities of the politicians who made up the regime.[5] All Jews in Vichy France, including French-born Jews, were prohibited by Vichy legislation from holding public office; banned from the judiciary, teaching, the military, banking, real estate, and the media; severely limited from entering the professions; and subjected to expropriation of their property and the dissolution of their organizations.

Of the 350,000 Jews in the French prewar population, approximately 90,000 were deported or executed or perished in internment camps.[6] Of the 90,000, 76,000 were in deportation convoys that left France for concentration and extermination camps of Eastern Europe. Of the 76,000, only 2,500 survived.[7]

Wherever the Nazis went, they relied heavily on local police, administrative personnel, and homegrown fascists organized into militias to round up Jews for the death camps. In France, the police and administration in both the north and the south participated on a massive scale. Jacques Doriot's Parti Populaire Français assisted in the roundups.[8]

French history shows that the apparent political insignificance of the extreme right in prewar France was misleading. Even a small extreme right-wing group can become the engine of the machinery of death when political misfortune puts it into power.

After the war, de Défense des Commerçants et Artisans, led by Pierre Poujade, began as a pressure group rallying supporters to a right-wing agenda by attempting to organize a tax revolt and an anti-welfare-state movement. In the first election it contested, in 1956, it won 12.3 percent of the vote[9] and elected fifty-two members to the National Assembly.[10] With the advent of Gaullism in 1958, many supporters defected to Charles de Gaulle, and the movement disintegrated.[11]

In Britain, the first formal antialien organization, the British Brothers' League, was established in 1901 by William Stanley Shaw.[12] It claimed to have a membership in 1902 of 45,000 people.[13] The British Brothers' League did not run candidates in elections but instead functioned as a political pressure group, organizing racist meetings, rallies, and demonstrations. It played a key role in the buildup of political support that led to the passage of the Aliens Act of 1905.[14]

The next major extreme right-wing political movement, the British Union of Fascists, became active in 1934 and was headed by Oswald Mosley. In the London City Council elections of 1937, the British Union of Fascists contested several East End constituencies and, in a few wards, won substantial support.[15]

Mosley and other British fascists were interred by the British government during World War II. After the war, Mosley reconstituted his party as the Union Movement. The Union Movement sporadically contested both local and national elections, mostly in the East End of London, from 1949 to 1970. Its highest vote was 20 percent in a London East End ward in 1968. However, that 20 percent represented only 160 votes.

An attempt at coalition in the United Kingdom of various right-wing groups led to the formation of the National Front in 1966. John Tyndall, one of the founders, had a history of overt associations with Nazism. Some elements of the National Front wanted to disassociate from Nazism as much as possible for electoral reasons. However, Tyndall was not to be denied, and eventually he assumed a position of leadership in the party.

The National Front, once formed, achieved variable success in elections it contested, reaching a high of 19.2 percent in the Bethnal Green and Bow constituency in the Greater London Council elections of 1977. This vote, however, dropped precipitously in the 1979 parliamentary election in Bethnal Green and Bow to 6.1 percent. Elsewhere the descent was similar.[16] The decline was attributable partly to an antifascist campaign prompted by the rise of the National Front. The initial response had been to ignore it, not to give it undue attention. As the group became stronger, neglect was replaced by active opposition. A concerted effort was made to expose the National Front as the neo-Nazi party it was, and the party was discredited.

When Uganda became independent from Britain, many Ugandan Asians had chosen to retain their British citizenship rather than take out Ugandan citizenship. When Idi Amin subsequently expelled ethnic Asians from Uganda, many ethnic Asian British citizens attempted to come to Britain. The then prime minister, Edward Heath, and the Tories decided to honor the British passports of these expelled Asians and allowed them to enter. British Labour and Liberals supported this decision, but the National Front did not. It became a political vehicle for the expression of opposition to this policy.

At the same time, the Tory Party took a sharp turn to the right with the replacement of its head, Edward Heath, by Margaret Thatcher. In January 1978, Margaret Thatcher appeared to endorse the opposition to the entry of Ugandan Asian British passport holders. She acknowledged that people were "afraid that this country might be rather swamped by people with a different culture." In the 1979 election campaign, after the Thatcher statement and apparently partly as a result of it, the National Front's support disintegrated and the bulk of the floating racist vote shifted to the Tory Party.

When the National Front splintered after the 1979 election, John Tyndall left and, after first forming the New National Front, formed the British National Party. The BNP became his vehicle and continues to serve that purpose.[17] The National Front remains as an entity but has lost the majority of its assets, has a much reduced membership, and is split into various factions.

In 1986, the Thatcher government introduced legislation into parliament to amend the Nationality Act. The amendments, once passed, had the effect of making it more difficult for some British passport holders, including some Ugandan Asians, to enter Britain.

Contemporary Overview of Far-Right Groups

The far right in the United Kingdom presents a quite different picture than the far right in France. In France, the Front National predominates. The far right in the United Kingdom has been characterized by factionalism. There have been myriad small groups with a few hundred members. The divisions have been prompted by personality squabbles, differences in ideology, and differences in strategy.

Britain

The BNP is now the largest of the far-right groups in England. However, its estimated membership is only 2,500. Other elements of the far right in the mid-1990s in Britain are Western Goals, Revolutionary Conservatives, the British National Socialist Movement, Combat 18, Blood and Honour, Church of the Creator, the International Third Position, the Ku Klux Klan, and the League of St. George.[18]

The Church of the Creator and the Ku Klux Klan are offshoots of U.S. organizations. The Ku Klux Klan is estimated at 400 members. Blood and Honour is estimated at about 2,000. Blood and Honour is the organized focus for the Nazi skinhead movement in Britain. Combat 18, the most violent group, is estimated to have only 80 people. There are a number of publications put out by these various organizations, including the *British National-*

ist and *Spearhead*. The groups also have a number of rock groups—the Elite, Straw Dogs, Violent Storm, Skullhead, Screwdriver, No Remorse, and Dirlewanger.

One technique the far right has used in Britain both for publicity and for recruiting is racist chants at football matches. Monkey chants are shouted and bananas are thrown from the stands whenever a black player gets possession of the ball. Paper crosses, symbolic of the Ku Klux Klan, are burned. There are attacks on blacks after the matches, and far-right newspapers are sold outside the stadiums. The far-right instigators attempt to recruit those who seem willing to go along.

France

In France, the far right is virtually monopolized by the Front National. It has emerged from the factionalism that has traditionally characterized the far right and towers over the other groups, each of which has a membership in the hundreds at most: the Restauration Nationale, which calls for restoration of the monarchy; the Parti Nationaliste Français et Européen; the Faisceaux Nationalistes Européens, an openly Nazi faction; Troisième Voie; Nouvelle Résistance; Groupe Union Défense (GUD); the Parti Nationaliste Français; l'Oeuvre Française; Nationalisme et République; Alliance Populaire; Comités d'Action Républicaine; Chrétienté-Solidarité; and La Contre-Réforme Catholique. Skinheads are organized around a record-publishing company, Rebelles Européenes. Some of the French skinhead rock groups are Légion 88, Bunker 88, and Skin-Korp. In the universities there are Front National Jeunesse, Renouveau Étudiant, and the previously mentioned GUD. The GUD operates through violence and intimidation and the Renouveau Étudiant stands for elections. In the 1991 elections, Renouveau Étudiant elected four persons to the student council. In 1994 no one from this group was elected.

In contrast to these organizations that have membership in the hundreds, the Front National has from 50,000 to 60,000 members. In the regional election of 1992, the Front National received 13.9 percent of the vote and elected 239 regional councillors out of 1,829. The FN came second in two regions, Provence-Alpes-Côte d'Azur and Île-de-France.

Growth in Racist Incidents and Electoral Strength

Two indicators—the number of racist incidents and electoral results—point to growth of the extreme right in both countries. According to the first indicator, the far right is having a greater effect than before in England; according to the second, the far right is gaining strength in France.

Britain

Racist incidents in Britain, from insults to murder, are significant in number and increasing in recent years. From 1991 to 1992, reported anti-Semitic incidents rose 9 percent.[19] From 1992 to 1993, reported anti-Semitic incidents increased by 18 percent.[20]

For both 1992 and 1993 there were no anti-Semitic incidents of extreme violence. In the categories of assault, threats and abusive behavior, and criminal acts, there were increases for both 1992 and 1993. In the categories of damage and destruction to property and literature, there were decreases in 1992 and increases in 1993.

In 1988, the police recorded 4,383 racially motivated incidents in England and Wales against both ethnic minorities and whites. The figure for 1989 is 5,044; for 1990, 6,359; for 1991, 7,882; and for 1992, 7,793.[21]

The British crime survey estimates that in 1991 there were 130,000 such incidents against ethnic minorities. Jews are included as whites rather than ethnic minorities in this survey. So this 130,000 figure does not include incidents of anti-Semitism. This survey indicates that 50,000 of the 130,000 incidents were reported to the police but that most of those reported incidents were not recorded or, if recorded, not recorded as racially motivated incidents.

This survey concludes that crime generally is increasing and that the increase in racially motivated incidents follows the general increase; thus the percentage of racially motivated incidents has remained constant. In the opinion of the authors of the summary, the increase in the police-reported racially motivated incidents reflects a greater propensity of police to record incidents as racially motivated incidents rather than a disproportionate increase in such incidents.

In Britain, the definition of a racial incident for the purposes of police records is deliberately wide. The definition was first employed in 1985 and covers "any incident in which it appears to the reporting or investigating officer that the complaint involves an element of racial motivation or any incident which includes an allegation of racial motivation made by any person."

Many local police forces employ dedicated community liaison officers, a good deal of whose work in areas with high ethnic minority populations has been to increase the confidence of those communities in the police. In these areas, an increase in the number of reported racial incidents may be evidence of success of the community liaison officers because it indicates a growing confidence in the victims that the police may be able and willing to help.

The Home Office's view is that Britain has a good deal less racial violence than the Continent despite the large number of estimated reported incidents. The Home Office considers that in Britain many more incidents are recorded and considered as racially motivated than in France. British statistics pick up low levels of noncriminal harassment that undermine people's quality of life, whereas Continental statistics often refer to more serious criminal activities. Thus, the Home Office concludes that its figures reflect different reporting procedures rather than a greater problem with racism.[22] French statistics also tend to focus on racial incidents linked to the extreme right. There is little or no collecting of statistics of racially motivated violence where there is no such link. This may be a consequence of failure to face up to multiculturalism or evidence of freelance racism in France.

The British police reported 7,993 racially motivated incidents in 1992. Because reported incidents are considered to be only a small fraction of total incidents, the Home Office estimates the actual number of racially motivated incidents for 1992 to be 140,000.[23]

There is no sense of the development of the far right as a mass movement in Britain. Although electoral support for the extreme right has grown, its membership has remained stagnant and it remains electorally insignificant. The increase in the vote has been from an extremely low base. The far right contests very few seats in both national and local elections. For those seats it has contested, it generally registers a vote of less than 5 percent, usually in the range of 1–2 percent. It is uncommon for the extreme right to get votes for any one seat in more than the three-figure range. Until September 1993, the last time the far right had elected anyone in Britain was in May 1976, when two extreme right-wing candidates were elected as councillors in Blackburn. However, in September 1993, the BNP did succeed in electing a councillor, Derek Beackon from the Millwall ward, the Isle of Dogs, Tower Hamlets, in the East End of London. The Millwall ward is part of the Isle of Dogs subcouncil. The Isle of Dogs is one of seven subcouncils that make up the Tower Hamlets council area.[24]

Beackon received 34 percent of the vote, or 480 votes. The rest of the vote was split between Labour and Liberal Democrats. The Tories received only 3 percent of the vote and were not a factor in the election. In a previous by-election in the ward, in October 1992, the BNP received 20 percent of the vote. Beackon was the beneficiary of a protest vote over housing policy. British housing law gives priority in public housing to the homeless. In Tower Hamlets, 80 percent of the housing stock is public housing. Twenty percent of the borough's population is ethnic; 9.2 percent is Bangladeshi—the largest minority grouping. Bangladeshis also constitute 69 percent of the homeless.

Bangladeshis represent such a high percentage of the homeless because of their traditional pattern of immigration from Bangladesh. Adult family men came without their families to work in the UK, staying with friends or relatives. When their families joined them, the amount of low-rent housing in the UK was not sufficient and the families were homeless.

Giving priority to the homeless for public housing in Tower Hamlets meant, in effect, a priority for Bangladeshis. The initial reaction of the Tower Hamlets council was to refuse to recognize this priority in a number of different ways. The Bangladeshis were categorized as intentionally homeless and therefore not eligible for public housing—their families could have stayed in Bangladesh. The House of Lords in 1981, in the case of *Islam v. the London Borough of Hillingdon*, held that a person could not be considered intentionally homeless simply because he wished to be reunited with his family.

Another tactic that Tower Hamlets employed was outright discrimination, denying accommodation to Bangladeshi families for no other reason than that they were Bangladeshi. This tactic mobilized the Commission for Racial Equality, which in 1987 issued a nondiscrimination notice against the Tower Hamlets Council. Under the terms of that notice Tower Hamlets was required "to ensure that those applicants (for housing) whose dependents are separated and living outside the UK are assessed for waiting list purposes as if they (the dependents) lived in the UK."[25]

Between 1988 and 1993 the Tower Hamlets Council attempted to comply with this nondiscrimination notice; legally, it had no choice. This attempted compliance led in turn to charges from the extreme right that Bangladeshis were being favored in the allocation of public housing over whites. These charges and protest over attempted compliance with the nondiscrimination notice led to the election of Derek Beackon.

France

The Front National was founded in 1972 but took off electorally in September 1983.[26] Prior to its sudden electoral success, it was a splinter right-wing group, indistinguishable from the others, with a membership in the neighborhood of 500.

The breakthrough was in Dreux, a town west of Paris. Jean-Pierre Stirbois headed a Front National list in the municipal elections that got 16 percent of the vote in the first round. In prior elections, the legislative elections of 1981, the FN received 0.2 percent of the vote. The September 1983 Dreux results were quickly replicated elsewhere in France. In October 1983 the FN received 9.3 percent of the vote in a municipal by-election. In December 1983, the FN received 12 percent of the vote in a legislative by-election.

In the second round of voting in Dreux, the extreme right and the traditional right formed an alliance—a joint Rallierent Pour la République (RPR)-Union Democratique Français (UDF)-FN list. Because the FN candidates were on the list, they were able to get elected, in the second round, to the municipal council.

This election marked the real birth of the FN not only because of the electoral returns but also because of the alliance subsequently formed with the traditional right. The following debate about whether there should be alliances between the extreme right and the traditional right brought the FN to the center of French attention.

Although the FN experienced its first surge of growth in Dreux, the other FN successes followed too closely upon the Dreux results and were too widespread for the Dreux election to have been just a local phenomenon. The rise of the FN is best explained by the political situation in France during a particular time period. The left formed the government in 1981 at a time of massive unemployment. François Mitterrand was elected president for the first time. After his socialist government had been in power for two years, it was apparent that it was not able to turn the economy around.

In the meantime, the right had been discredited by its failures in office and had been defeated. The traditional right, when out of power, had radicalized its discourse, approaching the vocabulary of the extreme right. In this context, the extreme right appeared to offer, to a sizable minority of the electorate, a viable option. Of all the small groups that form the extreme right, the FN was the beneficiary of this shift in the electoral vote, largely because it was one of the groups that had chosen the electoral option as a strategy. At the time when the extreme right was getting less than 1 percent of the vote, as in 1981 and previously, it was not immediately obvious that an electoral strategy was the most fruitful. Other extreme-right elements were involved in violence, propagandizing, or in attempts to infiltrate the traditional parties.

The FN also had the advantage of Jean-Marie Le Pen, an accomplished speaker and a former member of the National Assembly. He had been elected in 1956 as a Poujadist and in 1958 for the Centre Nationale des Indépendants et Paysans, a group formed in 1949 that gathered together pro-Pétainist parliamentarians.[27] Altogether, Le Pen served six years as a member of the National Assembly. In 1981, Le Pen could not get 500 elected representatives from any elected office at any level of government to sign his nomination papers so that he could be a presidential candidate. In 1988 his papers were signed and he received 14.4 percent of the vote in the first round.

For electoral strategic reasons, the FN modified its discourse. It was not overtly pro-Nazi or anti-Semitic. It operated by way of coded messages rather than by explicit hate propaganda. There was a thin veneer of respectability to the Front National that allowed it to be a credible player on the political scene.[28]

Responses to the Growth of the Extreme Right

The United Kingdom and France have very different responses to the growth of the extreme right, because the extreme right has grown in the two countries in very different ways. In the United Kingdom, because the far right has remained a fringe movement, a significant component of the response has been legal. In France, because the extreme right is a political force, a significant component of the response necessarily has been political.

Britain

The initial response among the antiracist organizations to the election of the BNP in Tower Hamlets was to downplay the result. The general commentary was that the election did not represent a recrudescence of the far right.

In one sense that is so. Membership in the far right has remained at the same level. The election of Derek Beackon in Tower Hamlets had very much to do with the local issue of housing. It did not represent a racist national trend. Derek Beackon is himself an inarticulate security guard within the BNP. He has no real leadership potential for the far right even within the limited reaches of Millwall ward.

In another sense, though, this attempt to deemphasize the extreme right is wishful thinking. The election achieved massive publicity for the BNP and put the BNP head and shoulders above the other splinter groups of the far right. It had a mobilizing effect on the membership of the extreme right, and even if that membership has not increased, its activity has increased exponentially.

For the government, the election led to a change in its policy on homelessness. After the Tower Hamlets election, the Tories announced that they would ask parliament to amend the Homeless Persons Act so that the homeless would no longer have priority for public housing. The government denies that this change in housing policy was a response to the Tower Hamlets election.

The Liberal Democrats in Tower Hamlets have themselves been involved in distributing racist literature both before and after the Tower Hamlets election. This behavior of the Liberal Democrats can be seen not only as a reflection of racist attitudes in the area but also as a reaction to the growth of the extreme right and an attempt to counter it. The national organs of the party set up a commission of investigation under Lord Lester because of the alleged racist activity of their local group. This commission of inquiry confirmed the allegations that the local activities were indeed racist in nature.

Racist violence also increased in Tower Hamlets, in step with the increased electoral support. There were at least thirty identified incidents of voter intimidation by the extreme right against opponents before the vote was held. Racist beatings and threats after the election were at such a tempo that the minority community in the area lived in a state of siege. Members of this community lived under a self-imposed curfew and were afraid to leave their houses at any time. Roving right-wing toughs created a reign of terror.

One response to the extreme right in the United Kingdom has been the use of legal measures. In 1965, the British Parliament enacted a law dealing with the offense of incitement to racial hatred. The law was strengthened in 1976 with an amendment that removed the requirement of proving deliberate intention to stir up hatred. Despite the changes, the law has been ineffective. There have been few prosecutions under the law despite the volume and the virulence of hate propaganda circulating in the UK.

The increase in racist incidents throughout Britain that preceded, accompanied, and followed the Tower Hamlet's election has led to calls for strengthening of hate-propaganda laws. The Board of Deputies of British Jews recommended in 1992 that the Public Order Act, which criminalizes incitement of racial hatred, be amended in the following nine respects: (1) the offense should be expanded from hatred to hatred, hostility, or contempt; (2) the offense of "stirring up" racial hatred be expanded to cover encouragement or advocacy of racial hatred; (3) racist propaganda covered by the law should not be limited to racist material that is "threatening, abusive or insulting" but should cover all such material; (4) the offense of distribution of racist material to "the public or a section of the public" should be expanded to include "any member of the public"; (5) instead of the requirement for prosecution that racial hatred "is likely" to be stirred up, it should be enough if it is reasonably foreseeable that racial hatred may be stirred up; (6) the police should have power to arrest any person who is reasonably suspected of distributing racist material, power they do not now have; (7) the exception to the offense, when it is committed inside a dwelling, should be limited so that it does not apply when there is an invitation to the general public to attend a meeting on private premises; (8) the court should have the power to order that no future copies of the offending material be distributed; and (9) the consent of the attorney general for prosecution should no longer be required, but private prosecution should remain prohibited.[29] The Commission for Racial Equality has recommended the same changes in the law. [30]

The Board of Deputies also recommended four changes to the Malicious Communications Act. This act criminalizes the sending of letters or articles conveying a message that is indecent or grossly offensive; a threat; or information known to be false, where the purpose is to cause distress or anxiety.

The board recommended that (1) the offense of sending include delivery; (2) it be made clear in the act that the words "indecent or grossly offensive" are not intended to relate only to material that is pornographic; (3) the offense allow for imprisonment; (now the only possible punishment is a fine); and (4) the illegal purposes for conviction be expanded beyond causing distress or anxiety to causing outrage. The board also proposed a totally new offense of vilification of a member of an ethnic group. The Commission for Racial Equality expressed some support for this position.

Parliament passed the Football Offences Act in 1991. The act penalizes chanting of an indecent racialist nature by any person in concert with others. The Board of Deputies of British Jews proposed that an individual chanting alone should be guilty of an offense.

The Commission for Racial Equality launched a football antiracism campaign in August 1993. The commission proposed an action plan for football clubs that included public announcements condemning racist behavior, the removal of racist graffiti, disciplinary action against players involved in racist abuse, and the ejection of racist chanters and their banishment from later matches.

The government reviewed the Public Order Act of 1986, which prohibits the use of threatening, abusive, or insulting words or behavior with intent or likelihood to stir up racial hatred.[31] Although there have not been many prosecutions under this provision, a Home Office review of the legislation suggested that the provision was, nevertheless, an important deterrent. As well, the Act of 1986 creates an offense of threatening, abusive, or insulting words or behavior likely to cause harassment, alarm, and distress.[32] The government concluded on review that the powers under this provision were not sufficient to prevent the more serious forms of racial harassment. It accordingly took steps to strengthen the legislation: A new offense of causing intentional harassment has been created. The maximum penalty is six months imprisonment and a fine of 5,000 pounds. The police, under the new provision, have an immediate power of arrest in relation to the offense.

The Board of Deputies of British Jews recommended that the police be given the power to arrest any person who is reasonably suspected of distributing or storing racist material. This recommendation was implemented in the 1994 Criminal Justice Act.[33] In general, the board's main recommendations have been supported by the *Select Committee on Home Affairs Report on Racial Violence* of 1994, the Labour Party, the Liberal Democratic Party, the Commission for Racial Equality, the Bar Council, the Law Society, and, to a lesser extent, the commissioner for the metropolitan police.

Ministers of the crown have convened an interdepartmental racial-attacks group to review the effectiveness of legislative and other responses to date to the problem of racist violence and racial harassment and to consider what further guidance can be given to local agencies. The group's findings will be published.

The rise of the extreme right and the rise of racist incidents are, to a certain extent, coincident rather than connected phenomena. The number of racially motivated crimes is so large and the extreme right is so small that it is hard to believe that the extreme right is directly responsible for the bulk of racist crimes in the UK.

The linkage is, rather, indirect. Racist crimes and attitudes are promoted and supported by the extreme right, which represents an ideological home where racists can go. Racists are a potential recruiting ground for the extreme right. However, not every racist is neo-Nazi. There is an ideological resistance to the extreme right even among racists.

This hesitancy of elements of the numerically large but proportionately small racist population to join the extreme right has led to differing strategies to deal with the two phenomena of neo-Nazism and racism. One political strategy is to attack the two simultaneously. Not all racists are neo-Nazis, but all neo-Nazis are racists. Thus any serious strategy must be broad enough to include attacks on all types of racism. Others advocate a focused attack on Nazis. The Anti-Nazi League and the Anti-Racist Alliance— formed in 1991 in response to the well-publicized racist killing of Roland Adams in February of that year—reflect this difference in strategy. Both organizations are nongovernmental, and both combat Nazis. The Anti-Nazi League however, focuses on Nazism, and the Anti-Racist Alliance focuses on racism.

Another difference between the two organizations is that the leadership of the Anti-Racist Alliance is predominantly, although not exclusively, black or colored, and the alliance is viewed as a black organization. The leadership of the Anti-Nazi League is predominantly Trotskyite communist, and the league is viewed as an extreme left-wing organization. There is a rivalry between the Anti-Nazi League and the Anti-Racist Alliance for the leadership of the nongovernmental advocacy campaign against the extreme right. Each group is critical of the other. This division in the nongovernmental community of the 1990s has the effect of weakening the overall effort against the extreme right, which in the 1970s was united.

The political parties face similar, if not more acute, divisions. All major parties at the national level oppose racism, although the Tories have been less explicit about it than the others. The Tories have been reluctant to sign an antiracist manifesto proposed by the Commission for Racial Equality. The Labour Party and the Liberal Democrats have been quite willing to sign.

At the local level, both the Tories and the Liberal Democrats have had rogue constituency organizations that have attempted to appeal for racist votes. This local deviance is partly the result of racism that has infiltrated at the local level and partly a calculated political strategy to woo the racist vote away from the extreme-right-wing parties. It was this sort of local deviance that led to the Lord Lester Report for the Liberal Democrats on the racist political appeals of the local party members in the municipal elections in Towers Hamlet.

In the 1970s, all the parties came out against racism before the rise of Margaret Thatcher and her "swamping" speech. This united front did not help the parties at the polls. There is a tendency now for all the parties to soft-pedal their antiracism and to keep a low profile on the issue.

The Board of Deputies of British Jews sponsored and organized a united campaign against racism both in a manifesto and at a public meeting prior to the May 1994 municipal elections. The Tory home secretary, the Labour shadow home secretary, and the Liberal Democrats' spokesperson on race issues joined church leaders and leaders of the main religious groups in this campaign. However, this initiative was initiated by the board and did not emanate from any of the parties.

Because the problem of racist violence is so large and the problem of right-wing extremism is so small, there is a feeling both within the Home Office and the Anti-Racist Alliance that a focus on the extreme-right-wing is misdirected. Such a focus emphasizes a smaller problem at the expense of a much larger one. Without denying the linkages between the two, those who subscribe to this analysis emphasize the need to attack racism directly rather than indirectly by attacking right-wing extremism. The total membership of the extreme right of all its organizations in the UK is 3,000. As of this writing, it is impossible to show a direct responsibility of those 3,000 for any significant proportion of the more than 130,000 racist incidents a year.

Although right-wing extremists provide comfort and support to those involved in racist attacks, the police have no intelligence to show that racist attacks are planned by the extreme right with the exception of one group, Combat 18, which has fewer than 100 people. The extreme right has used these attacks as a recruiting tool, and particular efforts have been directed against this type of violence. The police view is that all other attacks are opportunistic, the result of free-floating working-class aggression.

Much of the antiblack activity is violent and nonideological. There is little antiblack literature. With the Jewish community, the opposite is true: There is little in the way of physical attacks against Jews but a good deal of anti-Semitic literature. With anti-Semitism, the notion that the problem is racism rather than right-wing extremism does not hold. Right-wing extremists actively promote anti-Semitism.

This variation is a further indication that the violence is opportunistic rather than planned. If the violence was planned by the extreme right, the Jewish community would not be spared; on the contrary, it would be the first to suffer. Where the Jewish community is visible, for instance in its cemeteries and gravestones, it is the victim of racist violence, just as the black community is. The Jewish community escapes racist violence insofar as it is not visible.

The British police have organized local advisory public committees to assist in the fight against racism. Municipalities employ antiracism advisers to work with both ethnic minorities and the police to resolve local problems.

France

The French response to the extreme right has taken three forms: resistance, co-optation, and repression. Resistance has involved trying to win back the electorate that has gone over to the Front National and persuade those leaning to the right not to support the Front National. Co-optation has involved an attempt to win over the electorate of the Front National by adopting some of its policies. Repression has been directed not at the Front National but at those at the fringes of the extreme right. There have been bannings of groups and publications and closings of bookstores as well as the traditional criminal prosecutions for acts of violence.

Faced with an electoral surge in the extreme right, the traditional parties have two alternatives. They can either mimic the policies of the extreme right and incorporate them in modified form or they can reject these policies in any form whatsoever.

Both alternatives have their dangers. Adopting policies of the far right gives extremism credibility and brings the extreme right away from the margins toward the center. It runs the risk of reinforcing the electorate of the extreme right. Voters who want extreme-right policies are more likely to vote for the originators of the policies than those who copy the policies.

Ignoring the policies of the far right leaves the protest voters with nowhere to go but the extreme right. The far right attracts voters who may come because of a single issue but end up staying. The vote becomes radicalized and loyal.

Given the choice between the two alternatives, the traditional French parties have picked the first. The rise of the Front National has caused a whole political spectrum in France to shift to the right. The traditional right is more right than before in matters such as immigration, citizenship, integration, and law and order, and so is the traditional left.

This shift to the right of the traditional parties has not undercut the core support of the Front National. It has, however, arrested its growth. The FN now has a vote of 10–12 percent across France. That core vote has remained steady during the early 1990s.

There is a third alternative other than adopting the policies of the FN or ignoring it altogether. That is to combat it directly by attempting to expose it as racist, fascist, and neo-Nazi. This effort started immediately after the election of Jean-Pierre Stirbois of the Front National in Dreux in September 1983. Left-wing parties, unions, and organizations held a large protest meeting after the election. In 1984, at the time of the European elections, there was a wave of anti–Front National demonstrations that were sometimes violent; a second wave followed in 1990 after the desecration of the Jewish cemetery in Carpentras and a third, in 1992 at the time of the regional elections.

There have been several groups specifically devoted to combating the FN. SCALP/Reflex (Sections Carrément anti–Le Pen), a radical antifascist movement, was started in 1985 and appeals to the young. Appeal des 250 with its newspaper, *Ras l'Front*, started in 1990. There are, as well, several hundred local anti–Le Pen groups, mainly in the cities and large towns. Within the classic left the effort has been undertaken by the organization Manifest of Jean Cristophe Cambadelis as well as by the Ligue des Droits de l'Homme, l'Union des Étudiants Juifs, SOS Racisme, Le Ligue Internationale Contre le Racisme et l'Antisémitisme (LICRA), B'nai Brith, Le Mouvement Contre le Racisme et Pour l'Amitié Entre les Peuples.

These organizations have had the effect of damping the appeal of the FN. At one time polls showed that up to 40 percent of the electorate would be prepared, either at the time of the poll or at some future election, to vote for the FN. That figure was down to 15 percent in a 1995 poll. More than two-thirds of the voters see the Front National as a danger for democracy. More than three-quarters see it as incapable of governing France and would not vote for it under any circumstances. In other words, the FN seems to have little hope of growing beyond its present levels unless the context shifts dramatically.

Repression produces a similar dilemma. Ignoring the extreme right allows it to flourish. Waiting for acts of violence may be waiting too long. The damage from violence may be beyond repair. But using the law to repress the extreme right, although effective against the most extreme elements, renders respectable that which is not repressed. And inevitably, no matter how strict the law is, there will be elements beyond repression. For instance, Holocaust denial may be a crime, and is in France, but Le Pen, the leader of the Front National, has attempted to skirt the law. He has not denied the Holocaust but has called it a detail of history. These words, as it turned out, are against the law in France, so Le Pen employs other subterfuges, speaking to his audiences with words such as "I prefer my sisters to my cousins and my cousins to my neighbors." Coded messages replace explicit ones.

Removing explicit racist hate messages from public discourse is a victory over racism. However, it is a victory with a cost. The extreme right, left to its own recourse, could degenerate into disreputable discourse that would marginalize it. Simply in order to avoid prosecution, it develops a discourse that is more respectable and that generates a broader support.

There is a third solution to this dilemma. The choice does not have to be between prosecution and inactivity. There can be, as well, an effort to expose the far right by decoding its coded messages.

For the media there is a comparable dilemma. One choice is to ignore the far right. However, that allows the far right to develop unnoticed. Speeches and literature can be outrageous in the extreme without the general public being aware and being outraged. The other choice is a full glare of publicity. That choice involves the risk of drawing attention to the extreme right, winning converts who otherwise never would have been aware of its existence. Political polling shows a strong connection between recognition and support. Simply by moving the extreme-right leadership from the unknown to the known, the media can make the extreme right into a political force it would not otherwise be.

The French media have oscillated between these two extremes. At one point when it was growing, the Front National and its leader, Le Pen, were given massive publicity. Now that it has reached a level of stagnation in its growth, the media are ignoring it. There is little, either electronically or in print in 1995, about the Front National. The most recent media neglect allows the Front National to radicalize its discourse among its followers without the public being aware of it.

Again, there is a third alternative. The media can report on and keep track of the extreme right without giving it headlines and without making its leaders into media stars. *Le Monde* is credited in France, alone among the media, with that sort of responsible reporting on the extreme right.

In the universities in France, there is a twofold response. Threats and beatings are dealt with by appealing to the police and to the administration. The police will provide protection for meetings when asked. However, they do not lay charges against the culprits. The administration of Assas, the Faculty of Law at the University of Paris, is a particular problem. The administration does nothing to prevent or discourage extreme-right activity among the faculty, where it flourishes.

The various student organizations opposed to the extreme right respond by encouraging participation in the electoral process. The rate of student participation in elections is very low, 3.41 percent in the 1991 student union elections. This low rate of participation provides an opportunity for the extreme right in that a relatively few votes can go a long way. It also provides an opportunity for the opponents of the extreme right in that an increase in participation can overwhelm the extreme-right vote. Renouveau Étudiant, a rightist group, went from four seats to none in the 1994 elections because voter participation increased 35 percent.

A successful political party attracts careerists. Failure repels all but the most dedicated. In politics, success leads to further success and failure leads to further failure. In France, changes in the electoral system have magnified the successes and failings of the Front National. At one time the changes helped to form a crowd behind the Front National bandwagon. At other times they helped to disperse the Front National parade.

In 1986, France switched to a system of proportional representation for the National Assembly, and the Front National elected thirty-five deputies. In 1988, the country switched back to double-round, majority-rule, single-member constituency elections, and the Front National elected only one deputy.

The double-round elections provided another type of opportunity to the FN, an opportunity to make alliances. Because its votes, though not enough to win, might be enough to give another party a majority, the FN had something to offer. Initially the moderate right engaged in these alliances with the FN in order to win in the second round; but with the electoral collapse of the left since 1992, the moderate right has found these alliances no longer necessary. The ending of both proportional representation and electoral alliances with the moderate right have led to a drifting away from the FN of those with ambitions for a political career.

In order to close off opportunities to the extreme right, a political system must represent not just one political color but the major political questions of the day. The FN in 1983 filled a gap in the political spectrum by responding to the problem of unemployment. The gap was created by the distrust of the political elites, the decline of the mainstream parties, and their own unresponsiveness to the less-privileged component of the electorate. Politics abhors a vacuum. The French political system created a momentary vacuum in 1983 and the extreme right rushed in.

Pushing the Front National out of the political spectrum now is not just a matter of attacking it or defending against FN attacks. Because the Front National is a political phenomenon and not just a fringe group of extremists, it requires a political response. The gap that the FN filled must be filled by others. The issues to which the FN responded must be dealt with by others. To a certain extent, all the traditional political parties are trying to do this, but removing the FN has been a formidable task. It is easier to deny an opening to a fringe party than to replace a well-established one.

Legally, France has a whole range of creative remedies available against the racism and violence of the extreme right. Aside from laws prohibiting racism and discrimination in employment, housing, and provision of services, there are laws against the public incitement of hatred.[34] Statutes prohibit racial defamation and racist slurs. Nongovernmental, antiracist associations are permitted to join as civil parties in prosecutions against those who commit racially motivated crimes.[35] These antiracist groups may also join as civil parties in prosecution for incitement to racial hatred, group defamation, or racial slurs. When these nongovernmental groups join in a prosecution and the defendant is convicted, the court decides on civil liability at the same time. The government also has the power to dissolve any organization that incites racial hatred.[36] Denial of the existence of a crime against humanity is an offense.[37]

Despite these apparent remedies, there are problems with the present law and a need for improvement. For example, although often the same people are convicted over and over again for the same crimes, the court is not entitled to look at past convictions in deciding on sentence. In addition, although the law allows for banning of groups as well as conviction for individual acts, there is no connection between the two. Banning is not a sentence that follows from conviction for individual acts or a sequence of such acts. The result is that some individuals operating through extreme-right groups are convicted repeatedly without the group itself ever being banned.

Despite the panoply of laws directed against racist expression and their active enforcement, there is no significant free speech debate in France of the sort revolving around the First Amendment in the United States. The antiracist laws are generally accepted as part and parcel of a normal democratic society. In antiracist circles there is some regret that the Front National was not banned in its early days when it was a small group. Now it is generally conceded that banning the FN is not practical—not necessarily wrong in principle but rather something that cannot be achieved because the FN is too big and too strong.

In each region of France the police have organized advisory public committees to assist in the fight against racism. Representatives of antiracist organizations participate in these committees. The committees examine racist incidents and literature and advise on what steps the police should take, whether to prosecute an individual, seek a ban of a publication, or close a bookstore.

The Impact of Extreme-Right Activities

In the United Kingdom, the small absolute number of extreme-right activities has meant that its impact has been largely limited to specialist governmental and nongovernmental organizations dealing with the extreme right and racism. In France, the larger absolute size of the extreme right has meant that its activities have impacted politics and society generally.

Britain

The success of the British National Party in Tower Hamlets has had an escalating effect on the vote prospects of the far right throughout Britain. In subsequent local elections, extreme-right-wing candidates won votes in double-digit percentages without doing much more than presenting candidates.[38] It is noteworthy that in the Isle of Dogs election of May 1994, Derek Beackon did lose his seat but in losing won 30 percent of the vote with a voter turnout of 66 percent.[39] In the previous election, which he won with 34 percent of the vote, the voter turnout was just 44 percent.

A distinction has to be made between the effect of the rise of racially motivated incidents and the effect of the rise of the extreme right. The former has meant an increase in efforts to combat racism in a myriad of ways. Every agency of government or virtually every agency both local and national has some aspect of its work directed toward the combat against racism. It would take far too long and take this chapter afield to present these efforts in detail.

The rise of the extreme right in British society and policy has had a more modest effect commensurate with the modest absolute size of the extreme right. There is a noticeable impact in those areas where the extreme right is strong, both in the atmosphere of fear and intimidation amongst minorities and in the policies of local councils and mainstream party constituency organizations either catering to or trying to combat right-wing growth. The nongovernmental sector has also been affected, mobilizing to some degree but not, to date, becoming unified. The rivalry between the Anti-Nazi League and the Anti-Racist Alliance continues. And the rise of the extreme right has not only mobilized efforts to combat it but has mobilized both the government and nongovernmental agencies to combat the racism on which the extreme right feeds. Both, however, have been a good deal more active than they once were. The rise of racism and right-wing extremism in Russia and Germany has generated a sense in Britain that it may spread to that country. Britain can do little about the growth of right-wing extremism outside the country. But it can prepare its defenses, and there is a sense of urgency about doing so as quickly and deeply as possible.

France

The rise of the extreme right has led to a rightward shift in French politics across the political spectrum. On issues of immigration,[40] law and order, and immigration citizenship, all the parties have become more right wing than they otherwise would have been. For instance, it was the leftist government of Michel Rocard that took away work permits from refugee claimants. The right, when it entered into power in 1995, embraced this legacy of the left.

Antiracist organizations in France regret the attempt by all the mainstream political parties to cater to racist components of the electorate by adopting policies that might please Le Pen and his followers. Antiracists view these rightist policies as validating the extreme right and giving it credibility rather than undercutting its support. Le Pen himself has said that voters will always prefer the original to a copy. On this point the political analysis of the Front National and antiracists is the same, the more the traditional parties have taken elements from the platform of the Front National, the better it is for the Le Pen forces.

Another effect of the rise of the extreme right is the widespread nature of a polite form of racism in French society. Crude forms of racism are not allowed, but the form of racist expression the Front National uses has ceased to shock and has become accepted as a daily part of French social and political discourse.

The FN equates immigration with unemployment, quite boldly and explicitly. For example, 3 million immigrants lead to 3 million unemployed. It calls for the removal of immigrants from France as a solution to unemployment. There are approximately 3 million people in France who now vote for the Front National. One could as easily infer a direct connection between that group and the 3 million unemployed. If the expulsion of 3 million people from France would solve French unemployment problems, expulsion of Front National supporters would have the added advantage of solving the problem of racism.

Unfortunately, the FN's faulty logic has been accepted through sheer repetition. As mentioned, such thinking is now a legitimate part of political debate and is a striking feature of the French scene.

Laurent Fabius, one recent leftist prime minister, has said that the FN is giving the wrong answers but posing the right questions. Edith Cresson, another leftist French prime minister, has talked about hiring charters to send asylum seekers from France to their home countries. The Front National has changed the terms of political debate in France and causes people to think in terms of racist categories and engage in racist discourse simply to address the issues that the Front National has raised.

The rise of the Front National has had an impact on the whole extreme right. Although many individual groups continue to exist, their members are, with few exceptions, also members or supporters of the Front National. The FN is an umbrella group for the entire racist and neo-Nazi movement in France. It is also the main point of contact with the international extreme right-wing movement.

There is a tendency to dismiss the political impact of the FN because its prospects for achieving national power in the near future appear remote. This dismissal by antiracists is part wishful thinking and part strategy in order to contain any bandwagon effect operating in favor of the FN. Even though it appears to have hit a ceiling in the polls, the FN is not declining in the popular vote. All that has happened is that its rate of increase of support has diminished. At least in terms of electoral results, if not in terms of polling, the FN is still increasing in strength. For instance, in the election for the mayor of Nice held March 6, 1994, the Front National candidate Jacques Peyrat received 37.64 percent of the vote in the first round, coming within 34 votes of winning. That compares with 31.16 percent in the first round in 1993 and 20.39 percent in the first round in 1988. In the second round, March 13, 1994, the FN received 43.52 percent of the vote, a drop from the 48.42 percent in 1993. However, the drop in the FN vote appears to be more the result of increased participation of the electorate rather than an abandonment by FN voters. The participation rate in the first round in 1994 was 44.72 percent; in the second round it was 51.91 percent. It must also be kept in mind that in the second round the National Front received 43.52 percent of the vote in the face of the united opposition of all the traditional major parties. Both the left and the traditional right supported the FN opponent, Jean-Paul Barety.

Local support for the FN can have an impact even without power at the center. One of the recent changes in immigration laws, the so-called Pasqua Law, named after the minister of the interior who proposed it, allows mayors to decide whether a French citizen may marry a foreigner. The mayor can decide whether the proposed marriage is a marriage of convenience for immigration purposes and prevent it from happening. This power in the hands of an FN mayor could be easily abused.

Traditionally, France has welcomed many more refugees both in absolute numbers and proportional to its population from noncolonial foreign-language countries than Britain has. This difference in welcome may be due to the fact that France, as part of the Continent, is easier to access than the island of Britain. This tradition, *"la France: terre d'accueil, terre d'asile"* (France: country of welcome, country of refuge), has come under siege by the extreme right. More generally, the impact on foreigners in France, particularly immigrants from Northern African countries, is direct and immediate. France prides itself on being a country of welcome, a country of asylum; yet for the Front National and its supporters, immigrants, particularly Arab Muslim immigrants, are decidedly unwelcome. The rise of the FN creates an atmosphere of hostility to the stranger that is direct, immediate, and independent of any future success or failure of the FN at the polls.

Notes

1. Hannah Arendt, *The Origins of Totalitarianism* (New York: Harcourt Brace Javanovich, 1951), ch. 4.

2. Ibid., 46.

3. R. J. Soucy, "The Nature of Fascism in France," in W. Laqueur and G. L. Mosse, eds., *International Fascism 1920–1945* (New York: HarperCollins, 1966), 30.

4. Marcel Ruby, *Le Livre de la Deportation* (Paris: Robert Laffont, 1995), 39–40.

5. Michael R. Marrus and Robert O. Paxton, *Vichy France and the Jews* (Paris: Calmann-Levy, 1981).

6. Lucy S. Dawidowicz, *The War Against the Jews 1933–1945* (New York: Bantam, 1976), 488–491.

7. Serge Klarsfeld, *Le Mémorial de la Déportation des Juifs de France* (Paris: Klarsfeld, 1978).

8. Michael R. Marrus, *The Holocaust in History* (New York: Meridian, 1987), 71.

9. St. Hoffman, *Le Mouvement Poujade* (Paris: Coln, 1956), 388.

10. Nonna Mayer, "Le Phénomène Le Pen," *L'Histoire*, no. 162, January 1993: 114.

11. Klaus von Beyme, "Right Wing Extremism in Post-War Europe," *West European Politics* 11(2), April 1988: 1, at 10.

12. C. Holmes, *Anti-Semitism in British Society, 1976–1979* (1979), 89–97.

13. U.K. Royal Commission on Alien Immigration, vol. 2, paragraphs 8612–8614, 289.

14. Christopher T. Husbands, "East End Racism 1900–1980," *London Journal* 8(1), 1982: 1–9.

15. Ibid., 13.

16. Mary Beal, London Weekend Television, "The Rise and Fall of the National Front," February 29, 1980.

17. Ray Hill with Andrew Bell, *The Other Face of Terror* (London: Grafton, 1988).

18. *Searchlight*, January 1993.

19. Institute of Jewish Affairs, *Anti-Semitism World Report 1993* (London: Institute of Jewish Affairs, 1993), 61.

20. Community Service Organization of the Board of Deputies of British Jews, anti-Semitic incidents breakdown by category, 1990–1993, unpublished typescript.

21. Anti-Racist Alliance, "Racial Harassment: Country Action, Legal Remedies" (London: The Alliance, June 1983), and Natalie Angemurraya and Catarina Mirles, "Racially-Motivated Crime: British Crime Survey Analysis," *Research and Planning Unit Paper 82* (London: Home Office, Government of the UK, 1993), 43.

22. Marion Fitzgerald, *Racialist Harassment: Forms of Measurement and Comparison* (London: Home Office Research New Policy Unit, November 1993).

23. "Racism and Fascism in the European Community," *Searchlight* Information Services, January 1994.

24. Community Service Organisation of the Board of Deputies of British Jews, *Derek Beackon and the British National Party* (London: The Organisation, undated).

25. Commission for Racial Equality, *Homelessness and Discrimination*, Appendix D, Paragraph 2c (London, July 1988), 58.

26. See Guy Birnbaum, *Le Front National en Politique* (Paris: Balland, 1992); Nonna Mayer, "*Le Front National,*" in Dominique Chagnollaud, ed., *La Vie Politique en France* (Paris: Seuil, 1993), 329; Christopher T. Husbands, "The Support for the Front National: Analyses and Findings," *Ethnic and Racial Studies* 14(3), 1991: 382.

27. Jean-Yves Camus and René Monzat, *Les Droites Nationales et Radicales en France* (Lyons: Presses Universitaires de Lyons, 1992), 280.

28. Mayer, "*Le Front National,*" 329.

29. See Board of Deputies of British Jews, *Group Defamation Report of a Working Party of the Law Parliamentary and General Purposes Committee* (chair, Eldred Tabachnik), February 1992.

30. Commission for Racial Equality, *Second Review of the Race Relations Act 1976, Recommendation 29* (London: CRE, 1992), 73–74.

31. Public Order Act of 1986, Part 3.

32. Ibid., Section 5.

33. Criminal Justic Act of 1994, amending Section 19 of the Public Order Act (1986).

34. U.K. Law of July 29, 1881, amended by the law of 1972.

35. U.K. Article 2.1 of the Code of Criminal Procedure, amended by statutes of January 3, 1985, and July 3, 1987.

36. Statute of October 1, 1936, Article 1, amended by statute 1972.

37. Article 24 of statute of July 29, 1981, amended by statute of July 13, 1990.

38. "Beyond Beackon," *Searchlight*, June 1994: 3.

39. Mary Braid, "BNP Failure Masks Growth in Support," *Independent*, May 7, 1994.

40. See Christopher T. Husbands, "The Politics of Immigration in France," *Ethnic and Racial Studies* 14(2), 1991: 171.

6

Contemporary Right-Wing Extremism in Germany

Ian J. Kagedan

An examination of the dynamics of contemporary right-wing extremism in Germany is of particular importance within a broader consideration of the problem in Western democracies and nascent democracies in Central and Eastern Europe.

The Nazi period demonstrated dramatically some of the vulnerabilities of the democratic system, and the democracy that has been forged in Germany since the defeat of the Nazis has demonstrated concern and sensitivity to extremist right-wing stirrings varying in intensity according to the type of extremist expression, era, and region. Germany's pre-Nazi history combined with the German postwar experience on the front lines of the East-West divide contribute to a heightened sensitivity to authoritarianism and extremism in general. All this considered, it would have been reasonable to have expected swift and decisive governmental action in the face of the most egregious expressions of right-wing extremism in Europe since the end of World War II.

In fact, the initial response of the German government to the early extremist incidents, on which I comment further on, was neither swift nor decisive. It is too easy, and wrong, to suggest that this reflected lingering Nazi attitudes in broad segments of the population. It is likewise too easy to attribute the delayed response to a system overloaded with the simultaneous pressures of half a million asylum seekers and reunification, although these factors play a role. It is precisely when overloaded that a system's weak

The views expressed in this chapter are entirely those of the author and do not reflect the views or opinion of the Immigration and Refugee Board of Canada.

points are most apparent. Some of the weaknesses identified are specific to German democracy, but many, if not most, are common to all postwar liberal Western democracies. To the extent that through study and analysis we may identify fundamental weaknesses, we would be in a better position to chart our national and international responses to the challenge of right-wing extremism. We would be better equipped, as well, to assist in the evolution of durable democracies in Central and Eastern European states of the former Soviet bloc.

Historical Background: 1945 to 1989

It is broadly recognized that the reunification of Germany in 1990 brought it a more formidable challenge than most had predicted. Among the most distressing features of the reunified state has been a surge in nationalistic feeling and xenophobia, which have found expression in violence directed at "foreigners" by right-wing extremist groups, and an expansion of the influence of a variety of such extremist political groupings, including some that operate within the normative political process.

In the West after 1945 the agenda of the Cold War rapidly overtook the denazification process that had been put in place by Germany's U.S., British, and French occupiers. Still, a combination of constitutional provisions, the evolution of broadly inclusive political parties, and rapid economic development relegated extremist right-wing groups to the periphery of national politics. The influence of the occupying powers is manifest in those developments.

The 1949 Basic Law, which serves as the united country's constitution, includes provisions essential to the maintenance of democracy. Beyond articulating inalienable rights and fundamental democratic freedoms such as the freedom of expression and freedom from persecution on the basis of race or religion, the Basic Law also includes provisions for the banning of antidemocratic political parties by the Constitutional Court (Article 21) and the banning of extremist organizations by the minister of the interior (Article 9). The Ministry of the Interior houses the Office for the Protection of the Constitution (Bundesamt für Verfassungsschutz; BfV), created in 1950, which is mandated to collect and refer information on potentially unconstitutional political activity. As well, various provisions exist within German criminal law that permit action against extremist groups based on their activities (e.g., the promotion of Nazism and Holocaust denial).

This legislative complex serves as the basis for addressing the right-wing extremist challenge and, on the level of electoral politics, is buttressed by a provision in the Electoral Law that creates a threshold of 5 percent of votes cast for any party to qualify for seats in the Bundestag (parliament), whose members are elected on the basis of proportional representation. This provision limited the potential chaos created by numerous small parties, as had been experienced in the Weimar Republic and at the same time in effect promoted the development of large political coalitions capable of sufficient breadth to include most voters. By the 1960s three major parties had emerged that satisfied this agenda: The Social Democratic Party (SDP; in German, SPD) incorporated a range of interests on the democratic left, the Free Democrats provided a liberal centrist option, and the Christian Democratic Party (CDP/CPD) provided a home to conservative and even nationalist interests.

The advance and entrenchment of democratic institutions has also been propelled by Germany's dramatic economic development since the end of World War II. Various economic aid efforts, including the Marshall Plan, contributed to the development of a dynamic social market economy that until recently had not faced the test of economic decline or threat of decline. The deutsche mark (DM) exists as a major world currency and is a symbol of national pride. Until recently, unemployment in Germany was low by Western standards. All this contributed to the development, in what was West Germany, of a liberal democratic culture capable of being a productive member in the European community and NATO, of forging relationships with the then communist states on its Eastern borders, and of resisting premature efforts at reunification with its Eastern *Länder* (provinces), which had come under communist rule and Soviet domination.

Right-wing extremist forces found little room for operation and no significant potential for the recruitment of new members in this milieu. National socialism had been discredited as a political option, and Germans enjoyed the prosperity and security the Bonn Republic had brought. Still, from 1949 onward, Germany saw a succession of right-wing extremist groups in operation. These lie in the background of current extremist right-wing activism and establish links with Germany's Nazi past.

It is estimated that in the 1949 elections, right-wing extremist groups attracted at least 1 million votes, or 5 percent of the votes cast.[1] Voter support declined on the federal and *Länder* levels until the late 1960s, then declined again until the period of reunification. From the late 1940s through the 1960s some seven of twenty-six extremist right-wing parties were able to elect members to the federal or state legislatures.[2] They ranged in membership from 4,500 to 33,000. Of these, the Sozialistische Reichspartei (SRP), founded in 1949, was banned in 1952. In general, these parties found their greatest support in the largely Protestant regions of Northern Germany and in the Protestant region of predominantly Catholic southern Germany.[3] Their support varied as economic and social conditions improved. The extremist right has been plagued by continual internal strife, and this complicated any effort to mount a unified front capable of competing with the mainstream democratic parties. Banished to the periphery of German poli-

Ian J. Kagedan

tics, right-wing extremist parties saw no real opportunity for electoral valida-
tion until the economic downturn in 1966–1967, when the leadership abilities of the ruling CDU/CSU-SDP coalition was called into question. In the
1969 federal elections the Nationaldemokratische Partei Deutschlands
(NPD; National Democratic Party), founded in 1964, gained 4.3 percent of
the popular vote, just missing the 5 percent threshold for representation in
the Bundestag. It had already won seven seats in *Länder* legislatures. These
political gains faded by 1972, although public sympathy for extremist right-
wing positions, or, at least, antidemocratic sentiments, remained significant:
Stoss reports a 1971 poll that found 50 percent of the surveyed population
agreeing that "National Socialism was, in principle, a good idea poorly put
into practice."[4] A 1977 poll reveals a 26 percent positive reply. A SINUS Institute survey in 1979–1980 found that 13 percent of German voters held an
extremist right-wing worldview. A 1982 poll suggested between 20 percent
and 30 percent of the population held anti-Semitic views; another in the
same year found 49 percent "clearly in its attitude hostile towards foreigners." The figure diminishes for younger, more educated people.

The 1980s saw further realignments on the extreme right wing in the political realm even as militant neo-Nazi youth movements (primarily skinheads) began to form. One noteworthy feature of the 1980s was the evolution of a right-wing extremism less married to the old Nazi model, focusing
more on nationalism, xenophobia (directed at "foreigners" [Turks, Vietnamese, Poles, and other imported workers] but also Americans and against
moves toward European unity generally), and traditional moral values.[5] One
alliance was formed in 1989 between the NPD and the DVU (Deutsche
Volksunion), founded by newspaper magnate Gerhard Frey in 1971. The
BfV estimated DVU membership in 1988 to be in the 12,000 range, making
it the largest extreme-right organization in West Germany; the NPD had an
estimated membership of 6,400. The DVU itself in 1989 claimed 28,000
members.[6] The Republikaner Party, founded in 1983 and led by Franz
Schönhuber, is of particular importance in this period and into the 1990s.
Careful to articulate a party program that would simultaneously preclude
proscription, satisfy the more extreme rightists, and still attract more moderate right-wing sympathizers, it has focused its attention on nationalism, including the imperative of German reunification, and on decreasing the flow
of immigrants and asylum seekers, two themes that gained it unexpected
support in local and European elections in 1989. These electoral successes
afforded the Republikaner Party state funding that has permitted it to further its campaign for electoral support.

Although a variety of extremist right-wing parties have been active since
the defeat of Nazi Germany in 1945, the most publicized activities of the extreme right are those for which groups outside the realm of normative politics are responsible. Michael Kühnen, who died of AIDS in 1990, figured

prominently in this context. Kühnen led various groups in West Germany (primarily the Gesinnungsgemeinschaft der Neuen Front) and in East Germany (mainly the Deutsche Alternative) that, alongside other groups, were estimated to include some 1,500 members in 1990.[7] Four such groups were banned in the 1980s only to regroup under new organizational banners.

Racist skinheads also figure prominently in some of the more violent expressions of right-wing extremism. The BfV estimated 5,000–6,000 violent skinheads evenly distributed between East and West Germany in 1990. The skinhead phenomenon, with its origins in the alienated youth in working-class areas of British cities in the 1970s, came as a sort of gift to the traditional extreme right, providing a vanguard of "shock troops" committed to violence and attracted by the ideology of the extremist right wing. It is principally to this grouping that the highly publicized incidents of racist violence of the early 1990s can be attributed.

Among the first of the most violent incidents perpetrated by right-wing extremists since 1990 were those that took place in the states of the former East Germany. Notwithstanding official claims that fascism had been eliminated in the GDR and replaced with socialism, racist skinhead gangs had been in operation for almost a decade by the time of the events in Hoyerswerda and Rostock. The events in Rostok follow the pattern of events in Hoyerswerda of one year earlier. At Rostock, in August 1992, during skinhead and right-wing extremist riots, police withdrew from the scene and the rioters burned down a refugee hostel. Residents had been evacuated, but Vietnamese refugees in a neighboring hotel were endangered by the fire. And Stasi files disclose the existence of a range of right-wing extremist groups and organizations and a host of antiforeigner and anti-Semitic incidents dating well back to the establishment of the state. These included attacks on guest workers from Vietnam or Mozambique and other socialist states, socialist Chileans who fled the 1976 military coup, and even Jewish targets, in this case Jewish cemeteries in Dresden, Zittau, and Potsdam that were desecrated during the 1970s. Communist doctrines of the equality of workers aside, many instances of antiforeigner sentiment are reported even where the hostility was expressed in more benign ways. Germans and foreigners would generally not mix, and even young people were discouraged from fraternizing in discos or other social settings.[8]

Against this background of latent antiforeigner hostility within the context of a highly repressive communist state, various alternative subcultures evolved among the youth coming of age in the late 1970s and early 1980s. The legitimacy of the GDR rested on its existence as a socialist state, thus distinguishable from the other Germany, which it cast as home to the fascist legacy, but this was an inadequate source of identity for this new postwar generation. Antiestablishment "punk" or "hippie" movements initially evolved with a decidedly apolitical inclination, eschewing confining structures and celebrating spontaneity. The skinhead movement provided an alternative that was especially attractive to those who, as products of a totalitarian socialist upbringing, had a decidedly authoritarian inclination. As well, it provided an opportunity for power, something "hippiedom" had rejected in favor of pacifism.

Skinheads in the GDR looked to nationalism as a response to communism and were among the most vocal proponents of reunification in the GDR. To the extent that one may speak of a skinhead ideology, their objective was not a westernized Germany along the lines of the FRG but a Germany where nationalism was combined with an intense commitment to community for the sake of a greater Germany for all. Skinhead gangs of ten to fifteen members became more apparent in Berlin, Leipzig, Dresden, and other centers and became increasingly involved in criminal attacks against minority group members, hippies, and other punks.

Although government sources were aware of these developments and had been secretly producing studies of the phenomenon for some time, the state tended to take a hands-off approach. Public sentiment tended to be far more positive toward clean-cut, disciplined right-wing extremist skinheads than toward hippies, and the skinheads' families, usually well established within the state apparatus, acted to protect them from harsh treatment when, for example, some were brought before the courts.[9] This changed on October 17, 1987, when a large force of right-wing extremist skinheads attacked a pacifist rock concert promoted by a coalition of dissidents, environmentalists, pacifists, and church groups in (East) Berlin's Zionskirche. The resulting violence could not be covered up, and within a few days police had arrested a large number of perpetrators. Trials for "rowdiness" initially resulted in mild sentences of between one and two years. These were later increased to almost double the initial penalty. It is noteworthy that even in the course of these trials the state made every effort to deny any particular political character to the skinheads' actions, for this would have entailed an acknowledgment that the regime's antifascist, socialist ideology had not penetrated this generation.

From the Zionskirche event through to the reunification, the East German skinhead movement saw an evolution in its thinking and an acceleration in attacks against property, including Jewish cemeteries and memorials to the victims of Nazism, and against members of foreigner communities, gays, and other groups. Anti-Semitic sentiment in the East was reinforced by the hostility toward Zionism, which was part of the culture of virtually all Eastern-bloc states, certainly after 1967.

Preeminent among the skinheads' concerns was the establishment of a unified German state in which order and security was ensured and strong leadership was available. As the collapse of the GDR accelerated, the extremist right-wing movement itself tended to split more clearly into various component groupings. Some, including the traditional Nazi skinheads, remained especially inclined toward street violence and vandalism and continued to express their affinity for Hitler and the Third Reich. Others, generally older and better educated, took a decidedly more strategic view. Recognizing the imminent collapse of the GDR, they looked to position themselves to assert power in a new political entity—if necessary, through the violent overthrow of the state. They functioned in a highly secretive manner, evading police attention by avoiding involvement in street violence; they relied on the skinheads for that.

Right-Wing Extremism in the Streets Since Reunification

The reunification of Germany on October 3, 1990, saw the beginning of a surge in extremist right-wing violence unparalleled in the recent history of the FRG or GDR. Reunification also saw a variety of political parties on the more extreme right of the spectrum gain sufficient electoral support to elect members to various levels of government. These parties also merited the attention of the traditional mainstream parties, whose past voters contributed, in varying proportions, to the extremists' success. Although in significant measure reunification stood to affirm the direction of contemporary German democracy, the many adjustments it occasioned on very practical and on psychological levels created conditions ripe for exploitation by old-time and contemporary, youthful right-wing extremists.

In 1990 the BfV estimated there were 1,500 neo-Nazis in western *Länder*, organized into twenty or more groupings, and a similar number in eastern *Länder*. Beyond these more organized neo-Nazi activists are an estimated 5,000–6,000 violence-inclined skinheads, also roughly equally divided between West and East, and perhaps 30,000 or more tacit supporters. This collection of extremists is generally seen to have been behind the demonstrations led by Michael Kühnen in October 1990 and the Dresden rally following the shooting death of neo-Nazi leader Rainer Sonntag in June 1991. As well, they were perhaps behind the most dramatic incident of the period, the September attack on an asylum seekers' hostel in the Eastern industrial town of Hoyerswerda.

Postwar Hoyerswerda's earliest foreigners were Mozambicans, Angolans, and Vietnamese, arrivals from sister socialist states who came in the early 1980s to supplement available labor for low-end jobs. Various sources suggest they were never accepted within the dominant social milieu, and as reunification came with all its attendant frustrations, they became the targets of the locals' discontent. When 200 additional asylum seekers were admitted by the new regime, hostility increased. It was mid-September 1991. After a few days of racist skinhead vandalism directed at Vietnamese shops, a large group of skinheads attacked a foreigners' residence. The racist rhetoric accompanying the violence left no doubt as to its objective. With ordinary citizens attending as approving spectators, the group attacked the building with bricks and other projectiles, terrorizing the residents. Police had to remove the foreigners under cover of darkness. No arrests were made. In the days following, additional skinhead groups and more organized political groupings including the Gubner Front from Guben and Deutsche Alternative from Dresden and Leipzig arrived and attacked other residences. Over 100 extremists were involved in the attacks, which included parading with Nazi flags and straight-arm Sieg Heil salutes. Official expressions of regret were slow in coming, as was determined police action. It was almost a week after the first serious incidents that GDR army units arrived to restore order. As Elliot Neaman and Hajo Funke point out, the event was a major victory for the extreme right: "They found that a cohesive group identity could be constructed around hate directed toward 'others' . . . realized how effective targeted violence could be in evoking support among ordinary citizens [and] discovered that police hesitated to enforce the law and, in some cases, even sympathized with their assault on foreigners."[10]

The experience of Hoyerswerda was repeated in other cities in the eastern *Länder* during the rest of 1991, including Zittau, Halle, and Cottbus, but right-wing extremist violence was not restricted to the former GDR. Over 1,000 acts of violence against foreigners were reported countrywide that year, among these 383 arson attacks and three deaths. Although most acts of violence are directed against visible "foreigners," that is, what are called "visible minorities," the traditional set of Nazi targets was not neglected. Homosexuals, Romanies, and Jewish persons and their property were targets as well, and the number of incidents was far larger than the combined figures for East and West Germany in the last year before reunification.

For 1991, the BfV reported some 39,800 people involved in right-wing extremist movements in Germany (up from 33,600 in 1990). They acted as individuals or as members of loosely knit groupings or as members of seventy-six (in 1990, sixty-nine) more organized groups. Of this number, 4,200 are classified as militant right-wing extremists or skinheads; 2,100 as members of thirty neo-Nazi groups; 24,000 as members of three National Freedom organizations; 6,700 as members of five National Democratic organizations; and 3,950 distributed among thirty-eight other extreme-right groups. (The figures provided total 40,950. The figure of 39,800 takes into account overlapping memberships in extremist right-wing groups).

Underscoring the inadequacy of the government's initial assessment and response is the fact that figures for racist antiforeigner and antiminority violence continued to climb in 1992. The German Government Press and Information Department in a February 1993 document reported seventeen deaths in 1992, including the deaths of seven foreigners, associated with extremist right-wing violence. The number of explosions and fire bombings rose to 701; assaults to 598 (in 1991, 449); and incidents of vandalism to 969 (in 1991, 648)—for a total of 2,268 violent incidents. More refined BfV data published in March 1994 provide somewhat higher figures in these categories for the same year—a total of 2,639 violent incidents. A further 5,045 offenses of a less directly violent nature, for example, propaganda distribution, were reported.

Participation rates in extremist right-wing groupings rose as well in 1992. The BfV reported about 41,900 people involved who acted as individuals or as members of loosely knit groupings or as members of eighty-two more organized groups. The overall figure included 6,400 individuals classed as militant right-wing extremists or racist skinheads, an increase of 2,200 over the year prior; 1,400 members of thirty-three neo-Nazi groups; 26,000 individuals involved in three National Freedom organizations; 5,300 involved in five National Democratic organizations; and 4,000 involved in forty-one other extremist right-wing groups. (Once again, the figures here total 43,100. The total provided earlier takes into account multiple memberships in extremist right-wing groups.) Finally, the BfV reports seventy-five extremist right-wing publications circulating in 1992 as against seventy-one in 1991. Of these, fifty-four were appearing at least quarterly with a combined estimated circulation of 7,848,500, up from 7,171,000 for fifty-seven publications in 1991.

In 1992, the most violent antiforeigner activity continued to take place in eastern *Länder*, although states of the former FRG were not immune. The August antiforeigner violence in Rostock, an almost week-long assault on Romani and Vietnamese foreigners and a running battle between over 500 extremist right-wing youth and over 1,500 riot police, exemplifies the problem. Rostock's mayor, affiliated with the nation's governing party, attributed the tension to an "uncontrolled influx of foreigners," in effect blaming the victims. The federal minister of the interior said virtually the same thing.

The most activist of the neo-Nazi youth groups identified by the BfV are based in the East. Deutsche Alternative (DA), led by Frank Hubner and with an estimated membership in 1992 of over 800, is based in Cottbus. Its newspaper, the *Brandenburger Observer*, has helped broaden its influence. The DA was banned on December 10, 1992. The Nationale Offensive (NO) with an estimated 1,000 members is based in Augsburg and was banned on December 22, 1992. The Nationalistische Front (NF), banned on November 27, 1992, with a smaller membership of some 150 has cells in various Eastern cities, as does the Freiheitliche Arbeiterpartei (FAP), which is credited with considerable influence over the racist skinhead movement. The National Democratic Party is also influential, particularly through its youth wing, Junge Nationaldemokratie, as is Deutsche Freiheitsbewegung, a producer of Nazi material. Other important sources of Nazi propaganda seized

in police raids on extremist operations are the U.S.-based National Sozialistische Deutsche Arbeiter Partei-Auslands Organisation (NSDAP-AO),
headed by Gary Lauck out of Lincoln, Nebraska; Liberty Bell Publications, a
U.S. operation led by West Virginian George Deitz; and Toronto resident
Ernst Zundel, whose publication of the Holocaust-denying *Leuchter Report,*
distributed by his Munich-based associate Bela Ewald Althans, is reported to
be the most widely read Holocaust denial tract in Germany. Finally, various
extremist right-wing rock bands play a significant role in whipping up antiminority sympathy and in solidifying the identity of the neo-Nazi youth
subculture. These include Störkraft, Frankfurt-based Bohse Onkelz, Volk-
szorn, and others.

According to the BfV, militant right-wing extremists, including racist skinheads, numbered about 5,600 in 1993; these extremists acted independently
or in small, informal groupings or were linked in four larger groupings. This
figure represents a drop of about 800 from 1992 estimates. At the same
time, about 1,500 extremists participate in twenty-seven neo-Nazi groups,
up 100 over 1992; 26,000 in three National Freedom groupings (no change
from 1992); 5,200 in five National Democratic groupings, down 100 from
1992; and 4,100 in thirty-eight other extremist right-wing groupings, up
100 in membership but down from the forty-one groupings reported for
1992. The total figures of 41,500 and seventy-seven groups, with membership numbers adjusted from 42,400 to account for overlapping memberships, are down marginally from 1992 but remain above the 1991 levels. As
we will see later, various governmental and local community initiatives contribute to this marginal yet positive change.

Similar marginal shifts in 1993 are reported in terms of incidents. A February 1994 government report notes that from January 1 to November 25,
1993, the BfV registered a total of 1,674 violent offenses with proven or assumed right-wing extremist motives (compared with 2,584 in 1992 and
1,483 in 1991). Eight people were killed as a result of these acts in 1993 (as
against 17 in 1992 and 3 in 1991). The Federal Criminal Police Office
(Bundeskriminalamt—BKA) registered a total of 6,721 xenophobically motivated offenses committed in 1993 (compared with 6,336 in 1992 and
2,426 in 1991), of which 1,033 were violent offenses (1,216 in 1992 and
574 in 1991). Federal Criminal Police Office statistics also show a total of
327 anti-Semitic offenses committed in the first half of 1993 alone, contributing to a 1993 total of 656 (as against 289 in 1992 and 267 in 1991);
five of these were violent offenses (as opposed to 13 in 1992 and 10 in
1991). The violent offenses do not include cemetery desecration. Prelimi-
nary figures issued by the BKA indicate there were 937 anti-Semitic incidents in the first nine months of 1994, contrary to overall trends for that
year. In 1993, 8,329 propaganda and similar offenses were attributed to
right-wing extremists, of which 5,112 were directed at foreigners. Although

violent crimes against foreigners declined in 1993 from the previous year, the number of such incidents against other targets increased significantly. And nonviolent extremist offenses rose whether against foreigners or others. The downward trend in violent right-wing extremist incidents reported by the Office for the Protection of the Constitution for 1993, a decrease of about 15 percent from 1992, continued into 1994. The BfV registered 413 violent incidents with proven or suspected right-wing motivation from January 1 to April 14, 1994, down from 663 such incidents reported for the same period in 1993. German government information from early 1995 showed incidents in this category totaling some 1962 for the period January 1, 1993, to December 12, 1993, with the same period in 1994 accounting for 1,309 incidents. This significant decline is reflected in all criminal categories measured, including homicide (where there was a decrease from 3 homicides and 18 attempts in 1993 to 8 attempts in 1994), arson (271 incidents in 1993 as against 88 in 1994), and assault offenses against property and otherwise (785 incidents in 1993 as against 526 in 1994). The same trends are apparent in comparing statistics on crimes motivated by xenophobia. For the period under discussion there are almost half as many violent acts in 1994 (723) as in 1993 (1,377). Contrary to the overall trends, although the number of desecrations of Jewish cemeteries and the number of violent incidents declined somewhat in 1994, there was a significant increase in total violations of laws concerned with anti-Semitism.

The downward trends in extremist right-wing and other xenophobic criminality are surely an indication of success in the overall efforts mounted to combat these phenomena, but the German government acknowledged that the racist riots in Magdeburg on May 12, 1994, underscored the need for continuing the various stringent anti-right-wing extremist measures put in place (see further on). The riots ranked among the worst of the various serious outbreaks of racist and xenophobic violence since reunification. The fact that all but two of the forty-nine rightists taken into custody in the course of the riots were released brought on a storm of criticism. President von Weiszacker declared the move "incomprehensible." On ZDF television he commented, "Were they supposed to go back the next day and carry on where they left off?" In defending the action, Justice Minister Sabine Leutheusser-Schnarrenberger explained that those released could still subsequently be charged. Within days the German government presented a legislative package designed to accelerate the crackdown on right-wing racist extremism, detailed further on.

Finally, it should be noted that the vast majority of violent incidents on record are reported as committed by youth, racist skinheads or others. BfV statistics published in 1994 characterize the "militant right wing extremist" category as consisting overwhelmingly of males (96% male vs. 4% female, on average, over the period 1991–1993). For 1993, 16.8 percent are under 18

(23.9% in 1992, 21.2% in 1991); 39.1 percent are 18–20 (43.4% in 1992, 47.8% in 1991); 36.5 percent are 21–30 (29.9% in 1992, 28.3% in 1991); 4.9 percent are 31–40 (2.5% in 1992, 2.2% in 1991); and 2.7 percent are over 40 (0.4% in 1992, 0.5% in 1991).

Right-Wing Extremist Political Parties Since Reunification

Although most of the violence directed at foreigners and other traditional targets of Nazism is perpetrated by racist youth, there is latent, if limited, public sympathy for their position, if not all their actions. This support not only is apparent in public opinion poll results in recent years but finds its expression in the support for various extremist right-wing political parties that often operate just within the line of political legitimacy and constitutionality. These parties present themselves as proponents of traditional conservative concerns, including, for example, the importance of tradition and the centrality of the family, but lay special stress on the importance of *Volksgemeinschaft*: the notion of a natural, genetically determined, closed community of Germans, wherever they may live, bound up by a common culture and common values. Within this context the basis for their antiforeigner sentiment becomes clear ("Germany for the Germans" means not for Turks even if they were born in Germany; members of German ethnic minorities, however, in Hungary or elsewhere, are part of this Germany). Even their recent preoccupation with environmental concerns has been cast in xenophobic terms.

The most successful of these parties in terms of electoral strength is the Republikaner, headed since 1983 by Franz Schönhuber. Its 1995 membership was estimated at 20,000, down marginally from figures for the previous few years. Cautiously respectful of the Hitler taboo, Schönhuber nevertheless argues that there are positive lessons to be learned from the Nazi experience, including the strength to be gained from open and proud attachment to traditional national values and symbols. These values are rendered inaccessible so long as recent German history is out of bounds; so, he suggests, one must abandon the traditional postwar shunning of recent history, if not its effective criminalization. For the "Reps," left-wing liberal influences in the FRG contributed to a decline in the status of the family and to lack of respect for traditional roles. As well, the massive influx of foreigners, made possible by the Continent's most liberal asylum laws (adopted in some measure as compensation for Nazi policies), was seen as threatening the very existence of a German Germany.

The Reps' greatest electoral successes came in the period immediately preceding reunification and in the first few years thereafter. The party received 7.5 percent of the vote in Berlin Landtag elections in 1989 and 9 percent in European Parliament elections that same year, establishing the party as a force in both bodies. It achieved 10.9 percent support in Baden-Württemberg elections in 1992, the highest result for a right-wing extremist party in postwar Germany, and 8.3 percent in Berlin local elections that same year. An analysis of the 1989 voting indicated that support for the party came from those sold on its antiforeigner position. In many instances, the districts that showed the heaviest Reps support were middle class or higher with small foreigner populations. Analysts suggest there is clear evidence in Germany of fear of the future on the part of people who see their status as unstable (Berlin interview with Bernd Wagner). From 1989 to 1994 the Reps elected 662 representatives to some 215 local and regional governments. In the June 1994 European Parliament elections, the Reps did considerably less well than before, gaining the support of 3.9 percent of voters as compared with the 7.1 percent support seen earlier. There is little doubt that the major parties' action to change the constitution in July 1993 to modify Germany's asylum laws, with a consequent precipitous decline in the number of asylum seekers, effectively took the wind out of the Reps' sails. Infighting among groups on the extreme right also would naturally play a role. As the most "moderate" of the extremist right-wing political parties, the Reps would be the most vulnerable to such a rightward shift in governmental policy. Finally, it would seem reasonable that some Reps voters may have been using their franchise to register a sense of disenfranchisement or frustration with existing parties and policies. Such support is readily transferred to other alternative parties when the latter show more promise as an alternative voice. This was apparently the case when the Reps gained less than 2 percent of the vote in German national elections in mid-October 1994. The strong showing of the Party for Democratic Socialism, largely former East German communists, might itself account for some of the Reps' losses. Possibly the largest extremist party and the next most electorally successful after the Reps, and generally seen as located to its right, is the Deutsche Volksunion (DVU), based in Munich and counting 26,000 members. Its *Deutsche National-Zeitung (DNZ)* has a weekly circulation of 50,000, and its *Deutsche Wochen-Zeitung/Deutscher Anzeiger (DWZ/DA)*, a weekly circulation of 30,000.

The DVU was founded in 1971 as an offshoot of the NPD and continues to be led by business magnate Dr. Gerhard Frey. In recent years allegations have been raised regarding Frey's connections with Russian extremist nationalist leader Vladimir Zhirinovsky. The DVU has argued for, in effect, a rehabilitation of the leaders of Nazism, espouses a strident antiforeigner position, and presses for harsh measures to halt what it argues is foreigner-inspired criminality. It is transparently xenophobic and anti-Semitic. The party received 5.3 percent support in Bremen elections in 1987, 6 percent in Bremen in 1991, and 6 percent in Schleswig-Holstein in 1992, where the Reps did not run that year.

The Nationaldemokratische Partei Deutschlands, (NPD), based in Stuttgart, is the oldest of the major extremist right-wing parties, advocating the restoration of all the Third Reich's territories and taking a strong antiforeigner stance. Its greatest electoral showing was in 1969, yet it retains some 5,000 members, has a youth organization, and publishes the monthly *Deutsche Stimme* with a circulation of 48,000. In the European Parliament elections in June 1994 the NPD gained only 0.2 percent of the vote, and in German national elections later that same year it fell below the dismal 2 percent showing of the Reps.

The Public Response

Apart from the strident denunciations of extremist right-wing activism emanating from traditional opposing forces on the left, the German public was slow to respond to the increasing level of antiforeigner and antiminority violence in the early 1990s, just after reunification. In many respects, the public's response, at least in the West, was no different than what one would find in Canada until recently, if not still: A large majority of good and fair-minded people recognized that some level of racism and racial hatred exists in society, that it will generate a certain number of incidents each year, and that these were essentially criminal incidents and thus the responsibility of the police. For those holding this view, the issue is essentially one of containment. Although not dismissing the role of education, they view it as a fundamentally passive long-term process. A more enlightened approach is exhibited by those who demand police vigilance but likewise call for a simultaneous broadened educational process and public discourse on the realities of racism and hatred in society.

One heard little worry expressed about the possible undermining of postwar German democracy, and not until late 1991 and early 1992, when the level of incidents mounted to the point that they were receiving considerable international attention, did large groups in many cities, Munich the first among them, gather to denounce racism and xenophobia in dramatic candlelight marches. German president Richard von Weiszacker played an important role and showed great leadership in this process of public consciousness raising. An Allensbach public opinion survey in December 1992 revealed that 53 percent of Germans (52% in the West and 57% in the East) were "very concerned" about the possibility that right-wing extremism could spread. The same survey revealed that the level of public rejection of right-wing extremists as undesirable had risen significantly since 1990. When asked to identify from a list which groups of people one would not want as neighbors, in 1990 drug addicts topped the list (66%), followed by heavy drinkers (64%), then right-wing extremists (62%). Those who would be classed as "foreigners" rated between 20 percent and 10 percent, and Jews, 7 percent. In 1992 right-wing extremists top the list (77%; 77% in the West, 79% in the East), followed by drug addicts (67%; 66% in the West, 72% in the East), heavy drinkers (66%; 64% in the West, 72% in the East), Gypsies (63%; 63% in the

West, 68% in the East), and left-wing extremists (61%; 62% in the West, 57% in the East). Those who would be classed as "foreigners" rated between 18 percent and 13 percent, and Jews remained at 7 percent (6% in the East). The survey suggests that by 1992, so far as the German population was concerned, as unpleasant a prospect as it might be to have drug addicts or drunks as neighbors, right-wing extremists do even more harm to the neighborhood. There was also a marginal improvement in attitudes toward traditional "foreigners," although the figure for Gypsies betrays a deep-seated prejudice that is not at all unique to the German population.

The negative international attention drawn to Germany on account of mounting incidents, combined with the growing domestic concern, contributed to the Kohl government's ultimate mobilization to deal aggressively with right-wing extremism. At the same time, over the past few years one witnesses an increasing mobilization of public sector elements in the same direction. The response takes various forms. Organized labor and school systems began to mount antixenophobia programs, community groups devoted greater attention to providing disaffected youth with positive alternatives to gang activity, and enhanced efforts were undertaken to expose the horror of the Nazi era and draw lessons for the present.

The Federal Government's Response

The German federal cabinet took steps on December 2, 1992, to coordinate all antiviolence and anti-right-wing extremism measures under the single Campaign Against Violence and Hostility Toward Foreigners. The move was long called for by domestic and international parties that had been critical of the government for its slow, if not dismissive, initial response to incidents in 1990 and 1991 and its ineffective response once actions began to be taken.

The first interim report of the campaign was released by the cabinet in February 1993 and its sequel, in January 1994. The latter addresses issues and identifies measures both within the mandate of the federal government and within the authority of the *Länder*. Special attention is paid to the problem of youth violence, employment, education, and antiextremism informational efforts; the integration of foreigners; police and internal security measures; and legislative initiatives to be taken to bolster federal and state capacities to confront right-wing extremism.

Youth

The second interim report observes that the broad challenges facing young people arising out of the breakdown of the traditional family, changing social roles and structures, and the like (a situation common in all Western democracies) cannot explain the surge in racist violence that "arise[s] from specific situations and circumstances but [is] also embedded in a broader social climate." It suggests that media attention given to the incidents may have played a role in encouraging such behavior by "rewarding" it. Alcohol is also noted as a contributing factor. The broader public concern over the massive influx of asylum seekers into the reunified Germany in the early 1990s is "wrongly described as xenophobia." At the same time this broad concern assuredly provided genuine xenophobes with a sense of legitimacy. Whereas the malaise of Western democracies is seen as contributing to youthful extremism in Western *Länder*, the dramatic shift from a communist dictatorship without time for reeducation in the ways of liberal democracy is noted as particularly significant in the East.

The recommendations include educating youth for democratic living; meeting employment needs; ensuring adequate support for those with social or educational problems; better equipping schools to educate toward nonviolent problem solving; and, especially in the eastern *Länder*, providing positive leisure-time opportunities. The report recognizes that the efforts to be made in these areas require the broad participation and investment of all segments of society.

Specific measures were taken in various areas. A wide range of antihate and antiviolence programs were launched and directed at German youth, and calls were issued for the media to reflect on the manner in which hate incidents were covered so as to ensure that the potential for inadvertently encouraging such behavior was minimized.

The enhancement of child and youth services was promoted and included new provisions to the Labour Promotion Act to permit financial aid for personnel costs incurred by voluntary private agencies in creating new youth and welfare infrastructures. For the eastern *Länder*, one program introduced in 1992 focused on the promotion of voluntary youth services and provided DM 50 million for social work services that year and a further DM 25 million for 1993.

Schools were the focus of enhanced efforts to combat xenophobic violence. Beyond promoting programs to improve social behavior, instill an interest in and teach tolerance, and instill a sense of responsibility, officials identified various special programs to promote the integration of foreigners. Governmental support was provided to the Federal Parents' Council, representing 10 million parents of schoolchildren, in support of a conference Violence: A Phenomenon of Our Society. New antiviolence curricular materials were prepared and widely disseminated, and schools were all charged with addressing relevant issues in the classroom and in school-based nonclassroom events. Finally, teacher-training leaders also took note of the antixenophobia agenda.

The report says that the issues of xenophobia and antiforeigner violence have figured prominently on the agenda of those political education efforts directed at youth that are organized by the various federal and *Länder* bodies charged with this responsibility. And since October 1991, "instructions have been repeatedly passed down the [armed] forces' chain of command that every effort must be made to counter and prevent xenophobia behaviour and extremist tendencies energetically, and, most particularly, through education measures."

Finally, the report addresses the benefit of using sports as a venue for positive intergroup relations and as a constructive leisure-time activity. It also notes the establishment of various bodies to address the problem of sports-events-stimulated antiforeigner rowdiness.

Community Relations Between Germans and Foreigners

The interim report comments on the German federal government's long-term commitment to integrating foreigners into the German mainstream. In particular, it notes that in 1993 the "Federal Ministry for Labour and Social Affairs alone provided some DM 92 million for integrative measures and counseling services for foreign employees and their families, as well as for measures in related public relations activities to advance good relations between Germans and foreigners." The report points out that these funds were supplemented by some DM 52 million from the western *Länder*. One might observe that the attitudes of Germans as represented in the public opinion surveys noted previously generally speak to the success of such efforts, although at the same time there is no doubt that many problems remain in the relationship between Germans and foreigners, including foreigners who have lived among the Germans for many years, if not many generations.

The report also calls on the media to emphasize the contributions foreigners make to the country's prosperity. Foreigners are consumers, pay taxes, make social insurance contributions, are businessmen and employers, are a source of skilled labor, and so on. The report notes that the greatest progress toward integrating foreigners has been in fact achieved in the workplace, partly, the report says, as a result of the fact that foreign employees have participated in the democracy of the shop floor. It recommends the continuance of a series of other projects, including those in the new *Länder*, directed at creating a positive working climate free of xenophobia and antiforeigner feeling; among these are seminars, vocational projects, and binational training projects. Finally, action was taken to rectify a situation in which foreigners who had been victims of violent crime in Germany could receive compensation only in the event that reciprocal arrangements existed in the victims' native country. Regulations were changed to permit foreigners who had legally resided in Germany for at least six months without interruption to claim compensation under the Victims of Violence Compensation Act with retroactive effect to July 1, 1990.

Police and Internal Security Services

The interim report begins with the premise that there has been no evidence to suggest that racially motivated violence in Germany is centrally organized.

At the same time, the report recognizes the importance of a coordinated national collection evaluation and channeling of information on xenophobic offenses and notes that the internal security department of the Bundeskriminalamt (BKA) and respective state offices have been mandated to collect, evaluate, and channel relevant information. The BKA's right-wing terrorism section was enlarged as well. Finally, efforts on the federal level were paralleled on the *Länder* level.

The report recognizes the problem of operational readiness of police and emergency forces to respond to xenophobic violence and urges state authorities to increase the size of their emergency forces to nationally agreed upon levels. The issue of training of squads is addressed, as is the creation of quick-response units modeled after those provided by the federal border guard. The necessity of accelerating the development of internal security services in the eastern *Länder* is recognized, and the federal government reversed its decision to make staff cuts at the federal Office for the Protection of the Constitution; instead, it enlarged departments involved in monitoring right-wing elements and created a special team to monitor emerging groups.

Under German law "extremists" are prohibited from becoming public servants or members of the armed forces. This prohibition derives from Article 33(5) of the Basic Law. Of course, the question arises as to where the defining line is drawn. Events of the early 1990s point to the need to draw the line most clearly. Legal instruments to keep left-wing and right-wing extremists out of the public service and armed forces already existed; nevertheless, the Federal Ministry of the Interior reemphasized the loyalty requirements for public servants in February 1993.

Article 10 of the Basic Law provides for intelligence services obtaining information about possible criminal activities by monitoring mail and telephone calls. The report notes that legislative initiatives were planned to amend elements of Article 10 to widen the grounds for surveillance of suspected extremist parties. The report also encourages recourse to those provisions of the Basic Law that permit the banning of particular groups on the basis of their extremism. It notes that the Federal Ministry of the Interior had to date banned the NO, the DA, and the NF and that the federal government had asked the Federal Constitutional Court to suspend the basic rights of two neo-Nazis because of their activities. A further banning of the FAP is also noted. Whereas a state government may also ban associations when their organization and activities are confined to the respective state, the report observes that in December 1992 the government of Lower Saxony obtained a ban on the right-wing extremist organization Deutscher Kameradschaftsbund, that in June 1993 Bavaria banned the Nationale Block, that in July the government of Baden-Württemberg banned the Heimattreue Vereinigung Deutschlands (HVD), and that in September the government of North Rhine-Westphalia banned the Freundeskreis Freiheit für Deutschland. The Hamburg senate requested in August 1993 that the Federal Constitutional Court rule on the unconstitutionality of a local extremist right-wing group, the Nationale Liste. Finally, in 1994 the federal government banned the right-wing extremist youth organization Wiking Jugend (Viking Youth).

Criminal Law and Procedure

The report goes into some considerable detail regarding statistics on criminal proceedings against people indicted for right-wing extremist or xenophobic offenses. In 1992, 12,039 investigations were instituted for these offenses, the majority of which were propaganda violations. Such offenses fall under Sections 86, 86(a), 130, and 131 of the penal code. Approximately 6 percent of the 11,627 persons charged were juveniles or young adults under the age of twenty-one. A total of 10,171 proceedings, some of which had been begun in 1991, were completed in 1992. These resulted in 1,490 convictions with 504 people being sentenced to penitentiaries or juvenile institutions. Sentences exceeding two years were handed down in sixty-one cases. Almost half of the cases that had gone forward had to be dismissed because suspects could not be established. The report says that in particular in the large number of cases involving juveniles, the juvenile court law provides a variety of legal options to be applied, including those that mandate education in addition to periods of incarceration.

A further government report issued by the Federal Ministry of Justice in February 1994 and brought up to date in a January 1995 Ministry of Information publication notes that in the period between January 1 and September 30, 1993, 18,729 investigations were initiated (1992 total: 12,039) against 21,384 accused persons (1992 total: 11,627). During this period, 345 warrants for arrest were issued (1992 total: 719). Of these investigations, 95 (86 in 1992) were for homicide (including attempted homicide), 1,343 for causing bodily harm (831 in 1992), 344 for arson (432 in 1992), 744 for civil disorder (847 in 1991), and 14,360 for propaganda offenses (7,089 in 1992). In this period 703 investigations were conducted into anti-Semitic activities (220 in 1992), and 21,568 criminal proceedings were completed (10,176 in 1992); 14,401 cases (as against 6,940 in 1992) had to be abandoned on account of evidentiary problems or inability to locate the suspect. Some 2,191 criminal proceedings ended in conviction in 1993 (1,490 in 1992). In 627 of these criminal proceedings, a prison sentence or youth custody was imposed (514 in 1992). In 108 of these proceedings, a prison sentence was imposed in excess of two years (61 in 1992). Finally, two investigations by the federal prosecutor general (Generalbundesanwalt) are noteworthy. Those convicted of the murders in Mölln on November 23, 1992, Michael Peters and Lars Christiansen, each received the maximum sentence, life imprisonment and ten years in youth detention, respectively. In the investigation of Christian Reher, Markus Gartmann, Felix Köhnen, and Christian Buchholz in connection with the murders committed in Solingen on May 29, 1993, and on December 20, 1993, the federal prosecutor general pressed charges with the Sixth Criminal Panel of Düsseldorf Higher Regional Court (Oberlandesgericht). The May 29 firebombing of a Turkish home, taking the lives of two adults and three children, had provoked massive protests in many German cities against antiforeigner extremism.

The report notes that the Ministry of Justice has reviewed xenophobic and anti-Semitic song texts in the possibility that charges might be laid, and searches were conducted of producers of racist music and publications. It also argues for an expansion of penal code Section 86 to permit action against organizations that modify symbols under which indictments are possible in order to evade the law. It suggests the importance of amending Section 130 of the penal code, which deals with criminal agitation, and Section 131, which deals with incitement to racial hatred, in order to make these sections more broadly applicable and to ensure the imposition of sufficient penalties upon conviction. It argues with regard to Section 223 and following and Section 340 of the penal code, dealing with bodily harm, that the current three-year maximum prison sentence for simple bodily harm should be extended to five years with a graduated scale of imprisonment based on the respective acts and their consequences. Prison sentences of up to ten years are advocated, in particular for cases of aggravated bodily harm. The report calls for an expansion of Section 112(3) of the Code of Criminal Procedure, which concerns custody prior to trial for particularly serious offenses, to include among these offenses willful grievous bodily harm and malicious arson, two sorts of criminality involved in the explosion of extremist right-wing violence. The report points out that in usual circumstances under Section 112(a) of the Code of Criminal Procedure, suspects detained have to be released once police have taken particulars unless there has been a prior conviction. The code provides no basis on which individuals may be remanded prior to trial. It is suggested that this provision be modified to permit remand prior to trial in the case of individuals arrested during the course of violent disturbances so as to limit the possibility of their quickly resuming their criminal activities. It is stated clearly that in undertaking such a move the action would be permitted only on the basis of preventive detention and that appropriate caution would be taken to ensure that individuals' constitutional rights are not breached. Finally, the report recommends that priority should be given to legislation to amend the Code of Criminal Procedure to provide for an interstate prosecution service information system to facilitate the prosecution of individuals apprehended and suspected of involvement in extremist right-wing activities barred by law.

A number of the recommendations made in the report were acted upon by the Bundestag and Bundesrat in September 1994 when they approved legislation that enhances the criminal code's provisions to combat organized crime and right-wing extremist violence. Most notable among the changes are those increasing the maximum penalty for bodily harm from three to five years; allowing for imprisonment of up to five years for distribution of constitutionally banned extremist propaganda, incitement, and Holocaust denial; and recognizing modified Nazi symbols as used by various skinhead and other groups to fall within the already existing prohibition against Nazi symbols. Procedural modifications enhanced the courts' capacity to expedite cases and impose administrative detention. As well, administrative practices were adjusted to facilitate the seizure of banned organizations' effects and facilitate the control of mail and telephone usage of members of violent extremist organizations.

An Assessment of the Effects of and Responses to Right-Wing Extremism

The Sociopolitical Context

The problem of the recent, violent expansion of right-wing extremist activity is not unique to Germany among the Western democracies. Still, the German situation has attracted particularly dramatic domestic and international attention. This surely is at least in part due to Germany's Nazi past and musings regarding the stability of postreunification German democracy. At the same time, the sheer magnitude of the problem—thousands of violent incidents reported to police, thousands more propaganda offenses, and the operation of transparently extremist political parties—justifiably commands attention.

Many German authorities consulted for this analysis were adamant that current extremist right-wing and xenophobic sympathies in the population, and even more so, the incidents, were totally unrelated to political trends in the late Weimar and Nazi periods. In my view, they are only partially correct.

There is little evidence of direct, ongoing links between the more formal extremist right-wing groupings and the generally youthful extremists who are the main perpetrators of acts of racist and xenophobic violence. This is also the case when it comes to the more public extremist parties like the Republikaners, groups whose leadership includes ex-SS men and others of the appropriate generation and whose ideology is drawn, albeit in some instances in modified form, from the Nazi era. Still, a German government response to an SDP inquiry in early June 1994 indicated that the Republikaner Party had been linked to fourteen crimes since December 1992, including at least one beating resulting in death. The response indicated as well that members of that party were under investigation for crimes ranging from libel to bodily injury resulting in death. Whereas the old-time Nazis provide a sort of ideological framework in which the young xenophobes' actions are justifiable, the young xenophobes do not appear to seek or need this justification. At the same time, there is little doubt that they take encouragement from what appears to be, and perhaps is, a measure of public approval for their ultimate purpose, if not precisely for their actions. For the more urbane extremists, the racist violence perpetrated by skinheads and others provides proof of the validity of their claims. What both groups do share is a fundamental rejection of the democratic model and an attachment to authoritarianism and rigidity, combined with or expressed in a deep attachment to the *Volk*.

All this said, one cannot point to the more formal extremist groupings' theorizing and propagandizing as ultimate triggers for the recent explosion in incidents. The fondness for authority and the conformist elitism that have been part of German culture, whether in its more formal and extreme expressions or in its more subtle, democratized expressions, contributes to a climate conducive to an expansion of xenophobic feeling. The ultimate failure of denazification, discussed previously, also contributes, as does the retention in the Basic Law of elements faithful to old-style *völkisch* nationalism. The denial of the reality of immigration and multiculturalism, on the one hand, and the special pride in the deutsche mark as an acceptable national symbol of success and power, on the other, attest to the vitality of this nationalism. But the roots of the current problem, it appears, are more properly to be found in the social and political dynamics of Western democracies, Germany among them, since the late 1960s and most especially in the 1980s and early 1990s. Added to this are the unique experiences of Germany in the late 1980s and early 1990s as the communist bloc collapsed and with it, the Wall, that powerful symbol of the conflict blocking German reunification.

One critically important factor, not uniquely German, is the reorganization of the political landscape in Western democracies. Although this is not the place for an exhaustive analysis of the relevant dynamics, the following is offered for consideration within the context of this study.

The postwar boom in the West set the stage for a dramatic expansion of liberal democratic thinking with a major emphasis, on the international political front, on human rights. The experience of the Nazi era contributed to this heightened emphasis. The totalitarian communist domination of the East did as well. The need to contain the communist menace provided a rationale for Western military expansion in the name of preserving democracy and contributed to an early abandonment of the denazification effort in West Germany. Various Western states undertook a variety of domestic measures to combat racism and bigotry (antihate, human rights, and civil rights legislation, desegregation, and so on), but in times of plenty these problems generally were treated as minor. After all, most of the residents of Western democracies were not encountering violent racism in the streets. The human rights focus also provided a rationale for foreign involvements, including strategic alliances (the "good guy" human rights–promoting democracies against the "bad guy" eastern bloc or Soviet-dominated third world dictatorships) supplementing those related more purely to trade. Many a Western leader made his or her name in international affairs, while domestic economies coasted onward and upward, with threats to continued expansion (the Arab oil crisis of the early 1970s, as an example) met and ultimately overcome, at least until the late 1980s.

After almost three decades of Western publics shifting in their political preferences from Conservative/Republican to Liberal/Democrat/Social Democratic/Socialist parties to serve as either the government or the opposition, opposing parties' policies came to seem more and more the same, or, at least, parties seemed equally unable to deal effectively with looming domestic social problems: Unemployment, especially among youth, had risen even if inflation had been beaten back, economies were in decline, and the threat posed by the Cold War "bad guys," which in the past could be relied upon to unify an otherwise fractious public, was gone.

If there was any domestic issue, which at the same time was an international issue, that could capture the Western public's imagination in the post–Cold War period, it was the environment. The issue had been on the agenda of many a Western state for some time by the late 1980s but, by that time, was ready to assume a more important place in the realm of domestic and international politics. If the H-bomb were no longer the major threat to human civilization, the poisoned global environment was.

In some states old-time parties adopted this issue effectively, but in others, new Green parties promoted the issue and propelled themselves forcefully into the political fray. The emergence of the Greens as an alternative voting address underscored the exhaustion of postwar democratic polities. Support for the Greens demonstrated the voting public's desire for new alternatives. This opening up of the process created an opportunity for other groupings to seek electoral support, especially on the right, populist end of the political spectrum. The support for Ross Perot's candidacy in the 1992 U.S. presidential elections, the Reform Party's accomplishments in Canada's 1993 federal elections, the election of commanding numbers of conservative Republicans to the U.S. House and Senate in 1994, and the solid 1995 electoral victory of Ontario's Conservative Party, more obviously populist in its orientation and more obviously right-wing than its most proximate Tory predecessor, have demonstrated public sympathy for a shake-up in the traditional political matrix with at least an initial preference for more "traditional" conservative alternatives than those presented by the Canadian Tories or by George Bush's Republicans. In Europe, conservative parties continued to get support through the late 1980s and mid-1990s. Most important for our purposes, in the reorganized political landscape of the West, especially in Europe, support grew as well for more extremist right-wing groups such as the Front National in France or the Republikaner Party in

Germany. As noted previously, such developments did not necessarily encourage antiforeigner attacks directly, but they tended to suggest to the attackers a measure of approval and encouragement for their actions. A second, more distinctly German, set of factors behind the rise in right-wing extremism is related to aspects of German *völkisch* nationalism within the changing European political context of the late 1980s and early 1990s.

A growing attentiveness to the insidious nature of racism in Western societies and to the need to deal with systemic racism and its many manifestations developed in the late 1960s. A major challenge was to recognize the realities of immigration and refugee flow in a highly mobile world and to recognize the degree to which Western states were increasingly becoming multiracial, multicultural societies. Different states attended to this challenge in different ways. In West Germany, despite the influx of millions of foreign guest workers, few or no changes were made in citizenship laws to permit even foreigners of long-standing residence or ethnic Germans from Eastern Europe to achieve truly equal status alongside native residents.

This situation did not change through the 1980s and into the 1990s. At the same time, European moves toward greater integration encouraged the abandonment of narrow blood-based nationalism and détente with the eastern bloc; and then, the fall of the Soviet Union opened the floodgates of asylum seekers. Some of these meet the terms of the 1951 Convention Refugee definition, but many others are economic migrants seeking fulfillment of their dreams in the West. Even as Germany was on the front lines of an East-West confrontation, it found itself on the front lines of a massive flow of people from the East. Provisions in the German Basic Law, drafted in response to attitudes and practices of the Nazi era, gave Germany the West's most liberal asylum policies. Its capacity would now be pressed beyond the level of any other Western state, and this at a time when priority attention was required to smooth the integration of the Eastern *Länder* into the Federal Republic's mainstream. With unemployment at new high levels and with the economy faltering, although not as much as some other Western economies, right-wing xenophobic arguments suggesting "X million foreigners equal X million unemployed Germans" gained popular support. The DM costs of accommodating asylum seekers until the normalization of their status or their removal were high, especially in the East; so were the political costs. Those involved in the articulation or support of antiforeigner attacks often observed that asylum seekers' accommodations and allowances made them better off than native Germans. And if West German *völkisch* nationalism was not already a strong enough force looking for more open expression, the reunification with East Germany amplified it. This amplification was not so much on account of the reunification itself but rather, it seems, more because of East Germans' recourse to passionate nationalistic identification as a means of asserting the legitimacy of their existence as full partners with their infinitely more successful Western brothers: "*Wir sind ein Volk.*"

Public Responses

Opinion polls conducted during 1992–1995 have demonstrated a troubling racist and xenophobic attitude among citizens in virtually all European states. One poll taken in Germany suggests that 25 percent of its respondents agree that the country would be better off were foreigners to leave, 50 percent would agree with the notion "Germany for the Germans," and about 32 percent agreed with the statement that the Nazi regime had some good features. This having been noted, one must observe that the majority of Germans are not in the racially motivated antiforeigner camp and that a large majority views right-wing extremists as undesirable neighbors. Large public antixenophobia rallies in many German cities underscored the commitment of Germans, certainly in the western *Länder*, to sustaining the postwar liberal democratic tradition. By 1996 in some quarters at least, even a suspicion of neo-Nazi involvement in an incident was enough to bring out a throng of demonstrators in support of the victims and in denunciation of the perpetrators. This was the case on January 18, 1996, when a disastrous and deadly fire at a Lubeck foreigners' hotel took ten lives and injured scores of other residents. The international media reported that victims were from Africa, the Middle East, and Eastern Europe. Mayor Michael Bouteiller's call for a show of support brought out 4,000 townspeople, no doubt concerned to counter a reputation already tarnished in 1994 when, during Passover, the city's synagogue was torched by Nazi thugs. (After two days of intensive investigation, authorities attributed the blaze to one of the hotel's residents, himself a foreigner, for unknown motives.) Considerable evidence also exists of grassroots mobilizations to combat racist and xenophobic attitudes and to ensure a sustained mindfulness of the criminality of the Nazi period. The abrupt end to the candidacy of Steffen Heitmann, Chancellor Kohl's favored presidential candidate, stands as an example of the latter. He had reflected, in effect, the view that with reunification a new era had commenced in which Germany could unload the burden of its Nazi past. Finally, lagging public sympathy for extremist right-wing parties, including the most normative among them, the Republikaner Party, has been demonstrated in German domestic electoral results since the June 1994 European Parliament vote. The decline in voters' support for extreme right-wing parties continued in the subsequent German federal elections. These are all very positive signs, yet unanswerable questions remain regarding the position of the significant percentages of eligible German voters who decline to exercise their franchise. An EMNID poll released on March 14, 1993, suggested that in that month about 40 percent of all Germans were nonvoters, a figure representing about 30 percent in the West and 40 percent in the East. My research indicates that a portion of this nonvoting group would probably mirror the voting patterns of the voting public, given the traditional German voter's ultimate comfort being achieved with electoral stability and predictability. But a portion, perhaps the most cynical, might be on the way toward opting out of the democratic system. This latter group is susceptible to single-issue populist appeals for which the extreme right is famous.

The Government's Responses

I noted earlier that the German central government's initial response to mounting antiforeigner hostility, especially in the eastern *Länder,* was slow, if not noncommittal, and that it took some time for leading authorities to recognize that the country was facing a crisis that bore domestic and international consequences. One can understand the initial difficulties in adequately meeting the racist skinhead challenge in centers such as Hoyerswerda given the weak, if not nonexistent, policing and educational infrastructures. At the same time, attacks quickly moved beyond those directed at asylum seekers' hostels to attacks on "foreigners" more generally and beyond attacks on what we would call "visible minorities" to attacks on Jews and gays. These attacks took place in the West (for example, the fatal attack on Turks in Mölln) as well as in the East, and indeed, proportionally there were far more in the East. This dynamic of a broadening of the group of victims and proportionately more tensions in the East suggests a more fundamental underlying problem than that which can be met by more effective anticrime legislation, more efficient policing, and enhanced prodemocracy antixenophobic educational efforts alone. I return to this issue further on.

Efforts on the criminal legislation and policing fronts have been considerable and have shown some positive effect, but attacks and arsons continue. It is hoped that additional measures adopted in light of the government's *Interim Report on the Campaign Against Violence and Hostility Toward Foreigners* will further enhance police capabilities and results. As we have seen, overall violent-incident figures have declined from the high levels of 1992; still, the level of nonviolent offenses (propaganda and the like) has increased. The decline in violent incidents may be attributed to better police coordination and a more determined effort to specifically target xenophobic crime for action, both of which have resulted in higher levels of arrests and convictions. Especially in the case of youthful offenders, the majority of those involved in violent incidents, arrest and conviction does appear to diminish their ardor. Often their ideological commitment to the racist cause is ambiguous and susceptible to positive influence, which, it is hoped, is provided in the education required by the courts in many cases. What is most required here is a more effective way of meeting young peoples' concerns and insecurities over their future, and this issue has received attention in government planning.

The government's recourse to constitutional provisions permitting the banning of extremist right-wing parties and other groupings appears to have a somewhat greater impact on the symbolic than on the practical level. On the symbolic level, bannings send a strong message of societal rejection of antidemocratic groups and a message of the government's determination to go to all necessary lengths to put such groups out of business, banishing them to the margins of society where they belong. On the practical level, bannings afford authorities more of a free hand in acting against such groups' organizing efforts and, ideally, encourage the public to be more openly rejecting of such groups and the causes they espouse, although it should be observed that banned groups are able to reorganize under new banners and thus continue their activities.

The proliferation of xenophobic and racist hate propaganda remains a challenge, as does the ongoing circulation of anti-Semitic hate propaganda, including considerable Holocaust denial material (in such material the Holocaust is called "the Auschwitz lie"). The 1994 increase in total violations of laws dealing with anti-Semitism, reported earlier, illustrates the problem, although we ought to consider that the elevated figures at least in part come as the result of heightened public vigilance and intensified resolve on the part of the justice system overall to recognize the relevant offenses in broader terms. German criminal law has for a long time included more provisions than has perhaps any other Western jurisdiction to attend to the spread of hate propaganda. As noted, successful prosecutions have been mounted against hatemongers and numerous seizures of hate materials effected. Enhanced legislation in this area to deal with groups' efforts to evade the law is very much in order. At the same time, it is important to note that much of the anti-Semitic material circulating in Germany arrives from U.S. and Canadian sources. This underscores the need for international cooperation in this area.

A new subarea in the hate propaganda field requiring international attention involves extremist right-wingers' use of the electronic highway to disseminate hate propaganda and accomplish various organizational objectives. Uwe Kauss, editor of *Chip*, a Munich-based computer magazine, has estimated that 1,500 of the country's right-wing extremists are involved in the Thule Network, a PC-based exchange used for sharing propaganda, making plans for rallies, and providing information on bomb construction and other rightist tactics. An Associated Press report suggests that the network is well protected with sophisticated encryption capabilities, that other security measures are taken to limit the possibilities of unwanted penetration, and that it facilitated a 500-strong Nazi rally in Fulda in 1993 that went on essentially unhindered. That same report quotes Baden-Württemberg police official Matthias Schenk as crediting the network with bringing hitherto disconnected groups together. "This is a very difficult realm for gathering solid evidence," and prosecutions are more than difficult. Intent on asserting at least some measure of control, at least over foreign-source offending materials, German authorities acted early in 1996 to press electronic highway–access facilitators to block access first to pornographic electronic bulletin boards and web sites and then, in mid-January, to Canadian Holocaust denier Ernst Zundel's web site. Initial reaction to these moves has been mixed, yet Germany's determination to control the electronic publication of hate material is groundbreaking and demonstrative of governmental commitment to action. The effectiveness of this approach remains to be determined.

The problem of hate networks is not unique to Germany, and there is evidence of extremist right-wing groups in virtually all Western countries linking up through such means. The problem requires intense domestic and international attention as a transnational challenge with political, security, and criminal aspects.

The Traditional Political Parties' Responses

While the CDU and SDP have been involved in developing the various legislative and policy responses to the surges in xenophobic hate activity, each has turned its attention to countering the electoral successes on the far right as well.

The CDU, especially through its affiliated Konrad Adenauer Stiftung, has conducted numerous studies on extremist right-wing phenomena, in part on account of very practical concerns over the Republikaner Party and other groups further to the right encroaching on its own traditional support base. For their part, the Social Democrats have mounted an especially impressive political education campaign directed at all age levels, with particular emphasis on the youth, to counter extremist right-wing attitudes. The extreme right is targeted, as are the topics of racism, xenophobia, anti-Semitism, and antiforeigner hostility, in broadly disseminated audiovisual and print materials designed for group and individual use. This effort merits special commendation.

This being said, the major parties' efforts to address highly sensitive and emotional—and more critical—issues are not nearly as adequate. The most pressing of the fundamental issues underlying and sustaining xenophobic, racist, and anti-Semitic hatred and bigotry are those concerning belonging and identity. Through my interviews with government and nongovernmental organizations' officials, it is clear that generally speaking, Germans do not see their country as an immigration country. Some even take the view that immigration is, in effect, a peaceful method of territorial occupation. Multiculturalism is a widely denied, or at least ignored, reality.

The extent to which the major parties have been unwilling to deal determinedly with these issues is most apparent in the SDP's support for the governing CDU's action in late 1992 to modify Germany's asylum laws. I noted earlier that Germany's asylum laws were perhaps the most generous in the democratic world. With the collapse of the iron curtain, this policy contributed to a massive influx of asylum seekers, creating a situation of particularly dramatic fiscal, political, and moral consequences. Although the SDP had traditionally taken the position that it would not contemplate any changes to the asylum laws without complementary changes to citizenship laws, in the face of mounting pressure to stem the flow of asylum seekers (in 1990 and 1991 Germany admitted 58 percent of asylum seekers in the European Community, or 47 percent of those coming to Western Europe, and in 1992 admitted 72 percent of the EC's seekers of asylum and 65 percent of Western Europe's), the SDP support for legislation limiting access gave the government the two-thirds majority it required, and no quid pro quo on citizenship or naturalization was demanded. In the shorter term, if we use the recent European Parliament, federal, and some *Länder* elections as indicators, stemming the flow of asylum seekers seems to have contributed to the traditional mainstream parties recapturing much of the voter support that had gone to the Republikaners. The Republikaners and those to their right lost their major public agenda issue, although some sought to view their electoral losses as proof of their influence: The losses resulted from their success at forcing the mainstream parties to act on the asylum-seeker issue. In search of a new thematic vehicle, Republikaners and others have attempted to repackage their message in an environmentalist wrapping. As some have observed, what we have in this circumstance is a rotten cucumber: green yet bruised on the outside and brown and seedy on the inside.

An estimated 7 million "foreigners" reside in Germany, about 8 percent of the country's population. Many falling into this category were born in Germany, speak German as their first language, and consider themselves German, yet on account of a system so restrictive as to allow perhaps only 10,000–20,000 in any given year to become naturalized, the vast majority are not German citizens. Although Turks, the largest "foreigner" group, and others are essentially shut out of German citizenship, ethnic Germans entering the country—an estimated 230,000 arrived from the former Soviet Union in 1992—are generally regarded as having natural, if not formal, legal rights to claims on citizenship. In effect, the citizenship law, laden with *völkisch* nationalistic spirit, creates a permanent class of others, *Ausländer*, available in tough times to bear the brunt of societal frustrations.

No real and permanent solution to the problem of extremist right-wing influence on the German polity is possible without serious soul-searching on the issues of belonging and identity, in particular, without soul-searching that results in significant changes to the citizenship laws. Michael Mertes, director of the policy analysis and speech-writing unit in the Federal Chancellery, writes, "Only since the end of 1992 has the federal legislature begun to search seriously for a reasonable path between uncontrolled mass absorption of newcomers and a too restrictive naturalization of foreigners. A more liberal approach to the naturalization at least of second and third generation 'foreigners' is badly needed. There are ample reasons for change, and not only in the 'new' *Länder*."[11]

Mertes goes on to report that the Kohl government took a first legislative step in the direction of a new citizenship law with provisions—effective since January 1, 1991, but rarely used—that, "capable of and needing further amendment . . . give a claim to naturalization without considering 'ethnic' criteria, such as descent or total assimilation."[12] These provisions remain rarely used, Mertes tells us, because of the stipulation that one must relinquish other citizenships as a requirement for naturalization. This policy, he observes, is not at all uncommon among the nations of the world. Finally, he tells us that "further liberalizing measures—also with regard to the problem of dual citizenship . . . —are currently being discussed."[13]

I share Mertes's view that a more liberal approach to naturalization is required, for many reasons. I recognize that the issue of dual or multiple citizenship is a complex and vexing issue, yet it is particularly relevant, if not urgent, in a Europe and a world whose conflicts have produced some 20 million refugees, where international migration of peoples is easier than ever before, where our economic interdependence is increasingly apparent, and, as a consequence of these and other factors, where national boundaries are increasingly blurred. Germany has much to gain in the process of reconsidering immigration and citizenship policies.

That the citizenship issue remains a live political issue is demonstrated by its having been a subject of the coalition negotiations between the CDU and Free Democrats after the October 1994 federal elections. Subsequently, FDP members of the cabinet proposed consideration of granting citizenship at birth to German-born children of foreigners and significantly reducing the residency period for applicants for naturalization. The proposals have the overall backing of the SDP. For all this, I remain uncertain as to how committed the government itself is to the required liberalization. With the flow of asylum seekers stemmed and with falling rates in antiforeigner violence, overt pressure to revise citizenship laws will naturally diminish. But the issue of a significantly liberalized citizenship law, and within it the issue of dual citizenship, does indeed require the attention of the German government. Its success in dealing with this issue will have profound bearing on the ultimate success or failure of the reunified Germany. Germany has a pivotal role to play in the democratization and economic reconstruction of Central and Eastern Europe. It is a proximate and natural model. As such, it is in the interest of partner democracies in the West to encourage Germany to sustain active and deliberate movement on these fundamental questions. At the same time, they will be most able to provide meaningful encouragement if they are ready to recognize that they played a major role in both the construction of postwar German democracy and its evolution; to the extent that they replicated in Germany the systems that existed in their own lands, they also must recognize that their own systems, under stress, will exhibit the same problems as has the German. The great challenge is to recognize that even as the defeat of Nazi Germany saw a rearticulation of democracy in the West and of democratic ideals, through the United Nations, throughout the world, now, over fifty years later, the world is experiencing considerable political change, and democracy must change as well.

Unique among the world's nations as one that as a matter of history and national policy is committed to existing as a multicultural, bilingual democracy, Canada has much to gain from this process and much to offer in it.[14]

Notes

1. Richard Stoss, "The Problem of Right-Wing Extremism in West Germany," *West European Politics* 11: (2), 1988: 34–36.

2. Ibid.

3. Ibid.

4. Ibid.

5. Geoffrey Roberts, "Right-Wing Radicalism in the New Germany," *Parliamentary Affairs* 45(3), July 1992: 327–344.

6. Christoper Husbands, "Militant neo-Nazism in the Federal Republic of Germany in the 1980s," in Luciano Cheles, ed., *Neo-Fascism in Europe* (New York: Longman, 1991), 86–119.

7. Roberts, "Right-Wing Radicalism in the New Germany."

8. Paul Hockenos, "Free to Hate," *New Statesman and Society* 4(146), 1991: 18–19.

9. Ibid.

10. Hajo Funke and Elliot Neaman, "Germany: The Nationalist Backlash," *Dissent* 40, Winter 1993: 11–15.

11. Michael Mertes, "Germany in Transition," *Daedalus* 123(1), 1994: 13.

12. Ibid., 26.

13. Ibid., 32.

14. The bulk of the research for this chapter was completed by June 1994. Additional research was completed in early 1996 to include recent developments.

7

The Incomplete Revolutions: The Rise of Extremism in East-Central Europe and the Former Soviet Union

Aurel Braun

It would have been unthinkable just a few years ago. The Soviet empire has collapsed, the Baltic states are now independent, and democratically elected governments have taken over in Poland, Hungary, and throughout much of East-Central Europe. Dissident poets, playwrights, historians, philosophers, and union leaders are heading various governments in the region. There are unprecedented opportunities, it seems, not merely to bring prosperity and economic stability but to ensure that the early glow of freedom turns into true and lasting substance.

This is a region rich in history, traditions, and achievements and surely has the ability to fully avail itself of this historic opportunity to ensure freedom and prosperity for its inhabitants. Stretching across two continents and encompassing hundreds of millions of individuals, it has produced not only scientists and artists who have made seminal contributions to human development but also individuals who have been profoundly concerned with the issues of individual freedom. Much is at stake. If transition to pluralistic democracy is successful, this will not only ensure the betterment of the lives of the people in the region but will also help instrumentally in achieving international stability. Conversely, if this region with its enormous potential, to say nothing of its vast military (including nuclear) capabilities, should disintegrate into extremism, a new era of terribly dangerous confrontation would begin. This is why various manifestations, large and small, of extremism are so worrisome. This is why there is a need to listen to, identify, and address the early warning signals of the dangers of extremism before they imperil the transition to democracy.

But what is extremism in East-Central Europe and the former Soviet Union? And what constitutes right-wing extremism in the region? The first question would seem relatively easy to answer. When skinheads attack and severely beat an Ethiopian youth in Hungary, when Polish ultranationalists burn down the homes of Roma (Gypsies) in a small town, when Romanian ultranationalists murder some members of the Hungarian minority, when one of the highest-ranking members of the Russian Orthodox Church, Metropolitan Ioann of St. Petersburg in Russia, puts out vitriolically anti-Semitic tracts, or when ethnic "cleansing" is practiced by any of the parties in Bosnia, there is little doubt that one is witnessing manifestations of extremism.

Extremism, though, takes on many forms. The most blatant, the most violent, will usually attract widespread media attention and will likely arouse at least some public concern. Such examples of extremism, though, are emblematic of a far larger problem where much is hidden, a great deal is ignored, and important elements are little understood. There have been attempts to categorize extremism and to describe its characteristics. Some have suggested that it may be useful to distinguish among different forms of extremism: ultranational, violent, political, and religious.[1] One may certainly sympathize with these attempts at analytic clarification, but the obvious problem of overlap greatly mitigates, if it does not entirely eliminate, the benefits. All too often it is simply not possible to make a valid distinction. Moreover, political extremism has come to be widely used as an umbrella term, and therefore it may be counterproductive to try to distinguish it, for instance, from ultranational extremism. This is particularly so in the region, which is undergoing a fundamental transformation that has political, economic, cultural, and psychological elements.

It would, therefore, seem more productive to limit these distinctions to instances where a case can be made clearly for such a distinction. It would be, however, both important and productive to use a broad and comprehensive approach to the examination of extremism in order to assess its full threat to freedom and individual rights. There is a caveat here too in that it would be a mistake to so broaden the definition of extremism that it would encompass any offense to the sensitivities of a particular group. That is, there is a danger of diluting the gravity of the threat posed by extremism if one incorporates all unpleasant or contentious activities in society. The risk of such dilution is particularly significant in societies engaged in fundamental transformation where democratic norms and language are being absorbed. This is not to excuse bad or insensitive behavior in these states but rather to recognize the importance of distinguishing between that which may be classified as bad political manners or personal insensitivities and policies or speech that presents a substantive danger to political freedom and communal, ethnic, and individual rights.

A substantive threat, though, may emanate not only from blatant acts of extremism but also from more subtle, yet perhaps even more insidious, activities. Especially in a period of transition, policies and activities that inhibit the development of democratic processes and the growth of democratic institutions can gravely endanger the health of emerging democracies. Those who analyze extremism in the region, therefore, need to examine both blatant and subtle examples of extremism, for the latter, in particular, may be even better early warning signs that democratic forces may use to address and resolve issues before extremism has an opportunity to take over that society.

It is even more difficult to answer the second question, yet it is important to address it at the beginning. With the fall of communism in the region, many parties and groups have emerged that have acquired the trappings, the symbols, and the language of prewar extreme right-wing parties, some of which could justifiably be classified as fascist. There is, of course, little difficulty in classifying Nazism and fascism as forms of right-wing extremism. Those who can be clearly associated with Nazism or fascism, though, represent but a minuscule portion of the population in these countries. The violence they engage in, and the language that they employ, are certainly reprehensible, but they represent a rather limited threat for the time being. That is, though these individuals and groups do present some danger, the threat is manageable in the region. What is far more worrisome is widespread and pervasive views and policies and persistent institutional activities that are not compatible with democratic principles and norms. It is here that one runs into the problem of distinguishing between right-wing and left-wing extremism. Indeed, in many cases, particularly in Russia, the democratic forces face a threat from what is called the "red-brown" forces.

There is a history in the region of a blending of the extreme right and left. In Hungary, for instance, many members of the fascist Arrow Cross Party, which had enthusiastically cooperated with Hitler during World War II, became avid communists after the imposition of Marxist-Leninist rule. An examination of the current political scene in the region reveals many examples of this kind of unsavory blend. In Romania, the ultranationalist mayor of Cluj-Napoca and the leader of the extremist Romanian nationalist party, the Party of Romanian National Unity (PRNU), Gheorghe Funar, who has stridently denounced the Hungarian minority and restricted its rights in the city, is a former communist apparatchik. Similarly, Ilie Neacsu, the editor of the ultranationalist and rabidly anti-Semitic tabloid *Europa*, is a former lower-level communist official in Romania. And in Poland, many disgruntled former communist officials found a comfortable place in Stanislaw Tyminski's anti-Semitic right-wing Party X.

It is, therefore, not easy to distinguish in the region between left- and right-wing extremism. The problem, perhaps, goes back to the definitions, or at least the descriptions, of what constitutes right-wing extremism. It is true that in general, aggressive nationalism and chauvinism, a quest for national purity, anti-Semitism, and violence have been associated with the extreme right.

Some of the most trenchant assessments of the danger of right-wing extremism have been made by scholars from the left. Theodor Adorno, writing in *The Authoritarian Personality*,[2] cited both the personality traits of those who are fallible and susceptible to right-wing extremism as well as the economic causes for it. The problem is not only that this Marxist approach assigns a deterministic value to economic factors, a connection that simply has not been justified historically, but it also leaves the impression that personality flaws and economic shortcomings result in right-wing extremism exclusively. The analysis, therefore, suffers not only from ideological rigidity but also from oversimplification in seeking a causal explanation that is limited exclusively to personality problems and the relationship to the forces of production. There is a problem in many of the other studies of extremism, even those that do not emanate from the left, such as Seymour Martin Lipset and Earle Raab's *Politics of Unreason*,[3] which attributed the rise of right-wing extremism to governmental, institutional, and social structural problems. Here, too, the difficulty of finding a causal relationship is quickly evident. In fact, the authors frequently confuse, or at the very least are not able to clarify, the distinction between correlation and causation.

More important for the study of this region, the characteristics attributed to right-wing extremism also appear to be largely prevalent in left-wing extremism. The emphasis on nationalism, of pitting one ethnic group against another, may be traced back to Stalin, even Lenin. In fact, Lenin's use of nationalism purely as a tactic for weakening capitalist states by encouraging anticolonialism was a cynical expression of the use of nationalism. This is why, superficially, communist nationalism appears paradoxical.

More recently, the Ceaușescu regime used ultranationalism as one of the principal ways in which to consolidate power and seek political legitimacy. Yet it repressed the ethnic minorities. Minority rights, in fact, were suppressed in communist countries, and attempts at communal autonomy were often quashed violently. In the 1970s, for instance, the Tito regime violently suppressed nationalism in Croatia. Still, national communism, though it may seem to be a political oxymoron, became increasingly the norm by the 1970s and certainly by the 1980s as the Marxist-Leninist regimes sought to hold on to power in the face of collapsing political legitimacy.

Anti-Semitism is certainly not alien to Marxist-Leninist systems. One may argue whether Marxism itself in its denial of ethnicity and in its rejection of religion is inherently anti-Semitic. Marx's own writing was suffused with contempt for his fellow Jews. There is little doubt, though, that anti-Semitism was employed systematically by the regimes in the region.[4] Repeated purges, whether in Czechoslovakia in 1951 and 1952 or Poland in 1968, focused on Jews. Instead of the Streicherian caricature of the Jew, we had the Zionist employing terms such as "rootless" and "cosmopolitan."[5] But anti-Semitism fit in with what may be not unjustly labeled as an ideology of hatred. It was hatred encouraged among classes, hatred of political opposition, and dissent and hatred of capitalist states, or at least their governments.

There has been, then, similarity and a considerable degree of continuity in the political values and culture of the extreme right and the succeeding communist systems.[6] Both the extreme left and right have rejected the liberal idea of the freedom of the individual, have been opposed to limited government, and have been profoundly suspicious of the market. Both have, instead, created a romanticized notion of the individual, either Marx's unalienated, complete human being or the unspoiled, premodern, and racially pure individual. The ideas expressed in the Helsinki Accord, and later in the CSCE (Conference on Security and Cooperation in Europe) Paris charter, have remained anathema to both groups. Therefore, an exclusive concentration on "the extreme right" in this region will present a distorted picture of the danger of extremism.

Great danger, in fact, emanates from any all-embracing, all-resolving doctrine, whatever its nature.[7] Identifying the threats to the development and entrenchment of democracy is far more important than categorizing them as left or right wing. It is not that this would be a useless preoccupation but rather that the effort at categorization may understate the danger, perhaps in part due to ideological biases. Not that it is impossible to justifiably label some activities as part of right-wing extremism, particularly various forms of nationalism that are exclusivist and also insist on racial purity. In most cases, though, the danger in the region is more complex, and "right" and "left" are more muddled. Therefore, this chapter is more concerned with identifying the problems of extremism in general and the danger that it poses to emerging democracies rather than focusing exclusively on policies, activities, and attitudes that can be categorized unequivocally as right-wing extremism.

Though it may be impossible to clearly identify the causes of extremism in the region, there are many indicators of both the symptoms and the disease. The manifestations of extremism vary significantly from state to state given the variety of historic experiences, the differences in political evolution over centuries, the level of economic development, ethnic composition, and the perception of external enemies. And although economic determinism and facile socioeconomic explanations do not suffice, some developments indicate at least the existence of strong causal relationships. For although the recognition of the enormous diversity in the region is essential to understanding the uniqueness of certain developments in specific states, it is equally important to appreciate that the states in East-Central Europe and the successor states in the former Soviet Union do exist in a specific, historic epoch and a particular geographic region.

The Region

Although the transition from Marxism-Leninism appears—as in the case of Czechoslovakia 1989—the image of a "velvet revolution," the legacy of common ties and political experience over more than four decades, particularly when these experiences were so radically different from that of countries in Western Europe, is bound to have a profound regional impact on postcommunist development. It is certainly not my intention to argue that extremism in the postcommunist states is merely a legacy of the communist regimes. Extremism, particularly in its right-wing form, had a powerful hold in Eastern Europe as well as in czarist Russia before the imposition of communist regimes. And if one measures the length of communist rule in these states compared to their entire history, such rule, in most instances, represents but a relatively small portion of those histories. Yet this kind of quantitative contextualization of communist rule distorts its importance.

First, Marxist-Leninism is a totalizing political system. That is, it not only sought to control the political and economic heights in a country but engaged in a vast experiment in social engineering. That it ultimately failed does not mean that it did not, or could not, have a long-term impact. It sought to reach into every facet of every individual's life, it demanded total allegiance and faith, and it sought to achieve a radical break with the past. And though there were growing differences among the various communist states in the region, they shared crucial political, economic, and social features. These commonalities were reinforced by a web of bilateral and multilateral ties, including the Council for Mutual Economic Assistance (CMEA) and the Warsaw Pact.

Second, it is extremely important that the Marxist-Leninist system was in place in Eastern Europe and for most of the history of the Soviet Union while profound democratic changes were taking place elsewhere in the world. During the postwar period, when communist regimes were largely imposed in Eastern Europe and kept in power through the threat of force, the three principal axis powers, (Western) Germany, Japan, and Italy, became vibrant, successful democracies. Moreover, fascism collapsed in Spain and Portugal, as did the dictatorship of the colonels in Greece. The rest of Europe embraced democracy and markets. Eastern Europe and the Soviet Union were left out of an enormous process of democratization and, in the case of the former, a process of Europeanization.

Therefore, there is very little likelihood that these states could emerge unscathed. To use an imperfect but, I think, still useful analogy, psychologically abused children may not necessarily show the effects of their abuse, but as adults, will carry the scars. And if the problem is not recognized, the damage can be particularly dangerous to the well-being of the individual. This is why, I would contend, an examination of extremism, including right-wing extremism, in the region has to start with the impact of Marxist-Leninism.

First, I will look at the communist legacy and, second, closely tied with that, the development of a "victimized majority" mentality. Third, I will examine the problems of transition and its impact on the development of extremism and how they, in turn, reflect the difficulties of identifying and dealing with extremism throughout the area.

Legacies of the Communist Era

Zbigniew Brzezinski, President Jimmy Carter's national security adviser between 1976 and 1980, has been harsh but not inaccurate in his assessment of the communist era, particularly regarding the way in which it addressed political, ethnic, and economic issues. He asserted that "forty-five years of history were wasted. Communism didn't deal with any of these problems. It froze them. It aggravated them. It prevented the development of a more mature political culture, of the sort that flourished in Western Europe. There's a lot of catching up to do."[8] In their quest for total power communist regimes ran roughshod over individual interests and all institutional forms. Though communist regimes were supposedly dedicated to the ultimate liberation of the individual, in practice the individual was a mere cog in the dialectical machinery that was to bring about the ultimate salvation of humankind.

These regimes, then, had an enormous impact on the role of the individual in society, on the psychology of the people, on political discourse and perception, on law and legality, and on status. With the exception of Czechoslovakia, none of the states in the region were democracies prior to the rise of Marxist-Leninist governments to power. Therefore, notions of individual rights were ill developed at best and too often ignored by the authoritarian states. But it would be a mistake to suggest that the region was characterized uniformly by dark reaction and that the czarist regime (which had been overthrown in the first revolution by social democrats in 1917) was nothing but a form of "oriental despotism." There were oft-expressed desires for individual rights, particularly by members of the intelligentsia, but on occasion even by bureaucrats in Hungary, Poland, Romania, and Bulgaria during the interwar period. In Russia, already in the nineteenth century, the liberal B. N. Chicherin and the great writer I. S. Turgenev argued for individual rights and a meaningful, legal order.[9] It is true that most of those who advocated individual rights in the region were, and remained, on the margin of political power. Yet although liberalism ultimately did fail, there was, before communism, some receptivity to the notion of individual rights.

When the communist regimes took over there was no middle ground for individual rights. Since only those in the vanguard party had acquired the necessary revolutionary consciousness, the rest of the population, that is, the vast majority, had to be educated, manipulated, and, if need be, coerced onto the "correct" road of social development. These regimes, however, demanded more than mere obedience. Indeed, they sought to scientifically restructure the psychology of the individual. This operated both at the ideological level and as grand policy. In terms of realpolitik, the regimes had to ensure that they maintained power without any possibility of opposition. Therefore, Lenin set up a structure of control that Stalin perfected and put to even more horrendous use through the widescale employment of terror. In the post-Stalin period, coercion became more subtle but no less pervasive. Control was enforced with the atomization of society. Individuals were prevented from organizing in groups, dissent was harshly dealt with, a system of rewards and punishment was employed to manipulate the intelligentsia, and mistrust designed to paralyze political opposition was sown throughout society through the pervasive use of an enormous network of informers. Though the severity of coercion differed from state to state, particularly by the 1980s, the model of coercion was fundamentally the same.

The individual, therefore, was made to feel unimportant, unable to reach fulfillment except through some communal action sanctioned by the ruling party. Any resort to law for the protection of rights, opposition to the communist parties, and even interest groups were all systematically discouraged. There was a penchant for gigantism with huge government buildings and factories or extraordinarily wide boulevards meant not merely to impress but to intimidate the individual. Therefore, the individual who emerged from socialist rule was traumatized and mistrustful. For such an individual it would be particularly difficult to deal with the vagaries of a market and with the uncertainties of a competitive political and economic system. Such individuals would naturally tend to have an exaggerated fear of disorder and chaos, a tendency for dependence, and an inclination to accept a "strong hand." All this would make the creation of a viable civil society with respect for individual rights more difficult.

As Brzezinski stated, communism inhibited the development of a more mature political culture. Although all societies entertain some myths, under communism the entire political and social system was imbued with bizarre and ultimately harmful ones: As well documented by Milovan Djilas, these included extraordinary economic progress supported by manipulated statistics; a free and universal availability of all key social services that, in fact, fostered an extraordinarily corrupt system of access; and social leveling and equality that, in fact, ignored the rise of a new class.[10] By the 1980s these myths, particularly in Eastern Europe, were increasingly challenged. Nevertheless, in the four decades in Eastern Europe and more than seven in the Soviet Union during which people were forced to publicly reiterate these myths, they had an effect. For instance, envy of enterprise and wealth have become deeply rooted. So is the belief that wealth can be acquired only by dishonest means.

It is not that the population was unaware of corruption and privilege in communist societies. But the privileged elites went to great lengths to camouflage their lavish lifestyles. The special health clinics where Western-style medical care was available were hidden in nondescript buildings. The stores, where consumer goods that the vast majority of people could not even dream about were available at remarkably low prices, functioned in restricted-access areas of buildings with no storefronts or signs to indicate their existence. The camouflage worked, in some ways, similar to that on airline flights where a curtain between first class and economy is closed as soon as the airplane levels after takeoff. People in economy class know that behind those curtains the higher-fare passengers are being served drinks and offered food well before they are. The curtain is more of a psychological barrier than a physical one. It is meant to ensure that privilege does not become too blatant, a source of humiliation or irritation to the less privileged.

With the fall of communism, the curtain was removed. Consumption now is conspicuous. Store windows are filled with high-priced, high-quality goods available to anyone who has the money. For the vast majority of the population, which cannot, at least yet, afford such goods, this can be both shocking and humiliating. For societies raised on class hatred or at least envy, these developments can be particularly frustrating.

The same problem applies in the case of crime and corruption. Marxist-Leninist societies were extraordinarily corrupt. This involved not only economic corruption, which was certainly widespread, but the most fundamental type, that is, the corruption of rights and principles. Elites, whether Nicolae Ceaușescu and his family in Romania or Todor Zhivkov in Bulgaria or Josip Tito in Yugoslavia, not only led lavish lifestyles but could dispose of opponents or rivals at will. There was no responsibility to citizens or to courts or law. The secret services arrested and tortured individuals without fear of repercussions. Somewhat paradoxically, although no citizen was safe from arbitrary arrest in any of these states, they felt safe on seemingly crime-free streets. Today, crime has become decentralized. It is in the streets, and there's more of it, or so it seems. One must not forget that previously under communism, street crime was not reported; family violence and organized crime were all viewed as exclusively diseases of the West. Still, the perception is what is important. Although reliable statistics show that in most postcommunist states crime is at a much lower level than in the West, the local view is that crime is now rampant.

The emerging democratic governments, therefore, need to address the problem urgently. But because their tenure is often fragile and they confront myriad problems, their responses are often inadequate. When the people in these states contrast the myth of law and order in the old communist states with the new myth of rampant crime and corruption, many may become susceptible to the blandishments of demagogues who promise order and safety.

This is not to suggest that there is a danger of a reversion to communism. That ideology has become too discredited. As the head of the Polish Democratic Left Alliance, the successor to the communist party in Poland, Aleksander Kwasniewski declared bluntly, if inelegantly, on the eve of the elections in September 1993 (in which his party won the largest number of seats in parliament), "If someone in our party proposed a return to a central command economy, he would have to be expelled, not for being a communist, but for being an idiot."[11] Rather, people may be susceptible to a type of populism that defies the left-right categorization. For as Václav Havel has argued, the danger is not that of a return to hard-line communism but rather the growth of increasingly authoritarian rule in certain of the postcommunist states. Moreover, as he stated, some former communists have traded in Marxism for nationalism.[12] Given that nationalism was either suppressed or manipulated for political purposes by communist regimes, it is not unlikely that it could be combined in its most negative form with extreme populism rooted in the mystique of Slav, Hungarian, or Romanian *volk*.

The third element that is likely to present problems for democracy and individual rights relates to the characteristics of political discussion in these states. Before communist regimes came to power in the region (with the exception of Czechoslovakia and the provisional government in 1917 Russia), political discourse and opposition were restricted. Nevertheless, there was at least some limited debate. Certain predemocratic conditions were extant. The communist regimes removed whatever possibility there was for legitimate political opposition and discourse. Lenin's institution of democratic centralism and the elimination of factions set the stage. Stalinism then completely closed the door. The post-Stalin period allowed for periodic flexibility but not on the central issue of the primacy and the infallibility of the Communist Party. Though some have argued, wrongly, that interest groups developed later in the Soviet Union and in Eastern Europe,[13] in fact these regimes, as noted, created mechanisms specifically designed to prevent effective formation and functioning of interest groups. Even in the East European states where formally (as in Poland) a coalition of parties were ruling the country, these were in essence fronts. The communists made all the important decisions.

Therefore, whatever prospect there was for the evolution of the notion of legitimate political opposition was stifled by communist rule. In sharp contrast, in Western Europe, whether in Germany, Italy, or Spain, there was a rapid evolution toward the acceptance of "the loyal opposition" and an emphasis on the art of political compromise, so essential to a healthy functioning democracy. This was entirely missing east of the Elbe River. The painful legacy can be seen now throughout the region in the difficulty that parties, whether in government or opposition, have in accepting the legitimacy of opposing views. It can be seen in the fragmentation of democratic parties because of the difficulty of tolerating factions. And it is in evidence in the difficulty of reaching political compromise, which is so essential for pushing through effective programs. Certainly, progress is being made in several of the East European states and, to a more limited extent, in Russia on accepting the legitimacy of political opposition and on recognizing the need for political consensus and compromise. But there is a great deal of fragility. And that fragility and uncertainty create fertile ground for the rise of extremism.

Fourth, the role of law remains a crucial question in the postcommunist states. One of the most important features of democratic societies and pivotal to protection of individual rights is that an independent legal structure permeates, and indeed dominates, society. In the precommunist era, certainly in most of these states, legal rights were restricted and there were all too many examples of reprehensible political and nationalistic extremism. Even in nineteenth-century Russia, though, law still served to shape society.[14] Communism represented a radical break not because it eradicated a healthy legal system but because it obliterated any substantive legal structure. This may seem odd in light of the extensive court system in all of these states and the enormous body of law that was passed. But what is important to understand is that in Marxist-Leninist societies, the role of law was, as Leonard Schapiro rightly asserted, purely an instrument in the hands of the ruling elite, the vanguard party.[15] Therefore, not only could the individual not seek protection for what in democratic societies is considered basic human rights, but it was not meant for the individual to have any such protection. This flows logically from the acceptance of one all-embracing, all-resolving doctrine where a regime seeks total control over the population. This instrumental use of law is characteristic of all totalitarian systems whether of the left or the right. A well-rooted legal system and a resolute and independent judiciary to safeguard it are seminal to the protection of individual rights and the countering of the ever-present danger of extremism in all societies.

One, therefore, cannot think of a more important task for the postcommunist government than to create competent and independent judiciaries that are committed to the protection of basic rights. Progress is bound to be difficult. As one East European wag put it, "There are no judges who were born after 1989." It is important, though, that these states should make every effort to bring lawyers into the judiciary who have not been tainted by service as activists in the communist party or as agents of the secret service. It would be essential as well to provide constitutional protection for the independence of judiciary. The government should then publicly demonstrate its willingness to accept that independence. The latter would signal to the judges who remained on the bench from the communist period that they needed to act independently and that their role was no longer to serve a political master and to the people that a new political and legal order was in place.

There is, therefore, a need for a two-track approach. Substantive changes have to be made, and the public's perception of the judiciary as merely an instrument of party power needs to be altered. This has been happening in several of the East European states such as the Czech Republic, Poland, and Hungary. And even though there are many problems in these states, there is a great deal to be encouraged about. Unfortunately, progress has been far slower in Russia, Romania, and Bulgaria. In Romania, most of the judges seem to have been rotated rather than replaced, and there is evidence of continued political interference in the judiciary.[16] Not surprisingly, there is little confidence among most Romanians that they have recourse to the judiciary for the protection of human rights or that the judiciary can act as a bulwark against the rise of extremism. In Bulgaria, progress has also been unsatisfactory. For instance, in June 1994, the National Assembly at the behest of the Bulgarian Socialist Party (the successor to the Communist Party) passed a controversial law stipulating that everyone occupying a top position in the Bulgarian judiciary needs to have served at least five years as a judge or a prosecutor.[17] This was done, it seems in part, to oust the country's present top jurists, the chairman of the Supreme Court, and the prosecutor general. But it may also ensure that only judges appointed by the communist regime could now retain office. This is a major step backward that not only politicizes the judiciary but signals to the population that this is not the body they can rely on as a barrier to extremism.

Fifth, communism created not merely a new class of the privileged but also status societies. Income differentials were not critically meaningful in societies where everything depended on access. To gain access, the required currency was influence, not coin. That influence, in turn, was derived from one's position. A rigid hierarchy provided some psychological security even though it demanded absolute obedience to one's superior—at least until that individual could be displaced. Conversely, there was little regard for the interests or dignity of subordinates. Since the only road to success led through the party, fundamental principles of fairness and merit were simultaneously violated. This arrangement, therefore, did not provide justice, but at least it created the impression of security and orderliness.

Individuals consequently had to content themselves with status. Holding on to that status both as an identity and as a necessary factor in surviving in such a grossly distorted political, economic, and social system, was crucial. In a sense it was a classic dilemma of honor versus principle, of liberty versus security. As fundamental transformations take root in these societies, though, there is bound to be widespread loss of status and, with that, frustration and disorientation. Moreover, for many, an increase in income or even the availability of a far greater variety of goods will not compensate for the loss of status, the right to command, and at least the illusion of respect. These individuals, again, are likely to be very susceptible to the manipulations of leaders who promise a new status based on nationalism or racial purity or a seemingly predictable economic structure. They may become avid believers in scapegoat theories explaining their loss of status. Since these individuals are not likely to regain their status as their countries progress toward democracy, they need to adapt to new conditions. This is rather difficult, though not impossible, especially for the younger ones. Those who do not could well fill the ranks of the extremist parties, which all democratic societies must strive to keep in check. There is a danger, moreover, that when all these frustrations, including loss of status, come to a boil, the majority may feel itself to be the victim.

The "Victimized Majority"

It is both fair and accurate to contend that the majority of the people in all the Marxist-Leninist societies in the region were victimized by the political elites. As we have seen, state control was pervasive and the violations of human rights were systematic. But to assume a *"majority as victim"* mentality in the postcommunist period presents significant dangers to the process of democratization throughout the region. And at the very least, it facilitates and more likely fuels the rise of political extremism in a number of ways.

First, a "victimized" majority will tend to absolve itself from the need for normal political intercourse and compromise. That majority may be a parliamentary or an ethnic majority, often both. The crucial element is attitude—a kind of self-righteous-victim category. Bronislaw Geremek, one of the key democratic leaders in Poland, voiced his concern in a recent personal interview that this kind of "majority as victim" mentality leads to a rigid ideological expression of politics instead of consensus building. It can be categorized, he suggested, by a blind anticommunism that reflects a lack of trust in and hatred of all politicians. This kind of anti-politics, Geremek rightly pointed out, can be easily exploited by demagogues.

Authoritarian and Leninist traditions combine, moreover, to create a tendency to refuse to accept differing points of view or to acknowledge the legitimacy of other political perspectives. The result is that often, as was the case under Lenin, factions are not tolerated within parties. Consequently, there is a fragmentation of the democratic movement into many ineffective parties that are unable to work together to successfully push through a viable political and economic program. This has been the case, especially in Romania and Russia. In Russia, with the approaching parliamentary elections, various democratic blocs and parties tried to consolidate and form coalitions in summer 1995. By September, however, the centrifugal forces were prevailing. For example, Yabloko, led by Grigorii Yavlinsky, who views himself as the democratic alternative to President Yeltsin, could not work with any other grouping, and consequently both the Social Democratic Party and the Republican Party left his group before the December elections, which proved so damaging to the democratic forces. Although there have been some improvements with attempts at building coalitions of democratic forces—"big tent" parties as in Slovakia and even in Romania—such efforts have enjoyed rather limited success and the resulting coalitions have been fragile. As each group feels victimized, it is difficult for it to engage in what is the essential art of political compromise, and rigid, self-righteous stands can become the precursors to extremist positions and policies. Furthermore, increased frustration as fragmented parties are unable to bring about sufficiently rapid recoveries leads to cynicism about democracy itself. It enhances the sense of continued victimization of the majority and makes those voters so much more susceptible to the blandishments of demagogues.

Second, there is throughout much of the region a dearth of political introspection and of any objective reexamination of the past. This is, of course, not unique to the region, but in a period of transition from a totalizing political system to democratic pluralism, the development of a mature political culture and an understanding of the past are important.

Any period of transition, of course, is difficult. There is a great deal of dislocation and the possibility of disorientation. It should not be surprising, therefore, that there would be some yearning for calm, orderliness, and some relief from the shock of change. What is striking, though, is the level of nostalgia and the magnitude of the illusion about the past in many parts of the region.

In the former German Democratic Republic, for instance, which since unification has been the recipient of one of the largest transfers of wealth in history (from Western Germany), there is a growing sense of dissatisfaction among large segments of the population that cannot be explained by high levels of unemployment. In fact, there has been an enormous improvement in the economic conditions of the people; even those who are unemployed have a higher level of purchasing power than they did when they were working under the communist regime. The sense of dissatisfaction, I would suggest, is due in large part to a lack of understanding among the people of the depth of political, economic, and moral bankruptcy of the former communist regime. The transformation happened quickly, and there have been few, and certainly not very successful, efforts at explaining to the population the disaster left behind by the communists. There is, therefore, nostalgia that sometimes takes on bizarre forms. Many eastern Germans have professed to miss the "closeness" of East German society. This is particularly odd given that we now know that there was systematic spying of friends on friends and even spouses on spouses. With the exception of some election campaigns, though, there has been a disinclination to delve into the past. Attempts to do so were both clumsy and dangerous. "Lustration," that is, exposing those who had collaborated with the secret services, entailed many risks and frequently backfired. Files that were left by the communists were often incomplete or deliberately doctored. Furthermore, it had been the habit of communist secret service organizations to make use almost exclusively of noncommunists in seeking information on dissidents or dissident organizations because communists would have little credibility. Therefore, individuals who sometimes engaged in rather innocuous actions were compromised and their political prospects were destroyed upon the revelation of information in secret service files. This is precisely what the communists in Poland gloatingly told the Solidarity activists when the new Solidarity government proposed to release secret service files.

More than just nostalgia for the communist era, all too often there is a glorification of a precommunist past. New myths are woven about authoritarian and extremist right-wing regimes and movements. As Adam Michnik suggested, many of these prewar governments were inherently chauvinistic.[18] The fondness expressed in some circles in Poland for the authoritarian Pilsudski regime or in Hungary for the Horthy government is taken to even greater extremes by praise for the fascist Arrow Cross movement under Ferenc Szalasi in Hungary and that of Ion Antonescu in Romania.

Even in the more stable states such as Poland and Hungary, this is dangerous romanticizing of a repressive past that can inhibit the development of a democratic political culture, encourage the worst antidemocratic instincts of the population, and make people more vulnerable again to the preachings of demagogues who are so readily willing to take advantage of any political, economic, or social crisis. It presents a particularly grave threat in countries where the movement toward political democracy has been much slower, such as Romania, Croatia, or many of the successor states in the former Soviet Union. Though democratic forces have spoken out occasionally, this has not been done often, or vigorously, enough. The French political scientist Olivier Duhamel is largely correct when he says, "In the East cruel and old-fashioned ideas are not confronted by a vigorous reaction stemming from any democratic or civil ideal."[19]

Third, the "majority as victim" approach can also have a very deleterious effect on the rights of minorities and on domestic stability. Majorities who continue to consider themselves as victims are not likely to be sensitive to the needs of minorities. Only Poland comes close to being an ethnically homogeneous state (and even there the minorities constitute up to 5 percent of the population). All the others have substantial ethnic minorities. By stressing a kind of self-righteous victimization, majorities can develop what some have called a type of social autism where governments representing such majorities end up overemphasizing the positive cultural attributes of that majority. Thereby they reinforce a sense of exclusion among minorities even if it is not their intention to do so.

Far too frequently, though, the "majority as victim" approach—the politics of identity—results in deliberate government policies to exclude the ethnic minorities from power. Even in countries where considerable progress has been made in democratization and marketization and, specifically, in Latvia and Estonia, the majorities have severely restricted the rights of ethnic minorities and in many instances outright disenfranchised them. In Latvia, for instance, where the 1990 census showed that there were 900,000 Russians to 1.4 million Latvians, the vast majority of the Russians (close to 600,000) have been excluded from citizenship.[20] Initially, the harsh laws passed by the Latvian parliament established a quota system that would have allowed only 2,000 resident aliens per year to become citizens. It was only as a result of great pressure from Russia and the threat to stop withdrawal of Russian troops from Latvia that the Riga government decided to amend, in July 1994, its extremely restrictive new citizenship law.[21] In early 1995 the parliament passed some amendments to simplify the procedures for naturalization.[22] But many obstacles remain to citizenship in Latvia. By the time of the October 1995 election only about 40 percent of the Russian-speaking minority managed to qualify for citizenship. Thus almost one-third of Latvia's adult population has remained disenfranchised.[23] In Estonia as well, very tough restrictions on citizenship were softened only somewhat under Russian pressure.[24] Yet on April 1, 1995, Estonia put into effect a new law, bitterly opposed by the noncitizen community, that imposed a new civics exam on top of the already mandatory language exam, thus again making access to citizenship more difficult.[25] In Romania, discrimination against the large Hungarian and Romani (Gypsy) minorities is continued in part because progress toward democratization has been very slow. All too often the government of Ion Iliescu has engaged in an exercise of avoidance when it came to the kind of domestic transformation that would lead to real democratic pluralism and markets. That is, concessions to democracy would be made by the government whenever Romania sought entry into international organizations such as the Council of Europe or sought aid from funding agencies such as the International Monetary Fund (IMF). After Romania received approval of IMF funding and gained entry into the Council of Europe, new restrictions were placed on the right of the Hungarian minority. It is little wonder that there is a strong sense of betrayal both in Romania and among many Western observers and organizations. In 1994 the Council of Europe, in a report drafted by Friedrich Koenig and Gunnar Jannson, criticized Romania not only for overly slow reforms but also for its failure to bring its policies on ethnic, religious, and sexual minorities up to European standards. It was particularly critical of the treatment (including curbs on education in their mother tongues) of the Hungarian, Romani, and other ethnic minorities.[26] There is little chance for legal recourse for minorities. In 1995, the Romanian Helsinki Committee Human Rights Center pointed out that the judiciary system in Romania is yet to be reformed and that legal impediments to legal redress are enormous.[27]

Since its early days in 1990 the Iliescu regime through its antidemocratic policies contributed to the recovery of ultranationalism in the country.[28] Not surprisingly, the regime became more dependent on extremist forces of the left and the right, both of which have been ultranationalistic. It pursued national policies or acquiesced to local ones that questioned the patriotism of ethnic minorities, rejected the right to dissent, and characterized any attempts to preserve ethnic cultural rights as a conspiracy to "victimize" the Romanian majority. This red-brown coalition of extremism, moreover, not only received a sympathetic hearing from the government but saw some of its wishes on restricting minority rights translated into policy.[29] In summer 1994, Romania's Chamber of Deputies approved a new law on education over the protests of the ethnic Hungarian minority, which contended that its cultural and educational rights would be gravely endangered.[30]

Furthermore, the government at first appeared to acquiesce to the provocative decision by Gheorghe Funar, the extreme nationalist mayor of Cluj-Napoca, the largest city in Transylvania, to order an archaeological dig to proceed in the city's Union Square, where the statue of King Mathias, a venerated Hungarian king, stands (it is also listed by the UN educational cultural and scientific organization as a protected monument.) The dig was a crass cover for Funar's political agenda, namely to prove the "Romanianess" of Cluj. The commission that the Bucharest government set up reached a compromise that satisfied no one and outraged the Hungarian minority.[31] But the Iliescu regime had to pander to the right-wing extremists of the Party of Romanian National Unity (PRNU) despite the risk of international condemnation and of endangering improved relations with the new Hungarian government—the Romanian government of Iliescu and Vacaroiu had become too dependent on the votes of the Funar faction. By August 1994 the Iliescu regime caved in further to the right-wing extremists of the PRNU. Prime Minister Nicolae Vacaroiu gave that party two cabinet positions, the Ministry of Agriculture and the Ministry of Communications.[32]

By 1995 a member of the extremist PRNU was minister of justice of Romania. He then declared his intention to initiate procedures for banning the party representing the Hungarian minority, the Democratic Alliance of Hungarians in Romania (DAHR).[33] The ruling Party of Social Democracy of Romania (PSDR) could not discipline its coalition partner. But the Parliamentary Council of the European Council denied the PSDR membership in the social democratic parliamentary group.

Following summer 1995 the government made some concessions on the new (1995) education law that angered its xenophobic and anti-Semitic allies from the extreme right. The PSDR then decided to sever its links with the Greater Romania Party (GRP). And in October 1995 the prosecutor general asked the Senate to start procedures for lifting the parliamentary immunity of Senator Corneliu Vadim Tudor, the leader of the GRP, so that he could be prosecuted for slandering the president.[34] Yet the split may be tactical and temporary. Tudor could be a competitor to Iliescu in the 1996 presidential elections and the latter may wish to capitalize on the potential domestic and foreign benefits of distancing himself from the right-wing extremists. Iliescu, however, has a history of *transcending* moderation as soon as it is no longer advantageous; thus unless Romania puts down much stronger democratic roots, the danger of extremism will not dissipate substantially.

Although minority rights are endangered in all states where majorities view themselves as victims, the situation is particularly acute in those countries where democratization is proceeding more slowly and less successfully. This is the case with the Greek minority in Albania, where the leadership of President Sali Berisha has become increasingly authoritarian. The Greek minority has scant hopes of legal protections: Berisha, in a blatant attack on the independence of the judiciary, on September 21, 1995, had his pliant parliament dismiss the chairman of the Court of Cassation.[35] In a further blow to democracy, he moved to enact lustration legislation that would prevent many members of the opposition parties from running for office in parliamentary elections in April 1996.[36]

Slovakia's treatment of its Hungarian and Romani minorities during Vladimir Meciar's tenure leaves much to be desired. For part of 1994 in Slovakia, conditions improved for the minorities after the fall of the Meciar regime. With the reelection of the *former communist* Meciar and his Movement for a Democratic Slovakia, conditions worsened again. Emblematic of his government's attitude to minorities is the language law that was promulgated in November 1995. Though many of its provisions are vague, it makes Slovak the only official language of the country, restricts the public use of other languages, and virtually excludes the courts from the process through which sanctions will be imposed.[37] It is little wonder that Slovakia's Hungarian minority, numbering 600,000–750,000 (representing 12–15 percent of the population), has felt threatened, as do many of the minorities in several of the states in the region. In sum, "majorities as victims" can lead to scapegoating, the avoidance of political reality, and, ultimately, dangerous delays in the development of democratic institutions and processes. Again, it cannot be too strongly emphasized that in these states we are witnessing a process of transformation rather than the achievement of full democratic conditions.

The Transition

There is little doubt that despite the enormous diversity of the region, the best protection against extremism, including right-wing extremism, remains the successful transition to pluralistic democracy—to a political system where there is a well-rooted legal order and a strong and independent judiciary to safeguard it. Such success, though, is dependent on at least four major domestic factors: momentum, direction, implementation, and sensitivity.

1. Momentum is vital. Even successful, stable democracies in the West must continually struggle against negative political elements, usually extrem-

ist forces on the periphery that can endanger both civil society and liberties. During a process of fundamental transformation in the region (yet to be completed anywhere), momentum is the first priority. Momentum, though, should not be confused with speed. The speed of transformation certainly is important, but it may vary. What is also crucial is sustainability. To sustain momentum governments need to maintain a rhythm of change. Once a government achieves a consensus and gains a mandate, it must clearly indicate that the goals of transformation are immutable. It must demonstrate continually the political will to implement the enunciated program. And last, it should always guard against the danger of the forces of reaction (which in some countries are present in great force) trying to regroup and block the transformation. Maintaining the momentum of transformation would deny these forces that opportunity.[38]

In order to maintain momentum, governments might indeed make certain tactical changes as long as the strategy of transformation is not imperiled. But a lack of political conviction in democracy, cynical compromise, and confusion present enormous dangers to successful transformation. This is quite evident in states such as Romania or Croatia. There Ion Iliescu and Franjo Tudjman, respectively, control, to use a Marxist term, the commanding heights of the political system and run, despite using the language of democracy, largely unreconstructed authoritarian governments. The loss of momentum can also be crucial in other states such as Slovakia, where the democratic forces that took over following the resignation of the authoritarian Prime Minister Vladimir Meciar on March 14, 1994, had at least a brief window of opportunity to try to entrench democracy and markets before new elections could and did bring the old guard back to power.

It is also important not to draw the wrong lessons about transitions. It has been argued by some that rapid economic transformation, which in Poland was called "shock therapy," generates inordinate pain and can fuel extremism. Yet a closer examination of transformations in Eastern Europe shows that this is simply not correct. Those countries in Eastern Europe that pressed ahead with transition most rapidly and consistently suffered the smallest economic cost. Procrastination, by contrast, raised the price.[39]

2. Direction ties in with momentum. Governments cannot be ambivalent about the ultimate goal of political pluralism and respect for individual rights. Attempts to find a third way between pluralistic democracy and Marxism-Leninism have invariablay failed. Vacillation during a period of transformation from the old totalizing systems would result in a most dangerous detour.

To maintain direction, democratic forces must articulate their vision of a pluralistic democratic future as something that is universally desirable. It is essential for the leadership to convey to the population that it is not witnessing the imposition of some external system, such as the communists imposed in Eastern Europe or a system enforced by a ruthless minority, such as the Bolsheviks imposed in the Soviet Union. Rather, leaders should convey that pluralistic democracy, in its various forms (as evidenced by diversity in the West) but nevertheless united on key principles, is a natural outgrowth of human desires everywhere. In order to achieve this pivotal task, however, the democratic forces must have both the skills and the opportunity to communicate with the people.

Unfortunately, many of the intelligentsia who are dominant in the democratic leadership have proven to be ill equipped to communicate the democratic vision to the people at large. Historically there has been a wide gulf between the intelligentsia and the people in the region. This was greatly reinforced by the communist tendency to alternately persecute and pamper the intelligentsia while excluding them from real power. Furthermore, ongoing government attempts to control the press in many of these states have restricted access, at times, to the most articulate exponents of democracy. Even in instances where democratic forces gained control, occasionally they have exhibited an unfortunate tendency to deny access to those with opposing political views (even if sometimes such views were also democratic), particularly access to national television and radio networks.

3. The implementation of a democratic vision has been difficult. After all, as it has been said, it is not possible to find judges and generals born after 1989. Therefore, during the period of transition, many members of the nomenklatura are bound to hold positions of power. But here, too, movement is vital. That is, there must be a clear sense that the intent is to fundamentally transform government institutions, especially the judiciary, the military, and the security forces, along democratic lines. The government must demonstrate an adherence to democratic behavior that includes a commitment to impartiality and a sense of responsibility and responsiveness.

Free, competitive elections and the adoption of democratic institutions are necessary conditions for the democratic transformation. However, they are not sufficient conditions. It requires continuing progress and vigilance. The latter means that the forces of democracy must listen to the early warning signals of danger from extremist forces. And this takes us to the fourth point—sensitivity.

4. Sensitivity, of course, is not merely a matter of language, though given the history of mistrust and persecution in the region and the fragility of the process of transformation, it would be wise for governments to be careful not to raise new fears or stir up old hatreds. Sensitivity involves governments being aware of the need to be proactive, to heal, and to build political confidence in all of these states. Under the Marxist-Leninist regimes, societies were atomized, and the vast network of informers, together with an efficient security service, ensured that people would have difficulty in organizing an effective political opposition to the rule of the vanguard party. Although

these regimes are no longer in place, the legacies of fear and mistrust have remained. Therefore, it is incumbent on the new governments to engage in political confidence-building measures to persuade the people that the new political order that is being created is meant to ensure their full rights as citizens. It is essential not only to formulate policies that help the process of democratization but also to ensure that there is an appearance of equity and legality. For even the appearance of governmental unfairness or illegality will likely shake popular confidence in the democratic process.

Furthermore, governments should be especially sensitive to minorities. They need to accept that ethnic minorities have two kinds of rights: individual and communal. Members of ethnic minorities have the same concerns about individual rights as all other citizens of the country. But as an ethnic group they also have communal concerns—preserving culture, language, and traditions. To guarantee these communal rights, governments may need to make some extra efforts to reassure ethnic minorities, and for this they need to gain the consent and the understanding of the majority.

Conclusion

Focusing on three states: Russia, Poland, and Hungary—provides a better understanding of both the specific problems and the difficulties throughout the region. Russia, stretching over eleven time zones, has inherited not only half the population of the Soviet Union but most of its natural resources and scientific talent. Despite its difficulties it remains the preponderant economic and military power in the region as well as a global nuclear superpower. Although democratic success in Russia will not guarantee its victory elsewhere in the Soviet successor states, the failure of democracy in Russia would most certainly gravely imperil it in those states. Poland is important not only as the most populous East European state but also as the first state to successfully abandon Marxist-Leninism and to introduce "shock therapy." It also happens to be the East European state that currently is at the front of the economic recovery with the highest growth rate. Hungary, in many respects, is the most Westernized and Western-oriented East-Central European state. Moreover, it was the first to successfully introduce reforms (Czechoslovakia's attempt was crushed by Soviet troops) that sought to produce a kinder, gentler communism—only to have this "half-step" massively rejected by the population as soon as the threat of Soviet intervention disappeared. Are Russia, Poland, and Hungary, then, as three pivotal states in the region, doing enough to ensure the victory of the forces of progress over those of repression?

The tasks outlined in this chapter are all difficult to accomplish and yet they are central to the success of a democratic transition in the region. It certainly is not the case that states engaged in a fundamental transformation should be held to higher standards than Western democracies. But precisely because the transformation is so difficult, and the risks so significant, the democratic forces must energetically endeavor to take advantage of a historic window of opportunity. The extremist forces can be defeated, or at the very least, marginalized and contained.

Notes

1. J. F. Brown, "Extremism in Eastern Europe and the Former Soviet Union," *Radio Free Europe/Radio Liberty* [herafter RFE/RL] *Research Report* 3(16), April 22, 1994: 1–4.

2. Theodor Adorno et al., *The Authoritarian Personality* (New York: Harper and Row, 1950).

3. S. M. Lipset and E. Raab, *The Politics of Unreason: Right-Wing Extremism in America 1790–1970* (New York: Harper & Row, 1970).

4. Paul Lendvai, *Anti-Semitism in Eastern Europe* (London: MacDonald, 1971).

5. Paul Hockenos, *Free to Hate* (New York: Routledge, 1993).

6. Ibid., 14.

7. See the brilliant work by Leonard Schapiro, *Russian Studies* (New York and London: Penguin Books, 1988), 16, 17.

8. *New York Times*, June 14, 1992.

9. Schapiro, *Russian Studies*, 60–65.

10. Milovan Djilas, *The New Class: An Analysis of the Communist System* (New York: Praeger, 1963).

11. *New York Times*, September 16, 1993.

12. *Le Figaro*, January 23, 1995; *Globe and Mail*, February 8, 1995.

13. Jerry Hough, *How the Soviet Union Is Governed* (based on Merle Fainsod's book, *How Russia Is Ruled*) (Cambridge, Mass.: Harvard University Press, 1979). For a devastating counterargument see Schapiro, *Russian Studies*, 21–23.

14. Schapiro, *Russian Studies*, 23–25.

15. Ibid.

16. Michael Shafir, "Romania: Toward the Rule of Law," *RFE/RL Research Report* 1(27), July 3, 1992: 30–40.

17. *RFE/RL News Briefs* 3(25), June 13–17, 1994: 17–18.

18. Louisa Vinton, "Solidarity's Rival Offspring," *RFE/RL Report on Eastern Europe*, no. 38, September 21, 1990.

19. *New York Times*, March 21, 1993.

20. *New York Times*, July 24, 1994.

21. Ibid.; *East European Constitutional Review* 4 (2), Spring 1995: 16.

22. *East European Constitutional Review* 4 (2), Spring 1995: 16.

23. *Economist*, October 7, 1995, 62.

24. *Economist*, August 27, 1994, 48.

25. *East European Constitutional Review* 4 (2), Spring 1995: 20.

26. *RFE/RL News Briefs*, May 16–20, 1994: 20.

27. *New York Times*, August 31, 1995.

28. Tom Gallagher, *Romania After Ceausescu: The Politics of Intolerance* (Edinburgh: Edinburgh University Press, 1995), chs. 3, 4.

29. Michael Shafir, "Romanian Politics in Turmoil," *RFE/RL Research Report* 3(29), July 22, 1994: 1–6; Michael Shafir, "Ethnic Tension Runs High in Romania," *RFE/RL Research Report* 3(32), August 19, 1994: 24–32.

30. Shafir "Ethnic Tension," 24–26.

31. Ibid., 31.

32. *Le Monde*, Paris, August 23, 1994.

33. *East European Constitutional Review* 4(2), Spring 1995: 22.

34. Open Media Research Institute, *Daily Digest*, Prague, October 26, 1995.

35. *East European Constitutional Review* 4(4), Fall 1995: 2–3.

36. Ibid., *Economist*, October 7, 1995, 58–59.

37. *East European Constitutional Review* 4(4), Fall 1995: 31; *Economist*, December 2, 1995, 54–56, and December 23, 1995, 6; *Globe and Mail*, Toronto, December 6, 1995.

38. Aurel Braun, "Political Developments in Central and Eastern Europe," in *U.S. Relations with Central and Eastern Europe*, Congressional Program vol. 9, no. 4, August 22–28, 1994, the Aspen Institute.

39. Keith Crane, "The Lessons of Transitions," in *U.S. Relations with Central and Eastern Europe*, Congressional Program, vol. 9, no. 4, p. 7.

8

Russia: The Land Inbetween

Aurel Braun

Russia is not merely the legal successor of the USSR. It remains a great power. In territory it is still far larger than any other state in the world, and it has a population almost twice as large as that of unified Germany. It possesses enormous natural resources and remains a nuclear superpower. Domestic developments in Russia, therefore, are bound to have a profound effect not only on regional development but on international stability itself.

Russia is certainly suffering a great deal of turmoil. The twin traumas of fundamental transformation and the loss of empire have had a profound effect. There is a tendency, at times, to view Russia as a pathetic giant immersed in its domestic troubles, engaged for the foreseeable future in a kind of domestic political cannibalism that disqualifies it as a principal player in the international system and diminishes it even as a regional force. This view, often expressed in Eastern Europe but on occasion even by some Western leaders, is mere caricature. Moreover, it represents a dangerous misunderstanding of the nature of the links between Russian domestic and foreign policy. It tends to disregard the impact of the past, distorts the assessment of the present, and leaves little hope of understanding the future of Russia.

There are difficulties in analyzing the momentous developments in Russia. It is frequently said in Russia that the country's past, the past itself, is unpredictable and therefore who would dare predict the future? Yet Russia is not necessarily more inscrutable than any of the other postcommunist states. And therefore, before one examines the problems and the dangers of extremism in Russia one should also be aware of the tremendously positive developments that have occurred during the past few years.

Much has been accomplished in Russia. It appears that the economy is beginning to stabilize. Certainly this has been the view of the International Monetary Fund (IMF), and it is the position of the government of Viktor Chernomyrdin. Despite some reservations, the IMF approved large-scale funding for Russia in 1996.[1] Inflation, which appeared in danger of spinning out of control, declined from 17.8 percent in January 1995 to 3.2 percent in December, the lowest rate since prices were freed.[2] The 1996 budget, which imposed limits on total spending and the deficit, was approved by parliament and signed into force.[3] Privatization has been viewed by many Western analysts as one of the great successes of transformation. Padma Desai, for instance, has gone as far as to claim that privatization in Russia was better planned and more effective than in Poland and Hungary.[4] It certainly appeared to be the biggest transfer of property to private hands in history.[5]

Furthermore, the severe decline in Russia's gross domestic product (GDP) seemed to have bottomed out in the second half of 1995.[6] In fact, the Organization for Economic Cooperation and Development (OECD) projected a positive growth of 2.5 percent for the Russian economy in 1996.[7] It should also be noted that the decline in the Russian GDP since 1992 may not be as severe as official figures indicate. There have been problems not only with the accuracy of the data but also with the methodology for assessing changes in production. Jeffrey Sachs, for instance, has suggested that if actual household behavior was examined instead of crude indexes of real wages, the assessment of changes in the living standards of the populations of the postcommunist states would be radically different.[8] Others have suggested that GDP is a poor indicator of changes in transition economies and that if other indicators are used (in particular, power consumption), the official economic statistics for Russia suffer from a gross downward bias with perhaps a threefold overstatement of the downturn in aggregate economic activity.[9] Whatever the debate over the statistics, what is undeniable is that a revolutionary change has taken place in Russian economic development in that the economy has become depoliticized to a degree that would have been unthinkable just a few years ago.[10] Better economic performance and economic opportunities in turn can aid in the political and social transformation from a totalizing system to democratic pluralism.

This is not to say that there may not be questions regarding the accuracy of Russian statistics or that political and social stability is a simple, direct function of economic progress and stability. Perception of improvement, however, is important. The obverse, a belief that things are getting worse economically, combined with other negative political or social indicators, has tended in the past to produce a kind of dangerous synergy that ultimately did lead to unrest.

It is possible, though, to go beyond these statistics to find encouragement. There is a flourishing of differing political opinions in Russia that would have been unthinkable just several years ago. Political groupings and parties express an enormous range of views and publicize them in myriad publications across the country. People are free to practice their religion without state interference. Numerous human rights groups operate freely.

Quite encouragingly, given the ecological disaster left by the communist regime, there has also been a rapid growth in the environmental movement throughout Russia. Freedom of movement has been dramatically liberalized, with Jews and other ethnic groups free to emigrate. Russian citizens can now travel widely abroad on vacations, to attend conferences, or to study. And what just a few years ago would have seemed impossible happened on June 22, 1994, when Russia's foreign minister, Andrei Kozyrev, signed a Partnership for Peace Agreement with NATO.[11] A recognition of these positive developments is necessary to an understanding of the changes that are taking place in Russia and as a balance to the problems confronting that state.

A tendency toward complacency and political apathy and inertia, though, can be just as dangerous as a failure to recognize the enormous positive developments that have taken place. In May 1994, for instance, former acting prime minister Yegor Gaidar warned of the rise of right-wing extremism in Russia. He called ultranationalist Vladimir Zhirinovsky "the most popular fascist leader in Russia" and urged the government to prevent his rise to power.[12] Despite predictions that Zhirinovsky and his Liberal Democratic Party would lose most of their support, in the December 1995 elections, the party came in second with 11.2 percent, ahead of any centrist or liberal party, and garnered fifty-one seats in the Duma (the lower house of parliament).[13] At least as worrisome, though, has been growth in influence of a barely reformed left. In the December 1995 election the Communist Party of the Russian Federation (CP-RF) received the largest percentage of votes, 22.3 percent, and gained by far the largest number of seats (149 out of 450) in the Duma.[14] Moreover, in alliance with two largely unreformed parties of the left, the Agrarians and Power to the People, the communists now control a majority of the seats in the Duma.

The situation in Russia remains fluid. The president rather than parliament has the preponderance of power. But President Boris Yeltsin is ill and may not survive his second term. Moreover, there are structural and procedural difficulties that are bound to have a seminal impact on the rise of extremism. Therefore, to assess the danger, I propose to examine five areas: the problem of momentum; the "majority as victim" syndrome; the status of minorities; laws and legality; and dealing with refugees.

Momentum

A qualitative assessment of the enormously positive developments that have taken place in Russia since the fall of communism rests on the assessment of the momentum of transformation. This, in turn, involves political, social, and economic aspects that often are intertwined. Again, the concept of transformation is crucial. Though there is a need for vigilance against extremism in all democracies, the movement from a totalizing system to pluralistic democracy is dependent on ensuring that reactionary forces are kept off balance and are marginalized. Conversely, a loss of momentum gives an opportunity for such forces to regroup. In Russia this would most likely involve a combination of red-brown groupings trying to organize, expand, and then stifle a democratic process that remains highly fragile.

The danger to democratization cannot be measured merely by the number of reactionary organizations, ultranationalists, proto-communists, or virulently anti-Semitic publications. And there are numerous extremist parties and organizations and publications.

With much greater political freedom since the collapse of the Soviet Union at the end of 1991, extremist parties and organizations have multiplied exponentially.[15] Several, though, were founded during the tenure of Mikhail Gorbachev as Soviet leader. For instance, the National Patriotic Front "Memory" (Pamyat), a highly anti-Semitic organization, was set up in 1986 on the basis of the Historical-Patriotic Association "Memory."[16] Since then the organization has split into several groups ranging from Vasilev's Pamyat, which openly described itself as monarchist and fascist, to Popov Brothers' Group, which promotes national Bolshevism. Russian National Unity (a militarized organization that has espoused the cult of Adolf Hitler), one of the more influential groups, is based in Moscow under Aleksandr Barkashov. Some smaller groups, such as Patriot, led by Aleksandr Romanenko, were set up in 1988 in St. Petersburg with a platform based on national Bolshevism, anti-Semitism, and a belief in a Judeo-Masonic plot.[17]

Though most of these parties appear to be centered in the two largest Russian cities, Moscow and St. Petersburg, in fact, they blanket the entire country. The National State Party, for instance, is based in Chelyabinsk. The Kuban Council of the Kossacks is based in the city of Krasnodar, and the Patriotic Party of Russia (or Nekrasov's Party), a small, highly anti-Semitic and anti-Western nationalist group, is based in the Siberian city of Tomsk.

There have been attempts to categorize these parties, and some have suggested that it may be possible to separate them into three groups: the monarchists, the neocommunists, and the aggressive Nationalist Parties.[18] This categorization is useful up to a point. But then it begins to break down. Groups such as Vasilev's Pamyat, the core of the original Pamyat, is not only monarchist and fascist but also profoundly nationalistic. One of the best-known parties, the neo-Nazi Russian National Unity (RNU) of Aleksandr Barkashov, is a spinoff from Vasilev's Pamyat. Another well-known ultranationalist party, the National Republican Party of Russia, was based in part on one of the wings of the Leningrad (now St. Petersburg) branch of Pamyat. It not only has monarchist connections but, despite its official anticommunist stand, has participated in the setting up of the National Salvation Front (but left it in summer 1993), which is led by a hard-line communist, Sazhi Umalatova.[19] Some parties, such as the People's Liberation Movement

"Hours," led by the well-known television commentator Aleksandr Nev-zorov, are openly nationalist and monarchist.[20] A breakaway wing, the People's Patriotic Movement, follows a more procommunist line. Thus, these parties and groups range from fascism and monarchism to paganism. Just about any form of extremism now has some organized form. The most common thread, though, is that of ultranationalism, anti-Semitism, and statism.

As disconcerting as the existence of these myriad unsavory groupings and parties may be, it should not be entirely surprising. Centuries of oppressive rule, which reached its most pervasive form during the more than seventy years of Marxist-Leninist control, inhibited the expression of normal political desires and fueled myths, conspiracy theories, and political paranoia. This makes even more remarkable the degree of success that democratic forces have enjoyed so far in Russia. Yet it also speaks to the dangers. The absence of what Zbigniew Brzezinski has called a mature political culture makes coping with the problems of transformation so much more difficult. The extremist forces may be able to exploit what have been called "bridge issues" and move into the key areas, the central arena of Russian politics.[21] In a political culture where there is a deep-rooted distrust of any form of opposition to authority, the moderate parties then would have a lot of difficulty in making their case.[22]

Is there cause for alarm? This would depend, in part, on how successfully the extremist parties and groupings are able to exploit fissures in the political system and the weaknesses of the democratic forces. There are already two large parties (and more groupings and parties are coalescing and emerging) that can be rightfully classified as extremist that appear to present a more immediate threat than the small groupings described before to the process of democratization in Russia: the Liberal Democratic Party (LDP), led by Vladimir Zhirinovsky, and the Communist Party of the Russian Federation (CP-RF), led by Gennadii Zyuganov.

Zhirinovsky's LDP was spectacularly successful in the December 1993 parliamentary elections. It gathered almost one-quarter of the votes and became the second largest grouping in the lower house of the parliament, the State Duma. And as noted, in the December 1995 parliamentary election, though the LDP's support was reduced by half, it still emerged with the second largest number of popular votes. The party is well organized and it clearly commands a core of loyal voters. To much of the world, Zhirinovsky comes across as a bombastic demagogue whose frequently erratic behavior casts serious doubts on his sanity. Yet in Russia (although I would argue that his party's chances of taking control in the future remain slim, as are his prospects for the presidency), he remains a major force and is much feared by democrats.

In a long, personal interview in Moscow, Zhirinovsky came across as a calm, calculating, manipulative politician and a most dangerous adversary of pluralistic democracy.[23] Although he tried to sound eminently reasonable and sought to portray himself as a moderate dedicated to the interests of the people, his responses regarding several issues pivotal to democratization left little doubt about his profoundly antidemocratic convictions. His explanations of his position on democracy, on the political role and rights of the people, on fascism, and on private property were clever. One could see how, in a country with little democratic experience where the people are suffering from the pain of transformation, his views would have widespread appeal.

In the interview, Zhirinovsky immediately declared himself in favor of democracy. However, he also stressed that democracy was for the future. He declared, "We had a winter of seventy-five years, a very strong, very cold winter. Now some people would like summer. It's impossible without spring. We need spring to prepare for the summer, the summer of democracy."[24] There would, of course, have to be a transition period. In his estimation, this would take ten years. During this "springtime for Zhirinovsky" interlude, he asserted there would need to be in place a strong, central government that would guide the people.

The people, therefore, were simply not ready to govern themselves. In essence, Zhirinovsky was rejecting the notions of popular sovereignty. Ironically, then, though he disparaged communism, he clearly has the same kind of Leninist attitude toward the people, namely that during the transition period to a higher stage of development, only the ruling elites understand the issues. Therefore the people could not possibly be trusted during this period to manage their own affairs.

On the question of fascism, Zhirinovsky again was clever but disingenuous. He professed to be an antifascist. As to the definition of fascism, he replied that it meant German fascism, which in turn laid claim to German racial superiority. Since he would never contend that the Russian people or Russian nationalism was superior, he concluded that, obviously, he could not be considered a fascist.

Last, on the issue of private property—which relates, in the period of transition, not only to economic matters but also to changes in political rights and attitudes—his answer was similar to that on democracy. Yes, he was very much in favor of private property, but only in the long term. Most likely, his grandchildren would understand private property as his son gradually acquires some of it. But for the time being, Zhirinovsky claimed it was impossible for people to understand it. "Our psychological situation goes against it," he declared.[25] In the meantime the state sector would need to be protected, particularly the military industry.

Superficially at least, Zhirinovsky's positions may not seem overly threatening. He merely seems to be advocating a preparatory stage leading to a future "summer of democracy." One can see how this would appeal to people who fear the turmoil of change and feel insecure during a period of transition. But socialism, which was also portrayed to the people as a period of transition, was a phase that lasted for more than seven decades, involved the murder of millions and the imprisonment of tens of millions, and ultimately brought social and economic disaster. So what Zhirinovsky is proposing is hardly new. But it is up to the democratic forces to counter these old authoritarian ideas effectively.

Alla Gerber, a journalist and a member of parliament in Russia's State Duma has been among the relatively few individuals in that assembly who has had the courage to stand up to and criticize Zhirinovsky, his party, and other antidemocratic forces. She is a dignified and courageous woman whom I had a chance to interview at length in Moscow in May 1994.[26] She was extremely concerned about the fortunes of democrats and democracy in Russia. As a member of Russia's Democratic Choice, the party headed by Yegor Gaidar, she has been in the trenches every day, working not only in parliament but also with human rights organizations. Her occasional despondency over the political situation was extremely distressing. At one point she suggested that although there are democrats in Russia, there is no democracy, so fragile is the process of democratization. She is extremely frustrated by the inability of the democratic forces to unite. She contended that primitive ambitions among democrats were destroying their effectiveness and hoped that the danger of fascism might function as a unifying force. As matters stood, anything put on the agenda by Russia's Democratic Choice, she said, would be immediately attacked by the antidemocratic majority in the State Duma, with Zhirinovsky and his ilk labeling it as merely "democratic fascism."

There is, in fact, a great deal of disarray among the democratic forces. Political parties, particularly democratic ones, have little if any role for the time being in the exercise of power. Yegor Gaidar tried to organize a broader coalition of reformers to support Boris Yeltsin in the 1996 presidential campaign. Due to dissension and apathy (the latter being one of the most powerful political forces in Russia), he had to postpone the holding of the organizing congress for a presidential party from September 1994 to spring 1995.[27]

But by 1995 Gaidar was estranged from President Yeltsin. They differed on the pace of transformation and the war in Chechnya. Following the strong showing of the communists in the parliamentary elections in December 1995, Gaidar called on Yeltsin to withdraw as presidential candidate and give some other leading democratic candidate a better chance of rallying the anticommunist vote.[28] Grave concerns about the effectiveness of the democrats was also expressed by some democrats working in the executive branch of government. For instance, Tatiana Smirnova, the first secretary of the Department of International Humanitarian and Cultural Cooperation of the Ministry of Foreign Affairs, considered Zhirinovsky extremely dangerous, clever, and intimidating.[29] She was very perturbed by the fact that relatively few members of parliament were willing to confront Zhirinovsky. Also, she felt that the population was exhausted and therefore more likely to be politically apathetic and defenseless in face of the activities of the extremist forces.

The head of the Department on International Humanitarian Cooperation and Human Rights of the Ministry of Foreign Affairs of the Russian Federation, Teimouraz Ramishvili, an urbane and articulate individual deeply committed to democracy, also expressed in an interview in Moscow his disquiet about the effectiveness of the forces of democracy. He contended that the fight was, in many respects, between westernizers and Slavophiles, the latter favoring different forms of authoritarianism.[30] Momentum was critical, in his view, for successful democratization, and he was clearly worried that the democratic forces were losing that momentum.

Concern and perhaps even alarm at the ineffectiveness of the democratic forces in the face of extremism were also echoed by several human rights activists, including Boris Altshuler, the chair of the Movement Without Frontiers group in Moscow, Vladimir Raskin, the executive director of that movement, and Alexei Smirnov, the director of the Moscow Human Rights Center.[31] Boris Altshuler, in particular, contended that the ministries were generally passive in the face of extremism and bureaucrats were often sympathetic despite the clearly fascist activities of such extremist leaders as Aleksandr Barkashov. They were also concerned that the human rights groups and democrats in general had few resources to track the links that the extremists had outside of Russia. Despite these problems the human rights groups are continuing their efforts to foster democracy. Moreover, there are vigorous leaders, such as Boris Fedorov, the head of Forward Russia and the former finance minister of Russia (he resigned in January 1994), who fearlessly oppose Zhirinovsky and remain courageous proponents of democracy in Russia.

The democrats' position, though, is weakened by the so-called centrists or pragmatists, who deem themselves "democrats," and by the forces on the left, not just by the attacks from right-wing extremism. The prime minister himself, Viktor Chernomyrdin, a former "red director," now runs day-to-day affairs in Russia. Though he portrays himself as a democrat and loyalist of President Yeltsin, democrats contend that although he is correct in claiming the latter, he is yet to prove that he is justified in claiming to be the former. Alla Gerber expressed the view of many democratic leaders that Chernomyrdin has a "very different" mentality from democrats.[32]

Among others who claim to support democracy "with a difference," one could number Sergei Shakhrai, an extremely ambitious deputy prime minister who lost his position as nationalities minister in May 1994 but continues to entertain presidential ambitions. His closest associates spoke of his desire for finding a third way (which, given the experience of the East Europeans, has proven to be not only a futile but also a dangerous detour) between democracy as advocated by "the liberals" and authoritarianism.[33] His associates admitted that on such issues as the stability of society, the role of families, law and order, respect for the state, and a strong stand on nationalism, Shakhrai came closer to Zhirinovsky.[34] Though there are, of course, very important differences between Shakhrai and Zhirinovsky, the strong authoritarian strains exhibited by Shakhrai make him, at best, a very doubtful democrat. The danger that Zhirinovsky presents emanates not only from his ability to play on the worst instincts of a people who have little experience of democracy but also from the resonance of his views among influential individuals who believe themselves to occupy the political center, who claim to be democrats, but who essentially are far more comfortable with authoritarian rule.

"No enemies on the left" is not a slogan that Russian democrats can afford. Though Marxism-Leninism as a political order has lost its legitimacy in Russia, communists retain important positions at the local level, and communist organizations remain potent. In fact, the CP-RF, led by Gennadii Zyuganov, is by far the country's largest political organization, claiming more than 550,000 members and 20,000 primary units.[35] It has 149 seats (out of 450) in the State Duma, but with its allies it is just a few votes short of a majority. The party has even greater strength in the strong network of local branches. Its claims that it is moving toward social democracy are rather dubious, though more recently the party has become politically more flexible.

The party has flirted with the extremist forces of nationalism. For instance, Zyuganov, in the first year of the CP-RF's existence, was both cochairman of the extremist National Salvation Front and involved in the red-brown opposition to President Boris Yeltsin.[36] After the collapse of the Soviet Union he served for a year on the editorial board of *Den* (Day), a newspaper widely viewed as fascist and anti-Semitic.[37] The party began to reach out to former vice president Aleksandr Rutskoi, following his release from prison (he had been jailed for his role in the 1993 coup) after a parliamentary pardon (in winter 1994). The CP-RF became more nationalistic and, in moving toward supporting Rutskoi's presidential ambitions, was linking up with someone who exhibited some of the worst characteristics of the red-brown coalition. Rutskoi repeatedly called for the restoration of "Great Russia" within the boundaries of the former Soviet Union by using "whatever means necessary."[38] Second, it is important to remember that in the October 1993 coup, Rutskoi, who proclaimed himself the president of Russia, appealed to crowds to engage in pogroms—"kill all journalists, etc."[39] In the crowds surrounding Rutskoi there were numerous armed guerrillas with swastikas on their sleeves. (Rutskoi and his party, Derzhava, [Great Power], failed miserably in the parliamentary elections of December 1995.[40])

By 1995, Zyuganov and the CP-RF did not need Rutskoi (a spent force). The party became a hybrid of "red patriotism" and extreme-left populism. In fact, it co-opted much of Rutskoi's and a portion of Zhirinovsky's constituencies. The communists increasingly began to occupy the territory of the nationalists, praising the Orthodox Church and calling for the restoration of the Soviet Union (voluntarily, they claim).[41] Nevertheless, the party and Zyuganov proclaim their support for reform and assert their commitment to social democracy. Despite Zyuganov's polished performance in meetings with Western leaders and businessmen, grave doubts remain about the communists' intentions. In two pivotal areas, ideology and economics, the communists have sent out, at best, mixed signals.

Zyuganov has stated that he did not wish to return Russia to the Brezhnevite system, and it is obvious that the status quo ante 1991 cannot be restored. There is, however, the issue of Leninism as a guiding ideology. Access to archives reveals unambiguously that Lenin was committed to totalitarianism, to the use of terror as an instrument of the state, and to the class struggle.[42] Russian democrats have abandoned any illusions about Lenin and Leninism. Put simply, Leninism and social democracy are just not compatible. Yet Zyuganov and the communists, despite some moderation in their language, remain, it seems, committed to Leninism in the wake of the December 1995 elections. Zyuganov proclaimed that he would look to Lenin for inspiration and that his ideas were extremely relevant for tackling Russia's problems.[43] In 1995, moreover, the party passed a resolution that declared that not only was the victory of the "bourgeoisie" not final but the twenty-first century would inevitably witness the triumph of Leninism.[44]

In economics the party has become more restrained in its condemnation of private property (as former factory directors enrich themselves), but in allying itself with the Agrarian Party it is opposing the privatization of the moribund collective and state farm system that still encompasses most of Russian agriculture. During the election campaign the communists, in fact, had made hostility to privatization one of their main planks. In the Duma, the communists not only put their man Gennadii Seleznev in the speaker's seat but captured three of the most influential committee chairmanships—those on legislation, security, and economic policy—after the December 1995 elections.[45] They have used their position to push for more subsidies and for more social welfare expenditures. More ominously, the communists prodded the Duma to amend the title of the commission set up to investigate privatizations for 1992–1996 by adding the McCarthyite phrase "and for the establishing of the responsibility of officials for its negative results."[46] Though the communists cannot take Russia back to the command system, it is also evident that they have no sympathy for the market system.

In fact, overall economic progress in Russia seems more tenuous than the earlier overview would tend to indicate. There is considerable evidence to suggest that the economic momentum for transformation itself may be endangered. Unfortunately, for economic transformation to succeed, there has to be progress on allowing ineffective and wasteful companies to go out of business. And subsidies must be drastically reduced, or at times eliminated altogether, in industry and agriculture in order to bring about economic stability (Chernomyrdin has moved slowly at best).

There are several problems with economic transformation in Russia. As the disastrous showing of the democratic forces in the December 1995 elections indicates, there is a widespread belief in Russia that reform has failed. That this perception ignores the enormous achievements in many areas of economic transformation does not make it any less relevant. It is ironic of course that in Russia there has been a growing belief that the transformations need to be slowed down just when there is increasing evidence not only that there is a close relationship between economic liberalization and political freedom but that the more quickly a postcommunist country proceeds with economic liberalization, the better chance it has to speed growth and check the inflation rate[47] and thereby ultimately diminish pain. Second, there has been real pain and people in Russia are suffering, income differentials have grown, pensions have fallen, and hundreds of thousands of workers have not had their salaries paid for months. By 1995, 23 percent of the Russian population (34 million people) had money income below the minimum subsistence level.[48] Though officially, unemployment stood at 2.24 million in mid-1995, according to Ministry of Economy data (cited by Radio Rossii), the number of unemployed and partly employed totaled 10 million, or more than 13 percent of the working population.[49] In a country that had no unemployment under communist rule, this is a particularly painful and humiliating experience.

Third, many mistakes were made. For instance, what appears to some as economic stability is likely to be undermined by the enormous interenterprise debts that keep companies afloat but consume the vitality of the economy as a whole. According to what are viewed as conservative government estimates, interenterprise debts reached 30 trillion rubles ($15 billion) by August 1994, and First Deputy Prime Minister Oleg Soskovets declared that the problem was so acute that "it must be solved without a single minute of delay."[50] There is little evidence that this is being done. Soskovets, who was heading Yeltsin's reelection campaign, not only asserted that "many mistakes were made in the course of reform" but attacked the substance of Western-style economic reforms.[51] It also appears that Prime Minister Chernomyrdin, who has proclaimed repeatedly the need for fiscal responsibility, does not have an adequate understanding of, and certainly not the willpower, to allow large, obsolete enterprises to go under. This was quite evident as far back as May 1994, when he outlined his economic vision in which he claimed a newfound attachment to the market.[52]

Furthermore, even though Chernomyrdin has been less than enthusiastic about providing subsidies to the military industrial complex, he has found new allies in state and collective agriculture. Massive subsidies are moving in that direction. Indeed President Yeltsin himself has pledged to bolster agriculture subsidies at Chernomyrdin's urging.[53] This has had the twin undesirable effects of impeding urgently needed budget reductions and of stifling— or at the very least significantly inhibiting—the desperately needed privatization of agriculture. It is little wonder that the OECD in summer 1994 suggested that the Russian government's policies reflect a lack of fiscal and monetary control.[54] The banking crisis of fall 1994 did have a salutary effect on the macroeconomic policies of the Chernomyrdin government, and the first half of 1995 did look promising. But in the fall, with parliamentary elections approaching, Chernomyrdin opened wide the spending taps and made lavish and clearly unaffordable promises to both industry and the population.[55]

Fourth, privatization, often cited as the great success of the Russian economic transformation, is more problematic than it would first appear. Although an estimated 120,000 enterprises have been privatized,[56] many of these assets were concentrated in the hands of a few, either the "red directors" or the banks. Often the changes yielded little improvement in efficiency, and the "private" firm has been back quickly to feed at the public subsidy trough. Moreover, many of the privatizations, especially in the energy sector, involved de facto management buyouts below market prices.[57] In the eyes of much of the population, privatization has been equated with corruption, with legalized theft. As such, privatization to many Russians represented a failure not only of marketization but also of democratization.

Criminal activity has been strongly linked with privatization.[58] Not only have some become terribly rich through inside deals at a time when there is widespread visible poverty in Russia but organized crime has infiltrated many businesses. Though many Russian entrepreneurs are honest, hardworking, and innovative and although the privatization program overall has yielded great benefits, the public perception is negative. Extremists, especially the communists, have been very effective (as the December 1995 elections showed) in exploiting this resentment.

Fifth, current economic trends in Russia give cause for concern. Yeltsin's apparent decision to base his presidential reelection campaign on denouncing both communism and his own government's past economic policies threatens the country's economic transformation or, at the very least, creates significant doubt and erodes credibility. Following the December 1995 elections, Yeltsin forced the resignation of Anatolii Chubais, the minister in charge of the economy and a man who had given the Russian economic transformation credibility and also happened to be the last deep reformer in the government. Chubais was a convenient scapegoat, but Yeltsin's choice of replacement suggests that

Chubais's forced resignation was more than a symbolic move. Vladimir Kadannikov, the new deputy prime minister, was in charge of Avtovaz, a disastrously mismanaged automobile manufacturer that illustrates much of what is wrong with old-style Soviet management.[59] Though Kadannikov may choose to follow many of his predecessor's policies, his approach to economic development appears to differ significantly. His call for a prompt change in economic philosophy to making the government responsible for supporting industry suggests a radical turn that (if implemented) not only would fuel inflation by handing out new subsidies but would endanger macroeconomic stability and stall or break the momentum of economic transformation.

Mixed signals or outright threats to privatization also present danger to the transformation. For instance, though Yeltsin has maintained that he remains committed to privatization, his interior minister, Anatolii Kulikov, calls for the nationalization of some top companies[60] in the wake of the December 1995 elections. Further, the probe of privatization ordered by the new communist-dominated Duma is bound to have a chilling effect on the whole process.

Further, Yeltsin's election promises and wage concessions at a time when fiscal responsibility should be the order of the day can only damage economic transformation. His concessions to striking coal miners and his promise to pay all back wages[61] may help him in his reelection campaign, but even if he wins, the economic damage and the loss of momentum will be difficult to repair and may further fuel the chaotic political and social conditions in Russia.

Last, another factor at play in the preservation of momentum and the restraint of extremism is the press. The much welcomed increase in the freedom of the press, however, has also unleashed a virtually unrestrained stream of viciously anti-Semitic and ultranationalistic writing. By October 1993 there were about 180 ultranationalistic newspapers and magazines published in Russia, many of them rabidly anti-Semitic.[62] At the end of 1993, after parliamentary elections, ultranationalistic associations and papers were relegalized and a number of new extremist issues were also started. The most important paper that can be justifiably characterized as fascist, *Den* (Day), was renamed *Zavtra* (Tomorrow). It is profoundly anti-Western and anti-Semitic. It is edited by Aleksandr Prokhanov, who significantly also happens to be very close to Rutskoi. These papers are widely disseminated and help fuel paranoia about minorities and Western plots. Many clearly enjoy significant financial support from a variety of extremist groups and even from a number of church leaders. There has been little effort on the part of the state prosecutors to use antihate legislation to restrain attempts to whip up national hatred and divisions. It is little wonder, therefore, that many democrats perceive a shift of momentum toward extremism. Consequently, many democrats all too often seem to oscillate between depression and despair.

The Majority as Victim

A loss of momentum is combining with an increasing sense of majority victimization. That is, Russians, as the predominant ethnic group in Russia and as formerly the hegemonic ethnic group in the Soviet Union, tend to feel a tremendous sense of deprivation. First, they have suffered the trauma of losing an empire. Second, in what is proclaimed to be a very wealthy country, the majority live impoverished lives that are no longer camouflaged by the glorification of state achievements. Third, about 25 million ethnic Russians who remain outside the borders of the Russian Federation have lost their predominant status and have often been humiliated by the loss of citizenship or displacement from their jobs by the ethnic majorities in the new successor states. There is, therefore, a great susceptibility on the part of the majority to view themselves as losers, as victims in a transformation where they find themselves at the end of the queue for benefits. This susceptibility, then, is heavily played upon by extremist politicians, not least of all by Vladimir Zhirinovsky and Gennadii Zyuganov.

Zhirinovsky's approach to the issues shows how cleverly he has manipulated the vulnerabilities of the people. For instance, in our interview he denounced nationalism as a negative force. Yet he declared that nationalism was a must for Russia because it needed to defend itself. "We are against this nationalism, but in Russia now we must use the same weapon—nationalism."[63] The Russian people, he argued, are the main victims and, as such, are entitled to *restitution*. Moreover, they bear no responsibility toward ethnic minorities because it is the majority, according to Zhirinovsky, that is suffering the most.

Furthermore, he argued that all the Soviet ethnic groups but the Russians received some benefits upon the dissolution of the Soviet Union. Only Russians wound up with nothing, relegated to a northern territory with ten months of winter where, he claimed, they have little chance of succeeding. He implied, therefore, that there was a vast conspiracy to deprive the Russian people of what was rightfully theirs. Consequently, the problems in the region could not be resolved unless the "legitimate" rights of the Russian majority were satisfied.

This is the approach of many others in extremist groups, including Rutskoi's. What is particularly disconcerting, though, is that this sense of majority deprivation is also evident among the more moderate forces. These contemplate the more peaceful reintegration of the successor states of the Soviet Union. Though at the level of furthering general economic development, this is understandable, it nevertheless betrays a nationalistic streak when even democrats have a great deal of difficulty in accepting the breakup of the Soviet Union. They are, of course, concerned about discrimination against Russian minorities in the "near abroad." But as a consequence they are too reluctant to confront the ultranationalists and thereby become insufficiently sensitive to the problems of the ethnic minorities.

It is not that democrats are not aware of this danger. As Alla Gerber worried, the notion of a majority as victim feeds the impulse for extremism, and that, in turn, is a key issue in Russia.[64] Under Soviet rule there had been a very reassuring sense of belonging and of security, she contended, a popular belief that everyone was part of a great state. This is part of the myth about the past, but such a sense of loss makes it easy, according to Gerber, to move from the subconscious to the conscious—and this, then, creates possibilities for extreme nationalism. The extremists welcome the opportunity to keep the majority in fear, fear of the outside world (particularly the West, with democracy portrayed as a purely Western construct) and fear of ethnic minorities within as a fifth column.

The Status of Minorities

With more than 30 million individuals belonging to ethnic minorities in Russia, some of whom have not only territorial attachments but also claims to sovereignty, ethnic tensions remain an explosive problem. Many democrats have recognized the need to deal with the ethnic issues. In a country with more than 100 nationalities it is incumbent, particularly on the majority group, composing roughly 80 percent of the population, to show sensitivity toward the individual and the communal needs of all minorities. That, of course, is an ideal democratic vision that is difficult to fulfill under the best of circumstances. In a period of transition, particularly when the democratic forces appear to be losing momentum and when the majority feels that it is the primary victim, prospects for peace and conciliation diminish.

In Russia, though, extremist forces have been particularly adept at exploiting the biases and fears of the majority in order to demonize the minorities. Zhirinovsky, for instance, as he was making a case for a greater Russia to solve the problems of nationalism by creating a multinational state based on citizenship, argued simultaneously that as a matter of self-defense, Russians had to protect themselves from the criminality of "outside nationalism." It was these outside criminals, he contended, that caused the increasing problems of crime inside Russia: "It's all from the Caucasus, from the Trans-Caucasus camp, and not our inside criminals."[65] In Russia the term "Caucasians" usually is a code name for the ethnic minorities from the southern part of the country, in particular the Chechens. Thus for Zhirinovsky it was not a case of the majority discriminating against or being insensitive toward small ethnic minorities but rather one of the bulk of the population needing to defend itself against systematic criminal attacks by subversive minorities. Extremist Chechen leaders did not help the cause of their people when they encouraged, or at least condoned, brutal terrorist actions such as taking Russian civilians hostage in Budyonnovsk and Kizlyar.[66] General Russian revulsion at such acts merely reinforced negative stereotypes.

The mistrust of the non-Slavic people from the Caucasus has a long history in Russia. Many of them are visible minorities. Extremists have gained a great deal of political mileage by using them as scapegoats. Newspapers are full of stories of "Caucasian" criminals. Even the mayor of Moscow found that he could increase his popularity by ordering the expulsion of traders from the south who did not have residency permits for the city. Thus there has been a constant reinforcement of the negative attitudes of the majority of the population toward ethnic minorities, particularly ethnic refugees from other republics. To make matters worse, police in their reports on crime regularly identify criminals as coming from the Caucasus.[67]

Extremists, of course, have not neglected to vent their venom against Jews. Zhirinovsky and others have repeatedly claimed that there are too many non-Russian faces on television. And since it is the contention of many extremists[68] that wealth is acquired only through criminal activities, Jews and Caucasians are invariably singled out as examples of individuals who have achieved economic success through crime.

Even with minority groups that are being rehabilitated after long persecution in the past, such as the Cossacks, the end results are both disappointing and dangerous for democracy. The majority of Cossacks have declared their loyalty to Yeltsin, and some members of government, such as Sergei Shakhrai, proudly allude to a Cossack heritage. These formerly persecuted people, numbering perhaps 3 million, are not being readmitted into society on democratic terms. In the past they were used by the czar as shock troops. Later they were terribly persecuted by Stalin, deprived of education, and denied the right to foster their communal culture. Now democrats worry that they are being politically manipulated to support en masse (that is, as a bloc) certain political factions rather than being given an opportunity to become members of a civil society as individual free citizens of a multiethnic state.[69] Instead, they have been encouraged to elect tribal leaders. The latter have little understanding or sympathy for democracy, either for the Cossacks or for the country as a whole.

Ultimately, though, progress on the minorities issue is tied to the overall protection of human rights in Russia. Assessments of the status of human rights in the Russian Federation are hardly encouraging. The 1994 report issued by the Presidential Human Rights Commission, chaired by the former political prisoner Sergei Kovalev (who is attached to the office of the Russian president), stated that the number of human rights violations in Russia had not decreased in the past two years.[70] Among its many criticisms, the report noted that often state and government officials at the federal, regional, and local levels ignored existing legislation concerning human rights.

In 1995 the Council of Europe, responding to reports of gross violations of human rights in Chechnya and clearly influenced by Kovalev's denunciations of the government's excesses, temporarily suspended membership talks with Russia as an act of protest.[71] Kovalev's commission report for all of 1995, moreover, was scathing on the treatment of minorities (as well as human rights in general).[72] It denounced the use of force in Chechnya and contended that racism is on the upswing along with "increasing aggravation of the problem of ensuring the rights of minorities and small indigenous groups in the north, Siberia and far East".[73]

Laws and Legality

There certainly is no shortage of laws in Russia. There has been a proliferation of legislation on all conceivable issues, and a large number of decrees and counterdecrees have been issued by the State Duma and the president. A new constitution was adopted in December 1993, and the State Duma has moved to appoint a commissioner for human rights who would be answerable to the legislature. In February 1995 an expanded Constitutional Court with the requisite nineteen justices was resurrected with a respected jurist, Vladimir Tumanov, as chair.[74] Individual and minority rights, therefore, ought to be amply protected given the apparent legal and constitutional guarantees. But laws and constitutional assurances should not be confused with legality, that is, a deeply rooted legal system in which the population has faith and in which a competent and independent judiciary provides impartial adjudication and enforcement of natural rights.

Unfortunately, one of the greatest shortcomings of the process of democratization in Russia has been the grossly inadequate progress toward legality. This involves, first, the judiciary system and, second, the laws, the decrees, and the constitution of the state. After more than seven decades of socialism, it is only to be expected that there would be problems in the judiciary. After all, anyone who would serve on the bench or in the prosecutor's office would be someone who would have received all, or most, of his or her legal training under communism before the collapse of the Soviet Union at the end of 1991. Therefore, the judiciary could not be transformed overnight. Yet at the same time, one should expect strenuous efforts on the part of a democratic government to bring into the judiciary individuals from private practice or the universities and to lay down stringent rules for adjudication and for the independence of judges and prosecutors. This has not been the case. There are very few jury trials, though some progress is being made,[75] and in criminal cases, the judges overwhelmingly accept the briefs presented by the prosecution. Over 90 percent of the defendants are convicted.[76] By Western standards, prosecutors (rather than judges) who are given the responsibility to ensure that a trial is fair have too much power.[77] When it comes to human rights, the record of judges is no better. Human rights groups have protested that courts, including the appeal court, regularly dismiss hate cases.[78] Prosecutors, in fact, have been reluctant to pursue hate-crime cases. In the few instances where they did proceed, the prosecution was unsuccessful. But the lack of enthusiasm of prosecutors derives, according to many observers, from an attitude that views hate crimes against minorities as a relatively insignificant matter.[79] Adjudication in commercial cases adds to the problem. There is widespread corruption with many judges selling verdicts to the highest bidder.[80] Though this practice does not impact directly on human and minority rights, it adds to the image of an incompetent and corrupt judiciary, one in which the citizenry, not surprisingly, has little confidence.

The second problem creates a negative synergy with the first. The new constitution granted the president of Russia very strong powers. But the parliament that was elected in December 1993 is dominated by antidemocratic forces from the left and the right. (The democratic forces became even weaker in the Duma after the December 1995 elections.) There has been, therefore, a battle of decrees and an inability to clarify the laws or the constitution. The Constitutional Court, created in 1992, was largely discredited when its chair, Valery Zorkin (fired in fall 1993), actively and vociferously supported the coup leaders against Yeltsin. A law passed by the Duma at the end of June 1994 further reduced the court's power (it had not, at any rate, met since the coup). Therefore, the constitution does not provide enough guidance and there is no independent constitutional interpretation to settle the validity of laws. This has caused confusion not only in the business world, where Western investors have been driven away en masse because of the arbitrary interpretation of contradictory commercial laws and decrees, but also in cases dealing with individual and minority rights and hate issues. The inadequacy of the legal framework and of antihate laws has been readily admitted by a number of government officials.[81] Human rights groups, for instance, have repeatedly argued that Article 74 of the Criminal Code,[82] which deals with hate-related crimes, is too vague.[83]

Some progress was made in all areas in 1995, but the overall situation remains unsatisfactory. Legal protection for property has been increased but remains tenuous, as the Federal Security Service (the domestic successor to the KGB) retains the right to search businesses with a judge's prior approval.[84] True, the new Constitutional Court is beginning to establish some authority. For instance, in December 20, 1995, it ruled unconstitutional Article 64 of the Criminal Code, which classified as high treason, punishable by death, the decision of Russian citizens to leave the country and stay abroad.[85] In another ruling, though, the court displayed evidence of both the potential and the pitfalls of judicial review in Russia. On November 20,

1995, the Constitutional Court refused a Duma petition that sought to lower the 5 percent minimum for party list representation in the December 1995 elections.[86] The chair, Vladimir Tumanov, referred to the fact that the constitution was silent on the electoral system, but he also declared that the court should not become a "key campaign actor."[87]

Thus it remains difficult to entrench a legal system in Russia for all the reasons previously cited. What complicates matters even more is the difficulty of changing attitudes to rights and legalities. After seven decades of Soviet rule, Russians continue to distinguish between *zakon* (law), which they tend to view as an instrument of state control, and *pravo* (right), natural justice, true justice. It is still little understood that the *zakon* is meant to protect people and that individual right can override those of the state.

In these circumstances, the propagators of hate feel largely unencumbered by legal restraints. Metropolitan Ioann of St. Petersburg, the second highest churchman in the Orthodox Church in Russia, felt free to publish a strongly anti-Semitic article, "Creators of Cataclysms," in one of the most popular procommunist newspapers.[88] He had already published a number of other articles in smaller-circulation newspapers, citing with great enthusiasm the notorious czar's forgery, "The Protocols of the Elders of Zion." The head of the Orthodox Church, though, it must be pointed out, did not endorse Metropolitan Ioann's views but went only as far as to say that these were not the official church views.[89] Gleb Yakunin, a priest, a former dissident, and now a member of the State Duma, however, strongly condemned Metropolitan Ioann's article and, in an open letter to President Yeltsin, advocated prosecution under Article 74 of the Russian Criminal Code.[90] No such prosecution, however, has taken place.

Unfortunately, even in cases where attempts are made to bring about greater legality, often the effects are negative. For instance, confronted with rising crime that not only drives away foreign investments but has been so effectively exploited by extremist forces, President Yeltsin, in June 1994, issued a decree on combating organized crime. Then he and the parliament approved amendments to the Criminal Code in July 1994.[91] The decree on combating crime, though, is very broad, and changes to the Criminal Code granted far too many rights to law protection agencies. In fact, Sergei Kovalev condemned Yeltsin's June decree (even though Kovalev's commission was attached to the office of the president) for violating the new Russian constitution and infringing on human rights.[92] Kovalev resigned in the wake of the December 1995 elections. His commission issued a distressing assessment of legal protection in Russia. It contended, "In Russia's internal politics, political expediency increasingly dominates the fundamental principles of law, respect for human rights and dignity."[93]

Yet as distressing as this picture of legality in Russia may be, conditions in most of the other successor states are significantly worse. The protection of human rights in general and the status of ethnic minorities in particular is such that many individuals have sought refuge in Russia. Not only Russians but Ossetians and others have tried to escape conflict and persecution by seeking to flee to Russia.

Coping with Refugees

A majority that feels victimized, that is, insensitive to the rights and aspirations of the minorities within the state, is not likely to be sympathetic to the plight of minority refugees from beyond its borders. Although life for average Russians may not be quite as bleak as statistics indicate—there are so many unofficial ways to earn income and to gain access to goods and services—they do lead difficult lives in most cases. There is a widespread perception that only the old nomenklatura and the criminal elements are doing well. Demagogues, as noted, have played very cleverly and effectively on the reality and, even more so, on the perception of deprivation. Consequently, xenophobia has grown tremendously and conspiracy theories have multiplied exponentially. Refugees from the Caucasian republics find it virtually impossible to gain refugee status in Russia no matter how great the political persecution they may suffer at home.

These attitudes are very difficult to change. There certainly is no incentive on the part of the extremists to stop demonizing Caucasians. It is up to the democratic forces to take the lead. Some democrats in various nongovernmental human rights organizations and even some governmental organizations such as the Ministry of Foreign Affair's Department of International Humanitarian and Cultural Cooperation have indeed spoken out against hate, prejudice, and discrimination. These, however, remain largely isolated voices. For the majority of democrats it seems there is too difficult a fight for survival to focus on the issues of minority and, especially, refugee rights. There does not seem to be an adequate understanding that *such rights are, in a way, a litmus test for a successful process of democratization*—that, ultimately, minority and refugee rights cannot be separated from other fundamental democratic rights.

Some progress has been made on granting asylum, but much of it may prove to be ephemeral. A July presidential decree provides that asylum may be granted to foreigners if they face persecution in their country, but it also contains the stipulation that it may be denied on grounds of national security.[94] Conditions, though, are so difficult in Russia that even ethnic Russians from the "near abroad" who seek refuge in Russia have encountered enormous difficulties. Laws and regulations are largely meaningless in the face of local interpretation. It is local officials who determine matters of residency, work, and access to social services. Despite enactment of a law in 1993 stipulating the abolition of *propiska*, the system of residence permits, Russia's big cities have retained the system. As far back as July 1994, the Human Rights Commission, chaired by Sergei Kovalev, was highly critical of the retention of the *propiska* system and deplored the fact that many state and government officials at the federal, regional, and local levels ignored the existing legislation concerning human rights, particularly those relating to refugees.[95] There is a danger, therefore, that even positive steps such as the move to create a position of commissioner for human rights could be negated by the unwillingness of officials to abide by the law and, more basically, to recognize the fundamental rights of internal minorities and legitimate political refugees.

Conclusion

It is very difficult to find the right balance in assessing developments in Russia, but it is essential. Social autism, a self-righteous "majority as victim," the politics of identity, and the virtually unrestrained propagation of hate literature have cumulatively helped create a good deal of despair in Russia. It is easy, therefore, to become pessimistic about the prospects for human rights, the containment of extremism, including right-wing extremism, and the prospects for democracy. Yet such pessimism would ignore just how far Russia has come since the collapse of the Soviet Union, how many more opportunities there are for democracy, that so many people in Russia have vigorously joined the political debate, and how many have availed themselves legitimately of the new economic opportunities.

Yet Russia is a kind of "land in between." The momentum for democratization and marketization has slowed and is endangered. There are warning signs, blatant and subtle. And the latter may ultimately turn out to be the more important. Unless reformers are aware of the need for self-examination, appreciate the need to ensure human rights for everyone, and are willing to accept the legitimacy of opposing political views (as long as those holding opposing views do not attempt to deny others basic human rights), democracy is endangered. It is encouraging, though, that human rights activists and many democrats in Russia do increasingly recognize the universality of human rights. They understand that extremism threatens not only minorities but democracy itself, and a threat to democracy in Russia is a central threat to international stability. Democracy, of course, comes in many forms, and there are differences among Denmark, France, and the United States. There are, however, no fundamental differences in basic individual rights and in the recognition of the need for a civil society and a deeply rooted legality. It is important, therefore, to heed the words of the most committed in Russia, individuals such as the former finance minister Boris Fedorov, who warned, "Don't pretend that democracy in Russia is something else than in the West,"[96] and Sergei Kovalev, who urged, "First, in no event should the West turn away from Russia and leave it to its fate."[97]

Notes

1. *Economist*, February 24, 1996, 6.
2. *Economist*, November 1995, 79, and January 1996, 48.
3. *New York Times*, January 17, 1996.
4. Padma Desai, "Russian Privatization: A Comparative Perspective," *Harriman Review* 8(3), August 1995.
5. *Economist*, January 20, 1996, 48.
6. *Economist*, November 25, 1995, 79.
7. OECD, *Transition Brief*, no. 1, Autumn 1995: 2.
8. Jeffrey Sachs, "Post Communist Parties and the Politics of Entitlement," *Transition* (World Bank's *Transition* Economies Division, Washington, D.C.) 6(3), March 1995: 1–4.
9. Istvan Dobozi and Gerhard Pohl, "Real Output Decline in Transition Economies—Forget GDP, Try Power Consumption Data," *Transition* 6(1–2), January-February 1995: 17–18.
10. In fact, Anders Aslund contends (perhaps a little too prematurely) that the Russian economy "has become depoliticized." "Prospects of the New Russian Market Economy," *Problems of Post-Communism*, Fall 1994: 17.
11. *RFE/RL News Briefs*, June 20–24, 1994.
12. *Izvestia* (Moscow), May 17, 1994.
13. *Economist*, February 3, 1996, 42; "Constitution Watch: Russia," *East European Constitutional Review* 4(4), Fall 1995: 25.
14. Ibid.
15. Vladimir Pribylovsky, "A Survey of Radical Right-Wing Groups in Russia," *RFE/RL Research Report* 3(16), April 22, 1994: 28–37.
16. Ibid., 32.
17. Ibid., 33.
18. Wendy Slater, "Russia," *RFE/RL Research Report* 3(16), April 22, 1994: 23–27.
19. Pribylovsky, "A Survey of Radical Right-Wing Groups in Russia," 31.
20. Ibid.
21. Paul Goble, "Russia's Extreme Right," *National Interest*, no. 33, Fall 1993.
22. Walter Laqueur, *Los Angeles Times*, May 30, 1993.
23. Vladimir Zhirinovsky, interview with the author, Moscow, May 25, 1994.
24. Ibid.
25. Ibid.
26. Alla Gerber, interview with the author, Moscow, May 24, 1994.
27. *Economist*, September 3, 1994, 54.
28. *Economist*, February 17, 1996, 44–45.
29. Tatiana N. Smirnova, interview with the author, Moscow, May 24, 1994.
30. Teimouraz Ramishvili, interview with the author, Moscow, May 24, 1994.
31. Boris Altshuler, Vladimir Raskin, and Alexei Smirnov, interviews with the author, Moscow, May 23, 1994.

32. Gerber interview.

33. Jahan R. Pollyeva (principal adviser to Deputy Prime Minister Sergei Shakhrai) and Yuri V. Tavrovsky (press secretary to Sergei Shakrai), interviews with the author, Moscow, May 25, 1994.

34. Pollyeva and Tavrovsky interviews.

35. Wendy Slater, "The Russian Communist Party Today," *RFE/RL Research Report* 3(31), August 12, 1994: 1.

36. Ibid.

37. *Economist*, May 6, 1995, 51.

38. *Globe and Mail* (Toronto), September 19, 1994.

39. Boris Altshuler and Vladimir Raskin, "Russian Neo-Nazi and Modern 'Munich,'" letter of Movement Without Frontiers Group, Moscow Research Center for Human Rights, April 20, 1994.

40. *Economist*, December 23, 1995, 59–60.

41. *Economist*, November 18, 1995, 53; *Nezavisimaya Gazeta* (Independent Newspaper, Moscow), November 25, 1995.

42. See the excellent book by Dmitri Volkogonov, *Lenin: A New Biography* (New York: Free Press, 1995).

43. *Globe and Mail*, January 22, 1996.

44. *Economist*, May 6, 1995, 5.

45. *Economist*, February 3, 1996, 42.

46. *Wall Street Journal*, February 12, 1996.

47. Martha de Melo, Cevdet Denizer, and Alan Gelb, "From Plan to Market: Patterns of Transition," *Transition* 6(11–12), November-December 1995: 4–6.

48. *Transition* 6(1–2), January 1995: 21.

49. *Transition* 6(3), March 1995: 16.

50. *RFE/RL News Briefs*, August 8–12, 1994, 2.

51. *New York Times*, January 26, 1996.

52. Viktor Chernomyrdin "No Exits on the Road to the Market," *Financial Times* (London), May 16, 1994.

53. *RFE/RL News Briefs*, July 18–22, 1994, 4.

54. *RFE/RL News Briefs*, June 27–July 1, 1994, 6.

55. *Globe and Mail*, November 29, 1996.

56. *Globe and Mail*, February 7, 1996.

57. *Economist*, November 18, 1995, 68.

58. See the excellent book by Stephen Handelman, *Comrade Criminal: Russia's New Mafia* (New Haven: Yale University Press, 1995).

59. *New York Times*, January 26, 1996.

60. *Izvestia*, February 12, 1996.

61. *Toronto Star*, February 4, 1996.

62. Victor Zolotarevich, *Nazism in Russia: 1993–94 Survey* (Moscow: Moscow Research Center for Human Rights, April 15, 1994).

63. Zhirinovsky interview.

64. Gerber interview.

65. Zhirinovsky interview.

66. *Economist*, July 29, 1995, 35–37, and January 13, 1996, 50.

67. Smirnova interview.

68. Zhirinovsky interview.

69. Ramishvili interview.

70. *Nezavisimaya Gazeta* (Independent News, Moscow), July 22–26, 1994.

71. *East European Constitutional Review* 4(2), Spring 1995: 27.

72. *Toronto Star*, February 21, 1996; CBC Radio, February 20, 1996, 8: 00 A.M. EDT.

73. Ibid.

74. *East European Constitutional Review* 4(2), Spring 1995: 25–26.

75. *Economist*, September 2, 1995, 42–43.

76. *Economist*, September 3, 1994, 53.

77. Ibid.

78. Altshuler interview.

79. Smirnova interview.

80. *Economist*, September 3, 1994, 53.

81. Ramishvili and Smirnova interviews.

82. *Rossiiskaya Gazeta* (Russian News, Moscow), July 7, 1994.

83. Altshuler interview.

84. *Economist*, September 2,1995, 48.

85. *East European Constitutional Review* 4(4), Fall 1995: 29.

86. Ibid., 27.

87. Ibid.

88. *Sovetskaya Rossya* (Soviet Russia, Moscow), March 22, 1994.

89. Altshuler interview.

90. Ibid.

91. *Rossiiskaya Gazeta* (Moscow), July 7, 1994.

92. *RFE/RL News Briefs*, July 25–August 5, 1994, 5.

93. *Toronto Star*, February 21, 1995.

94. *Forced Migration Monitor*, Open Society Insitute, no. 8, November 1995: 2.

95. *Nezavisimaya Gazeta*, July 22–26, 1994.

96. Boris Fedorov, interview with the author, Berlin, August 26, 1994.

97. Sergei Kovalev, "How the West Should *Not* React to Events in Russia," *Transition* (OMRI) 1(9), June 9, 1995: 43.

9

Poland: The Vanguard of Change

Aurel Braun

In many respects, Poland is one of the great success stories in East-Central Europe. It was the first country in the region to abandon Marxist-Leninist rule. It quickly embarked on a fundamental political and economic transformation. It has gone through a number of successful democratic elections where power was handed over peacefully. Moreover, with a growth rate of 7 percent in 1995, Poland now has the fastest growing gross domestic product (GDP) in all of Eastern Europe.[1] The country also differs in important respects from other East-Central European states. It is by far the largest state, with almost 40 million people. It is more ethnically homogeneous than the other states in the region. And the Catholic Church has played an instrumental role not only in preserving national identity but also in shielding and sustaining political dissidence. There is reason, therefore, to believe that Poland is well on the way to rejoining a democratic Europe.

Yet Poland exists in a region of tenuous stability. It is affected by developments in the other East-Central European states and particularly in Russia. In crucial ways it has shared a common experience with the other Marxist-Leninist states. To claim that the past has had no effect, that Poland never left Europe,[2] or that its problems are unique is to misunderstand similarities in the region and run the risk of ignoring early warning signs of danger to democratization, particularly from political extremism. Poland may indeed be doing better than most other states, but it is still useful to look at the issues of momentum, transformation, the possibility of the majority viewing itself as victim, the status of minorities, laws and legality, and policies on refugees.

Certainly extremist political parties do not appear to present a grave or imminent danger in Poland. Whereas Stanislaw Tyminski, who founded the extremist Party X and expressed strong anti-Semitic and ultranationalist sentiments, garnered 23 percent of the vote in the 1990 presidential election,[3] in the parliamentary elections in 1993 his Party X managed to win only 2.74

185

percent of the total vote, thereby failing to reach the 5 percent threshold required for parliamentary representation.[4] According to reliable sources, another extremist group, Self-Defense, led by Andrzej Lepper, has contacts with Lyndon Larouche's group in the United States via the Schiller Institute in Germany.[5] Self-Defense has used violence repeatedly at local levels, on occasion successfully. The government has been reluctant, however, to clamp down on this group with the full force of the law.[6] It should be pointed out, though, that in the 1993 election Self-Defense won only 2.78 percent of the national vote.[7]

Other extreme groups are even more marginal. In March 1994 Janusz Bryczkowski set up the Polish National Front (PNF), which has many of the characteristics of a fascist organization. Bryczkowski, evidently, had links with the communist secret police. More recently, he has openly praised the Nazi Party as a model.[8] The PNF apparently has links with skinheads and has drawn memberships from other small extremist groups. Bryczkowski organized and financed Vladimir Zhirinovsky's visit to Poland in March 1994 and was invited to Saddam Hussein's birthday in Iraq.[9]

Extremism thus appears to be a marginal factor. Still, marginalization does have certain negative aspects. In the 1993 parliamentary elections, in which only 52 percent of the voters cast ballots, 34 percent of those who went to the polls gave their support to parties that failed to win any seats because they did not reach the required percentage threshold for entry.[10] Only part of these "nonrepresented" voters had supported extremist parties, but the failure of such a large group of the population to gain parliamentary representation, particularly during a period of transition (as successful as that may be to date), is inherently dangerous. It is only to be hoped that those parties that succeeded in getting into parliament will manage to act as political "sponges" that can absorb the support of the voters whose parties were left out of parliament.[11]

There are indicators, though, that suggest that all is not well, that there is a potential for extremism. For example, a poll taken in spring 1994 showed that, incredibly, 36 percent of the population in Poland believes that the minuscule Jewish minority wields too much influence.[12] Given the facts, this can hardly be viewed as anything but dangerous mass political fantasy and ultimately an obstacle to the development of what Zbigniew Brzezinski called a mature political culture.[13] Therefore, there are important questions to ask and warning signals to be evaluated. The first step is to assess the momentum of democratic transformation.

Momentum

There have been several significant developments in Poland that should provide valuable insights into the momentum of transformation. Reassuringly, there are, it seems, vital signals that indicate that the momentum of democratization has been maintained and remains sustainable. Although in the September 1993 elections the victors were a coalition of the Democratic Left Alliance (a successor to the former Communist Party) and a former partner of the Communist Party, the Polish Peasant Party, the vote was not one in support of the past. The two governing parties had undergone major changes and came to accept social democracy. There was no attempt to return to a central command economy or to alter the democratic structure that had been put in place. The government, led by Prime Minister Waldemar Pawlak of the Polish Peasant Party, emphasized that macrostabilization was to be achieved through a program of fiscal discipline designed to reduce the budgetary deficit significantly. Furthermore, the government strongly supported the enhancement of trade relations with Western European states. Last, the government continued to press strongly for Polish membership in NATO and in the European Union. Thus the Polish people had voted, in September 1993, for *a change of government, not of the political order*. In most respects, the Pawlak government seems to have honored that wish. Similarly, the election of Aleksander Kwasniewski—the leader of the Democratic Left Alliance—as president in the November 19, 1995, election was not a signal of a return to the communist past. Kwasniewski had run a slick American-style campaign and emphasized his commitment to democracy and political consensus.[14]

For the democratic political order to succeed, it must progress and it must maintain momentum. That is, democratic institutions and processes must be widened and deepened. In this regard, the signals become more mixed and democratic forces must be alert to potential dangers that can negatively affect the momentum of transformation. In particular, difficulties in accomplishing three democratic goals—the depoliticization of key ministries, the devolution of power to local governments, and separation of church and state—can cause considerable long-term damage.

Politics

First, when totalitarian systems, where political control is paramount, move toward democracy, where civil society emerges, depoliticizing the various ministries and building up an independent civil service is of primary importance. This depoliticization has been only partially achieved in Poland. The process, started by democratic forces in 1989, proceeded slowly and imperfectly and seems to have been slowed down further by Prime Minister Pawlak's coalition. By insisting, for instance, that Democratic Left Alliance deputy ministers be appointed to the Ministries of Defense, Foreign Affairs, and Internal Affairs in the government, Pawlak likely further politicized those ministries. In addition, in June 1994, the cabinet failed to approve guidelines designed to separate political from career posts in the Foreign Affairs Ministry. Instead, the new government gave the communist "professionals," who were ousted from the ministry after Solidarity took power in 1989, increasingly greater sympathy and encouragement.[15] Further, Pawlak placed his cronies not only in every available position in the administration but also on the boards of banks, industrial enterprises, and foundations created by government.[16]

Second, successful transformation requires both the support and involvement of the population in the process. Local government is the first and easiest level for the involvement of citizens. Democrats consequently introduced decentralizing reforms as early as 1989. Pawlak and Michael Strak, his minister of local administration, halted the reforms, including the measures introduced by the government of Hanna Suchocka. They replaced almost all incumbent local officials, promoting activists from their party whenever possible.[17] The Pawlak government, in power until February 7, 1995 (its policies were not substantially altered by the short-lived successor government of the former communist Jozef Oleksy), continued to block the devolution of power from the center to local governments. In part this was done by opposing the reintroduction of an intermediate level of government, the *powiat,* that would bridge the gap between the basic administrative unit, the *gmina,* and the *voivodship* (or *wojewodztwa,* meaning province).[18] During 1994 the Pawlak government strengthened its hold over the *gminas* and did well in local elections in early summer 1994. But the right-wing parties, some with questionable attachment to democracy, also did well in these elections.[19] These results indicate the potential for the rise of extremism in the absence of appropriate local channels to communicate local political concerns.

Third, the separation of church and state has also been problematic in Poland. Shortly before Prime Minister Hanna Suchocka's resignation, her government hastily signed a concordat with the Vatican that exempted the church from almost all taxation and gave it authority over marriage and divorce.[20] This was not merely an unpopular move in many parts of Polish society, where there is a rise of anticlericalism; it also violated the very fundamental principle of secular democracy. The accord is yet to be ratified, and the current debate over its ratification is proving to be politically damaging. The new left-of-center government that succeeded that of Hanna Suchocka's in 1994 was very reluctant to ratify the concordat and suggested that it would do so only after the adoption of a new constitution.[21] But making ratification dependent on a nonexistent constitution creates problems of legality within Poland and casts doubt on the state's ability to conclude international agreements.[22]

The church was angered by what it perceived as cynical delaying tactics by the leftist government to stop the ratification of the concordat. In the campaign for the November 1995 presidential elections the church, therefore, made an all out effort to block the election of Aleksander Kwasniewski. The tone was set by Pope John Paul II, who coined the slogan "Poland needs people of conscience" during his visit to his homeland.[23] This was designed to bring home the difference between President Lech Walesa, a believer who not only welcomed but encouraged the church's campaign, and Kwasniewski, a former communist "nonbeliever." The church mobilized its considerable resources to support Walesa, who nearly closed the enormous gap in the polls by coming within 700,000 votes of winning.[24] For example, the church issued a preelectoral pastoral letter that contained instructions and warnings to elect only a person of high moral standards and a guardian of the right to life.[25] Radio Maryja (Holy Virgin Radio), a network of very conservative radio stations owned by Redemptionist priests, threw its considerable weight behind Walesa.[26]

As mentioned, there is growing anticlericalism in Poland, particularly over such issues as abortion, and pre-election opinion polls indicated that 75 percent thought that the church should not attempt to influence elections.[27] But in the same poll 75 percent admitted that the church would, to some degree, influence their political decisions.[28] The election was in fact very bitter and divisive. Walesa refused to congratulate Kwasniewski or attend his inaugural, and his staff alleged fraud by the victorious former communist and threatened to seek an annulment of Poland's election results. Existing divisions thus are likely to be further exacerbated in the future.

Economics

There are problems as well in the economic realm. True, Poland is enjoying strong growth with a gross domestic product increase of 7 percent in 1995 and possibly 6.5 percent in 1996.[29] Yet despite the tremendous progress in marketization made by Poland, the process has been threatened at times with a loss of momentum. First, the privatization program envisioned by the Pawlak government and articulated by its finance minister, Grzegorz Kolodko, inhibited rather than freed market forces. He focused on "commercializing" enterprises, which in essence involved turning them into joint-stock companies in which all the shares are owned by the state.[30] Few, if any, of the shares were sold to the public, and contrary to market expectations, the state tightened its controls over the firms. This resulted in what has been called, "recombinant" property, that is, a form of ownership that cannot be considered either as private ownership with clearly defined property rights or as a continuation or reproduction of the old forms of state ownership.[31] In many instances the main beneficiaries of privatization were the members of the former nomenklatura (the party and managerial elites). Former party members, for instance, wound up holding 90 percent of the top banking jobs.[32] Though the finance minister presented this approach as a first stage toward privatization, there were reasonable concerns that it might instead be a substitute. Given that Poland has privatized less quickly than the Czech Republic or even Hungary, the approach did erode some of the momentum.

Second, even nominal privatization was greatly slowed by the Pawlak government. Whereas his predecessor had approved two earlier lists of 335 firms for mass privatization in 1993, Pawlak refused to approve the final list of 105 enterprises, in large part because his own party has been hostile to parts of the privatization program.[33] The Peasant Party remained firmly opposed to the privatization of important sectors related to agriculture, such as the tobacco industry. Pawlak's successor did begin to distribute free certificates that entitle Poles to indirect stakes in 514 state enterprises in November 1995. But this is a small operation in comparison with what the Czechs have done, and some worry that politicians will meddle in the administration of the funds.[34] Since funds from privatization are essential for economic transformation and budgetary control, the loss of momentum could threaten the relatively fragile macroeconomic stability that has been achieved, generating significant political difficulties.

The Majority as Victim

Complacency is dangerous in any democracy, but during a period of transition there is a particular need for democrats to be alert. It was reassuring to find that in Poland leading democrats and intellectuals, in sharp contrast to the sanguine assessments of change given by government officials (or on occasion by the odd unsophisticated Western diplomat), were concerned with the danger to democracy and were most interested in identifying early warning signals. In my interviews with Adam Michnik, a leading democratic thinker and editor in chief of the influential newspaper *Gazeta Wyborcza*, with Bronislaw Geremek (a brilliant academic and influential member of parliament and one of the key intellectuals who helped shape early Solidarity policy in 1989), and Konstanty Gebert (who writes under the pseudonym of Dawid Warszawski and is one of the best known political journalists in the country), there was a consensus about the need for vigilance, the danger of a majority viewing itself as the victim, and some of the important commonalities in the region in the postcommunist era.

First, the sense of the "majority as victim" in Poland, as in many other parts of the former Soviet Union and in Eastern Europe, has created a mistrust of politics in general that goes beyond the normal skepticism toward politicians prevalent in Western democracies. Even though communism has been defeated in Poland (the postcommunist parties are social democratic), the perception of victimization continues. Konstanty Gebert, for instance, suggested that it may even be appropriate to speak of the majority as "victorious victims."[35] The majority of the population was, indeed, victimized under the Nazis and under communists. It prevailed in both instances but there is, it seems, a widespread belief that the majority was indeed the primary victim.

This perception generates multiple negative political effects. The problem is not merely the all-too-often mixture of fascist-like rhetoric and communist terminology. There is in general a rigid ideological expression of politics. There is, as Geremek contends, a kind of blind anticommunism combined with a lack of trust in politicians that results in a dislike of both politicians and politics.[36] As Geremek rightly pointed out, this kind of antipolitics is occurring in all the postcommunist states, and there is even some evidence of it in longstanding democracies such as Italy. But in conditions of transition, especially where there aren't adequate national explanations of the pain of transition, such attitudes and consequent behavior can be exploited by demagogues. This is precisely what Geremek and others fear. As Geremek put it, "In social politics there is a battle between security and liberty . . . between social aggression and reform."[37] There are authoritarian temptations, polarization, and a danger of extremism.

Yet the dangers of authoritarianism can be combated. First, as in any democracy, politicians and society at large must foster the art of political compromise. Second, all citizens, but particularly the majority, must engage in an honest reexamination of the past that should include both the communist and the interwar era. But here too there are disturbing signals. In 1989 Solidarity organized a round table that emphasized the art of political compromise. The round-table philosophy, according to Geremek, helped win consensus on political reform, including changes in the army, and resulted in the creation of a seven-party coalition in 1990.[38] The intent was to transfer legitimacy from the "struggle," which involved the leading activists in the democratic movement, to the grass roots.

It is not merely that this particular consensus has broken down in Poland but rather that given the prevalence of a sense of victimization, there has been an unwillingness to acknowledge both the political imperative and the moral correctness of political compromise. Consequently, Polish politics have become characterized, according to Adam Michnik, by an anticonsensual approach.[39] A kind of majoritarianism prevails among most political formulations, and therefore, according to Michnik, who is perhaps somewhat more pessimistic than many other democrats, democracy itself in Poland is feeble and vulnerable. Michnik goes as far as to suggest that it is conceivable that Poland may be undergoing a kind of pre-Pinochet crisis where the danger of anticonsensual, "majority as victim" politics and the rise of mass psychology is inadequately recognized.[40]

To combat this danger, there is, as noted, a need to reexamine the past and particularly the assumptions of the majority as a perpetual victim. Here the warning signs, though, are all too frequently ignored in Poland. As Michnik pointed out, there is an aversion in Poland to reexamining not only the communist past but also wartime behavior and interwar politics.[41] And unexamined appeals to traditions, as Michnik rightly pointed out, are intrinsically chauvinistic.[42] Polish behavior during the war and in the interwar period, the latter time nostalgically alluded to by many in the country, remains largely unexamined. The opprobrium directed against Michnik and his newspaper whenever they tried to look at these issues or examine the dangers of nationalism[43] are evidence of the slowness in developing a mature political culture and in the building of a stable civil society. Consequently, the notion of the majority as victim remains widely accepted, and with it we witness the growth of a populism that tends to reject compromise and is insensitive toward minorities; the combination creates what Adam Michnik called a "dangerous undercurrent."[44]

The Status of Minorities

There is a tendency among Polish officials to downplay or dismiss minority problems because, unlike most of the other postcommunist states, Poland has a high degree of ethnic homogeneity. But their argument, based on the fact that minorities constitute no more than 5 percent of the population, misses the point. The treatment of minorities in general, and during a transition toward democracy in particular, is, as we have seen elsewhere in the region, one of the most important litmus tests of progress and sensitivity. As Adam Michnik argued perceptively in an editorial, the treatment of minorities is the "most sensitive test of tolerance, the democratic order, [and] the ability to resolve conflicts within the bounds of legal procedures."[45]

Yet there is no clear concept of minority rights in Poland.[46] This is reflected in the minister of justice's statement in 1993 that anything the majority wants is law.[47] This lack of an understanding of the fundamental linkages between minority rights and the success of democracy as a sustainable pluralistic system was reinforced in my interview with Marek Nowicki, the president of the Helsinki Foundation for Human Rights, in Warsaw.[48] If there was any dilemma in Nowicki's mind about the role of civil rights activists and that of the Polish patriot, he certainly seemed, throughout our interview, to have resolved this in favor of the latter. He was very concerned with the image of Poland. He was more embarrassed than outraged by the violations of minority rights. He argued that physical brutality against minorities was generally not a problem and that violations had tended to be exaggerated.[49] And in a country where the vast majority of the 3.5 million Jewish community was murdered during World War II by the Nazis and their collaborators, he made the astonishing statement that during the past few years Jews may have exaggerated anti-Semitic activities and suggested that they may be "overly sensitive."[50]

It is true that there have been few instances of physical violence against minorities or foreigners, or at least few that have been reported. There was a small pogrom against Roma in 1991 in Mlawa and an attack by skinheads against German truck drivers (in 1992 one of the latter died).[51] The main problem, though, may not be physical violence as much as other forms of intimidation, harassment, and exclusion. The attitude toward Roma and Jews as perennial outsiders, for instance, should be viewed as a warning sign regarding the health of the process of democratization. Roma tend to be visible. They are accused of begging and stealing. The influx of Romanian Roma further heightens those prejudices against the group. The undersecretary of state for the Ministry of Internal Affairs, Jerzy Zimowski, for instance, argued in an interview that Polish "sympathy" for Romanian Roma evaporated in face of aggressive begging and a rejection of offers of work.[52] But Roma have continued to complain of harassment and random acts of violence and about the difficulty of getting compensation for damages suffered during the anti-Roma riots in 1991 in Mlawa.[53]

Anti-Semitism, Nowicki assured me, was mainly a rural phenomenon. As in the case of many other issues in Poland, however, the reality is much more complex. Anti-Semitism takes on many forms. First, there is traditional anti-Semitism. At one level it involves hurtful words and deplorable deeds. It thus can be blatant. It includes openly voiced conspiracy theories put forth by the extremist parties and also occurs in casual conversation. Anti-Semitic graffiti on walls close to the small Jewish center in Warsaw declaring "Poland for Poles" is another blatant manifestation. But there is also the more subtle yet insidious problem of an ethnically exclusivist attitude. For a great many Poles, according to Dr. Stanislaw Krajewski, a leader in the Jewish-Catholic dialogue, an individual must be either a Pole or a Jew.[54] This attitude is one of the more extreme expressions of the old question of double loyalty. Instead of citizenship, the emphasis is on ethnicity. There have been some improvements in attitudes as the Catholic Church's appreciation and understanding of Judaism has grown. But Dr. Krajewski, for instance, worried that the more recent growth of antiliberal attitudes in the church will have an indirect, yet negative, effect on Jews.

Second, postcommunism has produced a new type of anti-Semitism in Poland. Its streak of authoritarianism does fit into an ideological pattern that is prevalent among far-right movements in the region and in Western Europe. It is not merely discriminating against Jews and the basis of the old Jewish stereotype but against the Jew as a concept. Both Geremek and Michnik viewed this as a basic political problem. Attacking Jews was rejecting "rootless cosmopolitanism" and what are perceived by Polish authoritarians as Western democratic values.[55] Anti-Semitism thus functions as a rejection of liberalism, of democratic values, and therefore threatens all of Polish society.

Third, there is legal, religious, and political insensitivity toward the primary victims of anti-Semitism. For instance, a law was adopted in December 1992 that required radio and television programming to "respect Christian values." This law was upheld in a June 1994 decision by the Constitutional Tribunal of Poland.[56] Many in Poland, including eighty-nine left-wing deputies in their legal challenge, had argued unsuccessfully that worldview questions should not be the subject of legal prescriptions.

Other manifestations of insensitivity toward the Jewish community abound. Although a major source of tension in Catholic-Jewish relations was defused when the pope intervened to instruct Carmelite nuns to leave their convent outside of Auschwitz, the former concentration camp where the vast majority of the victims were Jews, at many sites of former Jewish institutions, crosses or other Christian symbols have been erected. There are a vast number of such sites given the huge prewar Jewish community and the enormous contribution it made to Poland. And even though the present government has a positive attitude toward the Jewish community, there are slights that are extremely painful. For example, in a May 1994 interview, Pawel Wildstein, the head of the Union of Jewish Communities in Poland, complained bitterly that Jewish veterans who had fought valiantly against the Nazis and some who had also participated in actions by the Free Poles in Italy were not included in the Monte Casino celebration by the Warsaw government.[57]

Fourth, insensitivity often combines with economic difficulties in Poland to produce further negative outcomes for the Jewish community. It does not have adequate funds. Polish law stipulates that Jewish organizations can provide help only to the living. This means that they cannot take adequate care of cemeteries and other former Jewish community sites. Although there are young, vigorous, and active members of the Jewish community in Poland, the vast majority of the 8,000 Polish Jews, including much of the leadership, are elderly. The community leadership seems tired, frustrated, and at times even scared. If Jewish community property were returned, the few survivors would have more than ample funds to protect the Jewish heritage in Poland. But the Jewish community has no legal standing, although it is engaged in negotiating an agreement with the government.

The Polish government claims that it cannot afford to return all the communal property (although this has been done with most of the churches). There was also a fear expressed by Jerzy Zimowski that combined a plea based on economic difficulties with insensitivity toward Jews that easily bordered on anti-Semitism. Sitting in his huge office in the mammoth Ministry of Internal Affairs building, he suggested that surely everyone should understand that a return of Jewish property could mean that expatriate Jews would take advantage of this and give that property to relatives still living in Poland or make enormous profits.[58] Perhaps more could be done on Jewish communal property, he volunteered, as though this issue was something new rather than an ongoing problem that was several years old. Zimowski, assuming the role of the victim, then expressed outrage regarding Western accusations of anti-Semitism in Poland. He declared, "We don't get our anti-semitism from our mothers' milk. . . . The educated people, in fact, lean to the other extreme—they are philo-Semitic. Let me tell you one of the most popular writers in Poland is Isaac B. Singer."[59]

Reprivatization of Jewish property is a complex issue. There are economic problems, and the government does need to deal with a large budgetary deficit. Yet given the concessions it has made to the Catholic Church and given the minuscule size of the sad remnants of the once glorious Polish-Jewish community, it is not surprising the members of the community feel terribly hurt and ignored by governmental inaction.

Laws and Legality

Like the other postcommunist states, Poland suffers from problems in the implementation of laws. Most of the judges are from the communist era, and they do not have the proper training to implement the democratic laws.[60] In 1993, for instance, the Senate (Poland's upper house) Office of Intervention reported that it received complaints that Polish judges released or convicted defendants at their whim.[61] Some measures have been adopted to try to address the problem, including the introduction of the power to recall judges by the executive branch. But this amendment to the law and the court system caused resignations and protests not only from judges but also from the Association of Polish Lawyers and the Ombudsman.[62] There is, therefore, considerable confusion that ultimately can be clarified only through the adoption of a new constitution and rigorous efforts at recruiting competent and independent judges. Thus as far as protecting individuals against hate literature or punishing perpetrators of hate-induced violence, the court system in Poland is, for the time being, most inadequate.

There are, however, also problems with the kind of laws that have been passed and actions by the government to restrict freedoms. These could well provide fertile grounds for extremism. For example, the prime minister in July 1994 dismissed the chief of the Polish Press Agency, which, although a government-owned agency, had functioned as an objective and impartial service since 1990. Pawlak replaced him with a government appointee, so rather than diminishing political interference, the government signaled a move toward further politicization.[63]

There are laws in Poland that hardly help the cause of freedom. Article 270 of the Penal Code, for instance, provides for the punishment of anyone who "publicly insults, ridicules and derides the Polish Nation, Polish Peoples' Republic, its political system or its principal organs."[64] In 1993 the government used this law against its critics and a number of protesters were fined and arrested.[65] Fines and punishment are even higher if the acts prohibited by Article 270 are perpetrated through the mass media.[66] Given the stipulation in the law about respecting "Christian" values and the fact that television is still mainly under the control of the government, the latter can, therefore, exercise considerable influence to inhibit the kind of free discussion necessary in democracy, discussion that is required to combat hate and extremism.

The "Little Constitution," which President Lech Walesa signed into law in November 1992, is merely a transition document that, as noted, needs to be replaced by a permanent constitution. With Kwasniewski as president and his party and its ally holding a majority in the Sejm (the lower house of parliament) the potential for abuse is real. Not only can they change all laws by a majority vote but they could overcome a negative ruling by the Constitutional Tribunal because a law deemed unconstitutional can be returned to the Sejm, which can uphold it against the court.[67]

Ironically, with Kwasniewski (who had been chairman of the Constitutional Committee) as president, the chances for a new constitution have improved. Still, his draft could be rejected in a referendum. The country is polarized, and the church and Walesa may campaign strongly against it. But pending approval, there is considerable confusion about laws and the distribution of powers. Antihate measures cannot be very effective. With the slow movement in professionalizing the judiciary and ensuring judges' competence and impartiality, and given the populist instincts of the government, there are reasons to be concerned about legality in Poland.

Refugees

Poland is not a country of immigrants. But the Polish government signed the (1951) Geneva Convention on Refugees in 1991. These two points have been stressed repeatedly by government officials in Warsaw. As a largely homogeneous state, Poland does not encourage immigration, and officials such as Zimowski emphasized that as a signatory of the Geneva Convention Poland is fulfilling all the requirements on refugees.[68] But again, this situation is very complex. It is true that in the past few years most migrants from abroad viewed Poland as a country of transit on their way to the West. With difficult conditions in Russia, Belarus, and Ukraine, however, more migrants are seeking permanent employment, residence, or asylum.[69] There is a danger of extremist reaction unless the issue of immigrants and asylum seekers is handled carefully and equitably. For instance, although a public opinion survey taken in 1992 found that 55 percent of the respondents would accept refugees settling temporarily in Poland, *only 3 percent* said that they would like to see them stay in the country permanently.[70]

In the case of Romanian Roma, Warsaw reached a readmission agreement with Bucharest to send them back. This will be much more difficult to achieve, however, with the increasingly larger number of Russians, Ukrainians, and Belarussians who are coming to Poland. Though the majority will not wish to stay on a permanent basis, Poland does need to formulate new policies that will define the employment and residence status of aliens. Some, however, will invariably seek permanent residence and asylum. Therefore, Poland will not only have to ensure a careful and fair application of the Geneva Convention but the government will need to begin to foster change in the attitudes of the majority of the population.

Some Polish practices in dealing with immigrants and asylum seekers raise some concern. Zimowski claimed that only three Russians had applied for asylum.[71] He stated that Poland had appropriate procedures for asylum and that, moreover, asylum seekers had the right of appeal. This, however, does not tell the whole story. According to independent observers, the Polish government has been actively discouraging some refugees from applying for asylum. The Warsaw representative of the United Nations High Commissioner for Refugees (UNHCR) has found that the government has discouraged asylum seekers, especially citizens of the former Soviet Union, Bulgaria, and Romania.[72] Furthermore, contrary to the Geneva Convention, the government in 1993 stopped issuing permanent-residence documents to registered refugees, thereby limiting the refugees' ability to seek gainful employment. And to compound the problem, it has refused to allow undocumented refugees to apply for asylum.[73]

Given the current relatively small number of asylum seekers and the prospect for significant future increases, this would seem to be a propitious time for the government to deal with the problem. It needs to confront the issue of the rights of asylum seekers and immigrants and develop a comprehensive policy that the population would understand and accept. Given the high rate of unemployment in Poland, the tendencies toward populism, insensitivity toward minority rights, and the fear of crime, which is often attributed to foreigners, this is a very difficult task. But with increasing illegal migration and greater demands for legal access, refugees and immigration will be increasingly important issues. Yet the government is doing little to prepare itself and, even more significantly, the public. It would be most unfortunate if Poland's government were to continue to largely ignore the warning signs of impending danger to democracy in this area.

Conclusion

Many government officials in Poland contend that democracy is irreversible. Given the enormous sacrifices the Polish people have made, the great strides that they have taken toward the achievement of democracy, and the high degree of political legitimacy that has been achieved, clearly the odds are in Poland's favor. A great deal more remains to be done, however, before Poland achieves the level of democratic development reached in Western Europe. Since Poland wishes to become a member of the European Union, that is a fair standard. And since Poland is still in a transition period, Adam Michnik's arguments about the fragility of democracy in Poland are persuasive, at the very least as caveats. Second, even if Western European standards of democracy are reached, this is not a guarantee against extremism, particularly right-wing extremism. In all democracies society must continually struggle against extremist instincts, organizations, and activities. The most successful democracies cannot afford to be complacent on the issue of extremism.

In Poland the response to the warning signs of extremism is less than adequate. Some loss of momentum, perception of the majority as primary victims, insensitivities toward minorities, inadequate progress on law and legality, and an insufficient understanding of the issues of refugees and immigrants can spell major problems for the future. As has been discussed, the most visible manifestations of extremism, particularly of the right-wing variety, are clearly not the greatest danger in Poland. Poland needs to understand its past and deal with the changes in the region. Though some issues may be unique to Poland, Warsaw must also probe the same general transformational problems that the other postcommunist states are facing. Except for complacency and a refusal to take preventive measures, there is no reason Poland should not be able to resolve these problems successfully.

Notes

1. *Economist*, February 24, 1996, 112.
2. Louisa Vinton, "Poland," *RFE/RL Research Report* 3(16), April 22, 1994: 62–67.
3. Louisa Vinton, "Party X and the Tyminski Phenomenon," *RFE/RL Research Report*, no. 32, August 9, 1991.
4. Vinton, "Poland," 65.
5. Dr. Stanislaw Krajewski (co-chair, Polish Council of Christians and Jews), interview with the author, Warsaw, May 20, 1994.
6. Vinton, "Poland," 66.
7. Ibid.
8. *Gazeta Wyborcza* (Warsaw), March 10, 1994.
9. Krajewski interview.
10. Louisa Vinton, "'Outsider' Parties and the Political Process in Poland," *RFE/RL Research Report* 3(3), January 21, 1994: 13–22.
11. Ibid.
12. *Gazeta Wyborcza*, May 14–15, 1994.
13. *New York Times*, June 14, 1992.
14. *Globe and Mail*, Toronto, November 23, 1995.
15. *RFE/RL News Briefs*, June 22–24, 1994, 13.
16. Wiktor Osiatynski, "A Letter from Poland," *East European Constitutional Review* 4(2), Spring 1995: 36.
17. Ibid.

18. Anna Sabbat-Swidlicka, "Pawlak Builds Up Peasant Power," *RFE/RL Research Report* 3(24), June 17, 1994: 13–19.

19. *RFE/RL News Briefs*, June 20–24, 1994, 12.

20. *Economist*, January 15, 1994, 56.

21. *RFE/RL News Briefs*, August 8–12, 1994, 12–13.

22. *REF/RL News Briefs*, July 5–8, 1994, 9.

23. *Economist*, October 7, 1995, 57.

24. *Globe and Mail*, November 22, 1995.

25. *East European Constitutional Review* 4(4), Fall 1995: 19.

26. Wiktor Osiatynski, "After Walesa," *East European Constitutional Review* 4(4), Fall 1995: 38.

27. *Economist*, October 7, 1995, 57; *East European Constitutional Revie* 4(4), Fall 1995: 19.

28. Ibid.

29. *Transition*, 6(11–12), November-December 1995: 26; *OECD Transition Brief*, no. 1, Autumn 1995, 2.

30. *Economist*, September 3, 1994, 52–53.

31. See David Stark, "The Hidden Character of East European Capitalism: Recombinant Ownership," *Transition*, 6(11–12), November-January 1995: 13–15.

32. *Economist*, February 25, 1995, 55.

33. *RFE/RL News Briefs*, July 18–22, 1994, 10.

34. *Economist*, November 1995, 80.

35. Konstanti Gebert, interview with the author, Warsaw, May 18, 1994.

36. Bronislaw Geremek, interview with the author, Warsaw, May 19, 1994.

37. Ibid.

38. Geremek interview.

39. Adam Michnik, interview with the author, Warsaw, May 18, 1994.

40. Ibid.

41. Ibid.

42. Louisa Vinton, "Solidarity's Rival Offspring," *RFE/RL Report on Eastern Europe*, no. 38, September 1990.

43. Michnik was extremely disturbed by the unwillingness of most Poles to look at these issues and the vitriolic personal attack directed against him for questioning what he calls "little nationalism." Michnik interview.

44. Ibid.

45. *Gazeta Wyborcza*, July 1, 1991.

46. Gebert interview.

47. Ibid.

48. Marek Nowicki, interview with the author, Warsaw, May 18, 1994.

49. Ibid.

50. Ibid.

51. Marek Szyperski and Ireneusz Dudziec, "Gypsy Pogrom in Mlawa," *Gazeta Wyborcza*, June 28, 1921; and Marak Debicki, "Skinheads Sentenced," *Gazeta Wyborcza*, February 1, 1994; Vinton, "Poland," 62–63.

52. Jerzy Zimowski, interview with the author, Warsaw, May 19, 1994.

53. Department of State, *"Poland" Country Reports on Human Rights Practices for 1993*, February 1994, Washington, D.C., p. 1002.

54. Krajewski interview.
55. Geremek and Michnik interviews.
56. *RFE/RL News Briefs*, June 6–10, 1994, 15.
57. Pawel Wildstein, interview with the author, Warsaw, May 19, 1994.
58. Zimowski interview.
59. Ibid.
60. Department of State, "Poland," 995.
61. Ibid.
62. Ibid.
63. *RFE/RL News Briefs*, July 18–22, 1994, 14.
64. Department of State, "Poland," 996.
65. Ibid.
66. Ibid.
67. Osiatynski, "After Walesa," 44.
68. Zimowski interview.
69. Jan B. de Weydenthal, "Immigration into Poland," *RFE/RL Research Report* 3(24), June 17, 1994: 39–41.
70. Ibid., 41.
71. Zimowski interview.
72. Department of State, "Poland," 999.
73. Ibid.

10

Hungary: From "Goulash Communism" to Pluralistic Democracy

Aurel Braun

Budapest seems to be booming. In the center of the city, new luxury shops are crammed with expensive goods from the West. The major hotels are filled with Western businesspeople and tourists. Hungarians have always been voracious readers, and the newsstands are now crammed with an enormous variety of domestic and foreign publications. It certainly appears that Hungary has been successful in moving from "goulash communism" to political pluralism and markets.

There are many concrete indicators suggesting that this apparent success in democratic and market transition is real. In May 1994, Hungary held its second free and democratic elections. Power has been peacefully transferred to the Hungarian Socialist Party (HSP), which gathered an absolute majority of the 386 seats in parliament, and its junior coalition party, the Alliance of Free Democrats (AFD). The HSP, which is the successor to the Communist Party, has transformed itself into a social democratic party. Moreover, the new HSP-controlled government has declared its full commitment to democracy and marketization.[1] Such is Western confidence in Hungary's transition from communism toward democracy and a free market that although the country has only 10.5 million inhabitants, it has been the recipient of roughly one-half of the total Western investment in East-Central Europe.

Numerous human rights organizations and environmental groups now operate in Hungary without government restriction or interference. With about 10 percent of its population made up of minorities, Hungary has been a country that seems to have been able to keep extremism, particularly its right-wing variation, under control. True, the country has hundreds of skinheads and a number of extreme-right-wing parties and groups, such as the Hungarian National Front Line (which has contacts with Western neo-Nazis) and the World National Popular Rule Party (WNPRP). But none of these parties managed to gain representation in parliament during the May 1994 elections.[2] Of the two large and best known radical populist parties, Istvan Csurka's Hungarian Justice and Life Party (HJLP) and Jozsef Torgyan's Independent Smallholders' and Civic Party (ISCP), both of which hold certain extremist views, only the latter managed to gain representation in parliament by passing the required 5 percent threshold.[3]

The Hungarian population, therefore, appears to have rejected extremism. Given the relatively few outbreaks of violence against ethnic minorities, it would appear that there is little cause for concern about the dangers of extremism. Yet all of these positive developments, as encouraging as they should be, tell only part of the story. Hungary, which aspires to join the European Union (EU) and NATO, needs to progress further before it reaches the democratic standards extant in Western Europe and the level of economic development and stability that will allow integration. Moreover, the new government has made positive declarations but has had relatively little time to implement policies. There are, therefore, several areas that need to be examined in order to ascertain the nature of any extremist threat in Hungary and evaluate the danger it may present. As Hungary is a postcommunist state in transition, it should be useful to look at the areas of momentum, the possibility that there may be a "majority as victim" mentality, minority rights, laws and legality, and the treatment of refugees.

Momentum

Unlike Poland, the democratic government in Hungary, elected in 1990, did not opt for "shock therapy." Instead, it decided on a more gradualist approach to transition, hoping to avoid some of the pain of the wrenching changes in the political and, particularly, economic areas that "shock therapy" demanded. Nevertheless, the Hungarian Democratic Forum (HDF) government suffered an ignominious defeat in the 1994 elections. Hungary, therefore, refutes the often-made argument that former communists are brought back to power because people in the postcommunist states find the pain of "shock therapy" unbearable. The reasons for the defeat of the HDF government, however, can inform us about the nature of the momentum in Hungary and the problems of sustaining it.

The democratic leaders who took over in 1990 did not have a full understanding of the nature of the transition from Marxist-Leninist rule. Their attempt to diminish the pain of transition by employing a gradualist economic approach was well intended, but they failed to recognize that economic stress was but one of the elements of transformation. Economic arguments notwithstanding (and there is increasing evidence to suggest that those who press ahead with transition most rapidly and consistently suffer the smallest costs), there were all sorts of noneconomic shocks. As Deputy State Secretary of the Defense Ministry Zoltan Pecze observed quite perceptively, the country suffered and will continue for some time to be affected by overall cultural shock.[4] That is, regardless of the economic pace, the movement toward democracy and markets cuts the umbilical cord of dependence between the people and the state. Politically, the people needed to recreate civil society, which of course exists outside of government direction. Psychologically, they were now exposed to real political and economic risks. These were the issues that any democratic government would need to address. To succeed, it would need to both articulate a vision for the transformation and sustain the momentum to achieve it.

In fact, much of the pain that the people of Hungary have experienced since the transition to democracy began is not a result of the transition itself. More than four decades of a fatally flawed social experiment destroyed a great deal of the social fabric, prevented the development of a democratic political order that was occurring in Western Europe, and grossly distorted economic development. Hungary's economy was in far worse shape than most Western observers believed at the time the democrats took over in 1990. Inefficient and obsolete industries, subsidized agriculture, shoddy and uncompetitive goods, a terribly neglected infrastructure, and the loss of the work ethic were in part camouflaged by the faux prosperity of "goulash communism," which essentially floated on a sea of massive Western debt. This debt, the highest per capita in the Soviet bloc, not only helped hide the reality of disastrous economic development but also left a burden that continues to significantly damage the prospects for Hungarian economic development.

The HDF-led government should have communicated effectively to the people the scope of the disaster it had inherited and should have sustained a dialogue with the people on how to achieve the widely desired goals of the country: democratization, marketization, and eventual integration into the community of democratic and industrially advanced European states. And it should have engaged in political confidence-building measures so as to assure the population that rights were no longer ephemeral, that institutions were no longer arbitrary, and that it would try to the best of its ability to ensure that the inevitable pain engendered in implementing the basic goals (on which there seemed to be such a high level of consensus) would be shared fairly by everyone.

This would be an extraordinary difficult task in the best of circumstances. Any governing party or coalition is bound to make mistakes. But even if we take all these difficulties into account, the HDF was not quite up to the task. Many of the leaders of the HDF were honorable and well-intentioned individuals. They also were largely inexperienced intellectuals, were new to government after more than four decades of communist rule, and made numerous mistakes that not only resulted in electoral disaster for the party but also had an impact on the momentum of transformation.

First, the HDF leaders, often referred to as "the long beards" by an increasingly dissatisfied and contemptuous population, could not shake their image as incompetent and often uncaring intellectuals. They could not overcome the class and educational cleavages that have long existed and that were reinforced in Hungary under communist rule. Very cleverly the communist regime would alternately persecute and pamper the intelligentsia while excluding them from real power. The intelligentsia had little inclination and even less skill in communicating with the population at large. The HDF leaders, true to form, talked down to the population rather than engaging in genuine dialogue.[5] They raised exaggerated expectations of a rapid transformation and economic help from the West instead of impressing on the population the scope of the economic disaster the communists had left behind and the lengthy and painful period that would have to be endured before the country could be turned around politically, economically, and socially.

Second, the HDF exhibited some antidemocratic tendencies that clearly damaged its credibility in general and among urban liberals and social democrats in particular. For years the party refused to confront the fact that one of its founding fathers, the poet-playwright Istvan Csurka, was an extreme populist who had little respect for pluralistic democracy and was an anti-Semite.[6] It was only under extreme pressure, both from within and outside the country, that the HDF finally parted company with Csurka. Furthermore, in attempting to rule through a coalition, it built partnerships (that later disintegrated) with such unsavory authoritarian figures as Sandor Gyorivanyi.

Third, the HDF pursued an exclusive and clumsy nationalism. It sought to differentiate between "real Hungarians" and others.[7] Whatever the original intent, this impacted the minorities and in particular the Jews and Roma. Though many in the HDF leadership could not be viewed as anti-Semitic, they were nevertheless insensitive to the implications of their emphasis on Hungarian uniqueness and exclusivity.

Fourth, though committed to markets and economic normalization, the HDF did not take advantage of its gradualist approach to privatization to ensure fairness. Certainly there were difficulties. Perhaps it could be argued that the communists, in the months before they lost power, had engaged in even worse abuses by allowing "red directors" to reap enormous economic gains as firms were being privatized. But the HDF's own privatization program was very poorly handled. It created a sense of unfairness and an impression of corruption.

Fifth, the electoral campaign of the HDF in 1994 was particularly inept. It was characterized by a kind of raw anticommunism that took on such hysterical dimensions that it raised questions about the government's own commitment to fairness and democracy. Ultimately, it bordered on antipolitics, it damaged a belief in the emerging democratic political order, and, not least of all, it contrasted sharply with the smooth professional and confident campaign of the HSP.

Sixth, the government's attempts to use the media to discredit the opposition parties and to improve its own position both before and during the 1994 campaign proved to be counterproductive. The HDF government used budgetary control to influence television and radio. A number of programs were canceled for political reasons.[8] In March 1994, Hungarian radio, seemingly at the behest of the government, abruptly dismissed 129 editors and journalists (most of whom had been critical of the government and many of whom also happened to be Jewish).[9] The firings only two months before the national elections were widely viewed as a cynical attempt by the government to improve its electoral chances. And only one week before the first round of the general elections in 1994, the heavily government-influenced Hungarian television used two of its most popular programs to launch vitriolic attacks on the leader of the HSP.[10]

All of these policies, acts, and attitudes of the HDF government weakened its mandate and played an important role in its ultimate defeat. They also damaged the cause of democracy, not necessarily by blocking the momentum but by weakening it. Ironically, it is now up to the new socialist-led coalition to reinforce that momentum. This is essential because there is a danger of polarization and of exaggerated expectations that could result in violent political swings at the next election. Unless the momentum for democracy is reinforced, there is the danger that the parties that are out of power, including the HDF, could become more extreme.

It is a little premature to assess fully the policies of the new HSP-dominated government. It clearly has a very difficult task, but at least in terms of promises, it appears committed to democratization and marketization. In my interview with Dr. Imre Szekeres, the vice president of the HSP, he emphasized his party's commitment to pluralistic democracy and individual rights and promised sensitivity to minority concerns.[11]

Although the HSP-led coalition has been in power a relatively short time, there are additional clues to the new government's political and economic direction. One could not be but impressed with the sophistication and commitment to democracy of the younger HSP leaders such as Imre Szekeres. He is from a different generation than the prime minister, Gyula Horn, and there is little reason to doubt his sincerity. Most of his work and career experiences occurred during a period when, especially to those inside the system, it should have been fully obvious that Marxism-Leninism was a fatally flawed political order that could not be reformed. For such leaders social democracy is not merely a slogan but a clear break with a totalizing past. It is also encouraging that the HSP, despite an absolute majority of seats in parliament, chose to opt for a coalition with the AFD, a party clearly committed to democracy. In part, HSP may have sought a coalition in order to share any possible blame for difficult economic measures that it would need to take. It is also likely that it formed a partnership in order to enhance its legitimacy as a social democratic party. In terms of its promises, therefore, the HSP-led government should continue and may even enhance the momentum of democratization and marketization.

Some of the early measures by the HSP-led government, however, do raise questions about its ability and willingness to sustain the momentum for transformation in both the political and economic realms. The cabinet lineup in the Horn government, contrary to some expectations, consists mostly of professional politicians and party loyalists.[12] Though the average age is very low at 49.7 years, most of the key cabinet members, including the ministers of foreign affairs and finance and the minister without portfolio responsible for national security services, had served in high-ranking positions in the former communist government.[13] Significantly, the AFD's influence is limited to only three ministerial portfolios. It includes only one senior ministry, Internal Affairs, under Gabor Kuncze (who will also serve as the prime minister's coalition deputy). Furthermore, in contrast to its constant criticism of the HDF government, which is in part understandable, the Horn government has made no critical reference to the previous communist government. There is a concern, therefore, that the Horn government might view itself more as a successor to the (failed) reform communist government than as the second democratically elected one. That would clearly go against the expectation of the vast majority of Hungarians and would significantly damage the momentum of transformation.

There are some other disconcerting signs as well. The Horn government, as its first legal act, passed legislation that would supersede an earlier law that required mayors to resign after being elected to parliament.[14] The original law, which had sought to strengthen local government by ensuring that elected positions were full time, now has been weakened. Yet the devolution of authority and the strengthening of local governments is one of the best ways to enhance popular participation in governance.

Furthermore, the Horn government seems to be following the policies of its predecessors in trying to control state radio and television. It promptly appointed new radio and television heads without reaching consensus with the opposition parties.[15] The new directors then proceeded quickly to dismiss reporters who, they claimed, were politically biased and abolished a number of programs they claimed were politically unbalanced.[16]

In a seemingly positive development, in 1995 the Constitutional Court (case no.61/1995x.6 ABnat) struck down the Horn government's decree that had put the Hungarian News Agency under the government's direct supervision.[17] The court found that any direct government supervision of the media was an unacceptable restriction on freedom of expression. Yet because a comprehensive media law had not yet been enacted, the court suspended its decision, concluding (bizarrely) that a lack of regulation was more dangerous than no regulation, regardless of how poorly designed.[18]

In the economic realm as well, there have been mixed signals. The government has declared that its first priority is to speed up modernization and the transition to a market economy, which would include privatization, tax exemptions for domestic and foreign investments, improved tax collection, and reductions in state subsidies.[19] But at the same time the government committed itself to protecting the population from the harsh side effects of economic transformation. Since no country in history has been able to achieve both of these commendable goals simultaneously, there is reason to ask whether the government proclamations were anything more than declaratory statements. Such tactics are unfortunate because in order for momentum to be sustained, expectations must be lowered rather than raised.

Some of the answers came fairly quickly. Certainly there had been some signs of economic revival, such as the 9.4 percent growth in industrial production and the 30 percent increase in investment in the first quarter of 1994.[20] But in fact the Hungarian economy was in very poor shape. In 1994 the huge budget deficit stood at 7 percent of the GDP.[21] The current account deficit reached an untenable record $3.9 billion and the *net* foreign debt increased to $18.9 billion (from $13.3 billion in 1992), by far the highest per capita in Eastern and Central Europe.[22] Domestic demand exceeded production by 7 percent,[23] thus fueling already heavy inflationary pressures. Yet for more than six months the Horn government did not deliver a comprehensive or clearly defined plan.[24] The Finance Minister, Laszlo Bekesi, who wanted to introduce radical measures to restructure the economy and reduce social spending, was stymied at every turn by the left wing of the HSP. In January 1995 he resigned in frustration. Economic conditions were deteriorating so badly that by March 1995 Standard and Poor lowered the rating for Hungary's foreign debt to BB+ with a negative output.[25]

Faced with a domestic and foreign loss of confidence and pressured by his coalition partner, in March 1995 Horn appointed a no-nonsense banker, Lajos Bokros, as finance minister. Bokros moved quickly to implement a macroeconomic stabilization package that hinged on drastically reducing social spending. He argued, "A country as indebted as Hungary cannot afford to spend the equivalent of 27% of annual GDP on welfare and social services. . . . The universal entitlement will have to go."[26] The austerity measures were harsh and, in the typical fashion of the Hungarian intelligentsia, were poorly explained to the population.[27] The three-year plan for economic recovery included effecting severe cuts in social benefits, raising taxes, and reducing wages in conditions of high unemployment and inflation. Under the circumstances it is little wonder that social and political opposition to the austerity program grew quickly. Extremist forces on both the right and the left thus had opportunity to tap into popular discontent. The effectiveness of the program was diminished when the Constitutional Court struck down several provisions of the Bokros package,[28] and the left in the HSP quickly lost confidence in the package and pressured Horn to alter it drastically. In early 1996 Bokros resigned, casting new doubts about Hungary's economic stability and government attempts to maintain the momentum for economic transformation.

The new privatization program, which was meant to both improve economic performance and provide political reassurance that the process would be fair, has fallen significantly short of expectations. The new privatization law of May 1995 provides a transparent legal framework for pursuing privatization. But the second Organization for Economic Cooperation and Development (OECD) Hungarian economic survey claims that the government's implementational strategy, including employment conditions and poor asset backing for compensation vouchers, suggests a lack of commitment to the privatization process.[29]

There are, then, significant contradictions in the government's program as well as mixed economic signals. The Horn government still has an opportunity to regain and reinforce the momentum for transformation, but it can do so only if it enters into an honest dialogue with the population and makes a clear break with the Marxist-Leninist past. It can ill afford to engage in media purges for political reasons or to polarize politics in Hungary. The best prospects are the politics of inclusion. Though the vast majority of the people of Hungary have suffered in the past and are likely to feel for some time the pain of transition, the new government, as elsewhere in the post-Soviet states, needs to prevent the development or the continuation of the "majority as victim" syndrome.

Majority as Victim

For a long time, Hungary has been on the losing side of international conflicts. In two world wars and during the 1956 Soviet suppression of the Hungarian Revolution, its people suffered a series of terrible losses. In the first two instances Hungary was hardly blameless. Yet even in these cases vast segments of the population concluded that the country had been treated less than fairly.

From being a partner in one of the world's most powerful empires, Hungary was transformed into a small and relatively insignificant East-Central European state after World War I. Even today Hungary has more of its co-nationals living in neighboring states than any other East European country. At the end of World War II, the loss of territory and population was worsened by the gradual imposition of a communist regime by the Soviet Union.

It should not be difficult to understand or even empathize with a good deal of the suffering that the Hungarian people had endured. This is very different, however, from a perception that the vast majority of the people are victims and, moreover, victims of a conspiracy by internal and external forces involving foreign powers and domestic minorities. An honest reexamination of the past would not only reveal the extent to which authoritarianism contributed to the misfortunes of the Hungarian people but would also help develop a forward-looking policy, so essential to the successful entrenchment of democratic processes and institutions. There is at least an opportunity to fairly address everyone's grievances—again, democracy is a necessary (though not sufficient) condition.

The HDF's record, though, on ending what among many segments of the population was a "majority as victim" syndrome, is extremely poor. It encouraged nationalism and exclusivity throughout its rule and, for the better half of it, was in coalition with groups that took extreme populist stances. Torgyan's ISCP illustrates the problem, as does the prominent role that Istvan Csurka played for so long in the HDF.

Torgyan's ISCP, which in the 1994 elections finished ahead of the Alliance of Young Democrats, did not start out as an extremist party. Its long and often distinguished history spans more than eighty years. At times it opposed the Nazis and later the communists. Now it may be best described as an extreme populist party. The interview with Dr. Torgyan in May 1994 was disturbing but also had some of the elements of a comic opera. It was conducted in a very large room at Torgyan's headquarters. He sat across the table with three other cohorts. Together they exhibited a combination of old-world manners and some of the worst authoritarian biases. Seemingly unaware of any democratic sensitivities, lugubrious and pompous, they began the interview by insisting that the Hungarian majority was the perennial victim.[30] Like other East European ultranationalists, Torgyan insisted on the uniqueness of Hungarian suffering and the uniqueness of the "Trianon tragedy," the treaty following World War I that deprived Hungary of huge territories. Without any sense of history or irony, Torgyan then proceeded to explain the similarity of the fate of Hungarians deported from the Transylvanian city of Cluj following the Romanian takeover of that region after World War I and the deportation of the Jews during the Holocaust.

Under communism the Hungarian majority again was the victim of both internal and external forces. The Soviet Union, of course, imposed communism from the outside, but Torgyan also felt it important to point out that "too many Jews took part in the communist regime."[31] In more recent times, he contended, the Hungarian majority was insulted and slandered by statements made by the former chief rabbi of Budapest. He added that he had information that after Rabbi Landesmann left Hungary following widespread condemnation, he had been given a high position abroad.[32] The information about Landesmann's "important" position abroad, in fact, is incorrect (and the rabbi had insisted that his supposedly derogatory comments had been provoked and reported inaccurately),[33] but here was the Jewish conspiracy again, and in Torgyan's view the Hungarian majority was being victimized anew.

Given such views, it is noteworthy that popular support for Torgyan's ISCP skyrocketed in 1995 (due in large part to the popular dissatisfaction with the ill-explained austerity program). By September 1995 the opinion polls showed that support for the ISCP had surpassed that for the governing HSP.[34]

Csurka, as one of the HDF's founding fathers, has played an even more insidious role in perpetrating this myth of the "majority as victim" than Torgyan (who was merely associated with the ruling party). As far back as 1990, Csurka spoke of the victimization of the majority of Hungarians. In a 1990 pamphlet entitled "Wake Up—Hungarians!" he argued that a "dwarf minority" prevented Hungarians from realizing their true national essence.[35] The term "dwarf minority" was a coded but not too subtle reference to Hungarian Jews. Protests against Csurka in 1990 and the following year had little effect. Though the majority of the HDF leadership was not anti-Semitic, there were deep sympathies for the populist arguments about majority victimization. It was, in fact, a kind of competitive victimization; many in the HDF leadership equated Hungarian suffering under the communists with Jewish suffering under the Nazis. This problem was compounded by the HDF's reluctance to examine honestly Hungary's interwar and World War II past. If not glorifying outright the authoritarian rule of Admiral Horthy, the HDF government still conveniently forgot that, for instance, the early 1944 deportations to Auschwitz of Hungarian Jews occurred at the behest of the Horthy government.[36]

It is important and fair to reiterate that eventually the HDF did part company with Csurka (after more than two years in power). The HJLP, which Csurka founded in June 1993 shortly after he was expelled from the HDF, is clearly an extremist party, profoundly ultranationalist and anti-Semitic. It did not win enough votes in May 1994 elections to gain representation in parliament. None of the major parties, including the HDF, views it as a suitable partner. But the HDF's strong nationalistic and authoritarian tendencies could be reinforced during the HJLP's political exile.

Torgyan's ISCP, however, as noted, is in parliament, and I was interested in the HSP leadership's perception of this ultrapopulist party. I was surprised in my interview with Szekeres to find that he did not exclude cooperation with Torgyan's party.[37] Szekeres felt that Torgyan was a clever politician who could be "handled." Given Torgyan's extreme views, it seemed rather puzzling why the effort to handle him would be worthwhile. This became somewhat more clear when Szekeres began to talk about ethnic Hungarians living in the former Yugoslavia, Romania, and Slovakia. The HSP is also prepared to play the nationalist card. He and his party were concerned with nationalism in Hungary and particularly the possibility that the persecution of Hungarians in the surrounding states could create domestic as well as external security problems. Szekeres, in fact, suggested strongly that the inviolability of borders should be combined with some form of autonomy for Hungarians in Romania, Serbia, and Slovakia.[38]

The Horn government, though, clearly wishes to avoid the kind of confrontational relations with its neighbors, particularly Romania and Slovakia, that the HDF government had. Whereas the HDF prime minister, Jozsef Antall, had provocatively proclaimed that he was "in spirit the Prime Minister of 15 million Hungarians" (there are only 10.5 million in Hungary), Horn declared in May that he wanted to be the prime minister of 10.5 million Hungarians while at the same time sharing a "deep feeling of responsibility for the fate of Hungarians living abroad."[39]

It may indeed be the case that the foreign government is trying to finesse the problem of nationalism and security. In moving closer to Eastern Europe and becoming more lukewarm to integration into the EU and NATO, it may be responding to nationalist fears of westernization. But in dealing with Romania and Slovakia, in particular, it could face new problems. The danger is that without an honest examination of the problems of nationalism and without a rejection of the notion of the majority as victim, the Horn government may merely camouflage a problem that, with all the progress that Hungary has made, could still prove to be a seminal impediment to democratization. Though it is wise for a democratic government to take into account the full constellation of political forces, pandering to extremist parties or views is likely to prove dangerously counterproductive in the longer term.

The Status of Minorities

There is a duality in Hungary's approach to minorities. The policy at its most cynical level was summed up by Jozsef Torgyan. He declared that Hungary should give more rights to minorities so that it could *demand* more rights for ethnic Hungarians in neighboring states.[40] Neither the HDF nor the HSP-led governments have been or are quite as cynical or blunt, but both minorities appear to fall into two categories. The minute ethnic Romanian, Serb, Croat, and Ruthenian communities in Hungary have had few problems. Partly this may be due to their very small numbers, but there was also the component of demonstrating good faith and tolerance toward ethnic groups whose co-nationals form the majority in the neighboring states. There was at least an implicit expectation of reciprocity. It has been a different situation with two large minorities who do not have co-national majorities in neighboring states—Roma and Jews.

Even the statistical data on Roma and Jews are subject to some contro-versy. In the case of the Roma, the Hungarian government has been rather reluctant to provide an accurate assessment of the rapidly growing size of the community. In the case of the Jews, there has been a very high degree of as-similation and intermarriage. Often Jews themselves are reluctant to be iden-tified as part of that community. The most common estimate of the number of Roma is 600,000,[41] and official statistics generally refer to 80,000 Jews, although according to the Israeli law-of-return definition, there may be as many as 150,000.[42]

Both communities have suffered from discrimination and physical threats, but there are some significant differences. The Roma community is signifi-cantly poorer than the rest of the country. Its unemployment rate is esti-mated at 70 percent, more than five times the national average.[43] There are widespread prejudices against the Roma as untrustworthy and as responsible for high crime rates. They have often been subjects of attacks by extremists, particularly skinheads. There have also been reports of frequent police abuses against Roma.[44]

On July 7, 1993, the Hungarian National Assembly passed a new law on ethnic and minority rights (Act 77 of 1993).[45] It legally established the con-cept of the collective rights of minorities. It appears to provide generously for the rights of ethnic minorities. It explicitly permits organized forms of limited self-government in areas where ethnic minorities constitute a major-ity. It also allows associations, movements, and political parties based on an ethnic or national character and mandates unrestricted use of ethnic lan-guages.

The Roma and twelve other ethnic or national groups were included. Jews, because many in the community considered themselves purely a reli-gious group, were not included among the thirteen groups covered. For the Roma, who for the first time have received legal status as a national minority, Act 77 should have been a significant improvement. The benefits of the act in turn, however, hinged on changes in attitudes and the effectiveness of im-plementation.

In the December 1994 local elections, almost all designated minority groups (except the Ukrainians) nominated candidates for minority councils. The Roma were to form 264 minority councils, 163 of these in small com-munities (of under 10,000).[46] But there remains, unfortunately, consider-able confusion over the jurisdiction of minority (and local) councils and over how much funding is to go to the minority bodies.[47]

Attitudes, of course, are the most difficult to change. At the more populist level, prejudices remain deeply embedded. In our interview, Torgyan at first declared that the Romani problem was simply unsolvable.[48] He then con-tended that the best way to deal with the problem was to return to the old *vaida* system, where the Roma lived on the land under their own leadership but were separated from the rest of the population. The Romani leadership then would be held responsible both to the Romani population and to the state. In essence, Torgyan was suggesting that, since in is his view the Roma could not be integrated into society, the only logical solution was apartheid. And whereas Torgyan accused the Roma of heavy involvement in criminal activities, he vigorously attacked Roma claims of physical attacks and abuse as utterly false.

The HDF government's views on the Roma were certainly more sympathetic than Torgyan's. Nevertheless, its earlier concerns for human rights waned somewhat. The passage of the law on minority rights was positive but, as noted, would depend a great deal on implementation. Dr. Karoly Bard, the deputy state secretary of justice in the HDF government, seemed genuinely concerned in a May 1994 interview with the rights of the Roma.[49] But he also expressed his misgivings about the abilities and sensitivities of the leadership of the Ministry of the Interior (especially the then two deputy leaders), which was so important to effective protection.

Bard's fears proved to be fully justified in my interview with Dr. Fabian Jozsa, secretary of state, in the Ministry of the Interior.[50] Though a relatively young man, Jozsa came across almost like a caricature of the old communist apparatchik. First, in his view there was no problem. Race hatred in Hungary had been exaggerated, racially motivated crimes were statistically insignificant, and racially motivated abuses by the police were almost unheard of. Second, the law on nationalities passed in July 1993 and the Criminal Code, Section 156, dealing with racially motivated crimes, were perfectly adequate. Third, the implementation of the law and the code, he smugly contended (ignoring numerous concerns that have been raised in the newspapers and by human rights groups) was very effective. In sum, since there was no real problem, there was no need for real concern. Jozsa's obtuseness and insensitivity on these issues unfortunately seemed more typical of the HDF government than Bard's approach.

Szekeres indicated that the new HSP government would be more sensitive to the problems of the Romani minority.[51] He was aware of difficulties faced by both the Roma and the Jews. Nevertheless, although he seemed perturbed by the ineffectiveness of the police in protecting the Roma and was aware of occasional police abuses, he and his party do not seem to be driven by any urgency. Rather, he suggested that the Romani problem was part of the general conundrum of the transformation to a democratic society. In part this is correct, but the special difficulties of ethnic and religious minorities in Hungary, as elsewhere in the region, do go beyond the general issues and do require special solutions. The Roma can ill afford delays in addressing the problem.

In the case of the Jewish community, the concerns are somewhat different but no less dangerous or urgent. The HDF government sought good relations with Jews and provided funds to restore the main Budapest synagogue. But the community has been faced with two kinds of anti-Semitism: visceral (or traditional) and political.

The Jewish community in Hungary is by far the largest in Eastern Europe. A great many of the members of the community have been successful economically and some even politically. Ironically, though the community is very highly assimilated, it is far from accepted by society at large. The latter is not always adequately understood by Hungarian Jews. That is, there is a widespread belief among many Jews that they are invisible in Hungarian society, that they are indistinguishable from ethnic Hungarians.[52] This results in a kind of denial syndrome where many are reluctant to confront anti-Semitic manifestations. There is often a tendency to cover up the problem, to engage in self-censorship.[53] Despite its wealth, the Jewish community is fragmented and thus poorly organized.

Most Jews were reluctant to be registered as an ethnic minority because of the bitter memories of World War II, when they were singled out for persecution and extermination. Though there has been a Jewish revival among some of the younger members of the community, overall there is a reluctance to be openly identified as a Jew.[54]

Assimilation and self-censorship have failed to prevent anti-Semitism. The HDF government did not encourage or actively condone anti-Semitism, but neither was it sufficiently quick in disassociating itself from anti-Semitic attitudes. Traditional anti-Semitism, the view that Jews are an untrustworthy, conspiratorial, and ultimately very negative element in society, continues. It should be pointed out, though, that these negative attitudes are held by a much smaller percentage of the population in Hungary than in Poland.[55] But fairly widespread views of the majority as victim continue to encourage exclusivist attitudes. Moreover, various forms of prejudices may not show up in relatively simple surveys of anti-Semitism. In fact, there have been numerous manifestations of anti-Semitism in Hungary. These include desecration of cemeteries and physical assaults on Jews[56] as well as anti-Semitic graffiti and television programs with anti-Semitic jokes and anti-Semitic portrayals of Jewish characters.[57]

Political anti-Semitism remains powerful and in some respects is a growing force. Jews in Hungary, as in Poland, are associated with "rootless cosmopolitanism" and Western liberalism. Therefore, nationalist and populist forces reject Jews almost as a concept. The victory of the HSP in coalition with the AFD at first would seem to reverse an old trend. But paradoxically, since the AFD is very heavily associated, at least in the public mind, with Jews, leaders of the Jewish community fear that the new government may be less sympathetic to Jews because of a need to demonstrate to the majority that it is not *overly* sympathetic to a mistrusted minority.[58]

Laws and Legality

Hungary suffers from some of the same problems as the other East European states in its quest to ensure democratic legality. First, although Hungarian judges, in part as a benefit of reform communism, are better qualified than in other socialist states, these qualifications generally are quite low by democratic standards, and there remains a constant danger of bias.[59] The judges on the Constitutional Court are by and large an isolated group and have not shown in general an adequate determination to fight hate and racism.[60] The ombudsman's office is also weak. Therefore, the judicial system, which is so important to democracy, needs to be transformed. This is a time-consuming task. Some improvements have been made, but the relatively low status of judges (except those on the Supreme Court) and the holdover judges from the communist era create difficulties.

Second, there are also problems with the laws that were designed to fight extremism and ensure minority rights. Article 156 of the Criminal Code is supposed to deal with racially motivated attacks against minorities (defined by nationality, sex, religion, language, or color), but the law is rather vague and difficult to implement.[61] Further, the law on minorities, though well intentioned, fails to reassure those subject to persecution. Romani organizations complained that the new law made no provisions for setting up specific institutions to guarantee minority rights and did not supply minorities with electoral ballots in their mother tongue.[62] The new government, therefore, should move to improve both Section 156 of the Criminal Code and the law on minorities. This task should be approached in a comprehensive fashion given the inadequacy of current laws and the failure of piecemeal attempts in the past (such as a law banning the wearing and dissemination of Nazi symbols).

Third, much more needs to be done to ensure the implementation of even flawed legislation and sections of the Criminal Code that can provide protection against extremism. The record so far is not entirely encouraging. In the prosecution under Article 156 of skinheads accused of attacks against Roma and Jews, the judges instead sentenced the skinheads according to the law on hooliganism.[63] The police also tend to look on these acts as mere vandalism or hooliganism.[64] Though there has been some improvement among the police forces on the issue of human rights, there is still little sensitivity. In October 1993, for instance, the police chief of Budapest, in response to a skinhead's complaint that he could not get into the university because there were too many African students, answered that he himself did not want to see 2 million "yellows" in Hungary.[65] Some positive steps were taken in 1995 toward prosecuting hate crimes. Albert Szabo, the leader of the WNPRP, and Istvan Gyorkos of the National Socialist Action Group were charged with incitement of racial hatred, use of symbols of tyranny, and dissemination of Nazi propaganda.[66] Both, however, were acquitted for lack of sufficient evidence. One of the prosecutors concluded that the antihate law itself would need to be modified to make it more effective.[67]

Last, there is a potential danger in the overwhelming victory achieved by the coalition partners in May 1994. With more that 70 percent of the seats, the HSP-AFD coalition could easily amend Hungary's most important laws, including the constitution. There is no indication that this will be the case, but the country would certainly benefit from a constitution where an amendment would require a much higher degree of consensus than merely that of an overwhelming parliamentary majority.

Refugees

Hungary is not a country of immigrants, but it has received numerous refugees, particularly from the former Yugoslavia. In part, Budapest's foreign policy has been designed to prevent the development of conditions in neighboring states whereby huge numbers of ethnic Hungarians would seek to emigrate to Hungary. But in addition to refugees from neighboring states, there have been individual claimants from Asia and Africa.[68]

The general difficulty that Hungary has had in dealing with minorities, the insensitivity that arises from the notion of the majority as a victim, and government denials that the refugees are a significant problem have added to the problem. Both local and international human rights organizations, for instance, accused the HDF government of detaining aliens in unacceptable conditions for excessively lengthy periods at its main detention center.[69]

The problem of illegal residents in Hungary is growing; authorities estimate them at 150,000.[70] New laws passed by the HDF government in 1994, in fact, gave more powers to bureaucrats to screen immigrants and refugees.[71] Application for immigrant status has been made much more difficult, and those seeking refugee status also face more limitations. Given well-known police biases in Hungary, this is potentially a dangerous development.

Though the number of foreign citizens who have engaged in crime has represented a relatively small percentage of the total, there is a general perception of widespread involvement. In fact, of 122,000 convicted of crime in 1993, only 5,472 were foreign citizens. Over 2,600 of the latter, however, were expelled for various legal violations, and nearly 16,000 foreigners were deprived of their residence permits.[72]

There are foreign links to crime, though, and this fact is exploited by the extremists. Hungary, which had been only a transit country for drugs, now has become a drug-producing state. In the first eight months of 1994, 1,300 kilograms of narcotics were seized compared to only 6.4 kilograms for the whole of 1990.[73] With the right-of-center parties in opposition, there is reason to fear that unless the government acts vigorously to dispel the myth of primary foreign responsibility for crime, the more extremist elements within these parties will exploit the issue of crime in a manner that could be damaging to the long-term prospects of democracy.

Conclusion

Hungary has one of the best records in the region on dealing with extremism, yet it faces numerous dangers. There have been too many missed opportunities by the HDF government to change peoples' attitudes and move more quickly toward entrenching democracy and markets. The momentum has not been lost entirely, but it has been diminished. And ironically, it is the HSP, successor to the communists, that must reinforce the momentum for democratization and marketization.

It is also obvious in Hungary that the domestic problems of extremism, as in neighboring countries, cannot be separated entirely from regional security. It is indeed in the interests of all states to stop extremism and protect ethnic and religious minorities so that they can encourage more effectively elsewhere better protection for co-nationals (or co-religionists). Moreover, the avoidance of domestic ethnic strife also prevents mass refugee flows and provides political economic progress that will allow integration with Western Europe. The latter consideration clearly restrains governments from allowing extremism. East-Central European states that so eagerly aspire to membership in the EU and NATO need to meet certain political as well as economic standards.

The most important constraints on extremism, including right-wing extremism, in the postcommunist states however, are domestic. There has to be a realization that extremism ultimately hurts everyone. People who have suffered in the past must nevertheless look to a future that is not divided between victims and victimizers. Majorities that no longer view themselves as victims are bound to be more sensitive to the needs of others and are more likely to accept the principles of citizenship rather than seek refuge in ethnic exclusivity. But there has to be self-examination. The past and the present must be addressed honestly. The art of asking political questions, so atrophied under totalitarian rule, must be revived. Democracy, of course, will mean local diversity in the region. The universality of democratic principles is pivotal to controlling extremism. The words of Russia's former finance minister, Boris Fedorov, apply no less to Hungary and the rest of Eastern Europe—democracy cannot mean one thing in the West and something else in the postcommunist states.[74]

Notes

1. Dr. Imre Szekeres (executive secretary and vice president of the HSP), interview with the author, Budapest, May 16, 1994.

2. Edith Oltay, "Hungary," *RFE/RL Research Report* 3(6), April 22, 1994: 55–61; Edith Oltay, "Hungary's Socialist-Liberal Government Takes Office," *RFE/RL Research Report* 3(33), August 26, 1994: 6–19.

3. Ibid.

4. Zoltan Pecze, interview with the author, Budapest, May 15, 1994.

5. Paul Hockenos, *Free to Hate* (New York: Routledge, 1993), 105–133.

6. Ibid., 109–114.

7. Ibid., 111–112.

8. U.S. Department of State, Country Reports on Human Rights Practices for 1993, *Hungary* (Washington, D.C.: Department of State, February 1994), 912.

9. David Kraus (Israeli ambassador to Hungary), interview with the author, Budapest, May 13, 1994.

10. *RFE/RL News Briefs*, May 2–6, 1994, 13.

11. Szekeres interview.

12. Oltay, "Hungary's Socialist-Liberal Government Takes Office," 6–13.

13. Ibid., 9.

14. *Magyarorszag* (Hungary), July 8, 1994; *Nepszabadsag* (Freedom of the People, Budapest), July 15, 1994.

15. *RFE/RL News Briefs*, June 27–July 1, 1994, 19.

16. Oltay, "Hungary's Socialist-Liberal Government Takes Office," 11.

17. *East European Constitutional Review* 4(4), Fall 1995: 14.

18. Ibid.

19. *Magyar Nemzet* (The Hungarian People, Budapest), July 16, 1994.

20. Heti Vilaggazdasag, *World Economics Weekly* (Budapest), July 23, 1994.

21. Heti Vilaggazdasag, *Weekly World Economy* (Budapest), May 27, 1995.

22. *OECD Transition Brief*, no. 2, Winter 1996: 15.

23. Ibid.

24. Zoltan Barany, "Socialist-Liberal Government Stumbles Through Its First Year," *Transition* (Open Media Research Institute), July 28, 1995.

25. Lajos Bokros interview, "Hungarian Finance Minister Lajos Bokros Explains His Package," *Transition* (World Bank) 6(5–6), May-June 1995: 15.

26. Ibid., 13.

27. Zsofia Szilagyi, "A Year of Economic Controversy," *Transition* (OMRI), November 1995, 62–66.

28. Ibid., 65.

29. *OECD Transition*, no. 2, Winter 1996: 15.

30. Jozsef Torgyan interview with the author, Budapest, May 1994.

31. Ibid.

32. Ibid.

33. Dr. Peter Feldmajer (president of the Association of Communities and Synagogues), interview with the author, Budapest, May 15, 1994.

34. Szilagyi, "A Year of Economic Controversy," 65.

35. Hockenos, *Free to Hate*, 111–112.

36. Ibid., 132.

37. Szekeres interview.

38. Ibid.

39. Alfred A. Reisch, "The New Hungarian Government's Foreign Policy," *RFE/RL Research Report* 3(33), August 26, 1994: 46–47.

40. Torgyan interview.

41. Dr. Karoly Bard (deputy secretary of state, Ministry of Justice), interview with the author, Budapest, May 12, 1994.

42. Department of State, *Hungary*, 915; and Kraus interview.

43. Department of State, *Hungary*, 915.

44. Ibid., 911.

45. Ibid., 914–915.

46. MTI (Magyar Távirato Iroda [The Hungarian Telegraphic Agency]), Budapest, October 19 and December 12, 1994.

47. Edith Oltay, "New Election Dynamics," *Transition* (OMRI), May 12, 1995, 25; *Magyar Hirlap* (Hungarian Newspaper, Budapest), February 15, 1995.

48. Torgyan interview.

49. Bard interview.

50. Fabian Jozsa, interview with the author, Budapest, May 13, 1994.

51. Szekeres interview.

52. Feldmajer interview.

53. Martin Ill (executive director, Centre for Defence of Human Rights and Founder of the Martin Luther King Association), interview with the author, Budapest, May 13, 1994.

54. Kraus and Feldmajer interviews.

55. Hockenos, in *Free to Hate*, 143, cites 11 percent and 34 percent, respectively.

56. Department of State, *Hungary*, 916.

57. Feldmajer interview.

58. Ibid.

59. Bard interview.

60. Ibid.

61. Ill interview.

62. Department of State, *Hungary*, 915.

63. Ill interview; and Department of State, *Hungary*, 911.

64. Jozsa interview.

65. Ill interview.

66. *Globe and Mail*, November 13, 1995.

67. *Sajtoremle* (Foreign News, Budapest), March 5, 1996; *Magyar Hirlap* (Hungarian News Magazine, Budapest), February 24, 1996.

68. Judith Papaki, "The Recent History of the Hungarian Refugee Problem," *RFE/RL Research Report* 3(24), June 17, 1994: 34–37.

69. Department of State, *Hungary*, 912.

70. *Budapest Week*, May 11, 1994.

71. Ibid.

72. Ibid.

73. *RFE/RL News Briefs*, August 16–19, 1994, 18.

74. Fedorov, conversations.

11

The Internationalization of the Extreme Right

Michi Ebata

The Extreme Right as International Movement

It is inaccurate and irresponsible to propose that there is a far-right international movement with global objectives. Nevertheless, extremist groups are not confined within national boundaries. A wide array of international links confirm that extreme right-wing organizations in one country are aware of and in contact with parallel organizations in other countries. These groups did not develop and do not operate in isolation from each other. This apparent expansion and proliferation of right-wing extremists is alarming but needs to be kept in perspective. Although it is true that activists on the extreme right form a loose network of contacts, as yet the scope of right-wing extremist groups is still within their own national borders.

The transnational relationships evident among right-wing extremist groups stem from an international currency of hatred that bonds them all together. Assorted representatives such as David Duke, Ernst Zundel, Franz Schönhuber, Tom Metzger, and Vladimir Zhirinovsky, not to mention various neo-Nazi and skinhead factions, all draw inspiration from the same ideological heritage. This is visually exhibited by the shared symbolism of the extreme right, ranging from swastikas and other Nazi emblems, Klan hoods, shaven heads, and bomber jackets to more subtle business-suited figures giving Sieg Heil salutes. It can also be detected through the international appeal of racist music or by the homage paid to internationally recognized "martyrs" such as Hitler or the late Ian Stuart Donaldson of the Oi band, Blood and Honour. These surface tokens suggest that to an extent, the sundry manifestations of the extreme right share a common outlook and a common cause. It is the consciousness of this common cause that provides the basis for sympathy with each other's endeavors and for the international transport of ideas.

Each country's right-wing extremists can be encouraged, motivated, and inspired by their foreign counterparts in a number of different ways. Although it is difficult to measure the degree to which one group is influenced by another, there have been instances when a particular idea or strategy is apparently imitated by a foreign counterpart. For example, Jean-Marie Le Pen attained international acclaim after the sudden success of the Front National in the 1983 local elections, followed by the 1984 Euro-elections when it won 11 percent of the vote and ten of the eighty-one French seats.[1] His success was noted across Europe and was greeted by the extreme right in Germany as "foreshadowing an imminent change on the European political scene."[2] By entering the very center of mainstream French and European politics, Le Pen not only legitimized the movement but also legitimized the electoral strategy. Gaining entry into municipal governments and the European Parliament demonstrated the ingenuity and viability of seeking local and supraregional representation when other levels of governance were barred to the extreme right. Subsequently, in Germany, the Republikaners "built their party by mimicking Le Pen's Front National (FN) in France"[3] and ran in the 1989 Euro-elections, winning six seats. More recently, the Assembly for the Republic–Czechoslovak Republican Party was formed, based on the "ideas espoused by right-wing extremists in Western Europe, in particular Germany's Republicans."[4] Similarly, Le Pen and the FN also inspired and provided a model for U.S. extremists, drawing the praise of David Duke and inspiring the formation of the Populist Party.[5] David Duke's own transformation from neo-Nazi to professionally attired Louisiana State legislator in turn is a model for yuppie Austrian FPÖ leader Jörg Haider. Undoubtedly, the electoral breakthroughs in Russia, Italy, and, potentially, Austria will have similar repercussions across the spectrum of the extreme right. However, success doesn't necessarily bring rivals together; quite often it also fosters increased competition and jealousy.

Ideas, strategies, and experiences are also now more directly shared by one eager disciple of the extreme right with another. The extreme right's international awareness has largely been facilitated through the constant exchange of materials among the different groups. The result is a transcontinental trade and international circulation of neo-Nazi, anti-Semitic, and white supremacist propaganda. A British Nazi magazine entitled *The Order*, eponymously referring to a violent and criminal paramilitary organization that terrorized the Pacific Northwest, reprinted an outline of leaderless resistance written by Louis Beam, a member of the defunct Order and the Klan. He instructed Nazi groups to adopt "a non-centralized cell structure, [which] would protect them from being infiltrated and broken up by the state or their enemies. If one cell were exposed or destroyed this would have no effect on other cells."[6]

According to different reports, Gary Lauck, leader of the NSDAP-AO, based in the United States, has been instructing European neo-Nazis and is credited in the mid-1990s with circulating CD-ROM bomb-making manuals throughout Europe, including Moscow and Budapest.[7] Since Nazi propaganda and Holocaust denial are illegal in Germany, receiving such material from external sources is an important factor in the fortune and survival of German extremist groups. The BfV, Germany's Office for the Protection of the Constitution, which monitors extremist groups, says a large proportion of underground neo-Nazi pamphlets and magazines circulating in Germany originate in the United States.[8] A few individuals have devoted their energies to regularly supplying such propaganda. One supplier is Gary Lauck, who is "the largest distributor of neo-Nazi propaganda in [then] West Germany"[9] and is one of the world's largest printers of neo-Nazi materials. He "sells cassette tapes of Adolf Hitler's speeches and publishes Nazi literature in 10 languages, including German, Portuguese, Hungarian and Russian."[10] However, Lauck's recent arrest in Denmark and subsequent deportation to Germany to face charges of incitement to racial hatred and importing anticonstitutional propaganda should slow these activities. Ernst Zundel, founder of Samisdat publishers in Toronto, is another leading publisher and distributer of anti-Semitic, neo-Nazi, and Holocaust denial material, especially throughout Canada, the United States, and Germany. In 1981 "Zundel was named by West German investigators as one of the biggest suppliers of banned Nazi propaganda that had been seized in hundreds of raids on the homes of neo-Nazis in West Germany."[11]

It is through such key suppliers that *The Protocols of the Learned Elders of Zion*, *The Hoax of the Twentieth Century*, *Did Six Million Really Die?* and *The Turner Diaries* have been translated into several different languages and are available throughout the world, including South America, the Middle East, and Asia. Worldwide distribution of propaganda has clearly contributed to the process of internationalizing the right-wing extremist doctrine and making it more widely accessible.

In addition to the postal service, right-wing extremists have also taken advantage of other forms of communication to transport their message. They have set up telephone hot lines featuring racist diatribes on recorded messages that can be accessed locally but also across national borders. In British Columbia, Tom Metzger's White Aryan Resistance runs one of Vancouver's two far-right telephone hot lines; the second contains messages from Metzger and provides his hot line number in the United States.[12] Metzger and other white supremacists have also launched radio and TV programs, providing another forum for local and foreign extremists. "Nazi skinheads visiting from Europe have appeared as guests on Metzger's cable TV show, Race and Reason."[13] Ernst Zundel has appeared on *Truth for Our Times*, a U.S. TV show reaching 14 million Americans that was launched by Pete Peters, a Christian Identity preacher.[14] Never one to be outdone by others, Zundel himself "started shortwave radio programs broadcast from the United States in English and in German—the latter aimed at Germany, where Zundel has a growing following of right-wing extremists. He also launched a TV show, beamed from the United States to a satellite and disseminated to anyone with a receiving dish across North America."[15]

These examples highlight the extreme right's utilization of advances in modern technology to circumvent legal restrictions and promote its activities. The extreme right's foray onto the information highway of electronic-mail, computer bulletins, and the Internet has also enhanced its potential for greater coordination and organization. For example, "Many of the hundreds of neo-Nazis from Germany, the United States, Sweden, Denmark, and Britain who took part in an August 14 neo-Nazi march in Fulda [the sixth anniversary of the death of Rudolph Hess] were informed of the rally over E-mail."[16]

E-mail enables instant communication from any point in the world to another by computer to advertise such rallies and to solicit support. Computer bulletins are another avenue by which information, including the circulation of hit lists, is traded. "The magazine Der Spiegel recently reported that some [computer] files being traded among the right-wing radicals included the names, addresses, telephone numbers and descriptions of 'enemies,' categorized from a rating of 1 ('Political opponents') to 4 ('Shoot down freely')."[17]

Anyone with a computer can pay to access the Internet to find the thousands of messages, including hate messages, disseminated there. At very little expense, hate messages are disseminated by logging onto the following: alt.revisionism, alt.political reform, soc.rights.human, Banished CPU, and The Nile BBS, the last a take on the word denial. The *Journal of Historical Review*'s own message line normally features articles and advertisements of its publications. In contrast to printed hate material, messages on the Internet tend to be more sophisticated and more formal. One author, signed Rick Savage, has written a number of reasonably articulate essays that demonstrate the extreme right's manipulation and obfuscation of language, history, and the meaning of human rights and democratic freedoms. In one piece, "Political Correctness and Holocaust Revisionism: A Study of Thought Control and Modern Taboos," he wrote: "The Holocausters accuse Revisionists of being hate-filled people who are promoting a doctrine of hatred. But Revisionism is a scholarly process, not a doctrine or ideology. If the Holocaust promoters really want to expose hatred, they should take a second look at their own doctrines, and a long look at themselves in the mirror."

Other examples include misquotations from the Talmud and the Bible: "Jesus therefore said to those Jews which had believed him, . . . Ye (Jews) are of your father the devil." Through the Internet, computer bulletins, and E-mail, right-wing extremists potentially have access to millions of people around the world, giving them a truly global reach. The ease with which this medium can produce hate messages ensures greater proliferation and repetition, which in turn enhance the chances of finding a willing listener and also of convincing a sceptical one. Most of these newsgroups originate in the United States, but they are nonetheless extremely difficult to trace, granting and guaranteeing the authors' anonymity. Consequently, the incitement of hatred can be instigated in any part of the world to any audience, willing or otherwise, without any kind of accountability. The Internet, computer bulletins, and electronic mail are all completely unregulated, and for the moment, a strategy to combat this dissemination has not been devised.

Nevertheless, this concern over a larger potential audience must be tempered with caution of overexaggerating the potential danger, since hate material is but one of millions of bits of information found on the Internet. In reality, the size of the audience receptive to the message of right-wing extremists is still small. Furthermore, communication technology can also be utilized by those opposed to right-wing extremists as an educational tool to fight anti-Semitism; for example, British Columbian Ken McVay has used the Internet to refute Holocaust deniers.[18]

Beyond information sharing, there are also a number of personal links among members of extreme-right organizations. Contrary to the perception of right-wing extremists as unsociable egomaniacal lunatics, personal connections and contacts form the basis of a far-reaching international network. These connections operate on different levels. On one level, the rank and file of the extreme right regularly communicate with each other, writing letters, sharing mailing lists, and informing each other of current events and other organizational news. Evidence of this cooperation exists in the fact that members of the Canadian Jewish community have received anti-Semitic hate mail and propaganda originating in Sweden, Germany, Britain, and other foreign locales. Beyond this basic level of communication among the support personnel, the extreme-right network also operates at the highest levels of leadership. The strength of personal contact means that national leaders on the extreme right, leading propagandists, and activists all know each other and each other's organizations. Based in California, the *Journal of Historical Review*, for example, has an international editorial advisory committee that includes noted French revisionists Robert Faurisson and Henri Roques. Right-wing extremists also frequently visit each other and attend each other's gatherings, lending a sense of importance, endorsement, and momentum to the movement. David Irving, a leading British Holocaust denier, has his own international lecture circuit; he travels (although does not always gain entry) to the United States, Canada, Australia, and throughout Europe. Irving has "been listed as a featured speaker at IHR conventions, . . . has lent his name and presence to activities sponsored by Gerhard Frey (DVU), . . . and has taken advantage of many opportunities to speak in Germany, and has found a receptive audience in Germany's radical right."[19]

Jean-Marie Le Pen is also frequently invited to speak to the troops around the world; his deputy, Jean-Yves Le Gallou, appeared in Montreal in September 1993. John Tyndall, British National Party chief, toured throughout the United States in 1991. Gary Lauck frequently violates his entry restrictions by repeatedly visiting Germany, having met with Michael Kühnen (when alive) and Gottfried Küssel (when free).[20] Vladimir Zhirinovsky, on a visit to Austria, was the guest of Edwin Neuwirth, a former member of the Waffen SS.[21] "Stern magazine reported on Mr. Zhirinovsky's links with Gerhard Frey, leader of the far-right German People's Union (DVU) and referred to reports that 'a large part' of Mr. Zhirinovsky's campaign fund had come from the DVU."[22]

The highlight of these contacts are orchestrated international gatherings such as Holocaust denial congresses, commemorations of Nazi heroes, and protests at Holocaust memorials. For example, the Holocaust denial congress held at Hagenau, France, featured appearances by Zundel, Faurisson, Irving, Christian Worch, a German neo-Nazi leader, and Anthony Hancock, a British propaganda supplier.[23] These international gatherings, however, are not solely confined to academic or historical events. The late Ian Stuart Donaldson, British founder of the Oi band, Blood and Honour, was commemorated in February 1994 in Belgium by "250 Nazi skinheads from Belgium, the Netherlands, France, Germany, Britain, Italy, Sweden, Switzerland, and Romania."[24]

Further evidence of these interconnections has been documented by the Simon Wiesenthal Center in Los Angeles, which conducted a covert operation investigating German neo-Nazis. Yaron Svoray, an Israeli reporter, spent seven months undercover in Germany meeting with the movement's leaders. Throughout his investigation, Svoray listened to his German contacts list worldwide contacts, including Willis Carto, Gary Lauck, Léon Degrelle, Fred Leuchter, Tom Metzger, and Ernst Zundel. The fake newsletter *The Right Way*, set up to lend credibility to Svoray, was contacted by Mark Weber, a prominent member of the Institute for Historical Review, who could only have discovered the publication through German contacts.[25] For all this apparent camaraderie, this network is composed of a surprisingly small number of devoted individuals who travel around the world visiting each other. Again, it needs to be stressed that the size of this network still remains very limited with the same names appearing over and over again.

As this international network is quite personal, intergroup politics and dynamics can also be influenced; for example, Willis Carto and the Institute for Historical Review acrimoniously parted company. Not only has this public divorce attracted international attention among this select group, extremists have declared their allegiance to one side or the other; specifically, the institute has the support of Faurisson, Irving, and Zundel against Carto.[26] In another example of this close network, at Ernst Zundel's trial in Canada, the defense relied on testimony from leading Holocaust deniers like David Irving and Fred Leuchter, author of *The Leuchter Report: The End of a Myth,* which denies the existence of the Nazi gas chambers.[27] Doug Christie, Zundel's lawyer, represented Lady Birdwood, a committed hate propagandist in Britain.[28] These personal connections have also proven useful for some in escaping imminent prosecution by finding refuge with and getting assistance from their extreme-right associates. Thies Christopherson, a German neo-Nazi, fled prosecution in Germany for Denmark, where he maintains his operations.[29] The late Leon Degrelle, a Belgian SS officer, found refuge in Spain, where his activities also continued to flourish. Right-wing extremists have also physically aided and sacrificed for the cause in other countries; for example, right-wing extremist mercenaries fought in Croatia, and fascist activists joined the Afrikaner Weerstands Beweging (AWB) in South Africa.[30]

In some instances, members of the extreme right from different countries have attempted to harmonize their efforts by presenting a common front, as in the case of the formal alliance among members of the European Parliament. Under the chair of Jean-Marie Le Pen, extreme-right members of parliament (MEPs) from France, Germany, the Netherlands, Italy, and Britain formed the Technical Group of the European Right (DR). In terms of its effectiveness, the DR unsuccessfully opposed the formation of the 1985 Committee of Inquiry into the Rise of Fascism and Racism and has been "kept away from any role in the EP committees, but it did receive financing from the budgets allocated to organized parliamentary groups."[31] This ostensible alignment did not prove very cooperative, cohesive, or successful because of internal squabbling. Of the twenty-one members elected from radical right parties in 1989, only fourteen joined the alliance: ten from France, three from Germany, and one from Belgium. The Italian delegates did not come together on the issue of secessionism in South Tyrol, and Le Pen alienated German Republikaner members by aligning with Frank Neubauer over his rival for leadership of the Republikaner Party, Franz Schönhuber. However, after the June 1994 parliamentary elections, the fortunes of the radical right seem to have shifted; all Republikaner Partei (REP) members disappeared, and the Italian Alleanza Nazionale (AN) won eleven seats to Le Pen's ten delegates. "Despite the rise in the number of radical rightists MEPs (24) and in view of the statements already issued by the Italian AN, a radical right-wing group will not be formed"[32] given that there are not enough members to constitute a group. A considerable boost to the radical right did not occur, and this new alignment is putting various radical right-wing parties at cross purposes.

There have also been examples of extreme-right organizations attempting to expand their activities into foreign climates. Various factions of the Ku Klux Klan tried in the early 1990s to branch into Canada, Britain, Germany, and even the Czech Republic.[33] In Canada, the Klan has a long-established presence and is considered in many ways the forefather of white supremacy there, although it does not operate with any verve today. Under the direction of James Farrands, leader of the Invisible Empire, the Klan has been actively recruiting skinheads in Britain since at least 1990.[34] The British KKK was reportedly headed by Alan Beshella, a Briton who used to be a member of the Klan in the United States.[35] London's *Sunday Times* at one time speculated that "the Ku Klux Klan [is] to fund election candidates in Britain as part of a new strategy by American far-right extremists."[36] However, the foreign excursions of Farrands is very much in doubt given his financial and "political" decline in the United States. In 1991, German skinheads were targeted by Dennis Mahon, imperial dragon of the White Knights of the Ku Klux Klan.[37] After the initial controversy, not much more was reported on the KKK's presence in Germany. Presently, cultivating extremist elements in Russia and Eastern Europe has become a popular preoccupation for the American and West European extreme right. "Since the fall of communism, [Holocaust] deniers in North America and Western Europe have worked with like-minded groups in Eastern European countries to establish 'mini' Institutes for Historical Review (referring to the California-based pseudo-academic institution that is the bastion of denial activities and publications)."[38] There have also been rumors of overtures made by the American Christian fundamentalist right to groups in Eastern Europe. Whether this is of any significance is not yet apparent.

Although coordination and cooperation at the international level have been ineffectual, they have not deterred the extreme right from pretensions of consolidating an international movement. Gary Lauck was accused of directly coordinating German neo-Nazis by Ingo Hasselbach, a neo-Nazi defector who was once the leader of Berlin's largest skinhead group. According to Hasselbach, "Mr. Lauck has become a leading figure in the German rightist movement, not only calling for terrorism, but supplying the necessary instructions."[39] Lauck and the NSDAP-AO have also "launched a Russian organisation, the Front of National Revolutionary Action."[40] Third positionism, an anti-Semitic, anticapitalist, and anticommunist ideology, could also be said to be another foundation for an international movement. Extremists and extremist groups linked to third positionism include Nick Griffin of Britain, Tom Metzger, the Nation of Islam of the United States, the Nationalist Party in Canada, and Libyan strongman Khadafy. Khadafy is also credited with personally advancing the internationalization of the extreme right by providing material and financial support to these groups and organizing international conferences for them to attend.[41] Both examples, however, should be treated with a degree of skepticism given the impracticality and ineffectiveness of so-called leaders who are continents away from their followers.

Despite its xenophobic and nationalist tendencies, the extreme right is an internationally aware movement with an array of linkages and connections.

The new advances in information technology and other forms of technology exploited by the extreme right could potentially strengthen its capacity to operate in the international sphere. However, the negligible extent of activities of extreme-right groups beyond their particular home turfs proves that an international movement of the extreme right does not exist today. Central coordination, and even cooperation at the international level, to the extent that they appear, are amateurish affairs. The violence young extremists perpetrate is still localized, and the mass support political parties generate still "tends to ebb and flow according to country-level factors."[42] The international dimension has not changed the fact that the extreme right still remains a parochial and insulated group of zealots. The international reach of right-wing extremism is no more remarkable than any other sociopolitical idea that has spread simply because of the general trend toward increasing globalization and communication. Although this international dimension of the extreme right is disturbing and potentially threatening, it does not seem to have affected the extreme right's effectiveness in increasing its support. What is evident is that this process of internationalization has to some extent increased the ability of right-wing extremists to conduct their activities within their own territories. The transborder links provide encouragement and sustain their conviction of their own self-importance. The international exchange of ideas, practices, and information has improved the resiliency of the extreme right, which implies that the obstacles to combating and eliminating it are that much greater. Therefore, the extreme right's message and its capacity to disseminate that message have been strengthened and have attained a degree of permanence that it did not necessarily enjoy when confined within national borders.

International Human Rights Standards and Instruments

The message of hatred and intolerance that the extreme right represents has always been repudiated by the international community as contravening its underlying values and principles. Although the extreme right itself has not been of primary concern for the international community, it has usually been encompassed within the larger rubric of racism and racial discrimination. Thus the numerous international fronts derive their inspiration and authority to attack the extreme right from the international human rights instruments that represent the common standards of achievement to which all nations and peoples aspire. Originating in the aftermath of World War II, human rights laws reflect a consciousness of the atrocities committed by a leading industrial and so-called civilized society consumed by hatred. First embodied in the Charter of the United Nations, the recognition of human rights affirms respect for the fundamental dignity of every person. In 1948, the principles of human rights and freedoms were firmly entrenched in the Universal Declaration of Human Rights, which proclaimed that "human rights should be protected by the rule of law"(preamble). Although the declaration is not a binding treaty, as the ultimate standard of aspiration it exerts a powerful moral and authoritative force. In addition to establishing the basic principles of human rights and the equality and freedom from nondiscrimination in the enjoyment of those rights, the declaration offers a human rights strategy mirrored in later documents. This framework calls for "equal protection against any discrimination in violation of this Declaration and against any incitement to such discrimination" (Article 7). Should such violations occur, the declaration has a provision for effective recourse and remedial procedures (Article 8). It furthermore provides for the limitations of rights for the purpose of the general welfare of a democratic society and finally, in Article 30, stipulates, "Nothing in this Declaration may be interpreted as implying for any State, group or person any right to engage in any activity or to perform any act aimed at the destruction of any of the rights and freedoms set forth herein."

Nevertheless, the human rights declaration was drafted in an era when the assumption prevailed that the defeat of Nazism and fascism concomitantly signified the elimination of the hatred and hostility that fueled them. It wasn't until December 1966 that the persistent threat of racism was officially recognized. The adoption of the International Covenant on Civil and Political Rights by the General Assembly of the United Nations was the first postwar international human rights document to specifically address the issue of hate and racist activity. In Article 20, the covenant declares, "1. Any propaganda for war shall be prohibited by law. 2. Any advocacy of national, racial or religious hatred that constitutes incitement to discrimination, hostility or violence shall be prohibited by law." Unlike the human rights declaration, the Covenant on Civil and Political Rights is a legally binding treaty and demands that states "adopt such legislative or other measures as may be necessary to give effect to the rights recognized" (Article 2).

In the following year, the United Nations took another step against racism by adopting the International Convention on the Elimination of All Forms of Racial Discrimination. Reaffirming the principles of an earlier declaration of the same name, the convention stated that its signatories are "resolved to adopt all necessary measures for speedily eliminating racial discrimination in all its forms and manifestations, and to prevent and combat racist doctrines and practices in order to promote understanding between races and to build an international community free from all forms of racial segregation and racial discrimination"(preamble).

Moreover, the convention on racial discrimination makes clear that its provisions do not recognize "distinctions, exclusions, restrictions, or preferences made by a State Party to this Convention between citizens and noncitizens" (Article 1[2]). Legally binding for those states that ratify or accede to it, the convention explicitly outlines state responsibilities with respect to hate activity. Specifically, the convention on racial discrimination stipulates that its signatories must "condemn all propaganda and all organizations which are based on ideas or theories of superiority of one race or group of persons of one colour or ethnic origin, or which attempt to justify or promote racial hatred and discrimination in any form, and undertake to adopt immediate and positive measures, designed to eradicate incitement to, or acts of, such discrimination" (Article 4).

Article 4 also requires that state parties

> (a) Shall declare an offence punishable by law all dissemination of ideas based on racial superiority or hatred, incitement to racial discrimination, as well as all acts of violence or incitement to such acts against any race or group of persons of another colour or ethnic origin, and also the provision of any assistance to racist activities, including the financing thereof;
> (b) Shall declare illegal and prohibit organizations, and also organized and all other propaganda activities, which promote and incite racial discrimination, and shall recognize participation in such organizations or activities as an offence punishable by law;
> (c) Shall not permit public authorities or public institutions, national or local, to promote or incite racial discrimination.

Again, state parties must ensure for everyone within their jurisdiction effective protection against discrimination and recourse to just and adequate reparation, or satisfaction for any damage suffered as a result of discrimination that does occur. States are also compelled to provide more positive measures to combat prejudices that lead to racial discrimination in teaching, education, culture, and information.

By the end of 1993, the convention on racial discrimination had been ratified by 137 countries, including the countries of this study, with the exception of the United States. Ratification has proceeded despite the ambitious provisions of Article 4, which is "presently the most articulate provision in international law intended to fight not only racial discrimination but also related evils such as racial hatred, racist propaganda, and association with racist purposes."[43] However, there have been a number of objections to Article 4. Citing the primacy and necessity of First Amendment rights, the Americans did not approve of the article's lack of distinction between hate speech and hate violence. The United States issued the following declaration: "The Constitution of the United States contains provisions for the protection of individual rights, such as the right to free speech, and nothing in the Convention shall be deemed to require or authorize legislation or other action by the United States of America incompatible with the provisions of the Constitution of the United States of America."[44]

Similar reservations by France and the United Kingdom unfortunately rendered the unequivocal requirements of the controversial article meaningless. Nevertheless, the convention did establish a clear international guideline regarding the incitement to hatred as a punishable offense and a legitimate ground for limiting the freedom of expression. "Several [states] have enacted domestic legislation in the spirit of its provisions."[45]

In the time since, the UN and the international community have instituted a large and growing body of treaties addressing racism and discrimination. More recent declarations and conventions have specifically addressed the needs of certain vulnerable groups. In 1981, the UN adopted the Declaration on the Elimination of All Forms of Intolerance and of Discrimination Based on Religion or Belief, in 1990, the International Convention on the Protection of the Rights of All Migrant Workers and Members of Their Families, and in 1992, the Declaration on the Rights of Persons Belonging to National or Ethnic, Religious and Linguistic Minorities.

The issue of discrimination has also been a concern for other organs of the United Nations, whose mandates addressed different aspects of it, particularly the UN Educational, Scientific and Cultural Organization (UNESCO). UNESCO's educational arm focused its efforts on discrediting racist ideology and refuting the validity of pseudoscientific racist substantiation. Since 1950, UNESCO has issued four statements on race, culminating in the Declaration on Race and Racial Prejudice, adopted at its general conference of November 27, 1978. Reiterating the primary responsibility of the state, in Article 6(3) the declaration emphasizes:

> Since laws proscribing racial discrimination are not in themselves sufficient, it is also incumbent on States to supplement them by administrative machinery for the systematic investigation of instances of racial discrimination, by a comprehensive framework of legal remedies against acts of racial discrimination, by broadly based education and research programmes designed to combat racial prejudice and racial discrimination and by programmes of positive political, social, educational and cultural measures calculated to promote genuine mutual respect among groups.

Outside of the framework of the United Nations, regional arrangements have reaffirmed and have consolidated the general principles binding the international community. The European Convention of Human Rights, signed in 1950 and in effect since 1953, provides the framework of principles for the members of the Council of Europe. The European Convention incorporates the standards upheld in the Universal Declaration of Human Rights and the International Covenant on Civil and Political Rights but goes further in its strong and explicit commitment to a democratic society. Almost every article that prescribes a right does so in conjunction with the following proviso:

The exercise of these freedoms, since it carries with it duties and responsibilities, may be subject to such formalities, conditions, restrictions or penalties as are prescribed by law and are necessary in a democratic society, in the interests of *national security, territorial integrity or public safety, for the prevention of disorder or crime, for the protection of health or morals, for the protection of the reputation or rights of others, for preventing the disclosure of information received in confidence*, or *for maintaining the authority and impartiality of the judiciary* (Article 10, para. 2).

The European Convention does not contain an explicit provision against racial propaganda. Consequently, one has to rely on its general restriction clauses to deal with this issue.[46] The European Convention does not "contain any provision for the enactment of a national penal code,"[47] but it is implicit that a state's legal order must secure the rights expressed therein. Whereas it is the expectation of the European Convention that states will protect all freedoms, whether states are obligated to do so and under what conditions is a matter of interpretation that can only be resolved through case law, which shall be discussed later.

This commitment to democracy and human rights is reinforced by another regional framework, the Organisation on Security and Cooperation in Europe (OSCE), otherwise known as the Helsinki process. In the Helsinki Final Act, members of the OSCE agreed to uphold "respect for human rights and fundamental freedoms, including the freedom of thought, conscience, religion or belief" and reiterate a full commitment to "fulfill their obligations as set forth in the international declarations and agreements in their field." Presently signed by fifty-two countries, including all the countries in this study, the OSCE agreement and subsequent documents are not legally binding but are reached by consensus, thus lending the institution considerable force and precedent.[48] The OSCE is also unique in providing for follow-up conferences, which serve as a "forum to review compliance by the participating states with their OSCE commitments, and second, as a rule-making mechanism capable of expanding the body of OSCE commitments."[49] Thus, although the provisions of the Helsinki Final Act "are weaker than those of other international instruments [by speaking] only of incitement to violence, not of incitement to discrimination or hostility,"[50] subsequent conferences in Madrid (1980–1983) and Vienna (1986–1989) made the general commitments of states, relevant to racial and religious tolerance, increasingly more specific. In June 1990, the Copenhagen Document unequivocally "established democratic pluralism as the sole political system compatible with the new CSCE."[51] The Council of Ministers consolidated this commitment by "clearly and unequivocally condemn[ing] totalitarianism, racial and ethnic hatred, anti-semitism, xenophobia and discrimination against anyone as well as persecution on religious and ideological grounds. In this context, they also recognize the particular problems of Roma (gypsies). They declare their firm intention to intensify the efforts to combat these phenomena in all their forms and therefore will" (paragraph 40).

The Copenhagen Document is the first international instrument to specifically mention anti-Semitism and was followed by instructions declaring the OSCE's firm intention to combat this phenomenon. This denunciation was later confirmed by the Charter of Paris for a New Europe, signed by the heads of state of all participating members in recognition of the profound changes sweeping Europe following the collapse of communism. The charter also promised to "fully implement and build upon the provisions relating to the human dimension of the CSCE."

In March 1994, the UN Commission for Human Rights followed the precedent set by the OSCE by adopting the first international resolution condemning anti-Semitism, demonstrating how one instrument can inspire other legal standards.[52] Since the end of World War II, an extensive system of overlapping human rights instruments has been sending a clear and consistent message that racial intolerance and hatred have no place in the international community. The machinery of guarantees and enforcement instituted reflects the urgent concern accorded to the eradication of racism and discrimination. Moreover, the attention and efforts confronting this problem confirm the international character of right-wing extremism.

International Jurisprudence

Within the statutes of the European Convention of Human Rights, the International Covenant on Civil and Political Rights (ICCPR), and the International Convention on the Elimination of Racial Discrimination (ICERD), a number of international mechanisms were entrusted with the task of enforcing human rights. The European Commission of Human Rights (ECHR) and the European Court of Human Rights were the first two independent organs instituted under Articles 19–56; they were superseded by a single court in October 1993.[53] The ECHR was empowered to hear petitions from states alleging a violation of the ECHR by another state party, leaving the final decision with the Council of Ministers. In Articles 25 and 26, upon recognition of the relevant competence, the ECHR was authorized to receive petitions from "any person, non-governmental organisation or group of individuals claiming to be the victim of a violation." The commission, "with a view to ascertaining the facts, [shall] undertake together with the representative of the parties on examination of the petition and, if need be, an investigation" (Article 28). "When the Commission has declared an application to be admissible and has made a report on the alleged violation of the Convention, the case can be submitted to the Court which has the final binding decision."[54] Comparable appeals can also be made to the UN Human Rights Committee, created by the ICCPR, and the Committee on the Elimination of Racial Discrimination, created under Articles 11, 12, 13, and 16 of the ICERD. Through the decisions made by these organs, it becomes apparent how these instruments have been implemented.

Although the previous covenants and conventions were predominantly intended for individual victims whose freedoms had been violated in recent years, members of the extreme right have sought to use the law as a shield, even when exercised for undemocratic ends. Few courts have given the far right its desired latitude. On the international level in particular, tribunals have been reluctant to show any deference to extremist demands. Applications brought before the United Nations Human Rights Committee (UNHRC) and the European Commission of Human Rights (ECHR) have consistently been decided against extremist complainants. In general, these bodies have affirmed that fundamental freedoms are subject to justifiable conditions and that individual claims must be evaluated in proportion to the negative externalities their acceptance would engender. As such, the calculated libertarianism of the far right has been checked and the spirit informing democracy preserved.

Although few appeals proceed beyond the domestic sphere, sufficient reports exist to demonstrate the pattern of decisions since 1979, a pattern that has clearly disadvantaged the far right. Following are some representative cases.

1. *Malcolm Lowes v. United Kingdom*
Application 13214/87
Decision of December 9, 1988
European Commission of Human Rights

The applicant, a prisoner, sought to receive issues of a periodical called *Gothic Ripples* on a regular basis. Prison authorities, having determined that issue number 16–17 of the magazine was anti-Semitic, decided to censor the publication to preserve order and discipline in the institution.

The applicant submitted that *Gothic Ripples* is anti-Zionist rather than anti-Semitic in nature—critical of the Jewish state and not of the Jewish people. As such, he argued that the magazine should not be subject to the condition of Article 10(2) of the European Convention on Human Rights; namely, that the flow of information may be restricted "for the protection of the reputation or rights of others."

The commission found in favor of the respondent, noting that issue 16–17 encouraged racial prejudice without any serious discussion of Zionist thought. Containing advertisements for such works as *The Hoax of the Twentieth Century* by A. R. Butz and *Mein Kampf* by Adolf Hitler, the bulletin was held to foster public disorder. Moreover, other conspiracy theories and cartoons included in the brochure were found to promote racial hatred and therefore could justifiably be controlled in the interests of democratic society.

2. *Michael Kuhnen v. Federal Republic of Germany*
Application 12194/86
Decision of May 12, 1988
European Commission of Human Rights

In 1983, the applicant was a leader of the ANS/NA, an organization dedicated to the revival of the National Socialist Party in Germany. In its publications, the group advocated the reinstitution of the NSDAP ideology, a weltanschauung prohibited in modern Germany.

Initially, the applicant was convicted under s.86 of the German Penal Code, which forbids the dissemination of propaganda by means of unconstitutional organizations.

The complaint was brought against the state under Articles 9 and 10 of the European Convention of Human Rights, which protect individuals from punishment on the basis of beliefs or expressions. Furthermore, it was argued that Article 17, which proscribes the exercise of any one European Convention right to the detriment of another, ought not to apply because the NSDAP had been advocated as a legal party within the existing German political system.

In rejecting the applicant's claims, the commission held national socialism to be inherently opposed to the values of the German democracy, in which it professed to operate. In the commission's view, the applicant's proposals supported "the state of violence and illegality which existed in Germany between 1933 and 1945" and offended "the notion of understanding among peoples." Therefore, it was concluded that Article 17 could be raised against the applicant and that free expression of any one person cannot supersede the rights of any other to security and equality as provided by Articles 5 and 14.

Similarly, the commission found in favor of the state under Article 10(2). Although it was determined that the applicant's right to free expression was violated by the German Penal Code, the interference with that right was deemed necessary in a democratic society. The responsibilities incumbent upon those exercising free expression must include the duty to avoid racial and religious discrimination, the court held.

3. *X. v. Germany*
Application 9235/81
European Commission of Human Rights

This case involved an injunction against the applicant, preventing him from openly displaying right-wing publications on his property. Specifically, the applicant had posted a selection of pamphlets describing the

Holocaust as a Zionist fabrication. A neighbor whose grandfather had been killed in the Auschwitz concentration camp brought a successful defamation claim in response.

The applicant, a known member of a right-wing political organization, challenged the provisions of the German Civil and Penal Codes that authorized the injunction.

The commission declared the application to be inadmissible. In denying the historical fact of the Holocaust, the impugned pamphlets constituted "a defamatory attack against the Jewish community and against each individual member of this community." Articles 10(2) and 14 of the European Convention of Human Rights, drafted to inspire tolerance and to protect groups that have historically faced discrimination, directly apply to public statements of this nature. Accordingly, the commission ruled that the restriction imposed on the applicant was justifiable in a democratic society.

4. *M. A. v. Italy*
Communication 117/1981
Decision of April 10, 1984
United Nations Human Rights Committee

The complainant in this communication was a right-wing militant convicted for his attempts to reorganize a dissolved and prohibited fascist party. The essence of the claim was that M. A. had been convicted solely because of his ideas and political beliefs and that therefore the Italian law applicable in his case violated articles 19(1), 22, and 25 of the International Covenant on Civil and Political Rights (ICCPR).

In deciding against the complainant, the committee concluded that M. A.'s activities "were of a kind which are removed from the protection of the Covenant by article 5 thereof." More precisely, it was held that the complainant's advocacy of a totalitarian regime void of democratic freedoms was not amenable to national security or to the rights of Italian citizens. As a result, the activities of the complainant were deemed subject to state limitations as justified by Articles 18(3) and 19(3) of the ICCPR.

5. *J.R.T and the W.G. Party v. Canada*
Communication 104/1981
Decision of April 6, 1983
United Nations Human Rights Committee

Founder of the Western Guard political party, the complainant T. used recorded telephone messages to attract membership and promote party platforms. The recordings were accessible to any member of the public with the proper telephone number and warned callers of such dangers as "international finance and international Jewry leading the world into wars, unemployment and inflation and the collapse of world values and principles."

Pursuant to the Canadian Human Rights Act and Federal Court Act, the Human Rights Tribunal ordered the complainant to cease using telephone messages as a medium of communicating racial hatred. T. proceeded to violate this order and was consequently sentenced to a prison term for contempt of court. In his communication, T. argued that his conviction constituted a violation of Articles 19(1) and 19(2) of the ICCPR; namely, the rights to the freedoms of opinion, expression, and information.

The committee ruled, inter alia, that Canada is obliged to prohibit the advocacy of hatred "that constitutes incitement to discrimination, hostility or violence," according to Article 20(2) of the ICCPR. As a result, it was held that the submissions of the complainant were incompatible with the spirit of the ICCPR and thus inadmissable under Article 3 of the Optional Protocol.

6. *Glimmerveen and Habenbeek v. The Netherlands*
Application Nos. 8348/78 and 8406/78
European Commission of Human Rights

The applicants in this case had been convicted by Dutch authorities for distributing discriminatory leaflets. The leaflets, addressed to all "white Dutch people," called for the removal of all nonwhite immigrants and workers from the Netherlands.

The claims against the state party were brought under Article 10(1) of the European Convention of Human Rights, which guarantees the right to freedom of expression. The commission's response to the applications was negative. Opting not to rely on the responsibilities owed under Article 10(2), the commission instead focused on Article 17, which prevents "totalitarian groups from exploiting the principles enunciated by the Convention for their own benefit." Under that provision, individuals are forbidden to plead one European Convention freedom, such as expression, to the detriment of other freedoms enjoyed by society at large, such as nondiscrimination. As a result, the applications failed.

As the preceding cases illustrate, the international community has been unwilling to accept the extremist interpretation of democratic rights and freedoms.

The approach adopted by authorities has been both liberal and strategic in its protection of the public order. On one hand, the scope of claimed rights such as freedom of expression has remained broad; in every instance, the liberties of the claimants were recognized as having been violated. On the other hand, courts have not been hesitant to justify the violations using the conditions demanded by international covenants. Provisions such as Articles 10(2) and 17 of the European Convention of Human Rights and Articles 19(3) and 20(2) of the ICCPR have been employed unflinchingly for the exact purposes for which they were drafted. Extremist elements have been given notice that the enjoyment of rights must be accompanied by the acceptance of their concomitant burdens.

Activities by International Organizations

According to the documents from which they were instituted, the mandates of the International Convention on the Elimination of Racial Discrimination and the UN Human Rights Committee (UNHRC) are not solely limited to the role of judicial recourse. Both and CERD and the UNHRC are entrusted with the power to scrutinize the record of each state in implementing the provisions of the ICERD and ICCPR, respectively. Under Article 9 of the ICERD, states are obligated to provide "report[s] on the legislative, judicial, administrative or other measures which they have adopted and which give effect to the provisions of this Convention"—and ICERD is empowered to review these reports. On the basis of these reports, ICERD is expected to submit recommendations to the Secretary General and the General Assembly. Through the petition procedures, ICERD may also make suggestions and recommendations to the state parties, which must then respond to ICERD. Under Article 40 of the ICCPR, reports are submitted to the secretary-general, who then transmits them to the UN Human Rights Committee for assessment. The cooperation of state parties to both ICERD and ICCPR is indispensable in the fulfillment of this function. This cooperation has not been forthcoming. As of August 1990, "103 of 129 States Parties to ICERD were behindhand with the submission of one or more reports. Five states had submitted no reports at all, though they acceded to the Convention long ago. Many states (sometimes the same ones) have been dilatory in meeting their financial obligations too.[55]

It is important to also note that only 19 of the 137 presently ratified states recognize the competence of the ICERD. These include France, Hungary, and Russia, but other countries, such as Canada, have nonetheless submitted reports.

There is also a Center for Human Rights established under the auspices of the UN. This organization has published a series of booklets dealing with human rights issues that serve as useful reference tools. But on the whole, the center has suffered from a lack of priority and sufficient funding. This situation appears to be changing; the center is slated to become the focal point for reviewing information concerning activities carried out within the framework of the Third Decade of Action to Combat Racism and Racial Prejudice.[56]

These institutions are only a part of the broader system of UN involvement in eliminating racism and racial discrimination. The recent World Conference on Human Rights, held in Vienna, June 1993, reaffirmed that "the speedy and comprehensive elimination of all forms of racism and racial discrimination, xenophobia and related intolerance is a priority task for the international community."[57]

A number of UN organs and agencies are responsible for implementing the objectives set forth in the numerous proclamations condemning racism and intolerance. The General Assembly has adopted various resolutions and mandated responsibility to the different UN components, the secretary-general has been called upon to undertake specific reports and tasks, UNESCO in addition to its educational activities has proclaimed 1995 the Year of Tolerance, and so on. It is within the Economic and Social Council's Commission for Human Rights that racism and discrimination are the most prominent items on the agenda. Most of the commission's work in this area is conducted by its main subsidiary, the Subcommission on Prevention of Discrimination and Protection of Minorities, created in 1947.

In 1970, the General Assembly designated 1971 as International Year for Action to Combat Racism and Racial Discrimination, which led to the First Decade of Action Against Racism, instituted from 1973 to 1983 "to promote human rights and fundamental freedoms for all, without distinction of any kind." The program of action stated,

> To this end, appropriate measures should be taken to implement fully United Nations instruments and decisions concerning the elimination of racial discrimination, to ensure support for all peoples striving for racial equality, to eradicate all forms of racial discrimination, and to pursue a vigorous world-wide campaign of information designed to dispel racial prejudice and to enlighten and involve world public opinion in the struggle against racism and racial discrimination, emphasizing inter alia the education of youth in the spirit of human rights and fundamental freedoms and in the dignity and worth of the human person and against theories of racism and racial discrimination, as well as the full involvement of women in the formulation and implementation of these measures.

The program of action also called for a World Conference on the Elimination of Racism as well as other specific conferences and seminars and highlighted topics for research and study. Two world conferences were held in 1978 and 1983, where resolutions condemning neo-Nazi and fascist organizations were adopted. At the end of the decade, the principal objectives of the program of action had not been attained, leading to the designation of a Second Decade of Action from 1983 to 1993. As with the first, the second suffered from a lack of attention, resulting in less than satisfactory accomplishments. Subsequently, a Norwegian expert, Asbjorn Eide, was commissioned to submit a report reviewing the decades of action. In this report, entitled *Study on the Achievements Made and Obstacles Encountered During the Decades to Combat Racism and Racial Discrimination,*[58] Eide noted that an international system of human rights laws had been instituted and that racist ideology had been successfully discredited. But, he added, the Committee on the Elimination of Racial Discrimination had not been very successful. The primary recommendations of the report revolved around reinforcing and extending existing UN policies. However, under the direction of the Second Decade, the secretary-general did produce the Compilation of National Legislation Designed to Combat Racism and Racial Discrimination and prepared a Model Legislation for the Guidance of Governments in the Enactment of Further Legislation Against Racial Discrimination. This latter draft was intended to clarify and improve the drafting of national legislation needed to ensure the "adequate protection to the victims of racism and racial discrimination, through legislative guarantees, criminalization of racist acts, the development of recourse procedures and the establishment of independent national bodies to monitor implementation."[59] The secretary-general also submitted a report, *Measures to Combat Racism and Racial Discrimination and the Role of the Sub-Commission.*[60] The report was useful for examining the different measures directed against racism and racial discrimination taken in the legal, administrative, social, cultural, policing, and educational fields at different levels of government. UN-sponsored seminars have also been held around the globe, some leading to published reports such as the *Report of the Seminar on the Political, Historical, Economic, Social and Cultural Factors Contributing to Racism, Racial Discrimination and Apartheid,* which was written to explore the causes and current manifestations of racism.

In December 1993, a Third Decade of Action Against Discrimination was proclaimed, recognizing "new expressions of racism, racial discrimination, intolerance and xenophobia in various parts of the world. In particular [how] these affect minorities, ethnic groups, migrant workers, indigenous populations, nomads, immigrants and refugees."

It also stressed that primary responsibility and, therefore, potential success lies with states themselves. "International Action undertaken as part of any programme for the Third Decade should therefore be directed so as to assist States to act effectively." Such assistance is to be accomplished by ensuring that the standards established by the International Convention on the Elimination of All Forms of Racial Discrimination are universally respected and applied and that all states fulfill their reporting and financial obligations to ICERD. In March 1993, the UN Economic and Social Council Commission for Human Rights appointed for a three-year period "a Special Rapporteur on contemporary forms of racism, racial discrimination and xenophobia and related intolerance."[61] The special rapporteur's methodology incorporates three on-site missions for the collection of information on the manifestations of racism, the collection and analysis of legal and administrative provisions of states through the distribution of a questionnaire to governments, communications to states concerning evidence of violations, and the submission of a report to the commission on an annual basis. The mandate of the rapporteur is comprehensive, broad, and multidimensional but also thematic and intellectual, pointing out the need to "redefine or refocus, by further refining, the concepts or notions of racism, or racial discrimination, of xenophobia and of intolerance."[62] Currently, without staff and adequate financial provisions, the rapporteur has not been able to fully dispense his functions as delineated in his mandate, but he intends to hold an interdisciplinary seminar on the theoretical aspects of racism and xenophobia, technical workshops, and a global conference on consolidating international activities.[63]

The fight against right-wing extremism has not been limited to the United Nations but has been augmented by efforts of regional organizations. In addition to condemning racial and ethnic hatred and anti-Semitism, the OSCE framework has actively defended democracy against extremist elements. The Copenhagen Document, already cited, listed seven sections of instructions for member states to combat the phenomena of racism, hatred, and anti-Semitism, including the adoption "of such laws as may be necessary to provide protection against any acts that constitute incitement to violence," taking measures to protect persons or groups subject to threats or acts of discrimination, to promote understanding and tolerance, and to ensure full compliance with the obligations of international instruments, including the submission of periodic reports. This was followed by the Moscow Document, which specifically addressed the problems of migrant workers, condemning "all acts of discrimination on the ground of race, colour and ethnic origin, intolerance and xenophobia against migrant workers." The Moscow Document also incorporated the 1991 Geneva Report of the CSCE Meeting of Experts on National Minorities, which touched on almost all problems confronting minority groups in the CSCE. In December 1993, the Council of Ministers meeting in Rome included a declaration on aggressive nationalism, racism, chauvinism, xenophobia, and anti-Semitism. The ministers also urged enforcement of international humanitarian laws with the strengthening of the observance of such laws. They agreed "that the CSCE must play an important role in these efforts," keeping them high on the agenda. They called for a study on possible follow-up actions, pointed to the mandate of the high commissioner on national minorities in all aspects of aggressive nationalism, racism, chauvinism, xenophobia, and anti-Semitism, and finally provided a mandate for the Office for Democratic Institutions and Human Rights to attend to these phenomena. At the Vienna follow-up conference, the Human Dimension Mechanism was entrusted with the power to consider charges of noncompliance by states with their international obligations. It provides for third-party fact-finding and mediation through CSCE expert missions and rapporteurs. "This process is supplemented by a mechanism for publicizing the findings of the rapporteurs and for bringing them to the attention of the Committee or Senior Officials. Most significantly, the process can be invoked without delay in emergency situations, making it particularly useful for dealing with violence inspired by racial or religious hatred."[64]

Both the Office for Democratic Institutions and Human Rights (ODIHR) and the high commissioner on national minorities have been working toward intensifying functional cooperation with the Council of Europe in recognition of the active and aggressive fight against racism and intolerance conducted by the council.

Founded in 1949, the Council of Europe has thirty-two members, including all twelve members of the European Union, the European Free Trade Association (EFTA) countries, and the countries of Eastern Europe. From the very beginning, the raison d'être of the council was to prevent the repetition of Nazism, fascism, racism, and totalitarianism, which nearly destroyed Europe. In addition to the European Convention of Human Rights, the Parliamentary Assembly and the Committee of Ministers have both made a significant contribution to the fight against racism and xenophobia. As early as 1966, the Parliamentary Assembly adopted a recommendation (453) on "measures to be taken against incitement to racial, national and religious hatred" that invited members to prepare "effective legislation against such forms of incitement . . . and, in member states where such legislation already exists, to review and rigorously enforce it." The assembly also encouraged European governments to implement the UN Year for Action to Combat Racism and Racial Discrimination in 1971, established an ad hoc committee of experts, and also resolved to combat resurgent fascist propaganda and its racist aspects in 1980.[65] In May 1981, the Committee of Ministers adopted the Declaration Regarding Intolerance—a Threat to Democracy and held the Conference on Intolerance in Europe in Strasbourg. The Council of Europe has also attempted to empower foreigners by advancing their active participation in public life. Consequently, in 1992, the council adopted the Convention on the Participation of Foreigners in Public Life at Local Level. To ensure the equitable treatment of foreigners, the convention calls for each party to "ensure reasonable efforts are made to involve foreign residents in public inquiries, planning procedures and other processes of consultation on local matters." More recently, in 1993, the Parliamentary Assembly passed another recommendation on the fight against racism, xenophobia, and intolerance.

However, the increase in xenophobic activity and the pointed failure of past actions compelled the Council of Europe to intensify its efforts against racism by becoming more aggressive. In Vienna in October 1993, the heads of state of the member states met for the first time and issued a resolute declaration that recognized the destructive implications of intolerance and the violation of human rights. After reiterating their objectives and condemnations, they included in the Vienna Declaration a plan of action on combating racism, xenophobia, anti-Semitism, and intolerance. This plan of action stresses the importance of attacking racism by launching a "broad European Youth Campaign to mobilise the public in favour of a tolerant society based on the equal dignity of all its members and against manifestations of racism, xenophobia, antisemitism, and intolerance."[66] The youth campaign started in December 1994 and continued for the next three years. The Council of Europe also established a committee of governmental experts, to be known as the European Commission Against Racism and Intolerance. The committee had a mandate to review state legislation and policies with the view of reinforcing the guarantees against all forms of discrimination and thus assisting efforts to initiate intergovernmental cooperation within the council. Furthermore, the plan of action involves traditional council concerns in the areas of information, education, culture, and media. Representatives of these areas were invited to participate in a Europe-versus-intolerance seminar that was held in Strasbourg in March 1994. The considerable budget (19 million francs) allocated for the plan of action signifies the determination with which the council aims to combat racism, intolerance, and xenophobia.

Institutions of the European Union have also been involved in the fight against racism, particularly the European Parliament. Alarmed by the election of a number of candidates from far-right parties to the parliament, the European Parliament ordered an "inquiry into the rise of fascism and racism in Europe" in 1985. After a number of public hearings, submissions, and consultations, the committee of governmental experts released the Evrigenis Report. Based on an extensive survey of the situation in the member countries of the EU, the report emphasized the legal, administrative, educational, and cultural fields and made a number of recommendations to the European Commission, stressing a comprehensive and multilevel approach. One recommendation requested Eurobarometer to survey attitudes within the European Community regarding relations with members of different or foreign communities; since 1988, surveys on racism and xenophobia have been conducted every year. The Committee of Inquiry and the Evrigenis Report lead to a joint declaration against racism and xenophobia—issued by the European Commission, the Council of Europe, and the European Parliament in 1986—that vigorously condemned all forms of intolerance and resolved to protect members of society. Since the declaration, the European Parliament has denounced racism and fascism at every opportunity and reminded the European Community of its obligations, but little substantive action has followed the declaration. Recognizing the failure to implement the recommendations of the Committee of Inquiry and the need to update the information contained in the Evrigenis Report, the European Parliament convened a second committee, the Committee of Inquiry into the Rise of Racism and Xenophobia. In 1991, Glyn Ford released this report, which expanded upon and analyzed the previous report and included among the recommendations an appeal for an expanded and enhanced parliamentary role pertaining to racism, anti-Semitism, and xenophobia. It also encouraged the European Community to accede to the relevant human rights conventions in its own right. For the most part, the European Commission itself has not involved itself in the fight against xenophobia and intolerance, refusing to accept jurisdictional competence. But at the end of June 1995, at the Corfu summit meeting of the heads of state, France and Germany initiated an overall strategy to combat growing racism and xenophobia that was approved by the European Union leaders.[67] The plan of action included the creation of a consultative commission, the harmonization of national antiracist legislation among member states, the training of police and civil servants in the promotion of tolerance, improved cross-border cooperation and data collection exchange, and a global strategy at the European Union level in combating acts of racist and xenophobic violence. The consultative commission released its report in June 1995 to pave the way for negotiations at the 1996 InterGovernmental Conference. The report recommended that the Treaty of Rome be amended to include a specific reference to combating racism, granting the European Commission the authority to legislate in this matter; introduce a European race relations directive and a directive outlawing Holocaust denial and the distribution of racist and anti-Semitic material in written and electronic form; establish a racism and xenophobia monitoring center (RAXEN); ask EUROPOL to take responsibility for exchanging information regarding neo-Nazi and neofascist organizations; and continue the mandate of the consultative commission itself.[68] The report was endorsed unanimously with the exception of Great Britain. The European Commission has since put forward proposals to introduce Europe-wide legislation to combat racism and xenophobia.[69]

The Nongovernmental Sector

The institution of human rights instruments also led to the inception of nongovernmental organizations (NGOs) devoted to the protection and defense of human rights in all areas of life in the spirit that these instruments promoted. NGOs have a unique role in monitoring the conduct of governments and holding them accountable to their treaty obligations through public pressure and lobbying. Among the larger NGOs dedicated to the implementation of all human rights, Human Rights Watch monitors and combats right-wing extremism and xenophobia. Staff members travel to the respective countries, interview victims of xenophobic violence and government officials, compile reports, and submit specific recommendations to governments regarding steps to improve the situation and fulfill their international obligations. There are also a number of smaller, specific organizations devoted strictly to tracking hate-groups, neofascists, supremacists, and others. *Searchlight,* a British publication, is a leading expert on the extreme right throughout Europe, investigating and documenting extremists in connection with a network of contacts and informants across the continent. *Searchlight* has been involved with other antiracist and antifascist initiatives and has provided input into the planning of the Council of Europe's Youth Campaign Against Racism. *Searchlight* is also closely connected to the Center for Democratic Renewal, based in Atlanta, which is an authority on American hate groups. *Searchlight*'s editor, Gerry Gable, and the center's Lenny Zeskind have both provided testimony before the British House of Commons. *Searchlight,* France's LICRA, and MRAP also provided evidence for the 1991 European Parliament's Committee of Inquiry into Racism and Fascism. Both the New York–based Anti-Defamation League and the American Jewish Congress (AJC) are also keeping an eye on the situation in Europe. The AJC was instrumental in the Council of Europe's Seminar on Intolerance and is assisting with the plan of action. The Simon Wiesenthal Center in Los Angeles, after revealing its investigation entitled the Operation, submitted *A Special Report to the United States House Foreign Affairs Subcommittee on International Organizations and Human Rights* and was interviewed by officials in Germany.

Nongovernmental organizations operate at the grassroots level, compiling a picture of the situation from the people themselves, and are not always appreciated by either government officials or international organizations. The smaller NGOs also engage in directly confronting the extreme right's rank and file on the street, blocking its meetings, leading antifascist rallies and antiracist marches, and exposing its violent proclivities. Having honed their expertise, they share information with each other on different actors and different strategies. Unfortunately, at times NGOs are unable to coordinate their efforts under a united front because of parochialism and personal or political agendas. This can be detrimental to the extent that they distinguish their own quarry from other varieties without thinking of the whole phenomenon of right-wing extremism. Nevertheless, nongovernmental organizations do invaluable work in the service of the realization of human rights.

Conclusion

A wide-ranging system of international and regional human rights instruments has been instituted that clearly and unequivocally reject the hatred fomented by right-wing extremism as inimical to the values underpinning the international society of states. Countless resolutions, the establishment of effective guidelines, and the preparation of ambitious plans of action demonstrate the commitment of the international community. However, the international community is only as effective as its members allow it to be. These international instruments are hampered by the limitations intrinsic to all international activities: the difficulty of enforcement, the lack of direct jurisdiction, and the low priority allotted to them amid the many problems confronting the world. These obstacles stem from the reality that the ultimate responsibility rests with the states themselves to implement and realize the obligations of all international agreements. In ratifying these treaties, states have pledged themselves to certain norms of behavior and to the adoption of concrete measures in the legislative, judicial, administrative, and other relevant fields in the fight against right-wing extremism. Clearly, states have pledged themselves symbolically, but they have failed to accord the necessary priority to the problem and seemingly do not believe they are actually remiss in their obligations. International instruments are meaningless without strong leadership, political decisionmaking, and the willpower to maximize all the political effort necessary to see them through. Only with committed action on the part of governments and states in taking every opportunity within their own jurisdictions to combat the extreme right and xenophobia and racism will success be ensured.

Given that right-wing extremism flourishes by taking advantages of the weaknesses and tensions in the system, it is not really surprising that since the 1980s there has been a resurgence in the extreme right. The international community has perhaps not done all that it could in encouraging states to fulfill their obligations but remains uniquely placed to be able to do so. The international community is the arena in which the highest ideals can and should be aspired to; it serves as the highest source of authority providing a stimulus for action and acts as the global conscience reminding its members of their duties. The internationalization of the subject of extremism is useful for legitimizing the lobbying efforts and participation of nongovernmental, intergovernmental, and regional organizations committed to fighting the extreme right. It is the international community's responsibility to direct and mobilize these efforts in the launching of a broad, consistent, and persistent assault on the extreme right. International coordination and implementation must ensure the strongest and most determined response of states not only in enforcing universal principles but also in giving warning of potential dangers. Such coordination should include not only a review of the necessary legislation but assessments of the records of state activities in combating the extreme right. States must vigorously defend and protect democracy against forces threatening its very principles. It is absolutely imperative that the international community and its member states do not complacently take the health of democracy for granted but realize that it must still be protected and defended with all their effort.

Notes

1. Peter Fysh and Jim Wolfers, "Le Pen, the National Front and the Extreme Right in France," *Parliamentary Affairs* 45(3), July 1992: 309.

2. European Parliament, *Report of the Committee of Inquiry into the Rise of Fascism and Racism in Europe.* (Evregenis Report) (Brussels: European Communities, 1985), para. 27, 68.

3. *Monitor* (Center for Democratic Renewal), *Monitor,* May 1990, 2.

4. Jiri Pehe, "The Czech Republic," *RFE/RL Research Reports* 3(16), April 1994: 50.

5. *Monitor* (Center for Democratic Renewal), July 1988, 5.

6. "Leaderless Resistance," *Searchlight* (London), January 1994, 3.

7. Anti-Defamation League, "Extremist Groups Strengthen International Ties with Hi-Tech Communications: Poses New Threat of Anti-Semitism," press release, June 24, 1994. Also reported in *Searchlight,* January 1994, 4.

8. Government Secretariat of Israel, *The Anti-Semitism Monitoring Forum,* December 22, 1993, release following statement by FBI director Louis Freeh that "the United States would clamp down on American publishers of neo-Nazi propaganda."

9. Anti-Defamation League, *Extremism on the Right* (New York: ADL, 1988), 118.

10. George Rodrigue, "Ex-Neo-Nazi Says American Aids Cause," *Dallas Morning News,* February 5, 1994, 1A.

11. Anti-Defamation League, *Hitler's Apologists: The Anti-Semitic Propaganda of Holocaust "Revisionism"* (New York: ADL, 1993), 38.

12. *Canadian Anti-Racism Education and Research Society Bulletin,* July 1993.

13. James Ridgeway, "Wie Deutsch ist es?" *Village Voice,* December 3, 1991, 36.

14. Lenny Zeskind, "And Now the Hate Show," *New York Times,* November 16, 1993, A15.

15. Mary Nemeth and Tom Fennel, "Deny, Deny, Deny: Ernst Zundel Is Back in Action—and on TV," *Macleans,* August 30, 1993, 56.

16. Anti-Defamation League, "Extremist Groups Strengthen International Ties with Hi-Tech Communications." June 24, 1944, release.

17. Rodrigue, "Ex-Neo-Nazi Says American Aids Cause," 15A.

18. Maurice Lucow, "Internet Computer Network Used to Fight Anti-Semitism," *Canadian Jewish News,* October 27, 1994.

19. Anti-Defamation League, *Hitler's Apologists,* 19–25.

20. Gary Lauck, *The New Order,* as featured in the Center for Democratic Renewal package entitled "International Connections."

21. *The Globe and Mail,* "Zhirinovsky guest of ex-SS member in Austrian Alps," December 23, 1993: A13.

22. Ibid. According to *Searchlight,* February 1994, 18, Zhirinovsky was accompanied by Frey on this trip to Austria and, moreover, had been the guest speaker at the DVU's last two conferences.

23. Michael Schmidt, *The Truth Shall Make Us Free,* documentary 1992.

24. "Belgian Nazis Promote Family Events," *Searchlight*, April 1994, 17.

25. Simon Wiesenthal Center, "The Neo-Nazi Movement in Germany: An Eye-witness Documentary Report," June 15, 1993.

26. "IHR Split Reveals Corporate Misdeeds," *Searchlight*, May 1994, 23.

27. Anti-Defamation League, *Hitler's Apologists*, 39.

28. "Light Sentence for Birdwood in Second Trial," *Searchlight*, May 1994, 6.

29. Michael Schmidt, *The New Reich: Penetrating the Secrets of Today's Neo-Nazi Networks* (London: Random House, 1993).

30. *Searchlight*, reports on Spain and South Africa, May 1994, 20–21.

31. Government Secretariat: The Anti-Semitism Monitoring Forum (Israel), "The Elections to the European Parliament: The Radical Right," July 1994.

32. Ibid.

33. Jiri Pehe, "The Czech Republic," *RFE/RL Research Reports* 3(16), April 22, 1994: 53.

34. *Searchlight*, July 1990, 3, BBC Report, as found in the Center for Democratic Renewal's package "International Connections."

35. *Sunday Times* (London), "Ku Klux Klan to Fund Far-Right Candidates in British Elections," January 16, 1994, 7.

36. Ibid.

37. Stephen Kinzer, "Klan Seizes on Germany's Wave of Racist Violence," *New York Times*, November 3, 1991, 16.

38. Debra Lipstadt, *Denying the Holocaust: Assault on Memory and Truth* (New York: Free Press, 1993), 7.

39. Rodrigues, "Ex-Neo-Nazi Says American Aids Cause," A15.

40. "The Fascist Spectre That Is Haunting Europe," *Searchlight*, February 1994, 18.

41. For information relating to Khadafy's connections to the extreme right and the role of third positionism, see Warren Kinsella, *Unholy Alliances: Terrorists, Extremists, Front Companies and the Libyan Connection in Canada* (Toronto: Lester, 1992).

42. Christopher Husbands, "Racism, Xenophobia, and the Extreme Right: A Five-Country Assessment," revised lecture given to the Faculty of Social Sciences of the University of Amsterdam, May 9, 1995, 5.

43. Nathan Lerner, "Incitement in the Racial Convention Reach and Shortcomings of Article 4," Faculty of Law of Tel-Aviv University, *Israeli Yearbook on Human Rights*, vol. 22 (Dordrecht, Neth.: Martinus Nijhoff, 1992), 14.

44. Louis Greenspan, *Under the Shadow of Weimar: Democracy, Law and Racial Incitement in 6 Countries* (Westport, CT: Praeger, 1993), 189.

45. Nathan Lerner, "Incitement in the Racial Convention: Reach and Shortcomings of Article 4," *Israeli Yearbook on Human Rights*, vol. 22, 2.

46. Louis Greenspan, *Under the Shadow of Weimar*, 189.

47. Rudolf Bernhardt, "Human Rights Aspects of Racial and Religious Hatred Under Regional Human Rights Conventions," *Israeli Yearbook on Human Rights*, vol. 22, 22.

48. It is interesting that as a member of the CSCE (now OSCE), the United States has undertaken obligations in contradiction with its position regarding other human

rights laws, particularly with respect to Article 4 of the Convention on the Elimination of Racial Discrimination.

49. Thomas Buergenthal, "The CSCE and the Promotion of Racial and Religious Tolerance," 32.

50. Louis Greenspan, *Under the Shadow of Weimar,* 191.

51. Thomas Buergenthal, "The CSCE and the Promotion of Racial and Religious Tolerance," 38.

52. UN Resolution E/CN.4/1994/L.11 Add.7.

The resolution was concerned with the fact that despite efforts, racism, racial discrimination, anti-Semitism, xenophobia and related intolerance, as well as acts of racial violence, persist, are even growing in magnitude, continually assuming new forms.

53. Council of Europe Summit. Vienna Declaration October 1993. Appendix 1 "Reform of the Control Mechanism of the European Convention on Human Rights."

54. Rudolf Bernhardt, "Human Rights Aspects of Racial and Religious Hatred Under Regional Human Rights Conventions," *Israeli Yearbook on Human Rights,* vol. 22, 1992, 18.

55. Michael Banton, "International Action Against Racial Discrimination: A Briefing Paper," *Ethnic and Racial Studies* 14(4), October 1991: 550.

56. Implementation of the Programme of Action for the Third Decade to Combat Racism and Racial Prejudice, Draft Resolution 21.

57. World Conference on Human Rights, *Vienna Declaration and Programme of Action,* Article 15, June 25, 1993.

58. UN Doc. A/45/525 24 September 1990.

59. UN Doc. A/46/18 1991.

60. UN Doc. E/CN.4/Sub.2/1992/11.

61. Resolution 1993/20.

62. Report of the Special Rapporteur E/CN.4/1994/66.

63. In Resolution 1986/20, the Commission on Human Rights also created a Special Rapporteur for the Elimination of All Forms of Intolerance and Discrimination Based on Religion and Belief.

64. Thomas Buergenthal, "The CSCE and the Promotion of Racial and Religious Tolerance," 47.

65. Council of Europe. Resolution 743 (1980) on the need to combat resurgent fascist propaganda and its racist aspects.

66. Vienna Declaration, October 1993, Plan of Action, Section 1.

67. *European Union Statement on Racism and Xenophobia,* Corfu Summit, 24 and 25 June 1994 Annex IV.

68. *Searchlight,* May 1995, 23.

69. "Britain Stands Alone Against Plan for Racism Laws," *Financial Times,* December 13, 1995, 2.

12

Conclusions

Stephen Scheinberg

No fire bell in the night rings through the preceding pages. The authors have neither heard nor attempted to evoke the sounds of Nazi jackboots approaching any of the eight nations considered in this study. All share the concern that extremist groups pose an undeniable criminal menace and, additionally, recognize that in some of these countries they have the potential for greater political and social power. However, whereas there are indeed common features, the extreme right must be assessed within specific regional and national contexts.

Certainly the broad, historic traditions of democracy in the two North American and three West European societies considered offer a rather different picture from the three as yet fragile transitional societies studied in Eastern Europe. Thus our consideration of right-wing extremism in the democracies might be likened to the periodic checkup of normally healthy subjects; for Eastern Europe it is more like the anxious examination of those who have never had a record of good health and are recovering from a serious long-term illness.

Since the mid-1980s we have witnessed a significant rise of the extreme right in many parts of Europe and North America. The fascist banners, taboo for forty years, have been taken from their hiding places to be proudly borne by racist skinhead thugs or in some other cases to be refashioned in contemporary political styles. Fascism has become politically respectable once again. Masses of voters in Italy, Austria, Belgium, and France have voted for candidates whose appeal is to extreme nationalism and racial hatred. Even in the United States, large numbers of voters have responded to a similar appeal. In Russia extremist demagogues offer themselves to a dispirited and confused populace; in other sectors of Eastern Europe former communists now returned to power, often using the rhetoric of economic reform and democracy, have not yet had their democratic credentials sufficiently tested.

It would be a gross error and oversimplification, however, to offer this scenario as a rerun of the 1930s. The players and the context differ enormously. Even though a Jörg Haider in Austria may solicit the support of aging SS veterans and their families, this is not done to spark a revival but rather to politically capitalize on the enduring cultural fault lines of Austrian society. Professor Tony Judt perceptively writes that Haider and his counterparts are not "the ghosts of Europe past [but] something far more serious: they are the ghost of Europes yet to come."[1] The European extreme right of the 1990s has cultural and even family links to the 1930s, but after half a century it is certainly no revival of Hitler's legions. Moreover, the phenomenon goes far beyond the Western European heartland of the old fascism and in its first phase was particularly marked by the youthfulness of its participants.

In the late 1980s and early 1990s the most generally familiar face of the extreme right was its criminal element. Reports of assaults, arson, desecrations, and murders brought the skinheads and neo-Nazis to public and official attention. France was perhaps the only country in which the extremists also made a significant political breakthrough before 1990, and it is worth noting that the level of hate crimes there was comparatively low. Although the majority of hate crimes are not committed by those affiliated with racist organizations, such groups send out their message of violence well beyond their ranks to those inclined to spontaneously imitate their actions. Thus the first, or criminal, phase of the modern extreme right, which extended even into some still communist East European states, was primarily nonpolitical, scattered, and at best loosely organized.

It was Germany, because of its unfortunate past, that first drew world attention to criminal extremism. The 1987 skinhead attack at the Zionskirche in East Berlin stirred little interest in the West, but beginning in late 1991, the protracted antiforeigner violence in cities such as Hoyerswerda, Cottbus, and Rostock caught the attention of the world, as did the firebomb murders of Turkish residents. These outrages were accompanied by incidents of Jewish cemetery and holocaust monument desecrations as well as numerous cases of assault. The strong antirefugee stance of Chancellor Kohl's Christian Democrats and the allied Christian Social Union of Bavaria undoubtedly not only encouraged the violence, at least indirectly, but also used it to push the Social Democrats to approve a constitutional change of Germany's generous refugee asylum law. Over the past few years the incidence of hate crimes in Germany has declined, perhaps because police efficiency or diligence has increased or because Kohl has successfully co-opted an important share of extremist sentiment.[2]

It cannot yet be safely stated that there is a clear line of transition into a new political phase of extremism. The criminal side of extreme-right activities continues, but there are signs that the wave of violence is abating. Such signs must be treated very warily; the statistics for a year or two may be indicators but do not make a trend. For example, the data for 1995 could breed optimism. The ADL found that anti-Semitic incidents in the United States fell by 11 percent in 1995, the first decline in three years and the largest decline in ten years. Klanwatch reported a 61 percent drop in the number of skinhead organizations.[3] In Britain there was a 25 percent reduction in anti-Semitic incidents, but the number of racist incidents continued to rise.[4] Canada's League for Human Rights showed a decline in anti-Semitic vandalism of 13 percent (although the spread of hate propaganda led to an increase of incidents reported through 1995). Extremist groups in Canada were also clearly in disarray. However, even if in numerical decline, the extremists can be deadly, as the Oklahoma City bombing reminded the world.

Violence will undoubtedly continue to be attractive to important sectors of the extreme right in every country. It may serve various functions, such as a form of youth recruitment among the more criminally inclined of the youth, a means of intimidating enemies, or even a legitimation for those who have chosen the political path. In the United States in particular a strong paramilitary subculture is perpetuated by a media with worldwide influence.

Despite vast differences between the political cultures and the economies of Western and Eastern Europe and North America, there are common themes that underlie the rise of the extreme right in its political form. First, the collapse of communism and the end of the Cold War have not been an unqualified blessing. Communism leaves in its wake the difficult, often painful, construction of new economic and political orders. Populations long accustomed to a communist state giving them a minimum of security now must adjust to the vagaries of the market; many individuals are unable to do so. "Restructuring of industry" is not only a Western phenomenon; the often archaic industries of the East are often the battlefield where economic reformers and their opponents clash. The long-term promise of the free market may be realizable, and even now there are real signs of progress. However, in the short run hunger and deprivation are fuel for demagogues.

At the same time the envied populations of Western Europe and North America have also had their security disturbed, albeit on a lesser scale. Transnational structures—the European Union, the General Agreement on Tariffs and Trade (GATT), the North American Free Trade Agreement (NAFTA)—have promised much in the way of long-term mutual economic benefit, but the globalization of markets has either precipitated real job losses or provoked a greater sense of insecurity among all but the very rich. There is a fear that transnational bodies have removed or are in the process of removing the instruments of economic, political, and even military power from national parliaments and congresses. The extreme nationalist will feed on such fears.

Perhaps contemporary capitalism is a victim of its own immediate success, creating those "internal contradictions" beloved not by Marxists alone.

Globalization and new technologies have conspired, contends Edward Luttwak, "exposing hitherto more secure white-collar workers to the workplace dislocations, mass firings or at least diminishing employment prospects that have long been the lot of blue collar-industrial workers in mature economies."[5]

Corporate "reengineering" has led to the displacement of tens of thousands of white-collar jobs and to the declining wages in the same service sector that was to be the salvation for industrial decline. The promise of new information-age jobs to most unemployed industrial workers is illusory, and currently their frustrations are shared by now disposable middle managers who also feel, in the words of management theorist Michael Hammer, "trepidation and anxiety" and even "abject terror."[6] Traditional post–World War II security is rapidly disappearing in Western Europe and North America, and many are less prepared than generation X members to receive the kind of message that Andrew S. Grove, president of Intel Corporation, has for them: "If the world operates as one big market, every employee will compete with every person anywhere in the world who is capable of doing the same job. There are lots of them and many of them are hungry."[7]

Centrist politicians, whether of the social democratic or Tory variety, offer few convincing alternatives to the victims or the newly insecure who see their jobs being technologically eliminated or moving to Asia and Latin America. Debates among them about how much of the safety net can be salvaged or the efficacy of new training programs do not inspire hope. Moreover, both sides of the political center are committed to the very globalization that is at the heart of the new angst.

There is no convincing alternative emanating from a democratic left. The social democratic parties and many of the former communist parties of Western Europe, liberal Democrats in the United States, and Canadian Liberals all operate within the broad globalist consensus. In Eastern Europe the putative democrats tend to be economic reformers committed to the free market. For those, however, who have become the victims of the market, are apprehensive of its impact on their personal security, or fear competition on a remarkably unlevel playing field, there is an option.

There is political space today for the extreme-right alternative, which promises personal security to white- and blue-collar working people through restraints on globalization. Luttwak provocatively argues that this form of "fascism is the wave of the future."[8] Appeals to conservative cultural values can buttress the extremist (or fascist) approach along with the addition of chauvinism and racism, which may further enhance its allure. This enriched recipe constitutes the essential elements of the tasty dish that Haider, Buchanan, Le Pen, and Zhirinovsky have been serving up. The two former are classical opportunists who, recognizing the rising tide of middle-class fears and insecurity, jettison their older allegiances to transnationalism.[9] The cries of "Austria first," "America first," "The French first," and the call to restore "Great Russia" exploit legitimate fears to further chauvinist ends.

Xenophobic extremists have capitalized, often brilliantly, on the wretched masses of war- or terror-displaced refugees, economic immigrants, and guest workers who have found or threaten to find their way to more advantaged nations. Racist demagogues unite fear of the foreigner with real enough economic concerns to offer simple but attractive electoral platforms. In Western Europe and North America they promise to build higher fences, expel foreigners, ferret out illegals, and suspend or terminate immigration. In Eastern Europe the promises are to bring back the security of the past or, in the Russian case, to restore empire. Always there are available scapegoats—ethnic minorities, Romanies, Jews—or in the Polish case, only the shadow of them.

This study did not include Austria or Italy, two of the West European nations in which right-wing extremism seems to have enjoyed some of its greatest recent electoral successes. Italian fascism, led by Gianfranco Fini, has been newly legitimated first as a coalition partner entering government for the first time since World War II and second by casting off its old identity— at least for public consumption. Fini's mainstreaming tactics have enjoyed some considerable success, and it is possible that his National Alliance could even become the major partner in a coalition government in the near future.

Austria came perilously close to that situation in elections at the end of 1995. If Haider's popular support continued to grow, it was thought likely that he would lead his Freedom Party into a new coalition with the right-of-center People's Party, but this was not the case; it was Chancellor Vranitzky's Socialists that regained some lost ground. This likely cheered those moderate analysts who hoped that, as in France where Le Pen's vote seems to have leveled off, extreme-right politics throughout Western Europe would find a plateau where they would enjoy a more or less permanent minority status.[10] Of course, neither political pundits nor social scientists can take account of all of the social and economic factors that may either reduce or enlarge the extremists' vote. Regardless of what the political future may hold for the extreme right, it has already had a considerable impact on the Western European social environment.

Across Western Europe, immigration and refugee policies have taken on a new mean, if not racist, edge. It was not Le Pen but the conservatives in France who came down hard on both the illegals and the foreign residents of France. France's antiracist taboos yielded not only to the discourse of Le Pen but even to some of his prescriptions. Interior Minister Charles Pasqua unleashed his police against minorities and shared, along with his successor, Jean-Louis Debre, the extremist's desire for a "zero immigration" policy. The Socialists also shifted; their policies became indistinguishable from the right's on immigrant and refugee issues.

In Italy the Democratic Party of the Left, the Northern League, and the National Alliance have made common cause against the illegals to support a decree for their prompt expulsion.[11] German Green Party parliamentarians, with scattered support from FDP and SDP colleagues, failed to liberalize their nation's naturalization laws to extend citizenship to, as a government information bulletin puts it, "foreigners in the second generation if they are born in Germany."[12]

The European discourse on refugees and immigrants is not a calm, dispassionate appraisal of the numbers that each nation or the community can afford to admit. It is rather a shrill and often racist dialogue that draws liberally on the ideas and vocabulary of the extremists. Increased outrages against Jewish institutions and persons in Germany, France, Italy, and elsewhere over the past several years indicate that although the new extremist politicians are not overtly anti-Semitic, their message of intolerance creates an unsafe climate for all minorities. A new, meaner, more chauvinistic, often intolerant Western Europe has emerged with the rise of the extreme right.

North America has not been, at least as yet, so susceptible to the virus of extreme-right politics. Canada has no party of the extreme right; its moderately right Reform Party has resisted the infiltration efforts of radical elements. In the United States, Pat Buchanan has, at least since 1992, managed to pull together within the Republican Party a significant coalition that bears a strong resemblance to the followers of Le Pen, Fini, or Haider. However, the American political system has proved strongly resistant to extremism unless a major party, as in the 1950s era of McCarthyism, identifies its interest with that perspective. Still, the Buchanan cultural discourse, especially on immigration, may find an audience as receptive as the Europeans.

Eastern Europe and the post-Soviet states present very different prospects. Not only are extremist groups and political parties strong in Russia but perhaps more important, the true democrats are weak and divided. The appraisal of Alla Gerber that in Russia one can find democrats but not democracy may be too harsh, but it is worth repeating as a warning. Russian ultranationalism and anti-Semitism have flourished as the transitional economy falters, its military is humbled, and an empire is lost. In this atmosphere refugees, even ethnic Russians, find little succor, and minorities such as the Chechens are demonized. Communist Gennadii Zyuganov and the extremist Vladimir Zhirinovsky are but two of the better-known demagogues who exploit Russia's weaknesses. Among all of the countries included in this work, Russia is currently the most vulnerable to the extremist threat.

Poland seems to have its reform economy in hand, and the momentum of change seems sustainable. At present there is no strong right-wing extremist party. Moreover, in 1995 a genuinely democratic transition to an opposition took place, although with much bitterness expressed by former president Lech Walesa. The transition must be regarded as an important milestone in the democratic development of Poland.

Still, a democrat like Adam Michnik is pessimistic, seeing a strange anti-Semitism with fewer than 8,000 Jews living in the country, no real conception of minority rights, and a Catholic Church that seeks to undermine secular democracy. Too many Poles regard themselves, the majority, as the primary victims of both fascism and communism, breeding a kind of self-righteousness and rigidity that runs counter to democratic consensus building. These are disturbing factors, which to Polish democrats may be regarded as early warning signals; but Poland is not host to a visible extremism.

Hungary's government is presently dominated by reformed communists who seem sincere in their transformation to social democracy but may not be committed to stay the course with economic reform of the more severe variety. Jozsef Torgyan's Independent Smallholders was the only ultra-right-wing party to gain (some small) parliamentary representation in the May 1994 election, but he also understands how to utilize economic pain to his benefit and could be a serious contender for power.

Violent skinheads can be found in Hungary, and the government has not effectively checked them, classifying their crimes as mere hooliganism or vandalism rather than racist outrages. Anti-Semitism is not as strong there as in Poland, yet it is still conspicuous. The Jews of Hungary are reasonably integrated, but perhaps for that very reason they are reluctant to confront anti-Semitism. Hungary's Romani population has achieved official recognition but has not always been well protected by the government. There are disturbing signs of insensitivity toward minorities, and manipulation of the media by the government is reminiscent of the old communism. Hungary's transition has progressed reasonably well, but its political culture is not yet secure.

*   *   *

In 1935 the American novelist Sinclair Lewis's work *It Can't Happen Here* was published. Lewis warned Americans that fascism could triumph in their own land.[13] We are far from the social-political context of the 1930s, from Mussolini and Hitler. Still, in an amazingly short time the extreme right has made rapid gains. Fifty years after the Holocaust extremists have achieved a new prominence in Western Europe, appear almost as strong in the United States, and threaten to take power in parts of Eastern Europe. It is time to harken to Lewis's warning once again, but in a broader sense. Extremism does not pose an immediate political threat to take power in the nations included in this work. Yet prudence and respect for human rights demand that citizens and their governments act now, while there is still time.

Notes

1. Tony Judt, "Austria and the Ghost of the New Europe," *New York Review*, February 15, 1996.

2. Leon Mangasarian, "Neo-Nazi Violence Continuing to Decline, German Officials Say," *Globe and Mail* (Toronto), July 6, 1995. The high point for rightist attacks was in 1992 with 2,639 attacks, falling to 2,232 in 1993 and 1,489 in 1994.

3. Anti-Defamation League, press release, February 14, 1995; Klanwatch, *Intelligence Report*, March 1995.

4. Community Security Trust, *CST Annual Review 1995* (London, 1996), 3–4.

5. Edward Luttwak, "Why Fascism Is the Wave of the Future," *London Review of Books*, April 7, 1994. Professor Luttwak's stimulating essay is the basis for much of this argument. He is, of course, not a Marxist.

6. Michael Hammer and Steven A. Stanton, *The Reengineering Revolution: A Handbook* (New York: Harper, 1995), quoted by Simon Head, "The New, Ruthless Economy," *New York Review*, February 29, 1996.

7. Grove's statement appears in his book *High Output Management* and is quoted by Clay Chandler, "The Buchanan Factor: GOP Candidate's Success Chills U.S. Business," *Gazette* (Montreal), February 23, 1996, D4.

8. Ibid.

9. In summer 1992 a highly placed official in Austria's Foreign Ministry insisted on Haider's pan-German and pan-European commitments, but I was not convinced because the political opening was with the anti-Maastricht forces. Dr. Heinrich Gleissner, interview with the author, June 29, 1992, Vienna. For Haider's change, see Judt, "Austria and the Ghost of the New Europe." Buchanan was, of course, part of the globalist Nixon and Reagan administrations.

10. See, for example, the *Economist*, (October 21, 1995, 55–56), which takes the view that Fini and Haider "could win power only as junior partners in a coalition." However, some analysts did believe that Le Pen's xenophobic program would play well if the economy went sour (December 16, 1995, 43–44).

11. "No Room at Europe's Inn," *Economist*, December 9, 1995, 53–54.

12. "Greens Fail in Bid for Intra-Party Unity on the Issue of Dual Citizenship," *Week in Germany*, February 17, 1995, 2.

13. Sinclair Lewis, *It Can't Happen Here: A Novel* (New York: Triangle Books, 1935).

Appendix: List of Research Interviews

Ian Kagedan—Germany

Berlin

Rainer Erb	*Zentrum fur Antisemitismusforschung*
Bernd Wagner	
Hajo Funke	*Freie Universitat Berlin*

Bonn

Eleonore Linsmayer	Press Information Office of the Federal Government, Head of the Canada and U.S. Section
Lepszy	Konrad Adenauer Foundation
H. Blath	Federal Ministry of Justice
Gerd Schoen	Federal Ministry of the Interior
Rainer Zeimentz	Social Democratic Party
Michael Mertes	Federal Chancellory

Frankfurt

Ignatz Bubis	*Zentralrat Juden in Deutschland*
Szajak	*Judische Gemeinde Frankfurt am Main*

Strasbourg

Amedee Turner	MEP Tory, Chair of the Civil Liberties and Internal Affairs Committee
Glyn Ford	MEP Socialist Grouping, Rapporteur Committee of Inquiry on Racism and Xenophobia 1991

David Matas—England and France

London

Paul Mendel	Council of Christians and Jews
Gerry Gable	Searchlight Publications
Serge April	Canadian High Commission
Anthony Lerman	Institute of Jewish Affairs
Howard Spier	Institute of Jewish Affairs
Christopher Husbands	London School of Economics
Suhkdev Sharma	Commission for Racial Equality
Christopher Boothman	Commission for Racial Equality

Greville Janner, QC, MP	Chair Inter-Parliamentary Council Against Anti-Semitism
Michael Whine	Board of Deputies of British Jews
Catherine Lee	Police Quality of Service Section, Home Office
Marian Fitzgerald	Home Office, Research Unit Anti-Racist Alliance

Paris

Yann Galut	SOS Racisme
Haim Musicant	B'nai Brith International
Nonna Mayer	
Serge Cwejgenbaum	European Jewish Congress
Patrick Quentin	*Ligue Internationale Contre leRacisme et l'Antisemitisme*
Gerard Fellous	*Commission Nationale de Consultative de Droits de l'Homme*
Martial Anciant	Article 31
J.-C. Cambadelis	Socialist Party
David Sarment	*Union des Etudiants Juifs*
David Rozelle	*Union des Etudiants Juifs*
Patrick Lamy	*Ligue des Droits Humaines*

Stephen Scheinberg—Canada

Research in Canada was facilitated by the League for Human Rights of B'nai Brith Canada, which maintains extensive files on this topic.

Stephen Scheinberg—United States

New York

Randall Balmer	Barnard College
Irwin Suall	Anti-Defamation League
Tom Halpern	Anti-Defamation League
David Cantor	Anti-Defamation League
Marc Caplan	Anti-Defamation League
Alfred Ross	Planned Parenthood Federation
John Goetz	Planned Parenthood Federation

Washington, D.C.

Stephen Goldstein	Staff, Congressman Charles Schumer
Susan Caplan	Chief Counsel, Senator Paul Simon's Office
Michael Lieberman	Anti-Defamation League
Mira Bolen	Anti-Defamation League
Carol Keys	People for the American Way

Boston

Chip Berlet	Political Research Associates
Skip Porteous	Institute for First Amendment Studies
Jack Levin	Northeastern University
Jack McDevitt	Northeastern University

Montgomery, Alabama

Danny Welch	Klanwatch

Aurel Braun—Hungary, Poland, and Russia

Budapest

Karoly Bard	Deputy State Secretary of Justice
Martin Ill	Hungarian Human Rights Legal Consulting Centre
Miklos Palos	State Secretary in the Prime Minister's Office
Fabian Jozsa	Secretary of State, Ministry of the Interior
Jozsef Torgyan	President of the Smallholder's Party
Rodney Irwin	Canadian Ambassador to Hungary
Gustav Zoltai	President, Central Board of Hungarian Jews
David Kraus	Israeli Ambassador to Hungary
Imre Szekeres	Executive Secretary and Vice President of the Hungarian Socialist Party
Zoltan Pecze	Deputy State Secretary, Ministry of Defense
Peter Feldmajer	President, Association of Communities and Synagogues of Hungary

Warsaw

Anne Leahy	Canadian Ambassador to Poland
Audrey Glover	Ambassador, Director, ODIHR
Marek Novicki	Helsinki Foundation of Human Rights
Adam Michnik	Editor in Chief, *Gazeta Wyborcza*
Konstanti Gebert	Political Journalist, *Gazeta Wyborcza*
Bronislaw Geremek	Member of Parliament
Jerzy Zimowski	Undersecretary of State, Ministry of Interior
Pawel Wildstein	Head, Union of Jewish Communities in Poland
Stanislaw Krajewski	Cochair, Jewish-Catholic Dialogue

Moscow

Temuraz Ramishvili	Ministry of Foreign Affairs
Tatyana Smirnova	Humanitarian Cooperation and Human Rights
Boris Altshuler	Moscow Research Center for Human Rights
Vladimir Raskin	Moscow Research Center for Human Rights
Alexei Smirnov	Director, Moscow Research Center for Human Rights
Vladimir Zhirinovsky	Leader, Liberal-Democratic Party
Jeremy Kinsman	Canadian Ambassador to Russia
Beryl Lazar	Marina Roshia Synagogue
Alla Gerber	Member of Parliament
Jahan R. Pollyeva	Principal Advisor to Deputy Prime Minister Sergei Shakrai
Yuri Tavrovsky	Press Secretary to Sergei Shakrai

Berlin

Boris Fedorov	Former Finance Minister, Member of Parliament

Selected Bibliography

Right-Wing Extremism—General and Theory

Adorno, Theodor et al. *The Authoritarian Personality.* New York: Harper & Row, 1950.

Baker, David. "The Appeal of Fascism: Pathological Fantasy or Intellectual Coherence?" *Patterns of Prejudice* 20(3), 1986: 3–12.

Barkun, Michael. "Racist Apocalypse: Millennialism on the Far Right." *American Studies* 31, 1990: 121–140.

Billig, Michael. *Ideology and Social Psychology: Extremism, Moderation, and Contradiction.* New York: St. Martin's Press, 1982.

_____. "The Extreme Right: Continuities in Anti-Semitic Conspiracy Theory in Post-War Europe." In Roger Eatwell and Noël O'Sullivan, eds., *The Nature of the Right.* London: Pinter, 1989, 146–166.

Cheles, Luciano, Ronnie Ferguson, and Michalina Vaughan, eds. *The Right in Western and Eastern Europe.* London: Longman, 1995.

Connolly, William. *The Terms of Political Discourse.* Princeton: Princeton University Press, 1983.

Dandeker, C., and B. Troyna. "Fascism: Slogan or Concept?" *Patterns of Prejudice* 17(4), 1983: 19–30.

Eatwell, Roger, and Noël O'Sullivan, eds. *The Nature of the Right.* London: Pinter, 1989.

_____. "The Holocaust Denial: A Study in Propaganda Technique." In Luciano Cheles, ed., *Neo-Fascism in Europe.* London: Longman, 1991, pp. 120–146.

_____. *Contemporary Political Ideologies.* London: Pinter, 1993.

Falter, Jurgen, and Siegfried Schumann. "Affinity Towards Right-Wing Extremism in Western Europe." *West European Politics* 11(2), April 1988.

Gallie, W. B. "Essentially Contested Concepts." In *Proceedings of the Aristotelian Society* (London) 56, 1955–1956.

Hainsworth, Paul, ed. *The Extreme Right in Europe and the U.S.A.* London: Pinter, 1992.

Halliday, Fred. "State and Society in International Relations: A Second Agenda." *Millennium*, 1987.

Hockenos, Paul. *Free to Hate.* London: Routledge, 1993.

Johansen, Robert. "Real Security Is Democratic Security." *Alternatives* 16(2), Spring 1991: 209–241.

Krejčí, Jaroslav. "Introduction: Concepts of Right and Left." In Cheles, *Neo-Fascism in Europe,* 1–18.

Laponce, J. A. *Left and Right: The Topography of Political Perceptions.* Toronto: University of Toronto Press, 1981.

Lasswell, Harold. "The Psychology of Hitlerism." *Political Quarterly* 4(3), 1933: 373–384.

Maier, Charles. "Democracy and Its Discontents." *Foreign Affairs,* July-August 1994: 48–64.

Merkl, Peter, ed. *Political Violence and Terror, Motifs and Motivations.* Berkeley: University of California Press, 1986.

Merkl, Peter, and Leonard Weinberg. *Encounters with the Contemporary Radical Right.* Boulder: Westview Press, 1993.

O'Maolain, Ciaran. *The Radical Right: A World Directory.* London: Longman, 1987.

O'Sullivan, Noël. *Fascism.* London: J. M. Dent, 1983.

Policar, Alain. "Racism and Its Mirror Images." *Telos,* no. 83, Spring 1990: 99–108.

Rees, Phillip. *Biographical Dictionary of the Extreme Right.* New York: Simon and Schuster, 1990.

Rokeach, Milton. *The Open and Closed Mind.* New York: Basic Books, 1960.

Taguieff, Pierre-Andre. "The New Cultural Racism in France." *Telos,* no. 83, Spring 1990: 109–122.

Wilcox, Laird. "What Is Extremism? Style and Tactics Matter More Than Goals." In John George and Laird Wilcox, *Nazis, Communists, Klans and Others on the Fringe: Political Extremism in America.* Buffalo: Prometheus Books, 1992.

Canada

Anctil, Pierre. "Interlude of Hostility: Judeo-Christian Relations in Quebec in the Interwar Period, 1919–1939." In Alan Davies, ed., *Antisemitism in Canada.* Waterloo, Ontario: Wilfrid Laurier Press, 1992.

Barrett, Stanley. "White Supremacists and Neo-Fascists: Laboratories for the Analysis of Racism in Wider Society." *Canadian Ethnic Studies* 16, 1984: 1–15 .

_____. *Is God a Racist? The Right Wing in Canada.* Toronto: University of Toronto Press, 1987.

Betcherman, L. *The Swastika and the Maple Leaf: Fascist Movements in Canada in the Thirties.* Toronto: Fitzhenry and Whiteside, 1975.

Canada. Multiculturalism and Citizenship Canada. "Reported Incidents of Overt Racism in Canada, January 1, 1992, to April 30, 1993." Multiculturalism and Citizenship Canada.

Canadian Centre on Racism and Prejudice. "Anti-Racism at Work: Far-Right Network Exposed." *Bulletin,* nos. 3–4, April 1991.

Cuneo, Michael W. *Catholics Against the Church: Anti-Abortion Protest in Toronto, 1969–1985.* Toronto: University of Toronto Press, 1989.

Dunphy, Bill. "Canada's White Rights Groups Readying for Racial War." *Toronto Sun,* November 29, 1992, A2.

Kapica, Jack. "All Minorities Targets of Racial Violence, Experts Say." *Globe and Mail,* January 4, 1993, A3.

Kinsella, Warren. *Unholy Alliances: Terrorists, Extremists, Front Companies and the Libyan Connection in Canada.* Toronto: Lester, 1992.

_____. *Web of Hate: Inside Canada's Far Right Network.* Toronto: HarperCollins, 1994.

League for Human Rights of B'nai Brith Canada. *The Lyndon LaRouche Network: The Canadian Connection.* Toronto: League for Human Rights of B'nai Brith Canada, 1987

———. *Skinheads in Canada and Their Link to the Far Right.* Toronto: League for Human Rights of B'nai Brith Canada, 1990

———. *Audit of Anti-Semitic Incidents 1992.* Toronto: League for Human Rights of B'nai Brith Canada, 1992.

———. *Audit of Anti-Semitic Incidents 1993.* Toronto: League for Human Rights of B'nai Brith Canada, 1993.

———. *The Heritage Front Report.* Toronto: League for Human Rights of B'nai Brith Canada, 1994.

Loewen, Helmut-Harry, and Mahmood Randeree. "White Hoods: The Klan in Manitoba." *Canadian Dimension,* March-April 1993.

Mertl, Steve. *Keegstra: The Trial, the Issues, the Consequences.* Saskatoon: Western Producer Prairie Books, 1985.

Palmer, Howard. "Politics, Religion and Antisemitism in Alberta, 1880–1950." In Alan Davies, ed., *Antisemitism in Canada.* Waterloo, Ontario: Wilfrid Laurier Press, 1992.

Robin, Martin. *Shades of Right: Nativist and Fascist Politics in Canada, 1920–1940.* Toronto: University of Toronto Press, 1992.

Sher, J. *White Hoods: Canada's Ku Klux Klan.* Vancouver: New Star Books, 1983.

Wagner, J. *Brothers Beyond the Sea: National Socialism in Canada.* Waterloo, Ontario: Wilfrid Laurier University Press, 1981.

Weimann, Gabriel. *Hate on Trial: The Zundel Affair, the Media, Public Opinion in Canada.* Oakville, Ontario: Mosaic Press, 1986.

United States

Altemeyer, Bob. *Enemies of Freedom: Understanding Right-Wing Authoritarianism.* San Francisco: Jossey-Bass, 1981.

Anti-Defamation League. *Extremist Groups in the United States.* New York: ADL, 1983.

———. *Propaganda of the Deed: The Far Right's Desperate Revolution.* New York: ADL, 1985.

———. *The Hate Movement Today: A Chronicle of Violence and Disarray.* New York: ADL, 1987.

———. *Hate Groups in America: A Record of Bigotry and Violence.* New York: ADL, 1988.

———. *Anger on the Right: Pat Buchanan's Venomous Crusade.* New York: ADL, 1991.

———. *Hate Crimes Statutes: A 1991 Status Report.* New York: ADL, 1991.

———. *The KKK Today: A 1991 Status Report.* New York: ADL, 1991.

———. *Dukewatch 1992: The Failed Campaign of an Extremist.* New York: ADL, 1992.

———. *The Church of the Creator: Creed of Hate.* New York: ADL, 1993.

———. *Hitler's Apologists: The Anti-Semitic Propaganda of Holocaust Revisionism.* New York: ADL, 1993.

_____. *Young Nazi Killers: The Rising Skinhead Danger.* New York: ADL, 1993.

_____. *Armed and Dangerous: Militias Take Aim at the Federal Government.* New York: ADL, October 1994.

_____. *Extremism in the Name of Religion: The Violent Legacy of Meir Kahane.* New York: ADL, 1994.

_____. *The Religious Right: The Assault on Tolerance and Pluralism in America.* New York: ADL, 1994.

_____. *Liberty Lobby: Hate Central. A Case Study in the Promotion of Anti-Semitism and Extremism.* New York: ADL, 1995.

Applebome, Peter. "Rise Is Found in Hate Crimes Committed by Blacks." *New York Times,* December 13, 1993, A7.

Barkun, Michael. "Racist Apocalypse: Millennialism on the Far Right." *American Studies* 31, 1990: 122–126.

Bennett, David. *The Party of Fear.* Chapel Hill: University of North Carolina Press, 1988.

Bridges, Tyler. *The Rise of David Duke.* Jackson: University of Mississippi Press, 1994.

Buchanan, Pat. "As We Remember Joe." In Pat Buchanan, *Right from the Beginning,* Boston: Little, Brown, 1988.

Buckley, William F. "In Search of Anti-Semitism." *National Review,* December 30, 1991.

Centre for Democratic Renewal. *Far Right Violence, 1980–1986.* Atlanta: Centre for Democratic Renewal, 1987.

_____. *Ballot Box Bigotry: David Duke and the Populist Party.* Atlanta: Centre for Democratic Renewal, 1989.

_____. *When Hate Groups Come to Town.* Atlanta: Centre for Democratic Renewal, 1992.

Chalmers, D. *Hooded Americanism: The History of the Ku Klux Klan.* Durham, N.C.: Duke University Press, 1987.

Coates, James. *Armed and Dangerous: The Rise of the Survivalist Right.* New York: Hill and Wanger, 1987.

Cooper, Mary. "The Growing Danger of Hate Groups." *Editorial Research Reports,* May 12, 1989, 262–275.

Coplon, Jeff. "Skinhead Nation." *Rolling Stone Magazine,* December 1986.

Corcoran, James. *Bitter Harvest: Gordon Kahl and the Posse Comitatus: Murder in the Heartland.* New York: Penguin, 1990.

Cox, Michael. "Beyond the Fringe: The Extreme Right in the United States of America." In Paul Hainsworth, ed., *The Extreme Right in Europe and the U.S.A.* New York: St. Martin's Press, 1993.

Dees, Morris. *Hate on Trial: The Case Against America's Most Dangerous Neo-Nazi.* New York: Villard Books, 1993.

Diamond, Sara. "How 'Radical' Is the Christian Right?" *Humanist,* March-April 1994: 32–34.

_____. "Watch on the Right." *Humanist,* March-April 1994.

Dinnerstein, Leonard. *Antisemitism in America.* New York: Oxford University Press, 1994.

Flynn, Kevin, and Gary Gerhardt. *The Silent Brotherhood: Inside America's Racist Underground.* New York: Free Press, 1989.

Fredet, Jean-Gabriel. "Les Nouveaux Croises de l'Amerique." *Le Nouvel Observateur*, August 12–18, 1993: 32–34.

Friedman, Robert I. "The Brooklyn Avengers." *New York Review of Books*, June 23, 1994.

George, John, and Laird Wilcox. *Nazis, Communists, Klansmen, and Others on the Fringe: Political Extremism in America.* Buffalo, N.Y.: Prometheus Books, 1992.

Gibson, James William. *Warrior Dreams: Violence and Manhood in Post-Vietnam America.* New York: Hill and Wang, 1994.

Ginsberg, Benjamin. *The Fatal Embrace: Jews and the State.* Chicago: University of Chicago Press, 1993.

Glazer, Nathan. "Debate on Aliens Flares Beyond the Melting Pot." *New York Times,* April 23, 1995.

Hamm, Mark. *American Skinheads: The Criminology and Control of Hate Crime.* Westport, CT: Praeger, 1993.

Head, Simon. "The New, Ruthless Economy." *New York Review,* February 29, 1996.

Hunter, James Donavan. *Culture Wars: The Struggle to Defend America.* New York: Basic Books, 1991.

Johnston, David. "LaRouche Gains Federal Parole After the Minimum Term in Prison." *New York Times,* December 2, 1993, A13.

Judt, Tony. "Austria and the Ghost of the New Europe." *New York Review*, February 15, 1996.

King, Dennis. *Lyndon LaRouche and the New American Fascism.* New York: Doubleday, 1987.

Klanwatch. *Intelligence Report.* June 1995.

Langer, Elinor. "The American Neo-Nazi Movement Today." *Nation*, July 16–23, 1990.

Levin, Jack, and Jack McDevitt. *Hate Crimes: The Rising Tide of Bigotry and Bloodshed.* New York: Plenum Press, 1993.

Levine, Art. "America's Youthful Bigots." *US News and World Report,* May 7, 1990.

Lewis, Sinclair. *It Can't Happen Here: A Novel.* New York: Triangle Books, 1935.

Lipset, Seymour Martin. "Failures of Extremism: United States Politics and the Christian Fundamentalist Movement." *Society* 20, November-December 1982: 48–58.

Lipset, Seymour M., and Earl Raab. *The Politics of Unreason: Right-Wing Extremism in America, 1790–1970.* New York: Harper & Row, 1970.

Lutz, Chris. *They Don't All Wear Sheets: A Chronology of Racist and Far Right Violence, 1980–1986.* Atlanta: Centre for Democratic Renewal, 1987.

Martinez, Thomas. *Brotherhood of Murder.* New York: McGraw-Hill, 1988.

Marx, Paul. *Confessions of a Prolife Missionary.* Gaithersburg, Md.: Human Life International, 1988.

Mintz, Frank. *The Liberty Lobby and the American Right.* Westport, CT: Greenwood Press, 1985.

Moore, Leonard J. "Historical Interpretations of the 1920s Klan: The Traditional View and Recent Revisions." In Shawn Lay, ed., *The Invisible Empire in the West: Toward a New Historical Appraisal of the Ku Klux Klan in the 1920s.* Urbana: University of Illinois Press, 1992.

Page, Clarence. "Bringing Farrakhan into the Fold." *Chicago Tribune*, September 19, 1993.

Pantell, Laurie. "A Pathfinder on Bias Crimes and the Fight Against Hate Groups." *Legal Reference Services Quarterly* 11(1–2), 1991: 39–75.

Ridgeway, James. *Blood in the Face: The Ku Klux Klan, Aryan Nations, Nazi Skinheads and the Rise of a New White Culture.* New York: Thunder Mouth Press, 1995.

Rose, Douglas D. *The Emergence of David Duke and the Politics of Race.* Chapel Hill: University of North Carolina Press, 1992.

Slaughter, Michael. "An Interview with Sara Diamond." *Z Magazine*, January 1993.

Southern Poverty Law Center. *Hate Violence and White Supremacy: A Decade in Review 1980–1989.* Montgomery, AL: Klanwatch Project of the Southern Poverty Law Center, 1989.

_____. *The Ku Klux Klan: A History of Racism and Violence.* Montgomery, Ala.: SPLC, 1991.

Stanton, Bill. *Klanwatch: Bringing the Ku Klux Klan to Justice.* New York: Grove Weidenfeld, 1991.

Suall, Irwin, and David Lowe. "The Hate Movement Today: A Chronicle of Violence and Disarray." *Terrorism* 10(4), 1987: 345–364.

Terry, Don. "Minister Farrakhan: Conservative Militant." *New York Times,* March 3, 1994.

_____. "Seeking Statesmanship, Farrakhan Softens Tone." *New York Times*, October 25, 1995.

Wade, J. Craig. *The Fiery Cross: The Ku Klux Klan in America.* New York: Simon and Schuster, 1987.

Watts, Tim. *Politics of Hate: White Extremist Groups in the 1980's, a Bibliography.* New Orleans: Vance Bible, 1989.

Wilcox, Clyde. "Popular Support for the New Christian Right." *Social Science Journal* 26(1), 1989: 55–63.

Zatarain, Michael. *David Duke: The Evolution of a Klansman.* New Orleans: Pelican, 1990.

Zeskind, Leonard. *The "Christian Identity" Movement.* Atlanta: Centre for Democratic Renewal, 1986.

_____. "And Now, the Hate Show." *New York Times,* November 16, 1993, A15.

Europe—General

Bell, A. *Against Racism and Fascism in Europe.* Brussels: The Socialist Group of the European Parliament, 1986.

Betz, Hans-George. "The New Politics of Resentment: Radical Right-Wing Populist Parties in Western Europe." *Comparative Politics* 25, July 1993: 413–427.

Bohlen, Celestine. "A Survival of the Past: Anti-Semitism Is Back." *New York Times,* February 20, 1990.

Cheles, Luciano, ed. *Neo-Fascism in Europe.* London: Longman, 1991.

European Parliament. *Committee of Inquiry into the Rise of Fascism and Racism in Europe.* Luxembourg: Office for Official Publications of the European Commuities, 1985.

_____. *Committee of Inquiry on Racism and Xenophobia.* Luxembourg, 1991.

Ford, Glyn. *Fascist Europe: The Rise of Racism and Xenophobia.* London: Pluto Press, 1991.

Glenn, R., and A. Lerman. "Fascism and Racism in Europe: The Report of the European Parliament's Committee of Inquiry." *Patterns of Prejudice* 20(2), 1986: 13–26.

Gruber, Ruth. *Right-Wing Extremism in Western Europe.* New York: American Jewish Committee, January 1994.

Harris, Geoffrey. *The Dark Side of Europe: The Extreme Right Today.* Edinburgh: Edinburgh University Press, 1990.

Hill, R., and A. Bell. *The Other Side of Terror: Inside Europe's Neo-Nazi Network.* London: Grafton, 1988.

Husbands, Christopher. "Contemporary Right-Wing Extremism in Western European Democracies." *European Journal of Political Research* 9, 1981: 75–99.

_____. *Racist Political Movements in Western Europe.* London: Routledge, 1990.

_____. "The Other Face of 1992: The Extreme-Right Explosion in Western Europe." *Parliamentary Affairs* 45(3), July 1992.

Ignazi, Piero. "The Silent Counter-Revolution." *European Journal of Political Research,* special issue, "Extreme Right-Wing Parties in Europe" 22, 1992: 3–33.

Phillips, Andrew. "Europe's Nightmare." *Maclean's* 105, November 23, 1992: 28–32.

Tel Aviv University and Anti-Defamation League. *Anti-Semitism in Europe in the First Quarter of 1993.* 1993.

_____. *Anti-Semitism in the Second Quarter of 1993.* 1993.

_____. *Anti-Semitism in Western Europe: A Focus on Germany, France, and Austria.* 1993.

Von Beyme, Klaus. "Right-Wing Extremism in Post-War Europe." *West European Politics* 11(2), April 1988: 1–18.

Zariski, Raphael. "Ethnic Extremism Among Ethno Territorial Minorities in Western Europe: Dimensions, Causes and Institutional Responses." *Comparative Politics* 21, April 1989: 253–272.

United Kingdom

Angemurraya, Natalie, and Catarina Mirles. "Racially-Motivated Crime: British Crime Survey Analysis." Research and Planning Unit working paper 82, Home Office, Government of the United Kingdom.

Anti-Racist Alliance. *Racial Harassment: County Action, Legal Remedies.* London: The Alliance, June 1983.

Billig, M. *Fascists: A Social Psychological View of the National Front.* London: Harcourt Brace Jovanovich, 1978.

Community Service Organization of the Board of Deputies of British Jews. *Group Defamation Report of a Working Party of the Law of Parliamentary and General Purposes.* London, February 1992.

_____. *Anti-Semitic Incidents: Breakdown by Category 1990–1993.* London: The Organization, 1994.

Durham, Martin. "Women and the National Front." In Luciano Cheles, ed., *Neo-Fascism in Europe.* London: Longman, 1991, 264–283.

Eatwell, Roger. "Why Has the Extreme Right Failed in Britain," in Paul Hainsworth, ed., *The Extreme Right in Europe and the U.S.A.* London: Pinter, 1992.

Fielding, N. *The National Front.* London: Routledge, 1981.

Gable, Gerry. "The Far Right in Contemporary Britain." In Cheles, *Neo-Fascism in Europe*, 245–263.

Husbands, Christopher. *Racial Exclusion in the City*. London: Allen and Unwin, 1983.

_____. "Extreme Right-Wing Politics in Great Britain: The Recent Marginalisation of the National Front." *West European Politics* 11(2), 1988: 65–79.

Institute for Jewish Affairs. *Anti-Semitism World Report 1993*. London: The Institute, 1993.

Kusher, T., and K. Lunn, eds. *Traditions of Intolerance: Historical Perspectives on Fascism and Race Discourse in Britain*. Manchester: Manchester University Press, 1989.

Luttwak, Edward. "Why Fascism Is the Wave of the Future." *London Review of Books*, April 7, 1994.

Searchlight, special issue, "From Ballots to Bombs: The Inside Story of the National Front's Political Soldiers," 1989.

Taylor, S. *The National Front and English Politics*. London: Macmillan, 1982.

Thurlew, R. *Fascism in Britain*. London: Blackwell, 1987.

Troyan, B. "The Media and the Decline of the National Front." *Patterns of Prejudice* 14(3), 1981: 25–30.

U.K. Commission for Racial Equality. *Second Review of the Race Relations Action 1976*. London: The Commission, 1976.

_____. *Homelessness and Discrimination*. London: The Commission, July 1988.

Walker, M. *The National Front*. London: Fontana. 1977.

France

Billig, Michael. "Rhetoric of the Conspiracy Theory: Arguments in National Front Propaganda." *Patterns of Prejudice* 22(2), 1988: 23–34.

Brechon, Pierre, and Subrata Kumar Mitra. "The National Front in France: The Emergence of an Extreme Right Protest Movement." *Comparative Politics* 2563–2582, October 1992.

Camus, Jean-Yves, and Rene Monzat. *Les Droites Nationales et Radicales en France: Repetoire Critique*. Lyons: Lyons University Press, 1992.

de Brie, Christian. "Les Reseaux de l'Extreme Droite en Europe." *Le Monde Diplomatique*, January 1992: 16–17.

Fysh, Peter, and Jim Wolfreys. "Le Pen, the National Front and the Extreme Right in France." *Parliamentary Affairs* 45(3), July 1992: 309–326.

Hainsworth, Paul. "Anti-Semitism and Neo-Fascism on the Contemporary Right." *Social Movements and Protest in Modern France*. London: Pinter, 1982.

Husbands, Christopher. "The Mainstream Right and the Politics of Immigration in France: Major Developments in the 80's." *Ethnic and Racial Studies* 14(2), April 1991: 170–195.

_____. "The Support for the Front National: Analyses and Findings." *Ethnic and Racial Studies* 14(3), July 1991: 382–416.

LaFranchi il, H. "Mosque Project in Lyon Stirs Controversy." *Christian Science Monitor*, November 8, 1990.

Laxer, James. "France's Far-Right Puts Racism on Public Agenda." *Toronto Star,* March 24, 1992, A19.

Mayer, Nonna. "Le Phenomene Le Pen." *l'Histoire,* January 1990.

_____. "Carpentras and the Media." *Patterns of Prejudice* 26(1, 2), 1992: 48–63.

_____. "Explaining Electoral Right-Wing Extremism: The Case of the Le Pen Vote in the 1988 French Presidential Election." Paper presented at the Annual Meeting of the American Political Science Association, September 2–5, 1993.

Mayer, Nonna, and Pascal Perrineau. "Why Do They Vote for Le Pen?" *European Journal of Political Research* 22, 1992.

Mitra, Subrata. "The National Front in France: A Single Issue Movement?" *West European Politics* 11(2), 1988: 47–64.

Petifils, J-C. *L'Extreme Droite en France.* Paris: Universitaire de France, 1983.

Plenel, E., and A. Rollat. *L'effet le Pen.* Paris: Le Monde-La Decouverte, 1984.

Riding, Alan. "Inciting of Racism Banned in France." *New York Times,* May 4, 1990.

Rollat, A. *Les Hommes de l'Extreme Droites.* Paris: Calmann-Levy, 1985.

Singer, Daniel. "The Resistable Rise of Jean-Marie Le Pen." *Ethnic and Racial Studies* 14(3), July 1991: 368–381.

Vaughan, Michalina. "The Extreme Right in France: 'Lepenisme' or the Politics of Fear." In Luciano Cheles, ed., *Neo-Fascism in Europe.* London: Longman, 1991, 211–233.

Germany

Anti-Defamation League. "Neo-Nazi Skinheads: A 1990 Status Report [Prepared by the Anti-Defamation League of B'nai Brith]." *Terrorism* 13, May-June 1991: 243–275.

_____. *The German Neo-Nazis: An ADL Investigative Report.* New York: Anti-Defamation League, 1993.

Backes, Uwe. "The West German Republikaner: Profile of a Nationalist, Populist Party of Protest." *Patterns of Prejudice* 24(1), 1990: 3–17.

Birsl, Ursula. "Frauen und Rechtsextrismus im FRG" (Women and Right-Wing Extremism in the FRG). *Aus Politik und Zeitgeschicte* 3–4, January 10, 1992: 22–30.

Butterwegge, Christoph, and Horst Isola. *Rechtesextremismus im Vereinten Deutschland: Randerscheinung oder Gefahr für die Demokratie?* (Right-Wing Extremism in the United Germany: A Peripheral Phenomenon or a Danger for Democracy?) Berlin: LinksDruck Verlag, 1990.

Fawcett, Edmund. "Not As Grimm As It Looks: A Survey of Germany." *Economist* 323(58), May 23, 1992.

Funke, Hajo, and Elliot Neaman. "Germany: The Nationalist Backlash." *Dissent* 40, Winter 1993: 11–15.

Gress, Franz. *Neue Richete und Rechtsextremisus in Europa: Bundesrepublik, Frankreich, Grossbritannien.* Opladen: Westdeutscher Verlag, 1990.

Hafeneger, Benno. *Die "Extreme Rechte" und Europa: Herausforderung für eine multikulturelle Gesellschaft.* Schwalbach: Wochenschau, 1990.

Harnischmacher, Robert. *Angriff von Rechts.* Rostock: Hanseatischer Fachverlag fur Wirtschaft GmbH, 1993.

Heitmeyer, Wilhelm. *Jugend, Staat, Gewalt: Politische Sozialisation von Jungendlichen, Jugendpolitik und Politische Bildung.* Munich: Juventa, 1989.

Hockenos, Paul. "Free to Hate." *New Statesman and Society* 4(146), 1991: 18–19.

_____. "Return of the Right." *New Statesman and Society* 5(198), 1992: 25–26.

Husbands, Christopher. "Militant Neo-Nazism in the Federal Republic of Germany in the 1980's." In Luciano Cheles, ed., *Neo-Fascism in Europe*. London: Longman, 1991, 86–119.

_____. "Neo-Nazis in East Germany: The New Danger?" *Patterns of Prejudice* 25(1), 1991: 3–17.

Kinzer, Stephen. "Racist Attack on U.S. Athletes Upsets Germany." *New York Times*, November 2, 1993, A6.

_____. "Bonn Mayor, Blamed for Inaction in Violence Against Foreigners, Resigns." *New York Times*, November 13, 1993, A4.

_____. "Germans Sentence 2 in Firebombing." *New York Times*, December 9, 1993, A3.

Klusmeyer, Douglas. "Aliens, Immigrants, and Citizens: The Politics of Inclusion in the Federal Republic of Germany." *Daedalus* 122(3), Summer 1993: 81–114.

Kodderitzsch, Peter, and Leo Muller. *Rechtsextremismus in der DDR* (Right-Wing Extremism in the GDR). Göttingen: Lamuv, 1990.

Kollman, Doris. *Scharzbeucherbraun: Medienhandbuch Zum Thema (Neo) Fachisnmus*. AJZ, 1990.

Kramer, Susan. "Chaos in the Head." *New Yorker*, 1990.

Leggewie, Claus. *Rechtsextremismis auf dem Vormarsch?: Gib den Rechten Keine Chance*. Marbung: SP-Verlag Norbert Schuren, 1989.

Lepszy, Norbert. *Rechtspopulismus und Rechtsextremismus*. Bonn: Konrad Adenauer Stiftung, 1993.

Lepszy, N., and Veen, H-J. *Die Republikaner-Partei zu Beginn der 90er Jahre*. Bonn: Konrad Adenauer Stiftung, 1991.

_____. *Republikaner and DVU in Kommunalen and Landesparlamenten sowie un Europaparlament*. Bonn: Konrad Adenauer Stiftung, 1994.

Mertes, Michael. "Germany in Transition." *Daedalus* 123(1), Winter 1994.

Minkenberg, Michael. "The New Right in Germany: The Transformation of Conservatism and the Extreme Right." *European Journal of Political Research*, special issue, "Extreme Right-Wing Parties" 22, 1992: 55–81.

"Nazi International Declares War." *Searchlight*, January 1994.

Pfahl-Traughber, Armin. "Rechtsextremismus in den neuen Bundesländern (Right-Wing Extremism in the New German Federal Länder). *Aus Politik und Zeitgeschichte* 3–4, January 1992: 11–21.

Roberts, Geoffrey. "Right-Wing Radicalism in the New Germany." *Parliamentary Affairs* 45(3), July 1992: 327–344.

Schmidt, Michael. *The New Reich: Penetrating the Secrets of Today's Neo-Nazi Networks*. London: Random House, 1993.

Searchlight. Various reports on Germany

Stoss, Richard. "The Problem of Right-Wing Extremism in West Germany." *West European Politics* 11(2), 1988: 34–46.

_____. *Politics Against Democracy: Right-Wing Extremism in Western Germany*. New York: Berg, 1991.

Veen, Hans-Joachim. *The Republikaner Party in Germany: Right-Wing Menace or Protest Catcall?* Westport, Conn.: Praeger, 1993.

Webster, Ronald. "An Insurmountable Past? Xenophobia in Germany Today." *Refuge* 12(15–17), September 1992.

Westle, Bettina, and Oskar Niedermayer. "Contemporary Right-Wing Extremism in West Germany." *European Journal of Political Research* 22, 1992: 83–100.

Weusthoff, Anja, and Rainer Zeimentz. *Aktionen gegen Rechts.* Bonn: Vorwarts Verlag, n.d.

Whitney, Craig. "Bonn Presidential Nominee Quits in a Setback for Kohl." *New York Times,* November 26, 1993, A8.

Eastern Europe and Russia

Anti-Defamation League. *Anti-Semitism in Eastern Europe: Old Wine in New Bottles.* New York: ADL, December 1991.

Bauer, Yehuda. *The Danger of Antisemitism in Central and Eastern Europe in the Wake of 1989–1990.* Jerusalem: Vidal Sassoon International Center for the Study of Anti-Semitism, 1991.

Braun, Aurel. "Political Developments in Central and Eastern Europe." In Aspen Institute (Queenstown, Md.), *U.S. Relations with Central and Eastern Europe,* Congressional Program vol. 9, no. 4, August 22–28, 1994.

Brown, J. F. "Extremism in Eastern Europe and the Former Soviet Union." *RFE/RL Research Reports* 3(16), April 22, 1994: 1–4.

Cox, Michael. "After Stalinism: The Extreme Right in Russia, East Germany and Eastern Europe." In Paul Hainsworth, ed., *The Extreme Right in Europe and the U.S.A.* New York: St. Martin's Press, 1993, 269–285.

Crane, Keith. "The Lessons of Transition." In *U.S. Relations with Central and Eastern Europe,* Congressional Program vol. 9, no. 4, August 22–28, 1994, the Aspen Institute.

Djilas, Milovan. *The New Class: An Analysis of the Communist System.* New York: Praeger, 1963.

Fisher, Sharon. "Slovakia." *RFE/RL Research Reports* 3(16), April 22, 1994: 68–71.

Hockenos, Paul. "Dark Side of the Wall." *New Statesman and Society* 3(83), 1990: 16–17.

_____. "Bigot's Brew." *New Statesman and Society* 4(161), 1991: 20–21.

_____. *Free to Hate.* London: Routledge, 1993.

Hough, Jerry. *How the Soviet Union Is Governed.* Cambridge, Mass.: Harvard University Press, 1979.

Kamm, Henry. "In New Eastern Europe, an Old Anti-Gypsy Bias." *New York Times,* November 17, 1993, A6.

Lendvai, Paul. *Anti-Semitism in Eastern Europe.* London: MacDonald, 1971.

Mathews, Tom, Rod Nordland, and Carroll Bogert. "The Long Shadow." *Newsweek,* May 7, 1990, 34–44.

Schapiro, Leonard. *Russian Studies.* New York and London: Penguin Books, 1988.

Shafir, Michael. "Romania: Toward the Rule of Law." *RFE/RL Research Reports* 1(27), July 3, 1992: 30–40.

_____. "Growing Political Extremism in Romania." *RFE/RL Research Reports* 2(14), April 2, 1993: 18–25.

_____. "Romanian Politics in Turmoil." *RFE/RL Research Reports* 3(29), July 22, 1994: 1–6.

_____. "Ethnic Tension Runs High in Romania." *RFE/RL Research Reports* 3(32), August 19, 1994: 24–32.

Wilson-Smith, Anthony. "The Jew: Antisemitism Is on the Rise in the Soviet Union and Eastern Europe." *Maclean's* 103, January 1990: 20–26.

Russia

Antic, Oxana. "Successors to the USSR Council for Religious Affairs." *RFE/RL Research Reports* 1(35) September 4, 1992: 52–53.

Arzt, Donna. "Soviet Anti-Semitism: Legal Responses in an Age of Glasnost." *Temple International and Comparative Law Journal* 4(2), 1990: 163–183.

Bohlen, Celestine. "Russian Nationalist Adds Pitch for Women's Vote to a Flamboyant Campaign." *New York Times*, December 7, 1993.

Brown, Kathryn. "Sakhalin's Valentin Fedorov Makes Nationalist Allies." *RFE/RL Research Reports* 1(38), September 25, 1992: 33–38.

Chernomyrdin, Viktor. "No Exits on the Road to the Market." *Financial Times* (London), May 16, 1994.

Dunn, John. "Hard Times in Russia Foster Conspiracy Theories." *RFE/RL Research Reports* 1(46), November 20, 1992: 24–29.

Erlanger, Steven. "Greater Russia's Champion." *New York Times*, December 13, 1993, A6.

_____. "Russia Court Calls 'Protocols' Anti-Semitic Forgery." *New York Times*, November 27, 1993, A4.

Goble, Paul. "Russia's Extreme Right." *National Interest*, no. 33, Fall 1993.

Hirszowicz, Lukasz, and Howard Spier. "In Search of a Scapegoat: Anti-Semitism in the Soviet Union Today." Institute of Jewish Affairs research report, 1991.

Kamm, Henry. "Soviet Rabbi Tells of the New Anti-Semitism." *New York Times*, February 21, 1990.

Laqueur, Walter. *The Long Road to Freedom: Russia and Glasnost*. Boston: Unwin Hyman, 1990.

_____. "Russian Nationalism." *Foreign Affairs* 71, Winter 1992–1993: 103–116.

_____. *Black Hundred: The Rise of the Extreme Right in Russia*. New York: Harper-Collins, 1993.

_____. *Los Angeles Times*, May 30, 1993.

Pospielovsky, Dimitry. "Russian Nationalism: An Update." *Radio Liberty Research Bulletin* 2(6), 1990.

Prial, Frank. "Survey in Moscow Sees a High Level of Anti-Jewish Feeling." *New York Times*, March 30, 1990.

Pribylovsky, Vladimir. "A Survey of Radical Right-Wing Groups in Russia." *RFE/RL Research Reports* 3(16) April 22, 1994: 28–37.

Schmemann, Serge. "As Russian Vote Nears, Pessimism Rises." *New York Times*, December 11, 1993, A1, 4.

_____. "Yeltsin's Reformers Show Weakness in Russian Vote; Constitution Is Approved." *New York Times*, December 13, 1993, A1.

Slater, Wendy. "Russian Duma Sidelines Extremist Politicians." *RFE/RL Research Reports* 3(7), February 18, 1994: 5–9.

_____. "Russia." *RFE/RL Research Reports* 3(16): April 22, 1994: 23–27.

_____. "The Russian Communist Party Today." *RFE/RL Research Reports* 3(31), August 12, 1994.

Torbakov, Igor. "The 'Statists' and the Ideology of Russian Imperial Nationalism." *RFE/RL Research Reports* 1(49), December 11, 1992: 10–16.

Wishnevsky, Julia. "Nash Sovremennik Provides Focus for 'Opposition Party.'" *Radio Liberty Research Bulletin* 1(3), January 20, 1989.

_____. "Antidemocratic Tendencies in Russian Policy-Making." *RFE/RL Research Reports* 1(45), November 13, 1992: 21–25.

Zolotarevich, Victor. "Nazism in Russia: 1993–1994 Survey." Moscow Research Center for Human Rights report, April 15, 1994.

Poland

Cline, Mary. "Political Parties and Public Opinion in Poland." *RFE/RL Research Reports* 1(43) October 30, 1992: 66–69.

de Weydenthal, Jan B. "Immigration into Poland." *RFE/RL Research Reports* 3(24), June 17, 1994.

Sabbat-Swidlicka, Anna. "Poland Investigates Radical Farmers' Union." *RFE/RL Research Reports* 1(38) September 25, 1992: 19–25.

_____. "Poland: A Year of Three Governments." *RFE/RL Research Reports* 2(1) January 1, 1993: 102–107.

_____. "Warsaw Marks Fiftieth Anniversary of Ghetto Uprising." *RFE/RL Research Reports* 2(22), May 28, 1993: 28–34.

_____. "Pawlak Builds Up Peasant Power." *RFE/RL Research Reports* 3(24), June 17, 1994: 13–19.

Vinton, Louisa. "Solidarity's Rival Offspring." *RFE/RL Research Reports*, no. 38, September 1990.

_____. "Party X and the Tyminski Phenomenon." *RFE/RL Research Reports*, no. 32, August 9, 1991.

_____. "'Outsider' Parties and the Political Process in Poland." *RFE/RL Research Reports* 3(3), January 21, 1994: 13–22.

_____. "Poland" *RFE/RL Research Reports* 3(16), April 22, 1994: 62–67.

Hungary

Brown, J. F. "A Challenge to Political Values." *RFE/RL Research Reports* 1(40), October 9, 1992: 23–25.

Deak, Istvan. "The Danger of Antisemitism in Hungary." In Yehuda Bauer, ed., *The Danger of Anti-Semitism in Central and Eastern Europe in the Wake of 1989–1990*, 53–61.

Oltay, Edith. "A Profile of Istvan Csurka." *RFE/RL Research Reports* 1(40), October 9, 1992: 26–29.

_____. "Hungarian Democratic Forum Rent by Dispute over Extremism." *RFE/RL Research Reports* 1(47), November 27, 1992: 22–25.

_____. "Opposition Parties in the Parliament." *RFE/RL Research Reports* 1(48), December 4, 1992: 40–43.

_____. "Hungary Reforms Its Police Force." *RFE/RL Research Reports* 2(4), January 22, 1993: 50–54.

_____. "Hungary: Csurka Launches 'National Movement.'" *RFE/RL Research Reports* 2(13), March 26, 1993: 25–45.

_____. "Hungary." *RFE/RL Research Reports* 3(6), April 22, 1994: 55–61.

_____. "Hungary's Socialist-Liberal Government Takes Office." *RFE/RL Research Reports* 3(33), August 26, 1994: 6–19.

Pataki, Judith. "Istvan Csurka's Tract: Summary and Reactions." *RFE/RL Research Reports* 1(40), October 9, 1992: 15–22.

_____. "Hungarians Dissatisfied with Political Changes." *RFE/RL Research Reports* 1(44), November 6, 1992: 66–70.

_____. "Hungary: Domestic Political Stalemate." *RFE/RL Research Reports* 2(1), January 1, 1993: 93–95.

_____. "The Recent History of the Hungarian Refugee Problem." *RFE/RL Research Reports* 3(24), June 17, 1994: 34–37.

Reisch, Alfred. "Roundtable: Hungary's Parliament in Transition." *RFE/RL Research Reports* 1(48), December 4, 1992: 27–35.

_____. "The New Hungarian Government's Foreign Policy." *RFE/RL Research Reports* 3(33), August 26, 1994.

U.S. Department of State, *Hungary.* Washington, D.C.: Department of State, 912.

International

Anti-Defamation League. "Extremist Groups Strengthen International Ties with Hi-Tech Communications: Poses New Threat of Anti-Semitism." Press release, June 24, 1994.

_____. *The Skinhead International: A Worldwide Survey of Skinheads.* New York: ADL, 1995.

Anti-Semitism Monitoring Forum. "U.S. to Crack Down on Neo-Nazis." Government Secretariat of Israel, December 22, 1993.

Anti-Semitism Worldwide 1993. Tel Aviv University and the Anti-Defamation League. The Project for Anti-Semitism.

Center for Democratic Renewal. "New Laws on the Freedom of Association and Assembly." *Patterns of Prejudice* 23(1), Spring 1989: 46–48.

_____. "Advance in International Outlawing of Incitement to Racism and Religious Hatred." *Patterns of Prejudice* 24(2–4), 1990: 97–98.

_____. *The Neo-Nazi Movement in Germany: An Eyewitness Documentary Report.* Los Angeles: Simon Wiesenthal Center, June 15, 1993.

_____. "Zhirinovsky Guest of ex-SS Member in Austrian Alps." *Globe and Mail,* December 23, 1993, A13.

_____. International Connections Package. Atlanta: Center for Democratic Renewal, 1994.

_____. "Ku Klux Klan to Fund Far-Right Candidates in British Elections." *Sunday Times,* January 16, 1994, 7.

_____. *Searchlight,* various reports.

Barton, Michael. "International Action Against Racial Discrimination: A Briefing Paper." *Ethnic and Racial Studies* 14(4), October 1991: 545–556.

Bernhardt, Rudolph. "Human Rights Aspects of Racial and Religious Hatred Under Regional Human Rights Conventions." In Faculty of Law of Tel-Aviv University, *Israeli Yearbook on Human Rights*, vol. 22. Dordrecht, Neth.: Martinus Nijhoff, 1992.

Buergenthal, Thomas. "The CSCE and the Promotion of Racial and Religious Tolerance." In Faculty of Law of Tel-Aviv University, *Israeli Yearbook on Human Rights*, vol. 22. Dordrecht, Neth.: Martinus Nijhoff, 1992.

Greenspan, Louis, ed. *Under the Shadow of Weimar: Democracy, Law and Racial Incitement in 6 Countries*. Westport, CT: Praeger, 1993.

Kinzer, Stephen. "Klan Seizes on Germany's Wave of Racist Violence." *New York Times*, November 3, 1991, 16.

Lerner, Nathan. "Incitement in the Racial Convention: Reach and Shortcomings of Article 4." In *Israeli Yearbook on Human Rights*, vol. 22, 1992.

Lipstadt, Debra. *Denying the Holocaust: Assault on Memory and Truth*. Toronto: Maxwell Macmillan Canada, 1993.

Lucow, Maurice. "Internet Computer Network Used to Fight Anti-Semitism." *Canadian Jewish News*, October 27, 1994.

Nemeth, Mary, and Tom Fennel. "Deny, Deny, Deny: Ernst Zundel Is Back in Action—and on TV." *Maclean's*, August 30, 1993, 56.

Ridgeway, James. "Wie Deutsch ist es? *Village Voice*, December 3, 1991, 36.

Rodrigue, George. "Ex-Neo-Nazi Says American Aids Cause." *Dallas Morning News*, February 5, 1994, 1A.

About the Book

From the Oklahoma City bombing to the Vladimir Zhirinovsky phenomenon in Russia, manifestations of extremism remain a feature of the post–Cold War era, presenting a danger to both established and emerging democracies. This timely volume examines the threats to freedom and security posed by right-wing extremism in established democracies and by the blend of left- and right-wing extremism in postcommunist states.

Providing a strong theoretical framework, the contributors develop analytical tools for recognizing and assessing the dangers of extremism. Cognizant of context and the need for balance, they combine meticulous research and unique interviews with key individuals in case studies that identify the early warning signs of peril from Vancouver to Vladivostock. Written for upper-level undergraduate and graduate students, scholars, and policymakers, this book can be used either as a primary text or as a source of supplementary comparative case studies.

About the Editors and Contributors

Aurel Braun is professor of international relations and political science at the University of Toronto.

Michi Ebata was the project director for this study and is currently a doctoral candidate in international relations at the London School of Economics.

Ian J. Kagedan was formerly a professor at the University of Winnipeg, was director of government relations for B'nai Brith until June 1994, and currently serves as a member of the Immigration and Refugee Board in Ottawa.

David Matas is a Winnipeg refugee and immigration lawyer, an expert on war crimes, and a human rights activist.

Stephen Scheinberg is professor of history at Concordia University in Montreal.

Index

DATE DUE

GAYLORD			PRINTED IN U.S.A.